Cartesian Reflections

Cartesian Reflections

Essays on Descartes's Philosophy

John Cottingham

OXFORD
UNIVERSITY PRESS

OXFORD

UNIVERSITY PRESS

Great Clarendon Street, Oxford OX2 6DP

Oxford University Press is a department of the University of Oxford.
It furthers the University's objective of excellence in research, scholarship,
and education by publishing worldwide in

Oxford New York

Auckland Cape Town Dar es Salaam Hong Kong Karachi
Kuala Lumpur Madrid Melbourne Mexico City Nairobi
New Delhi Shanghai Taipei Toronto

With offices in

Argentina Austria Brazil Chile Czech Republic France Greece
Guatemala Hungary Italy Japan Poland Portugal Singapore
South Korea Switzerland Thailand Turkey Ukraine Vietnam

Oxford is a registered trade mark of Oxford University Press
in the UK and in certain other countries

Published in the United States
by Oxford University Press Inc., New York

© in this volume John Cottingham 2008

The moral rights of the authors have been asserted
Database right Oxford University Press (maker)

First published 2008

British Library Cataloguing in Publication Data

Data available

Library of Congress Cataloging-in-Publication Data

Cottingham, John, 1943–
Cartesian reflections : essays on Descartes's philosophy / John Cottingham.
p. cm.
Includes bibliographical references and index.
ISBN-13: 978-0-19-922697-9
1. Descartes, Rene, 1596–1650. I. Title.
B1875.C634 2008
194—dc22
2008016180

Typeset by Laserwords Private Limited, Chennai, India
Printed in Great Britain
on acid-free paper by
Biddles Ltd., King's Lynn, Norfolk

ISBN 978-0-19-922697-9

10 9 8 7 6 5 4 3 2 1

Preface

THE philosophy of Descartes is wonderfully rich and wide-ranging, and one of the fascinations of working on his ideas is that they take us into many diverse areas of philosophy. Probably best known in our own time for his philosophy of mind, and in particular for his widely criticized view that mind and body are two distinct substances, he also offers challenging accounts of knowledge and language, of freedom and action, of our relationship to the animal domain, and (though this aspect of his system has still not yet received the full attention it deserves) of human morality and the conduct of life. He is also a greatly misunderstood thinker. The Cartesian mind–body dualism that is so often attacked is only a part of Descartes's account of what it is to be a thinking, sentient, human creature, and the way he makes the division between the mental and the physical is considerably more subtle, and philosophically more appealing, than is generally assumed. The general character of the Cartesian system also offers much food for thought. Famous as an inaugurator of the scientific age, Descartes is often considered to be one of the heralds of our modern secular worldview, but here again the picture is far more complicated than is often realized. The 'new' philosophy that he launched retains many links with the ideas of his predecessors, not least in the all-pervasive role it assigns to God (something that is ignored or downplayed by many modern readers); and the character of the Cartesian outlook is multifaceted, sometimes anticipating Enlightenment ideas of human autonomy and independent scientific enquiry, but also sometimes harmonizing with more traditional notions of human nature as created to find fulfilment in harmony with its Creator.

In collecting these essays together, I am very conscious of how far they fall short of providing watertight interpretations of Descartes in these many different areas, and of how much there is that now seems to me to call for qualification and amendment. It is the fate of those working in philosophy (as no doubt in many other disciplines) that almost as soon as a given item appears in print one is aware of things that need correcting or would benefit from being put differently. But rather than tacking on a host of qualifications and retractions, whose effect would probably have been to impair whatever fluency and rhythm the essays may originally have possessed, I have been persuaded to offer these essays as they are, warts and all, and have contented myself with discussing some of the more important issues that seem to me to need further attention in the extended overview that opens the volume. The opening chapter is intended as more than a mere introductory summary of the essays: it attempts to flesh out many of my views on Descartes, and to present them in a more connected and perhaps slightly more persuasive way than was always possible at the time the original papers were being developed. At all events I hope that the opening chapter, together with the other essays included in this book, may at least offer some lines of enquiry to help the reader in coming to terms with the many-sided genius of a thinker who is, on any interpretation, one of the greatest philosophers of all time.

I have always been committed to the idea that philosophy should be as accessible as humanly possible, and that this often improves not just the presentation but the actual philosophical content as well. These essays were and are, for the most part, aimed at a wide audience. They were also mostly written as self-standing pieces, and as a result tend to contain quite a bit of scene-setting, which has inevitably produced some repetition now they are collected within a single volume. Rather than filleting this out, I have assumed that readers may want to dip into topics of their choice, with the relevant background information provided on the spot, either in the main text or in footnotes, rather than being asked constantly to refer backwards or forwards to other chapters. I have also made a point of reminding the reader of the original titles and dates of works of Descartes (and of other canonical figures) when they first appear in each chapter, and I have often provided quotations from the original texts, as well as the English translation. This is not just a piece of pedantry but is motivated by some considerations that seem to me important. First, in a world where English has become the international language for so much academic publishing, it is easy for philosophers to slip into a frame of mind in which they assume that a philosophical problem can have no other shape than that which it has when framed in the English tongue. It is vital to remember that Descartes wrote (with equal fluency) in Latin and in French; the terminology and phrasing of those languages were not just the external clothing for his thinking, but its very life and soul. As someone who has spent a considerable time translating Descartes's works, I am committed to believing that a decent part of his meaning can be transplanted to the very different soil of the English language. But the English version must never be mistaken for Descartes's own text; and those whose knowledge of the original tongues is lacking or imperfect surely deserve the courtesy of being given at least the option of looking at the some of the key terms in their original form, alongside the quotations in English.

As far as my frequent citing of original dates is concerned, this is a policy which I have consciously adopted for some years in the hope that the habit will spread. The way in which so many philosophers habitually refer to the classics of their subject is perplexing. What would we make of a literary scholar who used expressions such as 'see Shakespeare (1958)', when citing a passage in *Hamlet*, or who provided no dates other than that of the edition they happened to have on their shelves? And yet countless philosophy books appearing today will casually use references like 'Kant (1962)', very often with nothing, either in the footnotes or the bibliography, to give even the faintest indication that Kant was not an English or American philosopher writing in the latter twentieth-century. Such a reference system, apt enough for modern science journals, was never really suited for the humanities. Quite apart from issues of pedagogy (we surely owe it to our students to be a little more informative), there is something unappealingly parochial about a citation method that reduces the entire sweep of Western thought to a set of modern English editions.

I should like these essays to be of some use to students working in the history of philosophy, and I have indicated something of my debt to contemporary scholarship in the footnotes; but I have not on the whole seen it as my primary task to engage extensively with the massive and ever-growing corpus of secondary literature on Descartes. I have great respect for such specialist work, but in writing these essays I have tried (as with most of the other philosophy I have written elsewhere) always to keep in mind the needs of a more general philosophical readership. It is my hope that students and philosophers from a variety of interests and specialisms who find time to take up this volume may discover some of the standard caricatures of the Cartesian system starting to lose their appeal, and may be stimulated to take a fresh look at Descartes's actual ideas. I am certainly not aiming to recruit converts to Cartesianism; as the essays that follow make plain, there is much in Descartes's system that seems to me very problematic. But I do think that even when he is wrong, Descartes remains a thinker of enormous fertility and power, and that his ideas continue to repay close attention, not just by the seventeenth-century specialist, but by the contemporary student of very many of today's major branches of philosophy, including metaphysics, philosophy of mind, epistemology, philosophy of science, philosophy of religion, and ethics. Perhaps most important of all, the Cartesian system offers an extraordinarily powerful exemplar of what I regard as philosophy's most important task, the struggle to work out the extent to which the different areas of our conceptual landscape can be integrated into a coherent worldview. If we ever become such specialized creatures that such a task no longer interests us, then philosophy will have divided itself into extinction: the once great river of enquiry will have branched into so many isolated streamlets that eventually nothing will remain but a desert plain.

My thanks are due to Peter Momtchiloff at the Oxford University Press, and to the Delegates of the Press, for encouraging me to produce this collection. I should also like to express my thanks to the many friends, colleagues, and students who over the years have helped me in all sorts of ways towards whatever clarity of thought I have managed to achieve. Philosophy, despite Descartes's in many ways accurate description of it as a lonely struggle towards the truth, is nevertheless in important respects a collective enterprise, and nothing is more indispensable than the stimulus of having one's thoughts challenged and sharpened through dialogue with others. This collection is dedicated in gratitude to Anthony Kenny and to the memory of Bernard Williams. My debt to both philosophers goes back to the time, many years ago, when they were, respectively, supervisor and examiner for my doctoral thesis. The richness of their insights into Descartes seems to me greatly enhanced by the fact of their both being very much more than narrow Cartesian specialists. And though their styles and approaches are very different, the writings of both seem to me superb examples of what good history of philosophy can accomplish.

J.C.

Berkshire, England
December 2007

Acknowledgements

I AM grateful to the publishers and editors involved for permission to reprint material that previously appeared in other places. Chapter 1, 'Descartes, the Synoptic Philosopher', was specially composed for this volume, but a part of section 3(c) draws on material from my article 'The Ultimate Incoherence? Descartes and the Passions', in R. E. Auxier (ed.), *Essays in Honor of Marjorie Grene*, Library of Living Philosophers (Chicago: Open Court, 2003), 451–64; and part of section 3(d) appeared as a portion of 'The Mind–Body Relation: Matter and Morality in the Sixth Meditation', in S. Gaukroger (ed.), *The Blackwell Guide to Descartes' Meditations* (Malden, Mass.: Blackwell, 2006), 179–92. Chapter 2, 'A New Start? Cartesian Metaphysics and the Emergence of Modern Philosophy', first appeared in T. Sorell (ed.), *The Rise of Modern Philosophy* (Oxford: Oxford University Press, 1992), 145–66; Chapter 3, 'The Cartesian Legacy', in *Proceedings of the Aristotelian Society*, Supp. 66 (1992), 1–21; Chapter 4, 'Descartes on Thought', in *Philosophical Quarterly*, 28 (1978), 208–14; Chapter 5, ' "The only sure sign ..." Descartes on Thought and Language', in J. M. Preston (ed.), *Thought and Language* (Cambridge: Cambridge University Press, 1998), 29–50 (of which a part incorporates some material from my 'Descartes's Dualism: Theology, Metaphysics, Science', in J. Cottingham (ed.), *The Cambridge Companion to Descartes* (Cambridge: Cambridge University Press, 1992), 236–57); Chapter 6, 'Intentionality or Phenomenology: Descartes and the Objects of Thought', in T. Crane and S. Patterson (eds.), *History of the Mind–Body Problem* (London: Routledge, 2000), 132–48; Chapter 7, 'Descartes on Colour', in *Proceedings of the Aristotelian Society*, 90 (1989–90), 231–46; Chapter 8, 'A Brute to the Brutes? Descartes's Treatment of Animals', in *Philosophy*, 53 (1978), 551–9; Chapter 9, 'Cartesian Trialism', in *Mind*, 94/374 (Apr. 1985), 218–30; Chapter 10, 'The Intellect, the Will, and the Passions: Spinoza's Critique of Descartes', in *Journal of the History of Philosophy*, 26/2 (Apr. 1988), 239–57; Chapter 11, 'Descartes and the Voluntariness of Belief', in *The Monist*, 85/3 (Oct. 2002), 343–60; Chapter 12, 'Cartesian Ethics: Reason and the Passions', in *Revue Internationale de*

Philosophie, 195 (1996), 193–216 (much of which was subsequently incorporated into ch. 3 of my *Philosophy and the Good Life* (Cambridge: Cambridge University Press, 1998)); Chapter 13, 'The Role of God in Descartes's Philosophy', in Janet Broughton and John Carriero (eds.), *A Companion to Descartes* (Oxford: Blackwell, 2006), ch. 17, 287–301; Chapter 14, 'Descartes As Sage: Spiritual Askesis in Cartesian Philosophy', in I. Hunter, C. Condren, and S. Gaukroger (eds.), *The Philosopher in Early-Modern Europe* (Cambridge: Cambridge University Press, 2006), ch. 8, 182–201; and Chapter 15, 'Plato's Sun and Descartes's Stove: Contemplation and Control in Cartesian Philosophy', in M. Ayers (ed.), *Rationalism, Platonism and God* (London: Proceedings of the British Academy, 2007), no 149, pp. 15–34. For the requirements of the present collection I have standardized and where necessary updated the referencing system, added cross-references, standardized and sometimes supplemented section headings, and taken the opportunity to correct a few factual and typographical errors and stylistic infelicities.

Contents

Abbreviations

AT   refers by volume and page number to the standard Franco-Latin
      edition of Descartes by C. Adam and P. Tannery, *Œuvres de
      Descartes* (12 vols, rev. edn., Paris: Vrin/CNRS, 1964–76).
CSM   refers by volume and page number to the English translation by
      J. Cottingham, R. Stoothoff, and D. Murdoch, *The
      Philosophical Writings of Descartes*, vols. I and II (Cambridge:
      Cambridge University Press, 1985), and
CSMK refers to vol. III, *The Correspondence*, by the same translators plus
      A. Kenny (Cambridge: Cambridge University Press, 1991).

I

Overview

1

Descartes, the Synoptic Philosopher

1. Philosophizing with Descartes

Why should one study Descartes? There are large numbers of philosophers working today who see little if any reason to go back to the writings of a seventeenth-century thinker whose views they take to have been long since superseded. In so far as they mention Descartes at all, he is simply a dummy on which to drape various suspect doctrines (such as 'Cartesian dualism'), which enlightened contemporary work in science and philosophy prides itself on having abandoned. Far removed from subscribers to this progressivist conception of philosophy are those champions of the history of ideas who make it their life's work to pay meticulous scholarly attention to the philosophical works of past ages. Some of this labour is focused on the detailed study of the texts themselves—involving the production of scholarly editions, critical apparatuses, and the like—while other work addresses itself to the additional but in many ways complementary task of situating a philosophical text in its precise historical environs. The idea is that to understand a text properly we need to immerse ourselves in the intellectual and cultural context of an age, so as to gain a better idea of how the relevant doctrines took shape.

Both these sketches—that of the 'cutting edge' contemporary analytic practitioner and that of the scholarly historian of philosophy—perhaps represent somewhat extreme positions; so if we were to follow an Aristotelian model, we might suspect that virtue should lie somewhere in the middle. But I have no particular wish to impugn either of the approaches so far described. Vigorous engagement with the specialized and technical debates of contemporary philosophy (narrow and introverted though it may often be) can produce many stimulating arguments; and on the other side, historical scholarship (dry and fustian though it may sometimes seem) can succeed in throwing fresh light on crucial components of our intellectual inheritance. So in hinting at a middle way, I certainly do not want to denigrate anyone else's conception of philosophy, nor to stake out any particular claim to philosophical virtue. Nevertheless, I should like to say a few words at the start of this chapter about my own reasons for studying Descartes, since they diverge somewhat from the models so far indicated.

In the first place, to engage in philosophical enquiry is, whether we like it or not, to be involved in a cultural tradition. A tradition need not be construed in a hyper-conservative manner, as a set of sacred doctrines to be handed on unchanged and unchallenged; seeing our ideas as forming part of a tradition is simply to acknowledge that our ways of thinking about ourselves and the world have been partly shaped by the efforts of those who have preceded us. In the case of philosophy, the very idea of the 'love of wisdom'—a zeal for reaching beyond unthinkingly accepted beliefs towards a deeper and more rationally defensible understanding of things—is an idea with a fairly specific history. It was forged, like so many vital elements of our intellectual culture, by the thought of Socrates and Plato, and began to take shape as a systematic academic discipline under the towering genius of Aristotle. That our subject has classical foundations, that during the Middle Ages it underwent a prolonged and dynamic integration with the other great source of Western culture, the Judaeo-Christian worldview, and that in the seventeenth century it was subjected to seismic rumblings that gradually gave rise to what we know as modernity—these historical facts are part of the framework without which philosophy as we know it simply would not exist. So even in order to understand what we are doing when we embark on philosophy, it seems indispensable to have some grasp of these building blocks of our philosophical culture. Even today's most 'anti-historical' departments of philosophy seem partly to acknowledge this, in so far as introductions to classical and early-modern thought remain part of the syllabus for most if not all undergraduate courses in the anglophone philosophical world (not to mention the central role they continue to have for the universities of continental Europe).

Yet it is one thing to concede that the history of philosophy should remain somewhere on the academic syllabus, and another to make a serious attempt to understand the role of the great canonical writers in shaping our intellectual inheritance. Assigned to deliver routine introductory lectures on Descartes before serried ranks of easily distracted first-year students, the philosophy lecturer may be tempted to extract a few schematic arguments from the *Meditations* and then try to 'hook' the audience with glib philosophical challenges—'How do you really know you are not now dreaming?' The danger here is that the historical Descartes becomes just a surrogate for introducing the agendas of modern epistemology. Those agendas may of course have much philosophical value, but they can often become 'professionalized'—a routine obstacle course the aspiring student or academic is expected to navigate—rather than (like the agendas of a Socrates or a Descartes) part of an integrated search for genuine knowledge and self-understanding. However tempting it may be for the hard-pressed philosophy instructor to treat Descartes as if he was obsessed with puzzles about 'the existence of the external world', or to link his malicious demon supposition with Hollywood fantasy films such as 'The Matrix', such approaches manage in a certain way to trivialize his work. The First Meditation, to be sure, does raise radical doubts, but not in order to play an academic game, or to indulge in speculative science-fiction. The purpose of his arguments, Descartes observed in the preface to his *Meditations*, was not to prove 'that there really is a world, and that human beings have bodies and so on—*since no sane person has ever seriously doubted these things*' (AT VII 15–16: CSM II 11, emphasis supplied). The Cartesian quest did not spring into existence as a set of intellectual puzzles or diversions, but fits into a long tradition (going back to Augustine and beyond), which sees the philosopher as using doubt and self-discovery as the first step in the search for objective truth. The point of his arguments establishing the external world, says Descartes, is that 'in considering them we come to realize that they are not as solid or as transparent as the arguments which lead us to knowledge of our own minds and of God' (ibid.).

The reference to God in this last quotation signals something about Descartes that is often filtered out in the philosophical agendas of contemporary analytic philosophy. By secularizing Descartes's thought, treating his conception of the deity as if it was just an embarrassing piece of historical baggage, which he would have done better to discard in addressing the main epistemological and scientific questions that opened the door to modernity, we not only distort his philosophical achievement, but also destroy much of the point of studying his ideas. For part of the fascination of Cartesian philosophy is that it is a *system*: not just a discrete set of philosophical puzzles, grist for the specialized mills of today's fragmented analytic academy, but an integrated structure of thought that supports a complete vision of the world and the place of humanity within it. And for Descartes, God is right at the centre of that system, the guarantor of genuine knowledge, the source of the logical and mathematical framework according to which the cosmos operates, and the fountain of goodness that allows finite human creatures like us, weak and imperfect though we necessarily are, to lead flourishing and worthwhile lives.

Philosophy for Descartes is the key to understanding this divinely created order, which includes our own human nature. His organic metaphor for the philosophical enterprise is well known: philosophy is a tree of which the roots are metaphysics, the trunk physics and the branches the more specific fruit-bearing offshoots—medicine, mechanics, and morals.[1] That may sound very odd to anyone whose view of philosophy is limited to what is typically done in today's university departments. But Descartes's synoptic vision is not only integral to how he conceives of himself as a philosopher, but is also something that can be properly understood only by seeing his relationship to the philosophical culture in which he was nurtured. One of the textbooks he read as a schoolboy at the Jesuit college of La Flèche was the *Summa philosophiae quadripartita*, the 'Compendium of Philosophy in Four Parts', by the scholastic thinker Eustachius e Sancto Paulo. The parts comprised logic, physics, metaphysics, and ethics, and the enterprise Eustachius saw himself as engaged in, inspired in turn by the conception found in the great compendia of Thomas Aquinas in the thirteenth century, was directed towards the goal of achieving a unified understanding of who we are, what we can know, and how we should live. Only such a holistic conception could serve the final end of a complete philosophical system, which Eustachius declared to be nothing less that 'human felicity'.[2] In similar vein, Descartes saw his philosophical system as yielding a complete morality which would constitute *le dernier degré de la sagesse*—'the ultimate level of wisdom'.[3]

---

[1] Preface to the 1647 French translation of the *Principles of Philosophy* [*Principia philosophiae*, 1644], AT IXB 14–15: CSM I 186.

[2] Eustachius a Sancto Paulo, *Summa philosophiae quadripartita* [1609], Preface to pt. II. Translated extracts may be found in R. Ariew, J. Cottingham, and T. Sorell (eds.), *Descartes' Meditations: Background Source Materials* (Cambridge: Cambridge University Press, 1998), 68–96.

[3] Preface to French edition of *Principles*, loc. cit.

This may all sound very grand, not to say grandiose. But before we resign ourselves to resting content with the much lower-key ambitions of contemporary philosophy—unravelling conceptual confusions, mapping the logical structure of language, or serving the agenda of natural science as its 'abstract and reflective branch'[4]—it is worth seeing if the Cartesian picture has something to teach us. In the post-Darwinian climate of our modern age, many tend to see the universe as a randomly evolved process not in itself possessed of any intrinsic value or purpose, while our own lives are seen as not ordained towards any goal or end except that which we happen to choose to pursue. What is absorbing about Descartes is how some of his ideas foreshadow this bleaker modern picture, while at the same time other elements of his thought connect up with the more reassuring teleology that informed the worldview of many of his predecessors. In conceiving the physical universe as so much machinery, to be 'mastered' and utilized in order to improve the quality of human life,[5] he speaks with the voice of the modern scientific technocrat, less interested in the ancient philosophical aim of living 'in accordance with nature' than in making nature conform to our own needs and desires. But in trying to discern how humans can live as they are meant to, he holds fast to a vision of timeless objective goodness and truth that compels our assent whether we like it or not, and to a picture of our human nature as so ordered that 'there is absolutely nothing to be found that does not bear witness to the power and goodness of God' (AT VII 87: CSM II 60).

In short, when studying Descartes in a philosophically fruitful way we need to look in two directions—forwards to the ideas of our own age which Descartes's thinking helped to shape, and backwards to the medieval and classical culture which moulded so much of his own outlook. By

---

[4] The first of these three conceptions is represented by Ludwig Wittgenstein: 'what is your aim in philosophy: to show the fly the way out of the fly bottle' (Ludwig Wittgenstein, *Philosophical Investigations* [*Philosophische Untersuchungen*, 1953], trans. G. E. M. Anscombe (New York: Macmillan, 1958), pt. I §309); the second by Michael Dummett: 'only with the rise of the modern logical and analytic style of philosophizing was the proper object of philosophy finally established, namely... the analysis of the structure of *thought*, [for which] the only proper method [is] the analysis of *language*' ('Can Analytic Philosophy Be Systematic?' [1975], in *Truth and Other Enigmas* (London: Duckworth, 1978), 458). The third and most recent, described by Brian Leiter, is the now increasingly popular view that philosophy should 'either... adopt and emulate the method of successful sciences, or... operate in tandem with the sciences, as their abstract and reflective branch' (*The Future for Philosophy* (Oxford: Clarendon, 2004), Editor's Introduction, 2–3).

[5] *Discourse on the Method* [*Discours de la méthode*, 1637], Pt. Six (AT VI 62: CSM I 142).

deracinating Descartes, and extracting philosophical bullet-points out of his writings merely as ammunition for current philosophical sparring, we blind ourselves to that richness of texture that is indispensable for any but the shallowest understanding of the great philosophers. But on the other hand, by immersing ourselves in the historical detail to the point where his ideas become of merely antiquarian interest, connected backwards in time but not really meshing with our present philosophical thinking, we also remove the life from his ideas: grubbing round too much in the roots of an organism can be as life-threatening as trying to pull it out of its native soil.

These reflections are necessarily of a somewhat schematic nature, and one cannot satisfactorily explain what makes a given philosopher worth studying without delving into the specific content of the ideas and arguments. But let me add one more general observation before coming to the particular issues that have engaged my attention in the chapters that follow. In my undergraduate days, because of the peculiar structure of the Greats course at Oxford during the 1960s, I read the whole of two long masterworks of ancient philosophy (Plato's *Republic*, and Aristotle's *Nicomachean Ethics*), studying them in minute detail in the original Greek, and then jumped straight to R. M. Hare and P. F. Strawson and the latest puzzles of the (then) cutting-edge 'linguistic' philosophy, without pausing for breath or being asked by my teachers even to glance at anything in between. Not surprisingly, the resulting examination papers we had to sit, though extraordinarily intricate and demanding, seemed strangely isolated from each other, and indeed from virtually every other aspect of the cultural and intellectual landscape we inhabited. It was only later on, when coming to Descartes as a graduate student, that I started to become dimly aware of how those classical philosophical ideas had shaped the rise of modern culture, and, in turn, of why the debates of the latter-day philosophical luminaries were something more than a series of clever and abstract verbal games.

Descartes's pivotal place in the development of Western philosophy gives his ideas a unique importance. But on top of that, his thought also offers an unusually compelling picture of what it is to philosophize, and it is this that gives him such an enduring power to draw the reader into the philosophical quest. With Descartes, one is confronted by the challenge to question one's preconceived opinions and examine how much of what one claims to know can be justified. In a spiritual exercise of remarkable power, one is asked to imagine oneself quite alone, helpless, isolated, and ignorant, and to confront the possibility that this very helplessness and finitude is recognized only through a residual awareness of something greater and higher. By pondering on what is involved in the very act of wondering and reflecting, one is launched into an enquiry about one's own nature as a thinker, and its relation to the material world. Through reflection on how the essential structure of that world can be conceived in its clearest terms, one finds oneself confronting mathematical and logical ideas of such irresistible simplicity and transparency that it is impossible to doubt their validity. And by coming to terms with one's own intimate involvement with that corporeal world, one's essential and inescapable embodiment as a human creature of flesh and blood, one is forced to allow that such seemingly utterly alien domains as the realm of the mind and the realm of extended physical reality are somehow, mysteriously, intermingled, so as to make us what we are.

In every step of the Cartesian journey, and the scientific and ethical theories that come out of it, there are philosophical puzzles rich and fertile enough to occupy a lifetime's reflection. And almost every result that Descartes himself reached along his own journey has, as we are now too well aware, been strongly and repeatedly challenged by subsequent philosophers, right down to the present day. But his philosophy does nevertheless survive, not just as a historical curiosity, nor just as target practice, nor just because he is a writer of wonderful precision and eloquence, but as a model for what philosophy can aspire to. In Descartes's vision of how the reflective intellect can strive to achieve a systematic and coherent vision of reality, we find something that is unlikely to lose its hold on us completely, so long as the human impulse to philosophize continues. 'A good man,' he wrote in what may have been one of his last works, 'is not required to have read every book or diligently mastered everything taught in the schools. But he needs to rid himself of the bad doctrines that have filled his mind and discover how to raise his knowledge to the highest level it can attain.' And there then follows an extraordinary manifesto:

I shall bring to light the true riches of our souls, opening up to each of us the means whereby we can find within ourselves, without any help from anyone else, all the knowledge we may need for the conduct of life and the means of using it in order to acquire all the most abstruse items of knowledge that human reason is capable of possessing.[6]

It sounds impossible, arrogant, exaggerated; and even Descartes's most devoted disciples would surely dispute the vaunted self-sufficiency of that phrase 'without any help from anyone else'. But for all that, his manifesto captures something about philosophy that makes it diverge radically from subjects that require us to align ourselves with a recognized body of doctrine, a specific area of empirical enquiry, or a corpus of received wisdom. Everyone who tackles philosophy is in one sense on his or her own, in a way that is quite unlike what happens in any other discipline, whether scientific or humane. Just as Socrates learned to trust his 'inner voice' over the opinions of others or the lure of expediency,[7] so anyone who aspires to philosophize must, like Descartes, learn to set aside book learning and uncritical reliance on external authority,[8] in the struggle to achieve a rationally secure understanding of what we can know, how we should live, and what is our human place in the scheme of things. The Cartesian voice still calls to us, and it would be a sad day for philosophy if should ever fall silent.

2. Descartes's Position in Philosophy

The essays contained in the three remaining parts of this volume are thematically divided for the reader's convenience into three groups. Part II contains two chapters that look at Descartes's celebrated role as the 'father of modern philosophy' and ask exactly what this title means, and how far it is justified. The opening chapter, 'A New Start?', scrutinizes Descartes's claim to be an innovator. He highlighted that claim in 1637 in the brief intellectual autobiography he produced as part of his (anonymous) first publication, the *Discourse on the Method*, and it implicitly appears a few years later in his *Meditations*, in the graphic opening image of demolishing

---

[6] *The Search for Truth by Means of the Natural Light* [*La Recherche de la vérité par la lumière naturelle*], AT X 496: CSM II 400. The date and place of composition of this work are in doubt. It covers some of the same arguments as the *Meditations*, but the fact that it was unfinished, and that the (now lost) French manuscript is listed in an inventory of Descartes's papers made shortly after his death in Stockholm, suggests that it may date from the final year of his life.

[7] See Plato, *Apology* [c.390 BC], 40a2–c2.   [8] See *Discourse*, Pt. One (AT VI 4–11: CSM I 112–16).

all the old buildings and 'starting again right from the foundations' (AT VII 17: CSM II 12). I argue in this chapter that Descartes was quite genuinely an innovator in respect of the scientific programme he introduced to the public in the *Discourse*. Although he was not alone (Galileo has a just claim to be the co-inaugurator of the 'new' philosophy), there was something genuinely revolutionary in the idea that Descartes developed of a unitary template for understanding the physical world,[9] based on mathematical principles, and including not just the inanimate world but the world of physiology and even a large part of what we now call psychology.

Yet in the parts of the Cartesian philosophy for which its author is best known nowadays, the 'method of doubt' and the metaphysical enquiries that generate the foundations of Descartes's system, what is striking, by contrast, is the significant continuity between his ideas and those of his predecessors. The wholesale challenging of preconceived opinions by systematic doubt is a device found well before Descartes was born.[10] And as for his appeal to the light of reason, or 'natural light', Descartes's *lumen naturale* is no exception to the general principle that, however much philosophers may indulge the fantasy of having some kind of culturally detached hotline to the truth, their intuitions all too often reflect the intellectual atmosphere they breathed in their youth. Much of the background to Descartes's arguments for God's existence derives (as has often been pointed out) from the philosophical presuppositions of those medieval and Renaissance writers he studied as a young man, and the language of the *Meditations* bears unmistakeable traces of the scholastic philosophy that it was his stated aim to supplant.

Among the reflections I go on to offer towards the end of Ch. 2 are some thoughts about how Descartes's scientific revolution might have been carried through in a more radical way, without all this residual metaphysical lumber. The notion of *substance* is pivotal here. Though it figures prominently in Descartes's philosophical-cum-scientific compendium, the *Principles of Philosophy*, the way Descartes conceives of it has its natural home in the world of Aristotelian scholasticism—a world of discrete individual objects, each defined by its essential attributes. In the scientific vision presented in his earlier (suppressed)[11] physical treatise *Le Monde*, by contrast,

---

[9] See *Rules for the Direction of our Native Intelligence* [*Regulae ad directionem ingenii*, c.1628], AT X 378: CSM I 17).   [10] See the last two paragraphs of Ch. 2 sect. 2, below.

[11] Descartes withdrew *Le Monde* from publication on hearing of the condemnation of Galileo in 1633 (for advocating the heliocentric hypothesis, which he too supported). The *Principles* [*Principia*

the behaviour of matter can be explained and predicted in purely quantitative terms, via the specification of the 'motion, size, shape and arrangement of parts' out of which it is composed (AT XI 25: CSM I 89), and it seems that substances and attributes play no real role here. In fact this new perspective turns out to be reflected, albeit somewhat circumspectly, even in the *Principles*, where despite the prominence of the notion of substance, there are no genuine individual substances, only the single, all-encompassing plenum that is *res extensa*, extended stuff. The proviso is added, moreover, that there is no real distinction between material substance and its defining attribute of extension;[12] what this seems to imply is that once we have specified the various (quantitative) modes of the extended matter (motion, size, shape, and arrangement of parts), no further scientific work is done by invoking the idea of substance. There is thus a kind of tension between Cartesian science, which all but dispenses with substance, and Cartesian metaphysics, to which the notion is integral.

Some of the issues involved here are historical and textual ones, but, as is implied in my general introductory remarks above, the interest in studying Descartes's thought is, according to the approach taken in these chapters, never purely and simply historical; part of the fascination lies in seeing how the issues connect up with aspects of our own modern philosophical outlook. That outlook has been conditioned by a long and gradual eclipse of the notion of substance, accelerated in the eighteenth century by Hume's devastating dismissal of it as a 'metaphysical chimera'. It is of course true, as I should certainly have acknowledged when writing the paper under discussion, that the eclipse has never been total; indeed, with the current revival of traditional metaphysics, we find a good number of practitioners defending the idea of substance as still philosophically indispensable. Nevertheless, it remains striking that modern science has little use for the notion, nor, more generally, for the kind of philosophical-cum-scientific agenda that we find in Descartes (and some of his partial followers such as Leibniz), namely that of bolting a mathematically based physics onto something like a traditional metaphysical undercarriage. Part of what I aimed to show in this opening chapter is just how difficult it is to make these two elements mesh together in any satisfying explanatory

---

philosophiae, 1644] conveyed Descartes's views in a somewhat more cautious way, and was composed with an eye to getting it accepted as a university textbook. See AT III 276: CSMK 167 and AT IV 225: CSMK 252.   [12] *Principles*, Pt. I, art. 63 (AT VIII 30–1: CSM I 215).

schema, and how the tension between them is inherent in much of Descartes's work. Today's debates over alternative (non-substance-based) metaphysical frameworks such as that of 'trope theory' (attractive to some of its supporters precisely because it seems to cohere better with modern theoretical physics) suggest that the tension Descartes wrestled with is still being worked out; and it remains to be seen whether the ultimate structure of reality can be described in ways that can dispense entirely with what seems such an intuitively natural model—that of an object characterized by essential properties or attributes.[13]

In the second chapter of Part II, 'The Cartesian Legacy', the argument shifts to the (generally very critical) way in which Descartes's theories have been received in the modern academic world. 'Rationalism' and 'Cartesian rationalism' are labels that have often been used in a pejorative way; and though many of the confusions and exaggerations associated with such labelling have by now been exposed by those working in the history of philosophy, the widespread currency of the 'rationalist' tag has nevertheless left some distinctly negative impressions of Descartes's approach among the philosophical community at large. The most general implication of calling someone a rationalist is that they suppose that substantive truths about reality can be arrived at purely a priori. Descartes certainly supposed that the innate ideas implanted in our minds by God give us accurate knowledge of the general logical and mathematical principles in terms of which the universe is structured. But it is highly misleading to think of him as an 'armchair scientist': not only does he not deny the necessity of observation and experiment in science, but he goes so far as to stress their crucial importance in deciding between rival explanatory hypotheses.[14]

More interesting and complicated is the charge of what I called 'causal logicism'—the view that real causal connections are logically intuitable or demonstrable in the manner of the truths of arithmetic or geometry. As is quite often the case with the way we react to Descartes, we tend to look back on him through a Humean lens: we assume that he must have subscribed to a model of scientific knowledge whereby it was supposed

---

[13] Contrast the view of Peter Simons that 'with…the apparent irrelevance of the concept of substance for modern science it has lost its central position in metaphysics' ('Substance', in J. Kim and E. Sosa (eds.), *A Companion to Metaphysics* (Oxford: Blackwell, 1995), 481), with the view of Jonathan Lowe, in *A Survey of Metaphysics* (Oxford: Clarendon, 2002), which regards the category of objects, or individual substances, as indispensable.   [14] *Discourse*, Pt. Six (AT VI 64: CSM I 144).

to be a logical impossibility that a given effect should not follow upon a given cause (a view tailor-made to be demolished by Hume's acid observation that it hardly violates the law of contradiction to suppose that lunchtime's nourishing bread will not poison me at supper).[15] I argue that what is problematic here is not anything that Descartes proposed, but, on the contrary, the atomistic conception of knowledge and truth offered by Hume, which supposes that the logical status of a proposition can be evaluated in isolation from the system of which it forms a part. Descartes was indeed a deductivist in the sense that he conceived of explanation as the subsumption of phenomena under general laws that (in conjunction with various auxiliary hypotheses) entailed them—but one might add that this is pretty much how Hume himself conceived of it too,[16] together with most if not all philosophers of science down to the present.[17] This kind of hypothetical necessity (the necessity of an event given the laws that entail it) seems relatively unproblematic. What remains a matter for debate is the status of the covering laws themselves.

Here Descartes insists that we have innate knowledge of certain fundamental mathematical principles such that 'after reflection we cannot doubt that they are observed in everything that exists or occurs in the world'.[18] Clearly such optimistic apriorism as applied to physical reality diverges substantially from the way these matters have typically been thought about from Hume down to the present. Nevertheless, I continue to think it illuminating to notice a certain convergence between the two philosophical giants, one 'empiricist', one 'rationalist', when it comes to the status of the ultimate laws of nature. For Hume, these laws are purely contingent generalizations whose rationale, if any, must remain 'totally shut up from human curiosity';[19] while for Descartes, they are divinely decreed correlations, whose rationale we can never fully grasp, since they are subject to the 'incomprehensible power of God' (AT I 149: CSMK 25).

---

[15] David Hume, *An Enquiry concerning Human Understanding* [1748], from sect. IV pt. 2.

[16] In so far as he spoke of the power of human reason to 'reduce the principles productive of natural phenomena to a greater simplicity...and resolve many particular effects into a few general causes'. Hume, *An Enquiry concerning Human Understanding*, sect. IV pt. 1.

[17] For the standard 'nomological deductive' model, see e.g. Carl G. Hempel, 'Explanation in Science and in History', in R. G. Colodny (ed.), *Frontiers of Science and Philosophy* (London and Pittsburgh: Allen & Unwin and University of Pittsburgh Press, 1962), pp. 7–33.

[18] *Discourse*, Pt. Five (AT VI 41: CSM I 131).

[19] Hume, *Enquiry concerning Human Understanding*, sect. IV pt. 1.

Correlations decreed by the unfathomable will of God, or generalizations whose rationale is hidden from our knowledge: if we reflect on these formulations, I think we come to see that there is not in the end as vast a difference as might be supposed between the Cartesian and the Humean views of the nature of the scientific enterprise. Both philosophers are optimistic about the physicist's power to devise covering laws of maximum simplicity and generality, but both, in the end, have a certain humility about how deep our human understanding of the natural world can go.

The general moral to come out of this is that the 'Cartesian-rationalist' model of a scientific system emerges in tolerably good shape, if we take the core of that model to be what has since become the relatively uncontroversial view that the scientist's job is to construct precise quantitative laws under which the widest possible range of phenomena may be subsumed. Nevertheless, in rescuing Descartes from unfair caricatures, we should not try to gloss over genuinely problematic aspects of his system. As far as claims to certainty are concerned we do often get in Descartes's writings a whiff of the rather grandiose confidence that has tended to get his 'rationalism' a bad name. In offering his system to the world, he largely adopts the vocabulary that was still current in his day—the language of Aristotelian deductive certainty[20] (in contrast to Hume's preference, on behalf of the scientist, for the more reticent tone of the sceptic); though this is perhaps partly a matter of presentation on Descartes's part—of his wanting to advertise his scientific system as fully meeting the standards expected by the epistemic models of his day. Towards the end of the chapter under discussion I draw attention to what seems, with today's hindsight, another unwarranted element in Descartes's approach to explanation in physics—his confidence in the *transparent* nature of the underlying mechanisms of nature. This 'Cartesian simplicism', the insistence that 'nature always uses very simple means' (AT II 797: CSMK 215), led him to model the micro-world on familiar structures in our human-scale environment; and while Descartes can hardly be called to account for having failed to predict the astonishing strangeness of the micro-world as disclosed by modern physics, he can perhaps be charged with assuming too readily that, even at the macro level, what was familiar was somehow wholly transparent in its causal workings. This links

---

[20] Aristotle defines demonstrative knowledge in science as depending on premises that are 'true, primary, immediate, and better known than, and prior to the conclusion', *Posterior Analytics* [*Analytica Hystera*, *c*.330 BC], Bk. I ch. 2.

up with a major theme of our first chapter, namely the Cartesian failure to give systematic philosophical scrutiny to the concept of causation—an area where Hume was, so spectacularly, to earn his spurs. That said, the overall conclusion of the discussion is that there are central respects in which Descartes's 'rationalism' has stood the test of time far better than is often supposed.

3. Mind and World

The chapters comprising the third part of this volume are devoted to some of the most debated aspects of the Cartesian system. This part opens by looking at Descartes's account of the nature of thinking, in the context of his famous proposition in the Second Meditation that 'I am a thinking thing' (Ch. 4). There then follow two chapters that discuss Descartes's views on the relation between thought and language: the first deals with the common charge that Descartes subscribed to a fallacious conception of the 'privacy' of thought (Ch. 5); the second examines the contrast in Descartes between psychological and logical aspects of the thinking process, a correct account of which reveals the Cartesian view to be considerably less 'subjectivist' than is often supposed (Ch. 6). The next two chapters deal with Descartes's theory of colour (Ch. 7), a concept that has become particularly problematic in the philosophy of mind; and the Cartesian view of animals, focusing on Descartes's supposed denial of sensory faculties to the 'brutes' (Ch. 8). The final chapter in this part of the book looks at Descartes's conception of the human being as the subject of attributes not reducible either to modes of thought or to modes of extension, and offers a 'trialistic' framework for understanding Descartes's philosophy of mind, in contrast to the standard dualistic picture (Ch. 9).

(a) Thought

We have already noted how certain standard modern criticisms of Descartes involve distortions or oversimplifications of his ideas, and this is particularly true of his views on the mind. In Ch. 4, 'Descartes on Thought', I argue that there is good reason to be wary of the way many modern translators and interpreters of Descartes have understood one of the fundamental building-blocks of his system—what he called (in Latin) *cogitatio* or (in French) *la pensée.* Elizabeth Anscombe and Peter Geach, in a translation of the *Meditations* they produced in the 1950s, rendered *cogitatio* as 'consciousness'; and the rationale for this rendering was bound up with their highly suspicious attitude to certain moves they took Descartes to be making in the Second Meditation, as Anscombe makes clear in an article published some years later:

A huge trick has been successfully performed. Nutrition and locomotion are now purely material, mechanical; sensation, on the other hand does not essentially require the body. The acts of...immaterial substance are all those psychological states and events given expression in an indubitable first person present indicative: 'I feel pain', 'I see', 'I hear', 'I have images', 'I will', 'I hope', I reflect'. They are all sub-species of *cogito* ...[21]

So we are invited to suppose that when Descartes uses the verb *cogito*, he really means something like 'I am conscious' or (as the Anscombe–Geach translation sometimes has it) 'I am experiencing'.

This seems to me a classic case of retrojecting modern confusions back onto Descartes. Nowadays, philosophers of mind are preoccupied with the 'problem of consciousness', and in particular the so-called 'hard problem'—of whether certain dimensions of experiential awareness (what it feels like to have a toothache, or to smell a rose) can be explained in physical or functional terms. But it is vital to remember that Descartes was writing well before the term 'consciousness' had acquired its modern connotations. The term *conscientia* nowhere appears in the text of the *Meditations*, and the term *conscius* only once;[22] and when Descartes does, occasionally, use such terms elsewhere, they always, as one would expect given that they are cognates of the Latin *scire* ('to know'), relate to some kind of epistemic state—a kind of inner knowledge or judgement—*not* to some kind of experiential or phenomenological 'what-it-is-like-ness'.

Philosophers, after years in the seminar room, often end up with systematically distorted linguistic intuitions, and there is no more striking example of this than a widespread modern philosophical conception of the domain of the 'mental', such that if you ask a certain kind of philosopher for

[21] E. Anscombe, 'Analytic Philosophy and the Spirituality of Man' [1979], in Anscombe, *Human Life, Action and Ethics*, ed. M. Geach and L. Gormally (Exeter: Imprint Academic, 2005), 5–6.
[22] When Descartes says, in the Third Meditation, that if I had the power to preserve myself from moment to moment I should certainly be aware (*conscius*) of such a power (*Meditations* [*Meditationes de prima philosophia*, 1641], AT VII 49: CSM II 34).

an example of a mental state, he or she is as like as not to mention something as strange and ephemeral as a 'green after-image', or, even more bizarrely, a toothache—something that the ordinary dental patient would be baffled or highly irritated to have described as an event in the mind. Whatever justification can be concocted for this curiously stretched interpretation of 'mental', such an approach is miles away from Descartes. For Descartes, the mind is a *thinking* thing, and I argue in the chapter under discussion that there is good reason to suppose that by this Descartes means precisely what he says, namely something that engages in various kinds of intellectual and judgemental activity—doubting, understanding, affirming, denying, and so on. It is true that, almost as an afterthought, Descartes does in the Second Meditation tack on to this list 'imagining and having sensory perceptions', but this should not be read as implying any anticipation of the modern notion of 'consciousness', with its supposed philosophical intractability. Sense-perception and imagination count as cases of thinking only in a very special sense—a sense which requires us to read the *Meditations* as a whole in order to appreciate what is meant. So far from maintaining that 'sensation does not essentially require the body' (as Anscombe puts it), Descartes goes on to insist in the Sixth Meditation that sensations are the sure signature of our essentially embodied nature as human beings. It is true that we may, when performing the exercise of extreme doubt in the First and Second Meditation, 'slice off' a purely mental component of sensation, and talk of the judgement 'it *seems* to me that I see, or hear'; but this, as Descartes explicitly states, counts as a 'thought' only if *sentire* is understood not in its normal sense, but in this 'restricted sense' (AT VII 29: CSM II 19)—that is, as referring to the 'sliced off' judgemental component.[23] So far from extending *cogitare* to any conscious state, Descartes will count a conscious state as a *cogitatio* only if we restrict ourselves simply to the reflective mental judgement involved.

---

[23] 'For example I am now seeing light ... But I am asleep, so all this is false. Yet I certainly *seem* to see (*videre videor*). This cannot be false, and what is called "having a sensory perception" is strictly just this, and in this restricted sense of the term it is simply thinking' (AT VII 29: CSM II 19) The Latin says: *sentire ... praecise sic sumptum est cogitare*. The '*sic sumptum*' ('taken *in this way*') is significant. Descartes is *not* saying that from a proper and precise philosophical perspective sense-perception counts as a *cogitatio* because it is a psychological state, and any psychological or conscious state is a *cogitatio* (this is the anachronistic or 'retrojective' Anscombian view). Rather he is suggesting that (as will become fully clear in the Sixth Meditation) *sentire* is *not* properly a case of *cogitatio* unless we take it *sic precise*, in *this restricted way just specified*, namely as the mental act of supposing to myself that I see, or entertaining the judgement *videre videor*, literally 'I *seem* to see'.

(b) Privacy and Objectivity

The modern philosophical paradigm of the 'mental', as involving any 'conscious' item, is so firmly entrenched that we need to make a firm effort to leave it behind when approaching Descartes's theory of the mind. Given that consciousness in this modern conception is widely supposed to be characterized by a certain interior dimension, 'what it is like for the subject',[24] it is an easy step to suppose that it has an ineliminably *private* aspect; and if Descartes is then interpreted (in the way just described) as inaugurating the modern notion of 'consciousness', it is another short step to lumbering him with a doctrine of the 'privacy of the mental'—a doctrine that many modern philosophers, in the aftermath of Wittgenstein,[25] have seen as responsible for a host of conceptual confusions. In Ch. 5, on thought and language in Descartes, I examine the supposedly 'Cartesian' thesis of the privacy of thought and argue that such a view can be laid at Descartes's door only if we systematically ignore the approach he takes to mental phenomena in the vast majority of his writings. In his early scientific work, he is concerned to account for such psychological phenomena as sense-perception, memory, and voluntary action in a very objective and public way, without any reference to a supposed 'inner' or 'private' domain; indeed, in his work on vision, he explicitly *attacks* the 'homunculus' model that supposes we can explain someone's seeing an object by reference to a soul contemplating private images resembling external objects. The homunculus fallacy, so often foisted on Descartes, is one Descartes himself rejects as circular, when he scathingly attacks the view that makes it seem 'as if there were yet other eyes within our brain by mean of which we could perceive [an image resembling an external object]' (AT VI 130: CSM I 167). Daniel Dennett's lampooning of Descartes, for taking the pineal gland in the brain to be a kind of 'fax machine' transmitting images to the soul,[26] invokes the kind of picture that Descartes himself expressly repudiates.

It is of course true that the perspective adopted in Descartes's most famous work, the *Meditations*, is that of the solitary thinker, cut off from all contact with the outside world, and immersed in his own reflections. But

---

[24] Extremely influential in cementing this paradigm has been the famous (or notorious) paper of Thomas Nagel, 'What Is it Like To Be a Bat?' [1974], repr. in Nagel's *Mortal Questions* (Cambridge: Cambridge University Press, 1979), ch. 12.

[25] Wittgenstein, *Philosophical Investigations*, pt. I, §§256 ff.

[26] See D. Dennett, *Consciousness Explained* (Boston: Little Brown, 1991), 106.

countless 'ideas' of the meditator nevertheless have a publicly accessible structure—they are not dependent on the subjective psychological character of the meditator's experience, but relate to those 'immutable and eternal essences' that Descartes insists are quite independent of his own mind (AT VII 64: CSM II 45). The common complaint that Descartes 'psychologizes' ideas fails to take account of Descartes's own definition of an idea: an idea is not a thought, but the *form* of a given thought (AT VII 160: CSM II 113). What this implies is that an idea is not a subjective item in an individual's mind, but rather that it belongs in the intersubjective domain, in so far as two people's thoughts may have the same representational content.

In Cartesian metaphysics, the structure that grounds the objectivity of the essences so represented is none other than the mind of God—something as independent of the vagaries of any given individual's psychology as one might wish. But, once again, there is risk of missing this because of certain distorting paradigms that condition how Cartesianism is understood. Those who lambast Descartes for his 'private' theory of the mind tend to see him as doing philosophy 'all on his own' or 'from the inside', and implicitly contrast the more enlightened insights of those modern philosophers who have made the crucial links between ideas and language, and language and public rules; in short, the interpersonal domain of the social is taken to provide the necessary underpinning for objectivity that Descartes's approach supposedly lacks. But such a critique of Descartes's philosophical stance for its supposed subjectivism is only possible for the interpreter who implicitly secularizes Cartesian thought, subconsciously bracketing off the references to God as if they cannot really add anything substantial to the argument. If this is done, if the meditator is left adrift in the isolated world of his own psychology, then it is hardly surprising that the whole enterprise looks as if it is supposed to work in an entirely private domain. But that is not Descartes's way. His own philosophical journey is one that, almost simultaneously from its emergence from the morass of doubt and uncertainty, comes up against an objective reality that is the source not just of his own existence, but of those 'countless ideas' that relate to the 'determinate essences, natures or forms' which are 'not invented by me or dependent on my mind' (AT VII 64: CSM II 45).

Even if we leave aside the role of God as objective guarantor of the interpersonal domain of meaning and reference, there is a further independent argument for acquitting Descartes of being a 'privacy' theorist about the mind, namely that he explicitly links the phenomenon of thought to language use. Those who promote the myth of 'Cartesian privacy', and take this label as an apt way of condemning Descartes's approach to mental phenomena, are not well placed to explain his thesis of the linguisticity of thought. This thesis is advanced by Descartes (amongst other places) in the course of his arguments in the *Discourse* about animal behaviour, where he draws the firmest distinction between simply reacting to stimuli in a patterned way, and being able to respond in a thoughtful and rational manner to all the contingencies of life—something only genuine humans can do. And the relevant criterion for engaging in thought is *not* the occurrence of some inaccessible private process, but something perfectly public and observable, namely linguistic competence. Here once more our stereotyped notions of Descartes's philosophy may easily blind us to what he is actually trying to do. If we always focus on his dualistic theory of the mind, then the notion of a mysterious immaterial soul will tend to occupy the foreground; and we will then be tempted to make a swift inference that the workings of this soul must be something interior and accessible only to the subject; so the stage is set for the standard picture of 'Cartesian privacy'. But Descartes's writings become much more interesting if we first take off our Rylean spectacles.[27] In many passages both here in the *Discourse* and elsewhere, Descartes approaches things from the *outside*, and asks how various kinds of observable phenomena (in humans and in animals) can be explained. Thinking, in one sense, is a publicly manifested phenomenon, something revealed in the astonishing and infinitely variable outputs of the human language user; and it is not some modern behaviourist or linguistic theorist, but Descartes, the supposed 'privacy' theorist, who underlines the point. It is of course true that, since he was unable to envisage any plausible physical mechanism that could account for thought, and its linguistic manifestation, Descartes ended up attributing the relevant capacities to an immaterial 'rational soul'. Many modern readers may regard such a move with distaste; but one moral of the chapter under discussion is that they should not allow such distaste to divert them from recognizing Descartes's remarkable philosophical and scientific insights into the unique (and objectively accessible) character of our human capacities for thought, reason, and language.

---

[27] For Gilbert Ryle's famous attack on the Cartesian theory of the mind as invoking the idea of a 'private theatre', see Ryle, *The Concept of Mind* (London: Hutcheson, 1949), ch. 1.

In Ch. 6, I further develop some of the points already mentioned about the objective nature of ideas in Descartes. Modern views of the 'intentionality' of the mental (following on from the work of Franz Brentano)[28] focus on the representational content of our ideas—what they are *about*. If we construe Cartesian ideas along these lines, in a 'logical' rather than a psychological way, then much of what Descartes says about the relation between ideas and the 'things' they represent falls into place. Nonetheless, the term 'idea' is, and has always been, a somewhat slippery one in philosophy, and a look at some of the medieval antecedents of Descartes's thinking reveals a host of tensions and ambiguities, mainly centring on the question of whether an idea should be thought of as a mode of cognition or, instead, as its object. Taking the second line preserves the 'objective' or logical character of an idea, while taking the first may tend to encourage the assimilation of ideas to the domain of individual psychology. These tensions come to a head in some protracted and inconclusive debates about the status of ideas in the decades following Descartes's death; and I suggest that for help in finding our way out of this maze it is illuminating to follow the lead of Descartes's disciple, Nicolas Malebranche, who distinguishes between, on the one hand, ideas proper, objects of cognition which do not depend on the vagaries of human psychology, and, on the other hand, the purely mental phenomena of sensations (or, in Malebranche's French, *sentiments*).[29] Going back to Descartes, we find a clear distinction between those clear and distinct ideas which represent, for example, the self,[30] God, or triangles and other mathematical objects, and, on the other hand, those sensory ideas that are inherently confused, and, perhaps, do not represent anything at all. The examples Descartes gives are the ideas of 'light and colours, sounds, smells, tastes, heat and cold', which 'I think of only in a very confused and obscure way', so much so that I do not really know whether they are ideas of things or of 'non-things' (AT VII 43: CSM II 30).

The picture of 'Cartesianism' as dumping all conscious phenomena into a single catch-all container marked 'the mind' suffers another salutary

---

[28] F. Brentano, *Psychology from and Empirical Standpoint* [*Psychologie vom empirischen Standpunkt*, 1874], trans. L. L. McAlister (London: Routledge, 1974), Bk. II ch. 1.

[29] Malebranche, *Entretiens sur la Métaphysique* [1687], Dialogue III.

[30] Many philosophers would, of course, dispute that we have a clear and distinct idea of the self, including, interestingly, Malebranche. See Ch. 5 n. 38 below.

setback here. One of the themes to which I have often found myself returning is not the homogeneity but the radical *heterogeneity* of mental phenomena in Descartes's scheme of things. When we make an inventory of our ideas, we find a striking distinction between two types. In the first place there are those that have intentionality, representing objects that exist independently of ourselves, and are apprehended intellectually, through our grasp of their content—a content that we can understand and specify as rational, language-using creatures. In the second place, we find obscure modes of sensory awareness whose informational content is much harder to specify in language, and whose representational object is often far from clear.

(c) Colour Perception; Opacity; Animals

The point we have now reached, concerning the 'obscurity' of sensory awareness, lies as the heart of several vexed areas of Descartes's philosophy, including his account of colour perception. As I point out in Ch. 7, Descartes's treatment of colour plays an influential role in what can loosely be called the 'secondary quality' tradition—the idea found in different formulations in Locke, Malebranche, and Hume that external objects are not 'really' coloured, at least in the way we may ordinarily suppose them to be. In fact, the Humean way of putting the matter, that 'colours are not really in bodies',[31] is somewhat inept, or at least radically at odds with common-sense ascriptions of colour properties. Descartes puts things in a fashion less likely to violate ordinary ways of talking when he says, in the *Optics*, that 'in the bodies we call "coloured", colours are nothing but the ways in which bodies receive light and reflect it to our eyes'[32]—a formulation that does not deny that objects are coloured, but merely offers an account of what colour consists in. Consistently with his general view of the material world, he is prepared to attribute to objects only what

---

[31] See opening paragraph of Ch. 7, below.

[32] *La Dioptrique* [c.1630, first pub. 1637], Discourse I (AT VI 85: CSM I 153). In the English version of this work provided in CSM the title of Descartes's treatise was given simply as *The Optics*. Some scholars objected strongly to this, on the grounds that such a title is too general, and that the rendering 'Dioptrics' should have been used. (Dioptrics is the part of Optics that deals with refraction, while Catoptrics deals with reflection.) But not only is the less technical title more immediately informative to the general reader, but there is good reason to think that Descartes would have approved, since he described his work as one in which 'besides treating of refraction and the manufacture of lenses, I give detailed descriptions of the eye, of light, of vision, and of everything belonging to catoptrics and optics'. Letter to Mersenne of March 1636, AT I 340: CSMK 51.

can be defined in quantitative terms, as a function of the size, shape, and movement of molecules; and there is simply no room in this scheme of things for irreducible, *sui-generis* qualities such as redness. A colour properly understood, scientifically understood, is simply a disposition of an object 'which makes it able to set up various kinds of motion in our nerves' (AT VIII 323: CSM I 285).

It seems, then, that a full explanation of colour perception in human beings would have to add something not found in the physical account of the relevant causal chain of molecular motions from the object through to the human nervous system—namely the distinctive qualitative sensation that you or I have when we perceive, for example, a red rose. Both Descartes's conception of matter and his conception of causation[33] preclude this further event from being explained in scientific terms, so recourse has to be had to some wholly distinct type of explanation. This is precisely what we find in Descartes's *Treatise on Man*: the requisite qualitative sensation results from the fact that God has made the nature of the human soul such that this sensation will arise on the 'occasion' of the nerves and brain being stimulated in a certain way.[34] This may be regarded (as I point out in Ch. 7) as a striking anticipation of Malebranche's occasionalism. Actually, it may be construed in two ways: if God is thought of as causally intervening to make a sensation of redness 'arise' in your mind whenever a certain pattern occurs in your brain, it does indeed prefigure Malebranche; if on the other hand one thinks of God creating a soul with an innate and permanent structural disposition to come up with the right qualitative sensation when the body and brain are in a certain state, it is perhaps more of a pre-echo of Leibniz's pre-established harmony. Either way, we see Descartes, as so often, setting the agenda for the metaphysics and philosophy of mind of succeeding generations of philosophers.

But, to return to the point raised in the preceding section about the 'heterogeneity' of mental phenomena in Descartes, what is it, on his view, that makes the idea of redness 'obscure and confused', in contrast to the clear and distinct ideas of the intellect? Nothing, one might think, is more vivid and immediate than a colour sensation, and nothing more straightforward than the rules of language that determine the meanings of

---

[33] See Ch. 7 sect. 3.

[34] *Traité de l'homme* [c.1630, first pub. 1664], AT XI 143: CSM I 102. Cf. *Comments on a Certain Broadsheet* [*Notae in programma*, 1648], AT VIIIB 359: CSM I 304.

colour terms. So what it is about the intentional content of our judgements about colour that prevents them enjoying equal status with our judgements about, say, shape? It may be, as followers of Wittgenstein might be inclined to say, that Descartes has got himself into the fly-bottle here, allowing his (in itself perfectly reasonable)[35] scientific work on the corpuscular basis of colour properties in objects to confuse him into supposing that 'the sun is yellow' is somehow a more problematic judgement than 'the sun is spherical'. But I end this chapter by arguing that there is indeed something suggestive and defensible about Descartes's notion of a certain 'opacity' in our ideas of colour and other sensible qualities: the representational content of our idea of the sun as yellow does not provide us with a transparent representation of the nature of the solar property in question (as would be the case, for example, with our idea of it as spherical). As Descartes puts it, in a way that is a good deal more careful and philosophically plausible that the formulations of many of his successors, 'when we say that we perceive colours in objects, this is really just the same as saying that we perceive something in the objects whose nature we do not know, but which produces in us a very vivid and clear sensation which we call the sensation of colour' (*Principles*, pt. I art. 70).

Humans are not the only beings who have colour perception; common sense and science would readily concur in supposing that there is no difficulty in principle in identifying those animals with colour vision and those without. Would Descartes have had any problem with attributing colour-perception to animals? As is well known, he frequently described non-human animals as mechanical automata; and this has given rise to the common view that he regarded them as pure mechanisms, to which no conscious states whatever can be attributed. Marjorie Grene has expressed the standard interpretation very vividly:

[T]he doctrine of the *bête machine*, which denies feeling of any kind to beasts... relegates the human as well as the animal body to the status of an automaton. 'Nature' in the sense of the living scene made up of untold styles of life, nature in the naturalist's sense, is not only inferior to the geometer-mechanist's extended universe: it is illusory.[36]

---

[35] Reasonable, I mean, as far as the general methodology is concerned. The actual details of Descartes's proposed physical explanations of colour properties, and of the neurological basis for our perception of them, have, of course, long since been superseded.

[36] M. Grene, *Descartes* (Brighton: Harvester, 1985), 38.

But as I point out in Ch. 8, there is a host of reasons for being wary of reading too much into Descartes's mechanistic terminology. Interpreting it as a *relegation of* the animal 'to the status of an automaton' is misleading. All that the seventeenth-century use of the term 'automaton' properly implies is that the explanation of animal behaviour is to be found entirely in terms of (environmental stimulus plus) the organization and functioning of the various intricate internal organs, without reference to any external puppeteer (or indeed to any internal but incorporeal principle). And this, surely, is something that pretty much everyone now believes. One of Descartes's own contemporary critics, Alphonse Pollot, objected to what he took to be Descartes's view of animals, observing that animals 'function by a principle more excellent than the necessity stemming from the dispositions of their organs, that is by an instinct which will never be found in machines or in clocks, which have neither passion nor affection as animals have'.[37] Descartes, in reply, invokes a thought-experiment. Imagine someone brought up in a mechanical workshop, involved in the manufacture of ingenious working models of animals, who later goes out into the real world, and learns something of the wonderful intricacy of microstructure that supports the observed functioning of plants. If such a person is 'filled with the knowledge of God' (that is, understands how incomparably greater is the divine artifice than anything humans can devise), will he not easily conclude that real animals are 'automata, made by nature, incomparably more accomplished that any of those he had previously made himself'?[38] An animal is a machine, a mechanical structure, an automaton (that is, machine capable of movement without immediate external power source)—all this is granted. But does it really entail the 'ridiculous' and 'appalling'[39] doctrine that the beasts have no feeling?

Those who would answer this question in the affirmative may be inclined to cite Descartes's argument in Part Five of the *Discourse* (AT VI 56: CSM I 139, which closely matches the passage just discussed from the letter to Pollot). But the first thing that we need to notice about this line of argument, the main source of Descartes's notoriety concerning animals, is that it is *an argument about thought and language, not about animal sensation.* Descartes is speaking primarily as a scientist: we do not need to posit a

---

[37] Letter from Pollot to Descartes of February 1638, AT I 514; cited in Grene, *Descartes*, 36.
[38] Descartes to Reneri for Pollot, April or May 1638 (AT II 41: CSMK 100). Cf. *Discourse*, Pt. Five (AT VI 56: CSM I 139).   [39] Grene, *Descartes*, 38, 46.

rational soul in animals in order to explain their behaviour, since it can all be accounted for on mechanical principles; but we *do* need to posit a rational soul in man, since the infinite variety of human linguistic output could never be explained mechanically.[40] So far from being an absurd or repugnant set of claims, this argument embodies a great deal that everyone today fully accepts. No modern biologist, so far as I know, thinks that the attribution of a soul is needed in order to provide a full explanation of animal behaviour; and conversely, many (from Noam Chomsky onwards) maintain that human linguistic abilities defy analysis in terms of stimulus–response mechanisms.[41]

A further vital point to note is that scientific explanation of a phenomenon in terms of underlying structures is not necessarily 'relegatory' in the sense of eliminating the phenomenon to be explained or reducing it to the 'mere' operation of the underlying structures. If I explain the anger of my dog or the fear of my cat by reference to movements of vapour through the nerves (as Descartes does), or the rather more sophisticated apparatus of electrical impulses and the secretion of hormones (as modern biologists do), none of this denies the truth of the original statements, 'Rover is angry' or 'Tatiana is frightened'. There is no 'relegation' of Rover or Tatiana involved in such an explanation, any more than in explaining the properties of a medicine by reference to its molecular structure I am denying its genuine healing function, or somehow 'relegating' it to the status of a pseudo-medicine, a bunch of 'mere' chemicals.[42]

Despite all this, an objector may insist that if something is mechanically explicable, it must be a mere 'zombie' (this term has come to be used in modern philosophy of mind as a quasi-technical term, to denote a device whose functional organization and behavioural output is identical with that of a real living creature, but which, it is supposed, lacks any true consciousness). So is not Descartes after all lumbered with the thesis that animals are mere 'zombies'? The key premise in this argument, that if something is mechanically explicable it must be a zombie, seems to me highly problematic (not least because it is not clear how it could possibly

---

[40] AT VI 57: CSM I 140; see further Ch. 5 sect. 3.

[41] See Noam Chomsky, *Language and Mind* (New York: Harcourt, Brace, and World, 1986).

[42] I develop this argument further in my 'The Ultimate Incoherence? Descartes and the Passions', in R. E. Auxier (ed.), *Essays in Honor of Marjorie Grene*, Library of Living Philosophers (Chicago: Open Court, 2003), 451–64.

be established). But that aside, there are, as I point out in the chapter under discussion, plenty of places where Descartes does explicitly attribute all sorts of perceptual, sensory, and emotional states to animals. The sounds animals make, for example, are often their way of 'communicating to us their impulses of anger, fear, hunger'; an animal's movements may be 'expressions of fear, hope and joy'.[43] To these texts I would add a crucial passage in the letter to the Marquis of Newcastle of 23 November 1646, where Descartes is absolutely clear that the movements of the passions occur in animals just as much (or more so) than in human beings, the only difference being that there is no accompanying thought:

As for the movements of our passions, even though in us they are accompanied by thought because we have the faculty of thinking, it is nevertheless very clear that they do not depend on thought, because they often occur in spite of us. Consequently they *can also occur in animals, even more violently than they do in human beings,* without our being able to conclude from that that animals have thoughts.

(AT IV 573–4: CSMK 303, emphasis supplied)

Serious problems remain, of course, about how far these claims about animal passions sit well with Descartes's famous mind–body dualism—a doctrine whose precise interpretation I shall be discussing in a moment. But the main point to emerge for present purposes (which connects up with many themes already broached in this overview) is that the line Descartes is again and again concerned to draw is the line between thinking (rational, language-using) human beings and non-human animals—*not* the line, which so preoccupies modern philosophers of mind, between the 'conscious' and the 'non-conscious' domains. I was therefore somewhat unfair to Descartes when I said in the essay under discussion that he 'failed to eradicate a certain fuzziness from his thinking about consciousness and self-consciousness'. It would be better to say that he was writing well before these terms, in their modern sense, had started to play a central role in the philosophy of mind.

So obsessed has current philosophy of mind become with 'what it is like' to have a conscious experience that I think in a certain sense we have become more 'Cartesian'—more focused on the 'inner'—than Descartes himself ever was. We take it that notions like 'being in pain' stand for

---

[43] Letter to More of 5 February 1649, AT V 278: CSMK 366; letter to Newcastle of 23 November 1646, AT IV 574: CSMK 303.

the occurrence of a mysterious private *quale*, accessible only to the subject. We then infer from Descartes's mechanistic explanation of animal reactions that he must be denying that animals 'have' such in-principle-unknowable qualia, and swiftly proceed to accuse him of saying something monstrous and disgraceful. Yet one does not have to be a devoted Wittgensteinian to acknowledge that Wittgenstein's private language argument successfully disposes of the idea that the meaning of such terms as 'pain' and 'hunger' can be given by reference to a private beetle in my mental box[44]—a 'beetle' of a kind I can never, even in principle, know is occurring in the mental box of you, my fellow human, let alone Tatiana, my cat. Ascriptions of pain, and other mentalistic terms, must be subject to public criteria. Clear and compelling though this argument is, however, it does not quite settle the status of animal passions and sensations. For it seems very hard to deny that, when I have toothache, the damage to my tooth is signalled to me in a distinctive and urgent way, a way seemingly not captured even by the most exhaustive scientific description of my behaviour, or of what is going on in my brain; and this appears to allow me to ask meaningfully whether something similar is mirrored in your experience when your tooth is damaged, or in that of my dog when the vet probes its diseased tooth. Descartes, I have been suggesting, simply did not confront this issue as regards animals, and we should avoid retrojecting onto him the kind of position that, from our modern perspective, we are tempted to suppose he *must* have taken if he had addressed it. What may be said on Descartes's behalf is that in his role as a scientist he offers an explanation of all phenomena within the animal realm, including animal anger, fear, hope, pain and the like, which does not make any reference to supposed qualia; but in that respect he does not differ from any other subsequent natural scientist. For since such qualia are, by their very nature, not accessible to scientific scrutiny, it can hardly be a complaint against the scientist that he does not accommodate them, let alone a complaint against Cartesian science in particular that it does not refer to them.

(d) Descartes As Trialist

By now well entrenched in the way most philosophers think about Descartes is Gilbert Ryle's famous denunciation of Cartesian dualism as

---

[44] Wittgenstein, *Philosophical Investigations*, pt. I §293.

promulgating the myth of the 'ghost in the machine'.[45] I am not sure quite what Ryle meant by 'ghost', but it was not perhaps the happiest choice of term. A ghost, in normal parlance, is a departed spirit, a soul separated from its former body. So a ghost (if such things there be) still has, one would suppose, a certain hankering after its former life, a certain residual link with the corporeal state it once enjoyed. This has long been the common conception of a departed spirit—as something rather thin and incomplete and lacking.[46] Descartes's scholastic predecessor, Eustachius put it like this:

Separated souls are *not*, like angels, whole subjects that are totally and in every respect complete ... A soul, even when separated, it always apt to inform the body and to be substantially united with it; but this is not true of an angel.[47]

A human ghost or spirit, then, unlike an angel, cannot be conceived in utterly immaterialist or dualistic terms: it always retains that conceptual link with at least the possibility of embodiment. So perhaps 'angel in the machine' would have been a better phrase for Ryle to have used to characterize the Cartesian model he was attacking, in so far as his gripe was that Descartes conceived the mind in wholly dualistic fashion, as categorially distinct from the body. In fact, some twenty years before Ryle, the famous Thomist philosopher Jacques Maritain was already attacking Descartes along just such lines. 'The sin of Descartes', Maritain declared, 'is a sin of *angelism*. He turned knowledge and thought into a hopeless perplexity ... because he conceived human thought after the model of angelic thought. To sum it up in three words: what he saw in man's thought was *independence of things*.'[48]

Whatever the subtle differences between angels and ghosts, Eustachius in the above quotation is clearly reflecting the standard Thomist line in saying that a separated human soul is not a whole subject. According to Aquinas, a human soul is a *substantia incompleta*, an incomplete substance.[49] Unlike an angel, a human soul always in principle needs union with the body

---

[45] Ryle, *Concept of Mind*, ch. 1.

[46] The notion is a very ancient one indeed; see Homer, *Odyssey* [c.700 BC], 11. 465 ff.

[47] Eustachius, *Summa philosophiae*, Pt. III, third part, treatise 4, discourse 3, question 1; trans. in Ariew, Cottingham, and Sorell (eds.), *Descartes Meditations*, 91.

[48] Jacques Maritain, *Three Reformers* (London: Sheed & Ward, 1928, repr. 1947), 54–5.

[49] Thomas Aquinas, *Summa theologiae* [1266–73], pt. I qu. 75 art. 4, and qu. 118 art. 2. Cf. Francisco Suárez, *Metaphysical Disputations* [*Disputationes metaphysicae*, 1597] Disp. 33, sect. 1 §11: 'anima etiamsi sit separata est pars ... essentialis, habetque incompletam esssentiam ... et ideo semper est substantia incompleta.' (A soul, even if it is separated, is essentially a *part*, and has an incomplete essence, and hence is always an incomplete substance.)

that it 'informs' for its essential completion; and this is why the souls in purgatory are not (as popular myth perhaps represents them) human beings who have passed on to the 'next world', but are, rather, temporary beings or quasi-beings in a kind of suspended state, awaiting, indeed requiring as their very *raison d'être*, restoration to human status, when they will be rejoined to the body at the last judgement.

But where does Descartes himself stand on this question of the soul's completeness or otherwise? At times, most famously in Part Four of the *Discourse*, he seems clearly to reject the standard scholastic view of the essential incompleteness of the human soul. I can, he says, form a conception of the *complete and total me*, 'this me (*ce moi*), that is to say the soul by which I am what I am', as separated and distinct from the body. And from this I know I am indeed such a wholly independent incorporeal being.[50] This is (and was at the time) an extremely radical and controversial claim. And it shows that Maritain's indictment does indeed constitute a strong case for Descartes to answer. The 'sin' (or at least the philosophical error) with which he stands charged is, as Maritain saw, *not* that he supposed we were ghosts in machines—that the mind was an incomplete or partial aspect of our human existence—but rather that he supposed we were, like angels, complete incorporeal substances that only *happen* to inhabit bodies.

Descartes's brilliant contemporary Antoine Arnauld was on to this problem like a bull-terrier, long before Maritain (let alone Ryle). It seems, wrote Arnauld in the Fourth Objections, 'that [Descartes's] argument ... takes us back to the Platonic view ... that nothing corporeal belongs to our essence, so that man is merely a rational soul and the body merely a vehicle for the soul—a view which gives rise to the definition of man as a *soul that makes use of a body* (*anima corpore utens*)'.[51] I am not sure if Plato anywhere actually employs the Greek equivalent of this latter phrase, but it's a recognizably Platonic conception. And certainly Plato's disciple, Augustine, uses it: he describes a human being as a 'rational soul *using* a mortal and earthly body'.[52] In responding to Arnauld, Descartes firmly rebuts the Platonic

---

[50] *Discourse on the Method*, Pt. Four (AT VI 33: CSM I 127).

[51] Fourth Objections, AT VII 203: CSM II 143. Six sets of *Objectiones doctorum aliquot virorum cum responsionibus Authoris* [sic] (Objections of several learned men with the Replies of the Author) were published with the first edition of the *Meditations* in 1641; the second edition of 1642 included a seventh set of objections and replies.

[52] *De moribus Ecclesiae Catholicae* [387–9], 1. 27. 52. Cf. also the following passage on pain, which puts Augustine firmly in the Platonic camp and is strikingly at variance with Descartes's account: 'The

interpretation and refers Arnauld to the 'proof' in the Sixth Meditation that the mind is 'substantially united with the body'.[53] Writing to Regius the following year, he insisted that a human being was indeed a genuine unified entity, an *ens per se*, not merely an *ens per accidens*: mind and body are united 'in a real and substantial manner' by a 'true mode of union'.[54]

We are thus faced with a clear inconsistency, or at least a serious tension in Descartes's pronouncements. On the one hand he wants to say that the mind or soul is complete and independent in its own right. This is what we have come to call 'Cartesian dualism'. But on the other hand he wants to preserve the traditional scholastic idea that it is genuinely and substantially united to the body—that we are *not* incorporeal angelic spirits inhabiting mechanical bodies, but genuine human beings of flesh and blood. To set it out formally:

(1) *Pace* the Scholastics, the soul is a complete and independent substance (this 'me', by which I am what I am, is really distinct from the body).

(2) *Pace* the Platonists, the soul is really and substantially united to the body so as to form a genuine unit.

This, I take it, is the fundamental tension that any interpreter of Descartes must confront. And when I first called Descartes a trialist, in the paper that forms Ch. 9, I was in part groping towards a way of trying to resolve the tension. How can I, qua 'res cogitans' be a complete incorporeal substance, yet at the same time qua human being be really and substantially embodied?

Looked at in one way, there doesn't actually seem to be too much of a problem. Qua university professor, I am essentially attached to an academic institution; but qua person, I am not—I would still be the complete and total 'me' if I retired or resigned. So why not say that my body is like my affiliation: just as qua professor I have my affiliation essentially, but qua person I do not, so qua human being I am united to my body essentially, but qua thinking thing I am not? What makes the analogy hard to cash

---

soul itself, which by its presence rules and governs the body, can feel pain and yet not pass away ... If we consider the matter more carefully, pain, which is said to belong to the body, is more pertinent to the soul. For feeling pain is a feature of the soul, not the body, even when the reason for its pain existed in the body.' (*De civitate Dei* [413–26], 21. 3).

[53]   Fourth Replies, AT VII 227–8: CSM II 160.

[54]   For 'we perceive that sensations such a pain are not pure thoughts of a mind distinct from a body, but confused perceptions of a mind really united to a body'. Letter to Regius of January 1642 (AT III 493: CSMK 206).

out satisfactorily in terms of Descartes's position is his use of the language of substance, of real and *substantial* union. For supposing I said I was *really and substantially united* to my professorship, so that my professorship and I form a genuine and essential unity. An appropriately dry rejoinder would be that not even the notoriously cushy conditions of American academic tenure can deliver this strong a union. For once grant that the complete me could continue to exist without my Chair, it seems to follow that the link between me and my job can only be a contingent one—something that may be very important to me, but which cannot be deeply implicated in the kind of substance I essentially am. And so, *mutatis mutandis*, with the body. We seem to be back with Platonism.

In labelling Descartes a 'trialist' I was, in effect seeking to provide an interpretation of Descartes that preserves his commitment both to the independence of the thinking self (thesis (1), above) and to the essential union of mind and body (thesis (2)). The 'trialistic' classification implies that a complete list of the essential attributes of thinking things and of extended things would not include sensory experiences; and conversely, that human sensory experiences are not wholly reducible to, or fully analysable in terms of, the properties either of thinking or of extended things.[55] This is expressed by Descartes in terms of the claim that human sensory experience belongs to the 'third primitive notion' of which he spoke so emphatically to Princess Elizabeth.[56] Note the term: notion, *not* substance (a point to which I shall return in a moment).

Now the doctrine of the mind–body union as a 'primitive' may seem inconsistent with the official Cartesian position that humans owe their existence to just two basic substances, thinking substance and extended substance. But this criticism can be obviated by construing the 'primitive-ness' of the union as asserting that the mind–body complex is something that is the bearer of distinctive and irreducible *properties* in its own right; in this sense we might say that water is a 'primitive' notion, meaning that it is not a mere mixture but a genuine compound, possessing attributes 'in its own right' (distinctive 'watery' characteristics that cannot be reduced to the properties of the hydrogen or oxygen that make it up). Or as Descartes puts it in the *Principles*, while he recognizes only 'two ultimate classes of things',

---

[55] So far as I know, the use of the term 'trialism' in this connection was first introduced in my 'Cartesian Trialism' (1985), repr. as Ch. 9, below; cf. J. Cottingham, *Descartes* (Oxford: Blackwell, 1986), 127 ff.   [56] Letter of 21 May 1642 (AT III 665: CSMK 218).

thinking things and extended things, nevertheless appetites, passions, and sensations, which arise from the close and intimate union of the two, are items which 'must not be referred either to the mind alone or the body alone'.[57]

Several commentators have misunderstood me on this point. I never spoke of Descartes believing in three substances. The kind of trialism I espouse, then, is very different from the ontological thesis of Martial Gueroult, who claimed that for Descartes the mind–body union is a third substance—*une substance psychophysique*.[58] Instead, I suggest that we construe the trialism attributively; and so construed, Descartes's trialism, property trialism or attributive trialism, is not formally inconsistent with his ontological dualism.

A further advantage of this attributive trialism, indeed perhaps a key reason in its favour, is that it accommodates, with considerable success it seems to me, what Descartes says about the distinctive character of our sensory experience as embodied creatures. The appeal to sensations as proof of the union of mind and body is a recurring theme in Descartes. We know the distinction between mind and body, Descartes suggests to Elizabeth, but we *feel* the union (AT III 691–2: CSMK 227). A *pure* thinking being, like an angel, would have thoughts, but would not have sensations (AT II 493: CSMK 206).

But why not? Could not God implant sensations into the consciousness of an angel that inhabited a body? Presumably he could: on the occasion of bodily damage, he could give the angel an urgent and intrusive signal that threatened to disrupt the flow of its thoughts until the damage was attended to. This kind of 'angelic occasionalism' might seem a perfectly viable model for what happens when a Cartesian *res cogitans* feels pain in the body to which it is joined. And as we saw earlier, Descartes's way of talking about human sensations does sometimes contain pre-echoes of the occasionalist position.[59] But his prevailing view is that human pain is an *irreducibly psychophysical process*. The human mind–body complex is a genuine unit,

---

[57] 'I recognize only two ultimate classes of things, first intellectual things, i.e. those which pertain to mind or thinking substance, and secondly material things, i.e. those which pertain to extended substance or body ... But we also experience within ourselves certain other things [appetites, passions or emotions, and sensations] which must not be referred either to the mind alone or to the body alone' (*Principles*, pt. I art. 48).

[58] Martial Gueroult, *Descartes selon l'ordre des raisons* (Paris: Aubier, 1968), ii. 201 ff.

[59] Section 3(c), above.

not a separate soul making use of a body or endowed by its Creator to have certain kinds of awareness on the occasion of damage to the body it uses. When *my* body is damaged (and the 'my' is important for Descartes), *I* feel pain. And that gives us proof, the best kind of intimate proof—proof available, says Descartes, even to those who never philosophize—of the genuineness of the union.[60]

An important question remains. If the mind–body union is a genuine unit, how can the trialism be merely attributive? And indeed, does not Descartes's own use of substantivally flavoured language (such as *ens per se*)[61] to refer to the union create problems for my interpretation? One cannot deny that Descartes does sometimes use such language (though he always stops short of actually calling the mind–body unit a substance); but the reason for this seeming vacillation or imprecision lies, I think, in an ambiguity found in the original Aristotelian usage of the term 'substance'. Aristotle uses the term in at least two senses: first ontologically, to mean a basic unit of independent existence (e.g. an individual man, or horse, or tree), and second logically or grammatically, to mean simply a subject of predication (as opposed to that which is predicated).[62] So for Descartes, even if ontologically speaking the union consists of only two distinct substances, mind and body (substance being taken in the first Aristotelian sense of a basic unit of independent existence), he still allows himself to talk of the human being as a substance in Aristotle's other sense, namely a *subject of predication*—that subject in which attributes inhere. It is the human being, the mind–body complex (and not either of the ultimate substances that make it up), that is the subject in which attributes of a certain distinctive type (namely sensations, passions, and appetites) inhere, or to which they must be referred. This, it seems to me, gives us more than enough to support Descartes's use of the term 'substantial union' to characterize the human being, the mind–body complex, even though from an ontological point of view he always maintained there were only two ultimate kinds of existing thing involved, *res cogitans* and *res extensa*.

As with so much in Descartes, the germ of this way of thinking is derived from St Thomas Aquinas. Though Aquinas believed, like Aristotle, that the intellectual part of us could survive the death of the body, he

---

[60] Letter to Elizabeth of 28 June 1643, AT III 691–2: CSMK 227.
[61] Letter to Regius of December 1641, AT III 460: CSMK 200.
[62] Aristotle, *Categories* [330 BC], ch. 5.

insisted that a large number of basic human faculties (in particular, sensory ones) were irreducibly psychophysical: 'Some operations that belong to the soul are carried out through bodily organs, such as seeing (through the eye) and hearing (through the ear), and likewise for all other operations of the nutritive or sensitive part. Hence the powers that are the sources of such operations *are in the compound as their subject, not in the soul alone.*'[63] This last phrase seems to me to prefigure Descartes's position with uncanny exactness.[64] In a nutshell, then, Descartes's position is that ontologically speaking there are only two substances, but there are three distinct and irreducible types of attribute; and since the third type of attribute, comprising sensory and passional experience, inheres in the complete human being, as in a subject, we are justified in talking of a 'real and substantial union'. It is not, of course, a position free of all philosophical difficulty. But it is a considerably more subtle and interesting position than the exclusively dualistic caricature that is so often dismissed.[65]

4. Ethics and Religion

The fourth and final part of the book widens the purview to consider some highly significant, but often very neglected, implications of Descartes's thought for the realm of human life and the structure of ethical and religious belief. The opening two chapters in this part form something of a transition between Descartes's philosophy of mind and his ethics, by dealing with his account of the relationship between the intellect and the will. In Ch. 10, I address these issues in the context of Spinoza's famous critique of Descartes's view of judgement as a combined function of two supposedly distinct and separate faculties, intellect and will, while

---

[63] *Summa theologiae*, pt. I qu. 77 art. 5 (emphasis supplied). Peter King draws attention to this passage in an interesting article entitled 'Why Isn't the Mind–Body Problem Medieval?', in H. Lagerlund (ed.), *Forming the Mind: Essays on the Internal Senses and the Mind/Body Problem from Avicenna to the Enlightenment* (Dordrecht: Springer, 2005), 187–206.

[64] There are of course key differences between the two philosophers, of which the most striking one in the present context is Aquinas's grouping of nutrition with sensation as a function of the soul–body compound; for Descartes, it is a purely physiological function.

[65] For a different view, arguing that Descartes never succeeded in providing a satisfactory account of our distinctively human nature, and was increasingly prepared to accept some version of angelism, see Stephen Voss, 'Descartes: The End of Anthropology', in J. Cottingham (ed.), *Reason, Will, and Sensation* (Oxford: Clarendon, 1994), 273–306.

Ch. 11, 'Descartes and the Voluntariness of Belief' takes up the question of how far our beliefs are within our voluntary control—an issue that allows some significant conclusions to be drawn about the Cartesian account of religious belief. The focus then broadens out to the more general topic of the good life in Descartes. Chapter 12, 'Cartesian Ethics: Reason and the Passions', explores how Descartes utilizes the results of his scientific and psychological enquiries to tackle the ancient problem of how human reason can find a recipe for the good life that comes to terms with the often damaging influence of the emotions. Next, 'The Role of God in Descartes's Philosophy' (Ch. 13) argues that Descartes's religious commitments are an inescapable and central element of his worldview: a theistically inspired vision lies at the heart of his recipes both for reliable knowledge of the workings of the world and for the sound conduct of life. Continuing this theme, Ch. 14, 'Descartes as Sage: Spiritual Askesis in Cartesian Philosophy' argues that, despite the 'modernizing' aspects of his scientific thought, many of Descartes's deepest philosophical goals are best understood if we see his self-conception as a philosopher as stemming from the ancient idea of the 'sage'—one engaged on the search for wisdom and for a harmonious way of living. Finally, the concluding essay, 'Plato's Sun and Descartes's Stove: Contemplation and Control in Cartesian Philosophy' (Ch. 15), explores further aspects of the contrast between Descartes the proto-scientist, concerned to subjugate nature to man's understanding and control, and Descartes the contemplative, following in the footsteps of Plato and Augustine on a journey towards an integrated vision of reality.

(a) The Role of the Will

The opening chapter of this section, on Spinoza's criticisms of the Cartesian account of the will (Ch. 10), begins by noting the moral dimension involved in Descartes's strategy for the avoidance of error in the *Meditations*. No abstract exercise in epistemology, but part of an overall pattern of theodicy, Descartes's arguments follow tradition in putting the blame for our going astray on the improper use of our power of choice. Finite creatures should suspend judgement when the truth is not clear; instead, we rush in and give our assent to obscure or dubious propositions and get ourselves into trouble. Spinoza offers a sharp critique of this framework when he refuses to separate the intellect and the will, arguing that the apprehension of an idea and the affirmation of its truth are inseparable. But a proper reading of Descartes's arguments in the Fourth Meditation shows that Descartes's own position is surprisingly close to this Spinozan picture: clear and distinct perception goes hand in hand with automatic assent. But what of cases where the truth is *not* clear? Here Spinoza complains that the Cartesian recommendation of 'suspending judgement' lays bogus emphasis on the idea of an independent act of free will, when what is really going on is simply a recognition of the inadequacy of our perception. But I suggest that a careful reading of Descartes's arguments for doubting our ordinary beliefs (in the First Meditation) again reveals a considerable degree of convergence with the Spinozan view. Descartes's procedure is not a matter of urging us to exercise a supposedly sovereign and independent will, but that of devising arguments which will counterbalance the weight of our preconceived opinions until we perceive the inadequacy of our grounds for being sure of them.

So far from being a merely technical debate in the philosophy of mind, or simply a matter of textual interpretation, this dispute between Spinoza and Descartes connects with the vital question of what human freedom ultimately consists in. Spinoza, like Leibniz, took Descartes to be proposing a 'contra-causal' account—that the power of the will is entirely independent and undetermined. Many subsequent thinkers have been very suspicious of this kind of supposed two-way power—the power to X or not to X even when all the relevant antecedent conditions and circumstances surrounding the action are held constant. But the contra-causalist interpretation of Descartes by his close successors is in fact an early example of the phenomenon to which I have so often drawn attention in this opening chapter—the tendency for Descartes's ideas to be subject to systematic distortion by his critics. Except in the special case of God, whose infinite power he frequently insists is beyond our comprehension, Descartes is actually very far from insisting on such absolute contra-causal liberty as constituting the essence of freedom. Clarity of intellectual perception, as we have seen, he regards as irresistibly constraining our judgement (a 'great light in the intellect leads to a great propensity in the will');[66] while the 'indifference' we feel where the evidence is insufficient to establish the truth is, for Descartes, no indication of some supposed splendid two-way power

---

[66] Fourth Meditation, AT VII 59: CSM II 41. Cf. *Principles*, pt. I art. 42: 'whenever we perceive something clearly, we spontaneously assent to it and cannot in any way doubt that it is true'.

of choice, but on the contrary is a power of the 'lowest grade'—evidence not of any perfection but on the contrary of a mere 'defect or negation' (AT VII 58: CSM II 40).

Many of these issues return in the following chapter, which discusses the control we have over our beliefs (Ch. 11). The issue is one of considerable importance for religious faith, which many traditions hold to be to be something meritorious and hence, one supposes, within our voluntary control. Committed Christians, including Catholics (of whom Descartes was one) are required to accept certain revealed truths on faith, following the injunction of the risen Christ to the doubting disciple Thomas, 'Be not faithless, but believing!' (John 20: 27). But it seems doubtful whether we can believe at will ('just like that', as Bernard Williams once put it),[67] since belief appears to be a largely involuntary response to the evidence: I do not will, or decide, to believe that there is a cup of green tea beside me as I write this sentence. What is more, Descartes himself, as we have just seen, regards the judgement of the will as constrained by what the intellect perceives through the 'natural light' of reason. So is there not a tension between the picture of the independent and autonomous agent, in charge of deciding what to accept, and the seeming passivity or automatic nature of the belief process?

The answer seems to hinge, in part, on the kind of determination involved. When my beliefs are determined by some process that subverts the possibility of rational evaluation (as, for example, in a hypnotically induced belief-state), then I am indeed placed in the position of a passive pawn, who has, as it were, no control over which doxastic square (which belief position) it occupies. But when the will spontaneously responds to the clearness and distinctness of the evidence (as when I spontaneously assent to the proposition 'two plus two makes four'), then it seems that my agency and rationality, so far from being subverted, are protected and enhanced. Descartes's 'freedom of enlightenment' or *liberté éclairée*, as the distinguished Cartesian scholar Ferdinand Alquié has termed it,[68] seems exactly the sort of freedom we have most reason to desire.

Those who doubt that this kind of freedom of spontaneity amounts to 'all the freedom worth wanting',[69] may still hanker for some more robust and

---

[67] B. Williams, 'Deciding to Believe', in *Problems of the Self* (Cambridge: Cambridge University Press, 1973), ch. 9 p. 147.

[68] F. Alquié (ed.), *Descartes, Œuvres Philosophiques* (Paris: Garnier, 1963–73), ii. 461.

[69] See Daniel Dennett, *Elbow Room* (Oxford: Oxford University Press, 1984).

independent power, of the kind widely held to be necessary for supporting full moral responsibility. If we are to be properly praised for our beliefs, or properly condemned for making doxastic mistakes, do we not need this stronger kind of autonomous choice? Descartes provides, I think, an interesting answer to this question in the course of his discussion of doubt and of the meditator's contemplation of the clear and distinct truths that seem resistant to doubt. As I point out in the chapter under discussion, everything depends on the time dimension: as long as I focus on the relevant truths, I am unable to doubt them; but once I turn away from the light, doubts may arise. The mind, for Descartes, is a reliable instrument, but, like a lens, it requires attention and effort to keep it properly focused; and here there is scope for doxastic responsibility.

Descartes's overall theory of the will thus seems to be both carefully constructed and philosophically attractive, bringing into harmony the subjective and objective aspects of belief formation—as a response to evidence that can be both psychologically spontaneous and also rationally justified—while at the same time managing to preserve the idea that we can be held responsible for our beliefs. Yet, at the end of the day, the status of religious faith does not appear to allow it to be accommodated into this comfortable Cartesian schema without a certain unease. For what Descartes calls the 'supernatural light',[70] the light of faith (as opposed to the 'natural' light of reason), may induce a 'divinely produced disposition of my thought' (AT VII 58: CSM II 40), which makes me assent even when the evidence, by the normal standards of appropriate belief formation, is not perspicuous. This is the kind of faith the Christian disciple is supposed to have, and the kind there is no reason to doubt that Descartes himself held to throughout his life. But before condemning Descartes's support for this kind of belief as inherently unreasonable, we should remember that there are many instances, for Descartes (and indeed for all of us), where it is prudent for our ordinary welfare to put our trust in people and objects without waiting for epistemic certification of their reliability. We trust, for example, in the continued wholesomeness of certain foods, or the continuing trustworthiness of certain friends, without clearly and distinctly perceiving that they have not become poisonous, or treacherous, since we last encountered them. If this kind of confidence, in the absence of rational

---

[70] *Meditations*, Second Replies (AT VII 148 line 27: CSM II 106).

proof, is necessary for our material and emotional survival,[71] then it does not seem wholly unreasonable to suppose that something similar might apply to our spiritual well-being.

(b) The Good Life; the Place of God

Even in the rather specialized context just discussed, namely the Cartesian view of the voluntariness of belief, it should be clear that the position Descartes adopts is not simply a stance taken up for purposes of academic debate, but connects up quite closely with crucial elements of his moral and religious outlook. In the next two chapters, I move on to address directly the structure of Descartes's moral theory, and the position of God in his philosophical system. 'Cartesian Ethics: Reason and the Passions' (Ch. 12) fills in the main outlines of Descartes's theory of the good life. The management of the passions had of course been a long-standing concern of moral philosophers, going right back to Plato and Aristotle, and the Stoics, but in Descartes's substantial and under-appreciated contributions to this topic we see him applying many of the distinctive ideas we have already had occasion to refer to in connection with other parts of his system. One of the aims of Cartesian science was to provide a comprehensive explanatory account of the workings of the body and nervous system, and Descartes's ethics now proposes to draw on this in helping us to understand the physiological basis of the passions. But the earlier Platonic and Stoic programmes, whether for rational dominance over the passions or their complete suppression, are superseded in Descartes by a more sophisticated account. In discussing how we can learn to manage the passions, Descartes compares the way in which animals are trained; but he goes beyond the Aristotelian model of habituating children to virtue through the right kind of induced imitation and repetition,[72] since he envisages something more akin to a systematic process of reprogramming, undertaken in the light of the understanding provided by research into the workings of the nervous system. Yet it is crucial to see that this is not merely a matter of the application of Cartesian science in the way it might be applied to, say, bridge-building or medicine—that is, it is not merely a matter of the mathematical and mechanical analysis of extended

[71] Cf. Discourse, Pt. Three (AT VI 22: CSM I 122).
[72] Aristotle, Nicomachean Ethics [c.325 BC], 2. 1.

substance, and its manipulation so as to produce the molecular events we desire.

What provides the extra dimension here is the recurring theme of Descartes's conception of human nature as a union of mind and body, with the special and distinctive attributes that arise from this union.[73] While the body and its physiology is a part of Descartes's *res extensa*, and the mind, with its understanding and willing, and its resulting plans for the good life, belongs in the realm of *res cogitans*, human passions themselves are neither the clear perceptions of the mind, nor the mathematically analysable jostlings of physical particles. In contrast to the transparent domains of thinking substance and of extended substance, the passions have an inherent opacity, arising from the mysterious union of mind and body. One of the paradoxes of our human condition is that this opacity cannot be dissolved either by intellectual meditation or by scientific analysis; there is an inherent obscurity there that derives from our hybrid nature. We have already discussed Descartes's conception of a certain basic lack of transparency even in ordinary sensory states such as those we have when perceiving coloured objects,[74] but for Descartes there is now a further factor, attaching specifically to the emotions and passions, which makes them resistant to being fully understood in terms of purely rational inclinations or transparent desires. This further factor is one that Descartes, in a striking anticipation of Sigmund Freud, traces to early childhood experience:

The intellectual element in [our] joys and loves has always been accompanied by the first sensations which [we] had of them and even the motions or natural functions which then occurred in the body ... It is because of the confused feelings of our childhood, which remain joined to the rational thoughts by which we love what we judge worthy of love, that the nature of love is hard for us to understand.[75]

One might hope, as Freud did, that this opacity could be dissolved by delving back into the past, and dragging the forgotten memories of early childhood into the light of conscious reflection: 'where id was, there shall ego be'.[76] Descartes certainly notes in his own case that careful reflection

---

[73] See sect. 3(d), above.   [74] See sect. 3(c), above.

[75] Letter to Chanut of 1 February 1647, AT IV 606: CSMK 308.

[76] 'Wo Es war, soll Ich werden'; Sigmund Freud, *New Introductory Lectures on Psychoanalysis* [*Neue Folge der Vorlesungen zur Einführung in die Psychoanalyse*, 1933], Lecture XXXI, in *Standard Edition of Complete Works*, trans. J. Strachey (London: Hogarth, 1953–74), xxii. 80.

on childhood experience can help us to dismantle the distorting projections which afflict our emotional perceptions in adult life;[77] so there is evidence that he glimpsed the need to add something like what we have come to call psychoanalytic methods to his strategy for managing the passions. But it was by no means Descartes's aim to tame the power of the passions, or to reduce the passionate life to the life of pure reason. The overall picture to emerge from this part of his ethics is the extent to which Descartes embraces the affective dimension of our human experience, notwithstanding that it is often so hard to understand. Condemning the 'grimness' of those moral systems that reject them,[78] he accords the passions a primary place in the good life; when properly channelled, they can become, as they should be, the greatest source of joy in this life.[79]

The tone of many of these Cartesian pronouncement on ethics (in the *Passions of the Soul* and elsewhere) may perhaps leave the impression that Descartes is working within a largely naturalistic framework. It is true that considerations about ordinary human nature play a central role in his moral philosophy (as they do with so many moral philosophers, from Aristotle all the way down to such completely secular thinkers as J. S. Mill); and there is much in Descartes's fascinating account of the good life for humankind which does not invoke any direct support from theistic premises. Nevertheless, Descartes himself underlined the integral interconnections between his ethics, his physics, and his metaphysics; and (as will emerge in the final section of this overview) a full understanding of Descartes's moral theory requires close attention to the religious worldview that pervades his philosophy as a whole.

Chapter 13 prepares the ground for the two concluding essays of the volume by providing an introductory account of the role of God in Descartes's philosophical system. In some of the earlier chapters, I tended to show some sympathy for what is a fairly widespread view of Descartes's metaphysical interests, namely that they were motivated solely by his desire to provide an acceptable base for his scientific work.[80] But speculation on what may have personally motivated Descartes, or indeed any other great

---

[77] See Descartes's account of his tendency to be attracted to cross-eyed women (letter to Chanut of 6 June 1647, AT V 57: CSMK 323), discussed in Ch. 12.

[78] 'The philosophy I cultivate is not so savage or grim as to outlaw the operation of the passions; on the contrary, it is here, in my view, that the entire sweetness and joy of life is to be found.' Letter to ?Silhon of March or April 1648 (AT V 135).

[79] *Passions of the Soul* [Les Passions de l'âme, 1649], art. 212.   [80] See Ch. 2 n. 16.

writer, is probably largely beside the point. What can be said, by looking at the character of the writings themselves, is that the great bulk of the works produced in Descartes's early career were works of what we should now call natural science; moreover, when theistic metaphysics does enter the picture, in Part Four of the *Discourse*, the arguments initially offered are, to say the least, somewhat perfunctory.[81] But as so often happens in philosophy, ideas may have a life of their own, and arguments can lead us to destinations that were not at the front of our mind when we drew up our route map. Descartes was brought up as a Catholic, and his education had steeped him in the heavily theistic metaphysics of scholasticism, which was itself imbued with the thought of the early church fathers and with a pervasive knowledge of biblical scripture. As the overall structure of Descartes's world begins to be fleshed out, in the composition of his masterpiece, the *Meditations*, all manner of features that may initially have seemed less prominent start to occupy the foreground. God, the source of the 'light of reason' that drives Cartesian science, emerges not just as a kind of epistemic guarantor of the axioms for science, but as the fountain of all truth and goodness, the 'immense light' towards which finite creatures must reach, not just in a spirit of cold rational enquiry, but in awe and wonder, as their hoped-for future destiny and source of their present joy.[82]

Such language may seem to come from a mouth very different from that of the Descartes familiar from the standard historiography of philosophy, but if this is so it is a result of the systematic secularizing tendency that it is the aim of the chapter under discussion to question. Interpretative distortions, I argue, have arisen from two very different sources: first, the academic agendas of current philosophy, with their tendency to exclude anything that does not pass through the fine-grained mills of contemporary analytic specialisms, and, second, the image of Cartesianism purveyed by the ecclesiastical establishment, which encapsulate a wariness that the Church has long displayed towards one of its most famous philosophical sons. To those in the first camp, Descartes's 'modernism' is welcome, but only in so far as he can be fitted into the mould of a proto-natural-scientist, or a proto-analytic-epistemologist; to those in the second category, his

---

[81] See Ch. 2 n. 27.

[82] The former, says Descartes, is apprehended through faith, the latter known by experience. Third Meditation, AT VII 52: CSM II 36.

'modernistic' tendencies are the ominous early signs of a corrosive secular subjectivism that would reduce all reality, even the divine, to the scope of individual human consciousness. Yet, as should already have emerged several times in this overview, Descartes's philosophy is in fact far more objectivist than the latter picture suggests, and it is far less fragmented and more holistic than is suggested by the former picture. If we can manage to free ourselves from these pre-processed versions of Descartes, we may discover a thinker who is less familiar to our conditioned palates, but who may in the end give us a great deal more to chew on.

(c) External Control and Interior Discipline

The penultimate essay of the volume, 'Descartes As Sage' (Ch. 14), traces the roots of many central Cartesian ideas to conceptions that he inherited, ultimately, from Plato and Augustine. Descartes as a young man envisage himself entering the stage 'masked' (AT X 213: CSM I 2), and he remained extremely reticent about his philosophical aims, and also about his philosophical debts—something that has perhaps allowed many subsequent commentators to fasten onto him images of their own devising. Several of these images of Descartes have already surfaced to a greater or lesser extent in our discussion so far: the proto-epistemologist preoccupied with sceptical puzzles; the natural scientist struggling with the metaphysical debris of an earlier age; the subjectivist obsessed with the private theatre of the mind; the proto-secularist who would 'bring all reality within the ambit of the Cogito'.[83] But if, as there are several good reasons to do, we take the *Meditations* as the definitive statement of Descartes's philosophy, an unprejudiced reading reveals a quite different *persona*—that of the philosopher in the traditional sense, going back to Plato, of the searcher for truth and the lover of wisdom.

In the tradition Descartes inherited, 'wisdom' included knowledge of how everything is related to its ultimate causes;[84] and for Descartes, following in the footsteps of Plato and Augustine, the path that will lead to such wisdom involves the discipline of *aversio*, turning the mind away from the confusing world of the senses. This is the discipline that is begun on the first day of the *Meditations*, and its fruits are gathered in a great

---

[83] See the quotation flagged at Ch. 13 n. 8.
[84] Thomas Aquinas, *Summa theologiae* IaIIae (First Part of the Second Part), qu. 57 art. 2.

systematic sweep as the days proceed. The ultimate cause, God, 'supremely good and the source of truth' is provisionally acknowledged in the First Meditation (AT VII 22: CSM II 15), glimpsed again at the start of the Second Meditation (AT VII 24: CSM II 16), firmly proved to exist by the middle of the Third Meditation (AT VII 45: CSM II 31) and contemplated with joy and wonder at its end (AT VII 52: CSM II 36); declared at the start of the Fourth Meditation to be the hidden fountain of 'wisdom and the sciences' (AT VII 53: CSM II 37) and recognized by its end to be the perfect bestower of all we need to avoid error (AT VII 62: CSM II 43); shown near the start of the Fifth Meditation to be as firmly and demonstrably knowable as the truths of mathematics (AT VII 65–6: CSM II 45) and seen, by its end, to be the sole guarantor of 'the certainty and truth of all knowledge' (AT VII 71: CSM II 49); and finally, throughout the course of the Sixth Meditation, vindicated as the creative power of 'immeasurable goodness' (AT VII 88: CSM II 61) that shaped our human nature with a view to our survival and our flourishing.

This catalogue may seem strangely out of step with the list of topics that occupy today's typical lecture courses on Descartes's *Meditations*; but it is not meant to suggest that the familiar topics—doubt, the Cogito, thought and extension, freedom, mind and body—are not a perfectly valid way of carving up Descartes's arguments for expository purposes. What it does draw attention to, nonetheless, is the theistic thread that holds everything together, and which links the moral and epistemic domains in the prescribed search for truth and goodness—a search, I argue, that it is not inappropriate to call a genuinely spiritual one. Is this just fastening another mask onto Descartes, or imposing a spurious unity on a heterogeneous collection of arguments? I doubt if this criticism could survive a careful scrutiny of the pattern of references catalogued in the previous paragraph; nor, it seems to me, could it satisfactorily account for Descartes's own insistence on how he wanted the reader to approach his work. He stressed the holistic character of the *Meditations*, warning that little benefit would accrue from trying to extract individual arguments and assess them piecemeal; and he presented his work as a genuine exercise in meditation, urging no one to read the book 'except those who are able and willing to meditate seriously with me, and to withdraw their minds from the senses' (AT VII 9–10: CSM II 8). There are, of course, many ways of deriving benefit from a philosophical work, and we do not have to follow any prescribed method of study, even one proposed by the author himself. But Descartes's invitation to each individual reader to accompany him on his meditations remains a powerful one; and at the very least it may be worth considering whether light can be thrown on his metaphysical enquiries by seeing how they conform to an ancient and rather grand model of philosophical enquiry, as a subject that requires not just agility of mind and logical acumen, but a certain kind of moral seriousness.

The fifteenth and final chapter of the volume ('Plato's Sun and Descartes's Stove') attempts, in a certain way, to bring together distinct strands of Cartesian interpretation and exegesis that have been apparent through-out the collection. Two elements in particular emerge as prominent in Descartes's way of expressing himself: the contemplative and even devo-tional voice, deriving from Plato and Augustine, to which we have just been attending, and the more 'modernistic' voice, referred to earlier in the current discussion, of the Cartesian scientific innovator. One might suppose these elements to be wholly compatible: Descartes himself maintains, after all, that the scientist draws on the divinely implanted knowledge of math-ematics in order to understand the universe (AT VI 41: CSM I 131); so why should not Descartes have been attracted to a familiar kind of Christianized Platonism, seeing the natural world as a rational and value-laden cosmos, reflecting the beauty and order of its Creator? There are many reasons why he did not speak this way: his rejection of teleology in physics which he judged to be sterile from an explanatory point of view (AT VII 55: CSM II 39); his discarding of a qualitative account of matter (for similar reasons) in favour of a more neutral and 'bleached-out' quantitative framework (AT VIII 79: CSM I 247); and, perhaps most crucial, his vision that the 'ordinary laws of nature', the universal covering laws of matter in motion, would be all the physicist needs to explain the intricate order and organization of the natural world (AT XI 37: CSM I 92–3). None of this, of course, has in itself any tend-ency to undermine the theistic worldview; indeed, Descartes always insists that the power behind these laws of physics is God. But for all practical pur-poses this makes no difference to the physicist, whose job is to work out the simplest and most elegant covering principles to subsume the widest pos-sible range of phenomena.[85] The Cartesian methodology of physics opens

---

[85] In the case of Descartes's three laws of motion (*Principles*, Pt. II arts. 36–42), there is some attempt to derive the first law from the nature of God (whose immutable nature makes it 'most reasonable' to think that the quantity of motion is always preserved); but such appeals become less prominent with the remaining laws, and the reader is in any case left throughout with a sense that it is the physics, not the metaphysics, that is wearing the trousers. For example, if the behaviour of matter had been better

the door to the autonomy of modern science; and such autonomous knowledge of the workings of nature brings with it the possibility of a wholly
new and ultimately much less reverential relationship to the natural order.

Acknowledging these tensions brings us back to the Janus-faced character
of Descartes's thought—the way in which it looks forward to our own
time as well as back to the world of his predecessors. This theme recurs, as
we have seen, in Cartesian ethics, where the idea of technological control
that appears in his early scientific programme resurfaces in his blueprint
for the management of the passions, and seems to take him towards a
more manipulative view of how we might control our human destiny than
anything found in classical or medieval visions of the good life.

We could simply take note of these tensions and leave it at that; for a
philosopher's greatness is not necessarily a function of whether all aspects
of his thought can be made consistent, and the Cartesian system would lose
none of its interest for us if it offered us an unresolved tension rather than
a proposed reconciliation. Nevertheless, I think we can see in Descartes's
writings the wherewithal to resolve these tensions. The question he has
left us with, as I point out at the end of the final chapter, is whether we
should take charge of our destiny, leading our lives as would-be controllers
of our environment, and indeed our own human nature,[86] or whether we
should adopt the more 'spiritual' path of conforming our lives to the more
permanent values that command our allegiance whether we will or no. For
inhabitants of the twenty-first century, like those of the seventeenth, there
is no possibility of turning our backs on the increased knowledge, and
associated power, that the 'new' science has given us; but for all his implicit
commitment to the autonomy of the scientific method, Descartes never
makes the mistake of supposing that autonomy could be extended to the
ethical domain—at least not in the sense envisaged by Friedrich Nietzsche,
that we humans can somehow create our own values by an autonomous
act of will.[87] On the contrary, as we have seen, he firmly retains the older

---

explained on the assumption of a principle of curvilinear rather than rectilinear inertial motion, then,
one imagines, curved lines might have presented themselves to the author as more consonant with the
divine nature than straight ones.

[86] The possibility of genetic engineering has now given extra urgency to this essentially 'Cartesian'
question, in the light of the now vastly increased opportunity for technological manipulation and
control of our very genetic inheritance.

[87] See Friedrich Nietzsche, *Beyond Good and Evil* [*Jenseits von Gut und Böse*, 1886], trans. W. Kaufmann
(New York: Random House, 1966), §203.

vision of an objective domain of goodness that constrains our assent: we may turn away from the light, but we cannot deny it. In the end, then, the power of the new technology to change our world, and even our own psychophysical nature, remains of value, in the Cartesian scheme of things, only in so far as it is used in the service of that 'immense goodness' (AT VII 88: CSM II 61) revealed to us by the natural light.

At the end of our reading of Descartes we thus come up against a philosophical and indeed wider human problem of enormous importance. To put it at its most urgent, it is the problem of whether we can hope to survive as a species without the help of a moral vision powerful enough to guide us properly in the use of the increasing power we have over the natural world and our own nature. For Descartes, the requisite kind of moral vision was generated by Christian metaphysics, the objectivity of whose value system, for all his vaunted programme of doubt, he never seriously questioned. And so, finally, this believer in philosophy as an organic unity was able to achieve a truly synoptic philosophical vision. As understood by Descartes, the extended world of nature is one that we can understand and control as a result of the God-given power of reason; but that same power of reason also enables us to perceive what is objectively good; and a benevolent Creator has given every single human being the power to dispose their will so as to resolve to pursue that good.[88] This secure metaphysical underpinning for his ethics perhaps accounts, more than anything else, for the pervasive optimism we find in Descartes's moral writings, and his sense that true 'tranquillity of soul' was within the grasp of all.[89] Whether our own worldview, major parts of which Descartes so significantly helped to shape, can find a basis for sustaining that tranquillity is something that remains to be seen.

---

[88] *Passions of the Soul*, art. 154.   [89] Ibid. art. 148.

II

Descartes's Position in Philosophy

2

A New Start? Cartesian Metaphysics and the Emergence of Modern Philosophy

1. The Cartesian Image

In many of his writings, Descartes conspicuously presented himself as an innovator. Announcing his philosophical programme to the public in 1637, he likened himself to an architect, designing a town from scratch: ancient cities that have grown up over many years, with many different hands 'patching up (*raccommoder*) buildings by adapting old walls', are generally ill proportioned compared with those 'laid out by the planner on levelled ground' (AT VI 11: CSM I 116). The intellectual autobiography that opens the *Discourse* is that of a rebel who proposes not to build on the inherited wisdom of the past, but to demolish it and start afresh. And the sooner the better: 'as soon as I was old enough to escape from the control (*la sujection*) of my teachers, I entirely abandoned book learning' (AT VI 9: CSM I 115).

This direct and vigorous propaganda for the 'new' philosophy (as it came to be called in the later seventeenth century, and indeed even within Descartes's own lifetime) must have struck Descartes's readers more forcibly than we can easily imagine today. For nowadays, to break new ground is the goal of every aspiring writer whether in the arts or sciences—in some respects it is the very criterion of success. By the start of the eighteenth century the modern race for originality had begun to gather speed (witness the bitter priority dispute between the followers of Leibniz and Newton over the infinitesimal calculus). But the prevailing intellectual climate in Descartes's time was still largely characterized by suspicion of change and innovation. Renaissance culture was deeply imbued with the ancient classical tradition that tended to equate the new with the bad. Roman writers, expounding an earlier Greek theme that had appeared as far back as Hesiod, standardly depicted history as a steady regression from an earlier golden age; and a decade or so before Descartes's birth, Michel de Montaigne had composed elegant variations on the same tune:

The change and corruption endemic in all things makes us stray from sound origins and first principles. We can try to prevent this decline from going too far. But to try to reshape such a vast bulk, to change the foundations of such a great building, is to imitate those who ... wish to replace particular faults with universal confusion ... and to heal sickness by producing death.[1]

Descartes was of course aware of this tradition, and in writing the *Discourse* he evidently aimed to make a clean break from it.[2] The radicalism of the *Discourse* is immediately apparent even from the style of the writing; to the most casual reader, the contrast with earlier authors such as Montaigne is unmistakable. Lacking the protective cocoon of quotations and literary allusions with which so many writers of the late sixteenth and early seventeenth centuries typically surrounded themselves, Descartes's writing style is remarkably lean and unadorned. The self-professed aim is to speak directly to the reader of plain unencumbered 'good sense' (*le bon sens*, AT VI I CSM I 111); the intended audience, as the later *Search for Truth* makes clear, is not the learned scholar 'Epistemon' but the untutored 'Polyander' (Everyman). A 'good man' is 'not required to have read every book, or diligently mastered everything taught in the schools'; instead, the object of the exercise is to 'bring to light the true riches of our souls, opening up to each of us the means whereby we can find within ourselves, without any help from anyone else, all the knowledge we may need' (AT X 495: CSM II 400).

An important initial question to be raised here is whether this break with tradition is simply a matter of literary style and presentation, or

---

[1] Michel de Montaigne, *Essais* [1580], bk. 3 ch. 9 (my translation). The French text may be found in many editions including M. de Montaigne, *Œuvres complètes*, ed. A. Thiabaudet and M. Rat (Paris: Pléiade, 1962), 936.

[2] Though with his habitual caution he is careful to point out that his radicalism is not to be understood as having any political dimension: the enterprise is to be an individual one. It would be 'unreasonable to attempt to reform a state by changing it from the foundations up' (AT VI 13: CSM I 117). In this respect at least, Descartes wishes to avoid challenging the tradition for which Montaigne was a spokesman.

whether it has to do with substantive issues of content and philosophical conviction. The standard interpretation of Descartes as the 'father of modern philosophy' comes down firmly in favour of the latter hypothesis. '*Omnia evertenda atque a primis fundamentis denuo inchoandum*': the insistence, in the famous slogan at the start of the *Meditations*, on 'demolishing everything completely and starting again right from the foundations' (AT VII 17: CSM II 12) is seen as the very hallmark and *raison d'être* of Descartes's philosophy. Not all the evidence, however, squares with this interpretation. In his early work the *Regulae* (*c.*1628) Descartes was prepared to give at least a perfunctory nod of recognition to the 'original founders of philosophy' (*primi Philosophiae inventores*)—though significantly enough he cited not Aristotle but Plato, whose respect for geometry was reflected in the famous motto inscribed over the portals of the Academy (AT X 375; CSM I 18).[3] More importantly, he was careful to present his 'method for investigating the truth of things' as not entirely new and revolutionary, but rather as a revival of the *vera mathesis*[4] developed by the Alexandrian geometers Pappus and Diophantus, who 'though not of the earliest antiquity, lived many centuries before our own time' (AT X 376; CSM I 19). It might be thought that such denials of complete innovation are merely symptomatic of an early lack of confidence; but in fact the mature Descartes continued to maintain a similar position. 'My aim is not to retail arguments as novelties' (rationes pro novis venditare), he told Hobbes in 1641 (AT VII 171: CSM II 121); and later, after the Jesuit critic Bourdin had publicly, and with repeated relish, blasted his method for being 'either unsound or nothing new' (AT VII 532 ff.: CSM II 363 ff.), Descartes firmly declared: 'everything in my philosophy is old; for as far as principles are concerned, I accept only those which in the past have always been common ground among all philosophers without exception, and which are therefore the most ancient of all' (AT VII 580: CSM II 392).

Faced with this somewhat confusing mix of professions and denials of novelty, we might be tempted to conclude that the originality issue was

---

[3] *Mēdeis ageōmetrētos eisitō* (Let no one ignorant of geometry enter); Philoponus, *Commentary on De anima*, 117.

[4] The term *mathesis* in Descartes embraces much more than mathematics; it is a 'general science which explains all the points that can be raised concerning order and measure, irrespective of the subject matter' (AT X 378: CSM I 19). See further J. L. Marion, 'Cartesian Metaphysics and the Role of the Simple Natures', in J. Cottingham (ed.), *The Cambridge Companion to Descartes* (Cambridge: Cambridge University Press, 1992), 115–39.

not, after all, of central importance as far as Descartes's own attitude to his work was concerned. Rather, one might infer, it was essentially a matter of presentation: concerned above all to gain a sympathetic audience for his ideas,[5] he was keen at times to propagandize for the originality of his method, but equally happy, when the audience or the mood dictated that it might be more expedient, to present himself as following the best traditions of the past. Yet while Descartes was evidently an opportunist, always anxious to avoid offending the powerful and the influential,[6] it would be quite wrong to play down his evident commitment to establishing a genuinely new philosophical system. In at least four important areas, in particular, there is ample evidence that he was convinced that compromise was impossible and that his own method deserved to supplant entirely what had gone before. First, he aimed to propound a unified scientific understanding of the universe, in contrast to the compartmentalized and piecemeal approach of the scholastics.[7] Second, this science was to be based on mathematical principles, in contrast to the qualitative explanatory apparatus of his predecessors. Third (and closely connected with the second point) he wanted to develop a mechanistic model of explanation, avoiding wherever possible any reference to final causes and purposes; in this sense, Cartesian science was to stake its claim to a substantial degree of autonomy, in place of the traditional subordination of physics to theology.[8] And fourth, the new comprehensive system of scientific explanation was to embrace, for the first time, the realm of human existence, including physiology, medicine, and a very large part of what we now know as psychology.[9]

The above central planks in the Cartesian programme are 'philosophical' in the wide sense in which Descartes himself used the term; that is, they relate to what we should now call the scientific understanding of the

---

[5] For Descartes's concern in this regard, see the letter from the end of May 1637, where Descartes describes the publication of the *Discourse* as designed to 'prepare the way' for the reception of his physics, and to 'test the waters' (AT I 370: CSMK 58).

[6] Cf. AT VII 1 ff.: CSM II 3 ff.; AT VII 603 ff.: CSM II 397; AT V 159: CSMK 342.

[7] See AT X 215: CSM I 3; AT X 497: CSM II 401. For further discussion of this theme, see J. Cottingham, *The Rationalists* (Oxford: Oxford University Press, 1988), ch. 2.

[8] For the clearest statement of the Cartesian position on this issue, see *Principles*, pt. I art. 28; pt. III art. 3. (Not of course that God is dispensed with entirely in Descartes's physics; see *Principles*, pt. II arts. 36 ff.)

[9] The scope of Descartes's reductionism is often underestimated. See further my 'Descartes: Theology, Metaphysics and Science', in Cottingham (ed.), *Cambridge Companion to Descartes*, ch. 8, and see Ch. 5, below.

universe. And in this sphere at least, there is no denying that Descartes was a genuine innovator—not, to be sure the only such innovator of his time, nor so original as to have marked out utterly new territory unexplored by any of his contemporaries or immediate predecessors,[10] but for all that unquestionably meriting the title of one of the founders of the 'modern' world picture that still continues to dominate much of our culture. But from Descartes's valid claim to 'modernity' in the sense just sketched, it does not automatically follow that his philosophy as a whole was as revolutionary or 'modern' as is so often claimed.

Consider, in particular, the parts of Descartes's system that are 'philosophical' in the present-day, academic sense of the term—the epistemological and metaphysical ideas that form the basic structure of what we now think of as the Cartesian method of philosophizing. It is precisely these areas (the so-called 'method of doubt', the Cogito, the theory of clear and distinct ideas, the project for validating knowledge from the bottom up, and the defeat of scepticism about the 'external world') that historians of ideas characteristically focus on when they describe Descartes as the 'father of modern philosophy'. Yet to look carefully at the work of Descartes's predecessors in many of these areas is to realize that sweeping claims to originality are often misplaced. It is, for example, a salutary shock to those brought up to believe in the originality of Descartes's opening salvo in the *Meditations* to read such sixteenth-century writers as Francisco Sanches, the Portuguese philosopher and medical writer whose *Quod nihil scitur* was published in 1581.[11] Sanches begins his enquiry into the possibility of knowledge by 'withdrawing into himself' (*ad memetipsum retuli*) and 'calling all into doubt' (*omnia in dubium revocans*); this is the 'true way of knowing' (*verum sciendi modus*).[12] The parallels in phrasing and content with the start of the First Meditation are remarkable; and they do not stop there. Sanches, like Descartes, sweeps away traditional appeals to authority: Aristotle, for

---

[10] The most important names here are Francis Bacon, Galileo Galilei, and Pierre Gassendi. For anticipation of Cartesian physics in Galileo, see J. Cottingham, *Descartes* (Oxford: Blackwell, 1986), 103 ff.; for Bacon and Gassendi, see R. Woolhouse, *The Empiricists* (Oxford: Oxford University Press, 1988), 9 ff. and 48 ff.

[11] Francisco Sanches, *Quod nihil scitur* [Lyons, 1581]; Latin text established, annotated, and translated by Douglas F. S. Thomson, with introduction and notes by Elaine Limbrick (Cambridge: Cambridge University Press, 1988). Cf. also Thomas Hobbes's comments on the lack of the originality of the sceptical arguments in the First Meditation, in the Third Objections (AT VII 171: CSM II 121).

[12] *Quod nihil scitur*, ed, Limbrick, 92.

all his wisdom, was just wrong on many points; at the end of the day, *homo ut nos*—he was a man like us. To say 'thus spake the Master' is unworthy of a philosopher; better, in our reasonings, 'to trust nature alone'.[13] Sanches's motto, *solam naturam sequor* (I follow nature alone) sounds so Cartesian to the modern ear that we almost expect to find him appealing to the *lumen naturale*; but had he done so, this would not have been an anticipation, but a recapitulation, for the ancient metaphor of the natural light had been revived earlier in the sixteenth century by the Spanish humanist Joannes Vives in his *De disciplinis* (1531)—a work with which Sanches himself was almost certainly familiar.[14]

As far as the Cartesian approach to knowledge is concerned, then, any picture of Descartes as a lone innovator setting out on a new quest for certainty cannot survive serious scrutiny. What is more, when we come to Descartes's metaphysical solutions to the problems of knowledge, careful examination reveals that Descartes himself was often (though he seldom admitted as much) compelled to abandon the radical and progressive stance which he so proudly maintained in the other (more scientific) parts of his programme. In the remainder of this chapter I propose to look at one key test case: the role of God in Cartesian metaphysics. What I shall argue, in brief, is that what began as a seemingly straightforward exercise, that of supporting the trunk of his physics by unearthing its metaphysical roots,[15] gradually overwhelmed Descartes by its complexity; and that in attempting to complete the task, he was drawn, little by little, to fall back on the very scholastic apparatus that he so derided in his scientific work.

2. The Truth Rule and the Role of God

In the philosophy departments of today's academic world, whether of the 'continental' or the 'Anglo-Saxon' variety, Descartes is studied primarily as a writer of metaphysics. This is seen as the chief focus of his philosophy,

---

[13] *Quod nihil scitur*, ed, Limbrick, 93.

[14] For Vives, see further Limbrick's discussion in her introduction to Sanches, *Quod nihil scitur*, 32. The 'light' metaphor goes back much further—to Augustine and, ultimately, to Plato. For a detailed scholarly account of the Augustinian (and Platonic) influences on Descartes, see S. Menn, *Augustine and Descartes* (Cambridge: Cambridge University Press, 1998).

[15] For this celebrated metaphor cf. AT IXB 14: CSM I 186; it had been used earlier by Bacon, *De augmentiis scientiarum* [1623], 3. 1.

and the source of its abiding interest. But it is a major error to retroject this orientation and assume it captures the central preoccupations of Descartes himself. 'Non adeo incumbendum esse meditationibus' (you should not give such obsessive attention to metaphysical meditations) he told the young student Frans Burman (AT V 165: CSMK 346); he gave similar advice to that keen amateur metaphysician Princess Elizabeth of Bohemia (AT III 692–3: CSMK 227–8). In general, there is a considerable amount of evidence to support the thesis of Charles Adam that metaphysics was of merely subsidiary interest to the historical Descartes: 'Descartes ne demande à la métaphysique qu'une seule chose, de fournir un appui solide à la vérité scientifique.'[16] To say that Descartes's metaphysical concerns were subordinate to his scientific goals should not, however, be taken to imply that he launched into metaphysics merely as an afterthought. His celebrated brainstorm in the 'stove heated room' at the age of 23 had involved at least some thoughts on 'first philosophy',[17] and we know from the correspondence with Mersenne that by 1629 he had begun to compose a 'little treatise' on metaphysics which aimed to prove 'the existence of God and of our souls when they are separated from the body' (AT I 182: CSMK 29).[18] Nevertheless, it seems likely that Descartes did not give any systematic attention to establishing the metaphysical foundations of his philosophical system until he came to compose the *Discourse*—written, we should remember, as an introductory preface designed to smooth the way for the reception of the carefully chosen sample of mathematical and scientific work which he was finally venturing to release for publication.[19]

Although today we tend to 'fill out' the metaphysical arguments in Part Four of the *Discourse* as a result of all the attention that is accorded to a standard 'course text', if we look at what Descartes actually wrote there we

---

[16] 'Descartes requires only one thing of metaphysics, to provide a solid basis for truth in science.' C. Adam, *Vie et œuvres de Descartes* [1910] in AT XII 143. See further A. B. Gibson, *The Philosophy of Descartes* (London: Methuen, 1932), ch. 2.

[17] Cf. the section of Descartes's early notebooks entitled 'Olympica' (AT X 217 ff.: CSM I 4–5); the reconstruction of those early thoughts, presented in Part Two of the *Discourse*, contains a fairly detailed prolegomenon to metaphysics; but this may well incorporate reflections from a much later period of Descartes's life.

[18] 'Je ne dis pas que quelque jour je n'achevasse un petit *Traité de Métaphysique*, lequel j'ai commencé étant en Frise, et dont les principaux points sont de prouver l'existence de Dieu et celle de nos âmes, lorsqu'elles sont séparées du corps.' Letter to Mersenne of 25 November 1630. The treatise was never finished.

[19] After a long delay; see AT I 284 ff.: CSMK 42 ff. For the character of the *Discourse* as an introductory preface, see letter to Mersenne of February 1637 (AT I 349; CSMK 53).

find that it is schematic in the extreme. It is worth recalling, moreover, that (apart from the introductory autobiography in Part One), Part Four is the shortest section of the work; far more space is devoted, for example, to Parts Five and Six, containing the resumé of Cartesian physics from the suppressed *The World*, the problems of physiology and the circulation of the blood, and Descartes's future plans for scientific research. What we get in Part Four is a brief opening paragraph on the unreliability of previously accepted beliefs, culminating in the acceptance of 'je pense donc je suis' as the 'first principle of the philosophy I was seeking', a second, equally curt, paragraph sketching a (notoriously lame) argument for the essential incorporeality of the thinking self,[20] and then, without more ado, a breathtakingly bald and peremptory announcement of the decision to adopt the truth rule of clarity and distinctness: 'I decided that I could take it as a general rule that the things we conceive very clearly and distinctly are all true' (AT VI 33: CSM I 127).

We need to make a conscious effort to get back to the intellectual climate in which Descartes was raised if we are to understand his apparently cavalier adoption of a rule whose philosophical pitfalls are now so glaringly apparent after centuries of exhaustive critical dissection. For the ex-student of La Flèche, for the devout Catholic that Descartes was to remain throughout his life,[21] the matter was intuitively quite simple. The rationale for the truth rule was in the end the perfectly straightforward one that Descartes produced on many occasions when challenged. *Rectum ingenium a Deo accepi*:[22] the reliability of the human intellect is evident from its having been bestowed on us by a perfect and benevolent Creator. This is not the naively optimistic claim that human nature is somehow privileged or immune from error; Descartes frequently stresses the epistemological analogue of original sin—*naturae nostrae infirmitas est agnoscenda*.[23] Rather it is the simple point that, though our human limitations may often cause us to go astray through carelessness or lack of concentration, when we are using the divine gift of reason conscientiously and to the best of our ability, that gift cannot be inherently treacherous. If it were, the very source of our being would be

---

[20] For its fallaciousness see my, 'Descartes: Theology, Metaphysics and Science', in Cottingham (ed.), *Cambridge Companion to Descartes*, 236–57, at 241 ff.

[21] Cf. H. Gouhier, *La Pensée religieuse de Descartes* (Paris: Vrin, 1934), 300 ff.

[22] 'A reliable mind was God's gift to me' (*Conversation with Burman* [1648], AT V 148: CSMK 334). The wording in this formulation of the Cartesian response is as reported by Burman, but Descartes's own published formulations are closely similar; see Second Replies, AT VII 144: CSM II 103.

[23] 'We must recognize the weakness of our nature.' Sixth Meditation: AT VII 90: CSM II 62.

tainted with evil (AT VII 144: CSM II 103). The very truth rule that for the modern reader comes out of the blue as a crashingly bold postulate evidently appeared, for Descartes himself, to flow immediately and unproblematically from axioms that structured the very core of his worldview.

This last point should not be taken as implying (what is clearly false) that Descartes regarded the task of grounding his epistemology as a simple one. Although, for a believer, the matter was essentially simple, Descartes wanted his philosophy to be universally acceptable 'even among the Turks'.[24] What does follow is that the task of grounding science could, in Descartes's eyes, be almost completely boiled down to one single undertaking: proving the existence of God. It is this undertaking, therefore, after the brisk canter of the opening three paragraphs of Part Four of the *Discourse*, that occupies the whole of the remainder of the section. For, as Descartes himself admits with disarming frankness, 'if we did not know that everything real and true within us comes from a perfect and infinite being, then, however clear and distinct our ideas were, we should have no reason to be sure that they had the perfection of being true' (AT VI 39: CSM I 130).

But when Descartes does turn to the task of completing the sketch of his foundational epistemology by proving God's existence, the easy flow of the argument begins, for the first time, to suffer a check. The change of pace is immediately apparent in the long and tortuous third paragraph of *Discourse*, Part Four. The writing style, hitherto so clear and fluent, becomes rapidly clogged and murky: self-defensive jargon, previously entirely absent, begins to make its appearance, and in place of the device of the author appealing solely to his own inner light and speaking directly to the person of unencumbered 'good sense', we find the apologetic phrase 'j'userai, s'il vous plaît, ici librement des mots de l'école' (AT VI 34: CSM I 128).[25] Having

---

[24] *Conversation with Burman*, AT V 159: CSMK 342. Descartes prided himself on the transcultural appeal of his philosophy and also on its lack of technicalities and other obstacles to understanding; he hoped it would be readily accessible to untrained minds—'even to women' (letter of 22 February 1638, AT I 560; CSMK 86). It is worth adding that, despite this manifestation of the prejudice common to his era, Descartes can—if only on the basis of his remarkable correspondence with Elizabeth—be acquitted of the kind of unreflective sexism that is to be found in near contemporaries such as Spinoza (cf. Spinoza's pejorative use of the term *muliebris* ('womanly') e.g. at *Ethics* [c.1665], part 2, prop. 49, scholium IVc). Indeed, as far as the long struggle of the feminist cause is concerned, the influence of Cartesianism was, on the whole, a benign one. See Poulain's *L'Égalité des deux sexes* [1673] and the introduction in D. Clarke (ed.), François Poulain de la Barre: *The Equality of the Sexes* (Manchester: Manchester University Press, 1990).

[25] 'Here, if I may, I shall make free use of some scholastic terminology' (AT VI 34; CSM I 128). A similarly embarrassed throat-clearing, 'ut ita loquar' (if I may so put it), occurs in the corresponding

announced his liberation from the subjection of his teachers, Descartes is now reluctantly forced to employ the very apparatus of traditional learning which he had scathingly denounced earlier on in the *Discourse*.[26] So far from 'seeking no knowledge other than what could be found in myself or the great book of the world' (AT VI 9: CSM I 115), Descartes will now fall back on the arguments and methods of his scholastic teachers.

In a letter written during the year following the publication of the *Discourse*, Descartes ruefully admitted that the section on the existence of God was the 'least worked out section in the whole book' (AT I 560: CSMK 85); he also implies that it was produced in a hurry to meet the publisher's deadline.[27] But there is a certain disingenuousness here. The problem is not just one of speed of writing, or of lack of preparatory work. Rather, Descartes is genuinely bereft, in this area, of the kind of distinctively fresh approach he believed he had discovered in science. In the latter, he has a whole new apparatus, a quantitative, geometrically based methodology, which he hoped could replace entirely the Aristotelian way of describing and explaining the world. But in the field of natural theology, so carefully and systematically tilled throughout the preceding centuries, he cannot free himself from the influence of the long years of theological study he had dutifully completed at La Flèche.[28]

'Reflecting on the fact that my being was not wholly perfect ... I decided to inquire into the source of my ability to think of something more perfect than I was.' The opening of the fourth paragraph of Part Four of the *Discourse* takes us straight into a standard theme of medieval theology. 'How could the intellect know that it was a defective and incomplete being unless it had some knowledge of a being free from every defect?' The phrasing

---

place in the Third Meditation, just before the first introduction of the technical term 'objective reality' (*realitas objectiva*): AT VII 40 line 23: CSM II 28.

[26] A recurring theme in the early part of the *Discourse* is that scholastic terminology and methods are often little more than a smokescreen to conceal ignorance—'of less use for exploring the gaps in our knowledge than for explaining to others what we already know or ... prattling on matters of which we are ignorant' (AT VI 17: CSM I 119).

[27] 'I did not decide to include it until I had nearly completed it and the publisher was becoming impatient' (Letter to Vatier of 22 February 1638, AT I 560: CSMK 85–6).

[28] In Pt. One of the *Discourse* (AT VI 8: CSM I 114), Descartes hints at the possibility of dispensing with traditional theology: 'Le chemin [au ciel] n'est plus moins ouvert aux plus ignorants qu'aux plus doctes.' (The road to heaven is no less open to the most ignorant than to the most learned.) But he is also honest (or cautious?) enough to admit the 'reverence' for the subject that had been instilled in him ('je reverais notre theologie'; ibid.) and his respect for the value of the 'exercises done in the schools' ('je ne laissais pas toutefois d'estimer les exercises auxquels on s'occupe dans les écoles'; AT VI 5: CSM I 113).

of this latter question sounds distinctively Cartesian, but in fact it comes from St Bonaventure's *Itinerarium mentis in Deum* (1259).[29] In essence it is a variation on an earlier Augustinian argument (itself ultimately derived from Plato): the ability to make comparative judgements (*x* is better than *y*) could not exist unless we had within us a notion of perfect goodness, or God.[30]

The initial framework for Descartes's proof of God's existence is thus far from original. Nor could he plausibly claim (as he did when charged with lifting the Cogito from Augustine) that the principle was 'so simple that it might have occurred to anyone'.[31] For although it is certainly the case that the ability to make comparative value judgements presupposes the possession of some standard of comparison, it is far from self-evident that this in turn requires a positive concept of supreme goodness.[32] However that may be, when Descartes moves on and attempts to step from this notion of perfection to the real existence of its supposed author, his dependence on his predecessors becomes even more unmistakable. He invokes, in brief, two principles well established in the philosophical theology of the Middle Ages and Renaissance. The first of these, which we may term the *principle of the non-inferiority of the cause*, asserts that the more perfect cannot be caused by the less perfect: 'I recognized very clearly that the ability to think of something more perfect than myself had to come from a nature that was in fact more perfect' (AT VI 34: CSM I 128). Descartes attempts to soften the reader up for digesting this principle by slipping in the observation that, so far from

[29] 'Quomodo … sciret intellectus, hoc esse ens defectivum et incompletum, si nullam haberet cognitionem entis absque omni defectu?' Bonaventure, *Itinerarium*, III. 3. Cited in Descartes, *Discours de la méthode*, edition and commentary by Etienne Gilson (Paris: Vrin, 1925), 316.

[30] 'Neque enim in his omnibus bonis … diceremus aliud alio melius … nisi esset nobis impressa notio ipsius boni secundum quod … aliud alii praeponderemus. Sic amandus est Deus, non hoc et illud bonum, sed ipsum bonum.' (Nor in all these goods would we say something is better than another unless there were impressed within us the notion of the good itself, by reference to which we weigh one thing more highly than another. And hence God is to be loved not as this or that good but as the good itself.) Augustine, *De Trinitate* [*c*.410], 8, 3, 4, cited in *Discours*, ed. Gilson. For the origins of the argument in Plato (where essentially the same reasoning is used to establish the existence of the form of the good), cf. *Phaedo* [*c*.380 BC], 74a ff.

[31] 'C'est une chose qui de soi est si simple et si naturelle a inferer … qu'elle aurait pu tomber sous la plume de qui que ce soit' (letter to Colvius of 14 November 1640, AT III 248: CSMK 159). There are several anticipations of the Cogito in Augustine, the most striking being in the *De libero arbitrio* [388–95], 2. 3. 7: 'si non esses, falli omnino non posses' (if you did not exist you could in no way be deceived); other texts are discussed in *Discours*, ed. Gilson, 295.

[32] One may grade apples according to their freedom from defects without thereby presupposing the concept of a supremely perfect apple, entirely free from any defect. For Descartes's (unsatisfactory) attempts to reply to this line of criticism by insisting on the priority of the positive concept of perfection, see AT V 153: CSMK 338, and Cottingham (ed.), *Descartes' Conversation with Burman*, 72 ff.

presupposing any elaborate philosophical apparatus, it is in fact just a variant on the simple and universally accepted axiom 'nothing comes from nothing': 'it is no less contradictory (*il n y a pas moins de repugnance*) that the more perfect should result from the less perfect ... than that something should proceed from nothing' (ibid.). Now appeals to the notion of causality were of course a standard feature of medieval natural theology—the most celebrated example being the second of Aquinas's Five Ways.[33] But what Descartes in fact requires goes far beyond the common notion that everything must have a cause. As Marin Mersenne later objected, we may readily accept that flies and other animals must have some cause, without being forced to admit that this cause must be more perfect than they (AT VII 123: CSM II 88). Yet this is not the end of Descartes's difficulties. For in addition to the causal principle (even when that principle is construed in its controversial form as requiring not just the existence but the non-inferiority of the cause),[34] Descartes's proof requires an even more problematic principle, which we may term the *principle of transfer*. This principle (though Descartes refrains from stating it explicitly in the *Discourse*) asserts that the causal constraints operating in the real world are to be 'transferred' or carried over, so as to apply to the realm of our thought-contents. This principle of transfer mystified even those of Descartes's contemporaries who were thoroughly versed in the scholastic tradition,[35] and shortly after the publication of the *Discourse* Descartes was forced to admit that he needed to say a lot more to explain and defend it: 'I supposed that certain notions which habitual reflection had made familiar and evident to me would necessarily be so to everyone—for example that our ideas could not receive *their form or their being* except from some external objects ... [and] could not represent any reality or perfection not present in those objects.'[36]

---

[33] Thomas Aquinas, *Summa theologiae* [1266–73], pt. I qu. 2 art. 3. Cf. A. Kenny, *The Five Ways* (London: Routledge, 1969), 34 ff.

[34] When he came to write the *Principles* (1644), Descartes was prepared to come clean and admit explicitly that his argument in fact required a much stronger principle than the axiom that nothing comes from nothing: 'it is evident by the natural light not only that nothing comes from nothing, but also that what is more perfect cannot be produced by ... what is less perfect' (pt. I, art. 18 (AT VIII 11: CSM I 99), emphasis supplied). Contrast the earlier fudge in the Second Replies (1641) where Descartes claims that the two principles are just the same (AT VII 135: CSM II 97).

[35] See the comments of the Thomist critics who wrote the First Objections: 'a cause imparts some real and actual influence; but what does not actually exist [an idea] cannot take on anything and so does not receive or require any actual causal influence' (AT VII 93: CSM II 67).

[36] Letter to Vatier of 22 February 1638, AT I 560: CSMK 86 (emphasis supplied).

What finally emerges here, with Descartes's talk about the 'form' as opposed to the 'being' of ideas, is the complex network of metaphysical presuppositions that lurks beneath the surface of the supposedly self-evident reasoning of *Discourse*, Part Four. To be even intelligible, let alone convincing, Descartes's argument has to be read against the intellectual background of Renaissance scholasticism—the Thomist revival of the sixteenth century, which had transformed the study of Aquinas and led to the gradual supplanting of the traditional commentaries on St Thomas, and their replacement with more elaborate and systematic treatises on metaphysics, the so-called *cursus philosophici*.[37] This new tradition, in discussions of the existence and perfections of God, had deployed a complicated barrage of highly technical distinctions between various modes of being—most crucially, the distinction between actual (or 'formal') and merely representative (or 'objective') reality, and the distinction between the sense in which perfections were present in God ('eminently') and in his creatures ('formally').[38] In trying to satisfy critics of the *Discourse*, such as Father Vatier, Descartes was finally obliged to come clean and defend his reliance on this technical apparatus, and it was this task that led directly to the composition of the metaphysical arguments in the Third Meditation. But so far from being able to complete the job in a way consistent with the proud motto of the *Meditations*—*omnia semel in vita evertenda*,[39] Descartes found himself obliged to rely ever more deeply on the work of his predecessors.

3. The Metaphysics of Substance in the Meditations

It is striking that the term 'substance' has largely faded from the intellectual landscape of our own time. As far as science is concerned, the prevailing

---

[37] For an illuminating overview of these developments, which originated mainly in the Iberian peninsula, see F. Copleston, *A History of Philosophy* (London: Burnes Oates, 1947–75), iii. ch. 21.

[38] Cf. the discussions of being, causation, and perfection in Francisco Suárez, *Disputationes metaphysicae* [1597], Disp. 26, sect. 1, §§2–6 , trans. in R. Ariew, J. Cottingham, and T. Sorell (eds.), *Descartes's Meditations: Background Source Materials* (Cambridge: Cambridge University Press, 1988), 36–7. Descartes was well acquainted with Suárez; cf. AT VII 235: CSM II 164. For the antecedents of the terminology in Aquinas himself, see Descartes, *Discours*, ed. Gilson, 319, and Gilson's *Index scolastico-cartésien* (Paris: Alcan, 1916), s.v. 'realitas'.

[39] 'once in the course of my life, everything had to be demolished completely' (First Meditation, AT VII 17: CSM II 12).

models, whether of relativity theory or of quantum theory, operate (to put the matter crudely and schematically) in terms of covering laws specified by reference to mathematical equations; the way in which the variables in those equations are mapped on to the world simply bypasses the ancient (Aristotelian-based) framework of substance and attribute, and its ordinary-language analogue of subject and predicate. And as far as philosophy (in the modern sense) goes, the Humean critique of the notion of substance has, broadly speaking, triumphed;[40] in struggling to understand and analyse the material world or the nature of consciousness, we no longer assume that ontology must reflect grammar. In the philosophy of mind, to take but one example, talk about the mind is typically analysed either in terms of mental functions, states, or processes, or else adverbially (by invoking the subjective dimension, or 'what it is like' to be conscious);[41] substantival dualism has pretty well ceased to be a serious philosophical option.[42] In general, it would perhaps not be too much to say that the presence or absence of the term 'substance', and the explanatory frameworks associated with it, is the single most reliable indicator that divides the 'ancient' and 'modern' worlds.

If this criterion is applied to Descartes, the results are highly instruct-ive—all the more so because they are not always as simple or unambiguous as one might expect. The term 'substance' appears only once in Part Four of the *Discourse,* in the announcement of the essential incorporeality of the self: 'I realized that I was a substance (*une substance*) whose whole essence or nature is simply to think and which does not … depend on any material thing' (AT VI 33: CSM I 127). And even here, in the later Latin version, the term is immediately given a non-technical gloss; 'I realized that I was a *thing* or substance' (me esse *rem quamdam* sive substantiam; AT VI 558, emphasis supplied). There is in fact a good deal of evidence to suggest that Descartes would have liked to present his metaphysics in such a way as to dispense with this hallmark of traditional philosophy. The *Meditations* starts out in a self-consciously non-technical style: just as the *Discourse* had spoken directly to the simple man of 'good sense', so the *Meditations* invites the reader to share in the solitary reflections of the isolated thinker who

[40] David Hume, *A Treatise of Human Nature* [1739–40], bk. I pt. 4 sect. 3. See, however, my comments in Ch. 1 sect. 2.

[41] Cf. T. Nagel, *The View from Nowhere* (Oxford: Oxford University Press, 1986), ch. 1.

[42] Cf. R. Penrose, *The Emperor's New Mind* (Oxford: Oxford University Press, 1989), ch. 1.

proposes to strip himself of all *praejudicia*, or preconceived opinions.[43] And even when the systematic process of reinstating former beliefs begins, the language adopted is strikingly plain: 'I am a thing which is real and truly exists. But what kind of thing? As I have said, a thinking thing' (AT VII 27: CSM II 18). Not for Descartes the formal definitions of the Schools:

What is a man? Shall I say 'a rational animal'? No; for then I should have to inquire what an animal is, what rationality is, and in this way one question would lead me down the slope to other harder ones, and I do not now have the time to waste on subtleties of this kind. Instead I propose to concentrate on what [comes] into my thoughts spontaneously and quite naturally.   (AT VII 25: CSM II 17)

Not only did Descartes prefer to avoid scholastic definitions in favour of the phrase 'a thinking thing', but he even fought shy of such a seemingly non-technical term as 'soul' (*âme*) because of the misleading connotations he feared it might have for some readers.[44] And he was similarly chary of traditional terminology to describe the material realm: 'If we say that body is a "corporeal substance" ... these two words do not tell us any more than does the word "body"' (*Search for Truth*, AT X 517: CSM II 411). In the *Meditations*, the preferred phrase is the plain unadorned 'extended thing' (*res extensa, chose étendue*; AT VII 78 and AT IX 62: CSM II 54). Later, when Descartes presented his metaphysics in a form that he hoped might find favour in the schools and universities, he found it tactful to use traditional terminology; but even then he was careful to distance himself from its unwanted ontological implications. You can, he wrote in the *Principles*, consider thought and extension as 'constituting the natures of thinking substance and extended substance', but in effect (he suggests) this is just a rephrasing of ordinary talk about 'mind' and 'body'; there is no real distinction between the mind and the thinking which constitutes its essential nature.[45]

---

[43] Cf. *Meditations*, Synopsis, AT VII 12: CSM II 9.

[44] Compare Fifth Replies, AT VII 356: CSM II 246.

[45] 'Cogitatio et extensio spectari possunt ut constitutentes naturas substantiae intelligentis et corporeae; tuncque non aliter concipi debent quam ipsa substantia cogitans et substantia extensa, hoc est quam mens et corpus.' (Thought and extension can be regarded as constituting the natures of intelligent substance and corporeal substance; and then they must be conceived none otherwise than as thinking substance itself and as extended substance itself, that is, as mind and body.) (AT VIII 30: CSM I 215.) The distinction between substance and defining attribute is, Descartes goes on to say, merely a conceptual one ('distinctio rationis; une distinction que se fait par la pensée'). For further discussion of these passages, see J. Cottingham (ed.), *Descartes's Conversation with Burman* (Oxford: Clarendon, 1976), 77 ff.

In sum, while Descartes did not totally set his face against the traditional terminology of substance (and was even prepared to employ it himself in order to facilitate the reception of his work), the overwhelming message from the language used in the *Meditations*, and Descartes's own explanatory comments elsewhere, is that the terminology is, like Wittgenstein's cog-wheel,[46] unconnected to the rest of the machine; it does no work that cannot be better done in non-technical language. Cartesian metaphysics requires no training in scholastic jargon, but is founded solely on the simple direct perception I have of myself as a thinking thing, and my equally clear and distinct perception of physical objects as extended in three dimensions.[47]

But any attempt to read Descartes's definitive statement of his metaphysics *solo lumine naturali*—guided by the natural light alone, without recourse to any preconceptions from past philosophy—comes up against a brick wall in the Third Meditation. The same abrupt change of pace and style that marked the third paragraph of *Discourse*, Part Four is immediately apparent when we reach the argument for God's existence in the fourteenth paragraph of the Third Meditation; and, ironically enough, the change occurs in the very paragraph that opens with a disarming appeal to the simple light of reason: 'Iam vero lumine naturali manifestum est' (AT VII 40: CSM II 28). What we are asked to accept as 'manifest by the natural light' is the complex, not to say baffling, principle that 'there is at least as much [reality] in the efficient and total cause as in the effect of that cause'.[48] Descartes seems initially to repeat the manoeuvre in the *Discourse* of smuggling in the principle as nothing more than a variant on the simple axiom of causation—nothing comes from nothing: 'for where, I ask could the effect get its reality from if not from the cause, and how could the cause give it to the effect unless it possessed it?' (ibid.) Yet reflection soon reveals that much more is being demanded here than a simple acceptance of the deterministic maxim that everything has a cause.

---

[46] See Ludwig Wittgenstein, *Philosophical Investigations* [*Philosophische Untersuchungen*, 1953], pt.I §271.

[47] I have a clear and distinct perception of 'the whole of that corporeal nature which is the subject-matter of pure mathematics' (AT VII 71: CSM II 49).

[48] The original Latin of 1641 omits the word 'reality'. The omission invites the speculation (for which there is no other evidence, but which none the less has a certain plausibility) that when Descartes began to compose this paragraph of the Third Meditation, he still hoped to get by without technical scholastic terminology. If he did harbour any such hope it must have been short-lived; compare the jargon-laden last two sentences of the paragraph (AT VII 42 lines 20 ff.).

What Descartes needs is a traditional scholastic interpretation of that maxim which I have elsewhere called the 'heirloom principle'[49]—that the only way an effect can come to possess some property is by inheriting it, heirloom fashion, from its causes. It is not just that a stone cannot come to exist out of nothing, but that the cause of a stone must itself possess, in some form, all the properties to be found in the stone (AT VII 41 line 5: CSM II 28).[50] Elsewhere, at least as far as his physics was concerned, Descartes might have been able to claim that this principle had a certain intuitive plausibility. The Cartesian laws of motion, for example, rely on what Descartes seems to have felt was a perfectly transparent idea, analogous to the modern concept of the conservation of energy: a body with a certain quantity of motion cannot have got the motion from nowhere, but must have had it passed on from another body which itself possessed as much or more motion.[51] But unfortunately, the application of the principle to metaphysics requires something far more controversial and problematic. In the first place (as already noted above in sect. 2), Descartes needs the 'principle of transfer'—he needs to apply the heirloom notion not just to really existing objects, but to the representational content of our ideas. Even a mere *idea* of a stone could not be in me unless caused by something 'which contains everything to be found in the stone' (AT VII 41 lines 12 ff.). And in the second place, even this controversial move requires a complex qualification to cope with the obvious objection that, on Descartes's principles, there would have to be a genuine existing counterpart to *everything* of which I can form a clear idea. That would imply an altogether too swift and easy proof of the external world, which would violate the cautious scepticism of the First Meditation, and indeed contradict the whole Cartesian project of reconstructing science from the bottom up. So Descartes is forced to qualify, and admit that the fact that I have ideas of stones and other corporeal objects is not, at this stage in his reconstruction of knowledge, sufficient *tout court* to prove their existence.

[49] Cf. Cottingham, *Descartes*, 51.

[50] 'Non potest ... aliquis lapis ... incipere esse, nisi producatur ab aliqua re in qua totum illud sit ... quod ponitur in lapide': in the cause of the stone there must be 'all that which is present in the stone'. The principle is in fact complicated still further by the addition of the qualifying phrase 'formally or eminently' (to be discussed later).

[51] Cf. *Principles*, pt. II arts. 36 ff., and, for further discussion of Descartes's use of the principle of conservation and its relation to his ideas on causality, see Cottingham, *The Rationalists*, 201−2.

My ideas of stones need not have been caused by actual stones, since I might (he argues) simply have produced these ideas from within myself. Yet how, since I am simply an incorporeal 'thinking thing'? He answers: 'as for the ... elements which make up the ideas of corporeal things, namely extension, shape, position and movement, these are not formally contained in me, since I am nothing but a thinking thing; but since they are merely modes of a substance, and I am a substance, it seems possible that they are contained in me eminently' (AT VII 45: CSM II 31).

Here at a stroke the earlier aim of dispensing with technical terminology is unceremoniously jettisoned. So far from being an optional and unnecessarily complex terminological variant on 'thing', the term 'substance' is now employed with the full weight of scholastic metaphysics behind it. There is a hierarchical realm of categories, a chain of being, in which substances occupy a higher place than mere modes; and the principle of the non-inferiority of the cause is thus construed in a way that allows an idea of a mere mode to have as its cause a substance of *any* kind. A substance, being higher in the hierarchy of being, can be said to contain 'eminently' items such as modes even when it does not actually have anything in common with them. Descartes can no longer claim that his appeal to causation is nothing more than a reliance on the intuitively simple idea that effects inherit their features from causes which themselves possess those features (hot effects get their heat from hot causes). Nor can he rely any more on the supposedly self-evident notion that 'the effect is like the cause'.[52] Instead the very structure of his argument now stands or falls with the acceptability of a whole framework of ontological presuppositions derived in varying degrees from renaissance and medieval scholasticism and ultimately from Aristotle himself. Even before Descartes is ready to take the crucial step of inferring the existence of a supreme being as the source of his idea of perfection, he has given the game away: the supposedly unencumbered deliverances of the natural light are deeply tainted with the philosophical preconceptions that he had imbibed as a schoolboy at La Flèche.[53] So far from being an optional extra, the cog-wheel of scholasticism now drives the whole machine.

---

[52] 'Effectus similis est causae' (*Conversation with Burman*, AT V 156: CSMK 349–50)

[53] My phrasing in this sentence closely follows Anthony Kenny's highly illuminating comment in his *Descartes* (New York: Random House, 1968), 62. Kenny, however, applies the criticism to the Cogito argument, which he analyses (mistakenly in my view) as presupposing the scholastic maxim *nihili nulla sunt attributa*: see further my *Descartes*, 37 ff.

4. Science without Metaphysics: The Incomplete Revolution

It would be a mistake to conclude this chapter by leaving the impression that Descartes's failure to shed the philosophical preconceptions of his age was simply an isolated affair, connected with the (undeniably daunting) task of trying to construct a convincing proof of God's existence. For there is a deeper, more pervasive shortcoming in his challenge to preconceived opinion—one that is seldom discussed by commentators, perhaps because it amounts to a gap, an absence, rather than a visible flaw. What is missing is any serious analysis, let alone critique, of the concept of causation itself. That vital philosophical task was left to Hume, building on the work of the (much underestimated) Malebranche.[54] What Descartes failed to see was that his scientific revolution, the programme for the mathematicization of physics, required a fundamental re-evaluation of the way in which causality was to be understood. Physics, in the Cartesian system, is entirely reducible to covering laws which account for the qualities and dispositions of material things solely by reference to the shape, size, and motion of the portions of matter of which they are composed. No need here for natural kinds or elements;[55] no need for the Aristotelian plurality of substances, where things behaved the way they did because of their specific natures or essences. There was simply a material plenum whose behaviour at any given moment was derivable from the initial specifications of the 'motion, size, shape and arrangement of its parts' (*The World*, AT XI 25: CSM I 89). But what follows from this (and this is the crucial corollary of the new science that Descartes failed to grasp properly) is that what had been understood as causal transactions between individual substances—a kind of transmission either of form or matter between *x* and *y*[56]—could now be interpreted without making any use whatever of the traditional apparatus of substance, form, attribute, and quality. For the point of that apparatus, as far as the understanding of causation was concerned, was supposed to be that it revealed some transparent connection linking the properties of the effect with the nature of the cause that produced it. Yet in Descartes's universe

---

[54] See further N. Jolley, *The Light of the Soul* (Oxford: Clarendon, 1990), ch. 6.

[55] What Descartes sometimes terms 'elements' are in fact nothing more than classifications of (homogeneous) matter according to the shapes, sizes, and motions of the particles of which it is composed. Cf. *The World*, AT XI 26: CSM I 89.   [56] Cf. Jolley, *The Light of the Soul*, 41.

there are, properly understood, no such necessary connections. Matter, it is true, conforms to the necessary (deductively derived) laws of three-dimensional geometry; but to get real events (movement, efficacy) into the system, what is invoked is not a causal structure of interacting substances and forms, but simply an initial set of divinely ordained specifications concerning the quantity of motion of the system as a whole.[57]

The appropriate conceptual framework for the Cartesian universe would thus have been a radically new one which (1) dispensed entirely with the ancient terminology of substance, attribute, and mode, and (2) jettisoned the traditional model of causation which linked causes to effects by invoking the transfer of attributes or modes between substances. Descartes never devised such a new framework. With respect to (1) he got as far as dispensing with 'substantial forms', but (perhaps through caution) preferred to develop the main public statement of his physics in a way that did minimal violence to traditional substance-based science.[58] With respect to (2), he was prepared to jettison the traditional models of causality only when it came to interactions between mind and matter. Here, at least, he paved the way for the occasionalism of Malebranche and the regularity theory of Hume.[59] But elsewhere he was content to subscribe unreflectively[60] to a cluster of preconceptions—'the effect is like the cause' (AT V 156: CSMK 339); 'nothing in the effect which was not previously in the cause' (AT III 428; CSMK 192)—which were ill suited to the new scientific worldview he championed.

In a shadowy alternative universe we can imagine a seventeenth century in which Galileo escaped ecclesiastical censure and in which, as a result,

---

[57] Cf. *The World*: God's creation does not involve the bestowing on matter of any *form*, or *order*, but simply an initial specification of the divisions and motions of its parts (AT XI 34: CSM I 91). Compare *Principles*, pt. II, art. 36: all change and motion in the universe has one and one only true cause, specifiable in terms of the quantities of motion and rest initially imparted (and continually preserved) by God (AT VIII 61: CSM I 240).

[58] The physical world is sometimes described in the *Principles* as (a) corporeal 'substance', though Descartes underlines certain awkward ambiguities in the traditional use of the term; *Principles*, pt. I art. 51. See also ibid. art. 63. It is worth noting that the term does no work at all when it comes to the 'hard core' of Cartesian physics—the development of the laws of motion in pt. II arts. 36 ff.

[59] For Descartes's anticipations of occasionalism, see J. Cottingham, 'Descartes on Colour', *Proceedings of the Aristotelian Society* (1989–90), 231–46, repr. in Ch. 7, below. See also Jolley, *The Light of the Soul*, ch. 3.

[60] This may seem a harsh judgement, but there is no evidence that I know of which suggests that Descartes ever gave serious thought to the precise cash value of these maxims, or to the standard metaphors (of 'transfer', 'containedness', and the like) in terms of which causality was traditionally understood.

Descartes went public in 1633 with his *World*—a starkly radical vision of a new science largely free of the trappings of traditional metaphysics. In this alternative world he might have gone on to challenge the whole scholastic framework of substance. How different the subsequent history of philosophy would have been is difficult to say. Leibniz's reconciling project, it seems, would have been much the same; for many of his arguments for rehabilitating the 'substantial forms' discarded by the 'new philosophy' could, with a little adjustment, have been rephrased as a defence of the notion of substance in general.[61] As for Leibniz's contemporary Locke, who took so much of his conceptual apparatus from the Cartesians, his (notoriously problematic) views on substance[62] would no doubt have been clearer had Descartes and his followers provided a radical critique of that notion. The fate of Spinoza's *Doppelgänger* in our alternative universe is the hardest of all to predict. In many respects he is the most uncompromisingly 'modern' of the great seventeenth-century writers—in his firm allegiance to the principles of Cartesian science, in his vigorous rejection of finalism, in his independent-minded insistence that man must come to terms with his fate unprotected by the comforts of revealed religion.[63] Yet for all that it is almost impossible to conceive of the *Ethics* being composed without the metaphysical underpinning of substance and attribute that the actual Spinoza derived from Descartes's *Principles*.[64]

These reflections (fascinating or tiresome as they may be) must remain purely speculative; as we have seen, in the actual universe that we inhabit, Descartes's demolition job on scholasticism was only imperfectly carried through. Yet this result is itself important food for thought. For in the real world, paradigm shifts are rarely instantaneous; revolutions seldom

[61] 'Extended mass is not of itself enough...I was constrained to have recourse to what might be called a real and animated point or to an atom of substance which must embrace some element of form or of activity in order to make a complete being. It was thus necessary to recall and in a manner to rehabilitate substantial forms.' 'New System of the Nature and Communication of Substances' [*Système nouveau de la nature et de la communication des substances*, 1695]. An English version of the 'New System' may be found in G. W. Leibniz, *Philosophical Texts*, ed. R. S. Woolhouse and R. Francks (Oxford: Oxford University Press, 1998).

[62] Compare the lengthy and convoluted discussions in the *Essay concerning Human Understanding* [1689], bk. II ch. 23.

[63] For further discussion of these themes, see Cottingham, *The Rationalists*, 84 ff.

[64] Though of course with crucial modifications, See the comments in the preface to Spinoza's exposition of Descartes's *Principles* (*Principia philosophiae Renati Descartes* [1663], trans. in *The Collected Works of Spinoza*, ed. E. Curley (Princeton, NJ: Princeton University Press, 1985)).

occur as suddenly as is suggested in the retrospective schematisms of the historians. Descartes's greatness, the genuine originality of so much of his philosophy, remain immune from serious challenge, even though he was only one of the many *accoucheurs* at the long parturition of the modern age.

3

The Cartesian Legacy

1. Introduction

What does our present worldview owe to Descartes? Routine genuflections to the 'father of modem philosophy' do not help one bit to answer this question. It is true that nearly all philosophy students still cut their teeth on the *Meditations*; further, that its author's place in the historical canon of great philosophers is unassailable. But despite Descartes's prominence on the reading lists, if we look at the way philosophy is actually practised in our own day, it seems undeniable that the ruling conception of the philosophical enterprise is, and has been for some time, a powerfully anti-Cartesian one.

A brief sketch of how we got to where we are today might look like this. Hume punctured the pretensions of reason to underpin science;[1] Kant unmasked the fraudulence of foundational metaphysics;[2] and in the twentieth century the bludgeonings of the positivists,[3] the delicate scalpel work of the Frege-inspired philosophers of language,[4] and the baroque

---

[1] 'The utmost effort of human reason is to reduce the principles productive of natural phenomena to a greater simplicity...But as to the causes of these general causes, we should in vain attempt their discovery...The most perfect philosophy of the natural kind only staves off our ignorance.' David Hume, *An Enquiry concerning Human Understanding* [1748], sect. IV pt. 1, penultimate paragraph.

[2] 'The procedure of metaphysics has hitherto been a merely random groping, and what is worst of all, a groping among mere concepts.' *Critique of Pure Reason* [*Kritik der Reinen Vernunft*, 1781, 2nd edn. 1787] B xiv. For more on Kant's notion of the 'betrayal of reason', see Onora O'Neill, *Constructions of Reason* (Cambridge: Cambridge University Press, 1989), 6 ff.

[3] 'Among the superstitions from which we are freed by the abandonment of metaphysics is the view that it is the business of the philosopher to construct a deductive system...This is illustrated most clearly in the system of Descartes [who tried] to base all our knowledge on propositions which it would be self-contradictory to deny...The belief that it is the business of the philosopher to search for first principles is bound up with the familiar conception of philosophy as the study of reality as a whole.' A. J. Ayer, *Language, Truth and Logic* [1936] (2nd edn. repr. London: Gollancz, 1962), 46–7.

[4] 'Sometimes philosophers have claimed that they were investigating, by purely rational means, the most general properties of the universe...Descartes supposed that he had uncovered the one and only

flourishes of the post-modernists[5] have all converged on at least one undisputed theme: the collapse of the traditional project of Cartesian rationalism. In the philosophy of mind and of knowledge, it is true, some lingering traces of the Cartesian outlook remain.[6] But two things at least are clear: on the one hand, contemporary onslaughts on the puzzle of consciousness, whether from the 'neurophilosophical' or the functionalist camps, have all but eliminated Cartesian dualism as a serious contender for an account of the nature and workings of the mind;[7] and on the other hand, the Wittgensteinian revolution has undermined the very possibility of building a theory of knowledge *more Cartesiano,* from the inside outwards: the primacy of the subjective has given way to the primacy of the social.[8]

2. What is Cartesian Rationalism?

Before the burial rites are completed, however, it is as well to establish the identity of the remains which are being interred. 'Cartesian rationalism' is often used as a casual label for a variety of doctrines that are so preposterously silly that it can scarcely be a subject of warm self-congratulation for modem philosophers to have succeeded in demolishing them. The casualness with which the label is applied is a further reason for concern; for if we want to achieve a proper understanding of how modern Western philosophy evolved, it cannot be enlightening to attribute to one of its acknowledged precursors theses that he never came remotely near to advancing. One

proper philosophical method'; 'only with Frege was the proper object of philosophy established [the study of thought and the analysis of language]'. Michael Dummett, *Truth and Other Enigmas* (London: Duckworth, 1978), 457–8.

[5] 'The notion that our chief task is to mirror accurately, in our own glassy essence, the universe around us is the complement of the notion, common to Democritus and Descartes, that the universe is made up of very simple, clearly and distinctly knowable things, knowledge of whose essences permits commensuration of all discourses.' Richard Rorty, *Philosophy and the Mirror of Nature* (Oxford: Blackwell, 1980), 357.

[6] For example in Thomas Nagel's claim that there are 'facts' accessible only to subjective consciousness: 'What Is it Like To Be a Bat?' in *Mortal Questions* (Cambridge: Cambridge University Press, 1979). See, however, Ch. 5, below, for the question of whether such subjectivism about the mental represents Descartes's own true position.

[7] Though its poverty was already apparent to discerning critics in the seventeenth century: see Pierre Gassendi, Fifth Set of Objections to the *Meditations* [1641], AT VII 276–7: CSM II 192–3.

[8] See e.g. Ludwig Wittgenstein, *Philosophical Investigations* [*Philosophische Untersuchungen*, 1953], trans. G. E. M. Anscombe (New York: Macmillan, 1958)], pt. I §§293 ff. See, however, Ch. 6, below, for the question of whether the thesis of privacy of the mental can really be laid at Descartes's door.

unattractive 'rationalist' doctrine with which Descartes is still too often blandly credited is *apriorism*: the bizarre view that the whole of science can be spun out deductively from the armchair. Not only did Descartes never claim this; he explicitly asserted the opposite. 'The human mind', he wrote in the *Discourse*, 'cannot possibly distinguish the forms or species of bodies that are on the earth from an infinity of others that might be there if God had so willed.' He continues:

The power of nature is so ample and so vast, and [my] principles so simple and so general, that I notice hardly any particular effect of which I do not know at once that it can be deduced from the principles in many different ways, and the greatest difficulty is usually to discover in which of these ways it depends on them. I know of no other way of discovering this than by seeking further observations whose outcomes vary according to which of these ways provides the correct explanation.[9]

Descartes, in his philosophy of science, was no rationalist spider (indeed it seems doubtful whether any such a priori web spinners have existed except in the straw-man, or straw-arachnid, factories of over-hasty commentators). Whatever Descartes may have believed about the foundations of his system (I shall come to this later), the methodology he adopted in his physics is for the most part soberly and sensibly hypothetico-deductive in character.[10]

Another strand in 'Cartesian rationalism' as commonly understood is *necessitarianism*—the view that the job of the philosopher (and the scientist) is to uncover truths which in some sense cannot be otherwise; in its strong form, necessitarianism rejects the whole idea of 'contingent truth' as a fiction created by our lack of complete and adequate knowledge of reality.[11] The demolition of necessitarianism (except in the stipulative and merely conceptual realm of the analytic) is taken to be Hume's primary achievement; and in our own day, insistence on the 'contingency' of human knowledge is the battle cry of the enlightened post-modernist. The hallmark of such latter-day enlightenment is taken to be its emancipation from the Cartesian paradigm of philosophy as the master discipline that limns the ultimate, necessary structure of reality.[12]

[9] *Discourse on the Method* [*Discours de la méthode*, 1637], Pt. Six, AT VI 64: CSM I 144.

[10] For more on this see J. Cottingham, *Descartes* (Oxford: Blackwell, 1986), 91–2.

[11] Cf. Spinoza, *Ethics* [*c.*1665], pt. I prop. 33, schol. I: 'a thing is called contingent only because of a defect in our knowledge, when we can affirm nothing certainly about the possibility or impossibility of its existence because the order of causes is hidden from us'.

[12] Cf. Rorty, *Philosophy and the Mirror of Nature*, 300.

We need to be careful here. David Hume, one of whose principal targets, according to a recent commentator, was, *tout court*, 'rationalism',[13] did indeed assert that reason alone could never discover any connection between cause and effect. 'The bread which I formerly eat [*sic*] nourished me', but the consequence that 'other bread must nourish me at another time' is 'nowise necessary'. But why not? Because, Hume explains, the consequence cannot be logically demonstrated. Were its denial 'intuitively or demonstrably false' it would imply a contradiction; yet the denial 'is no less intelligible and implies no more contradiction, than the affirmation.' And so for any supposed necessary connection between cause and effect, or between one state of affairs and another.[14] Hume's target, then, is what may be called causal logicism—the view that causal connections are logically intuitable or demonstrable in the manner of the propositions of 'Geometry, Algebra and Arithmetic'.[15] (He has a second target, which I shall leave on one side, namely the view that empirical observation can warrant assertions of causal necessity; this cannot be, he tells us, since we have no sensory impression corresponding to the notions of 'necessity', 'power', 'force', 'efficacy' and the like.[16])

Now what is interesting about causal logicism is that it presupposes a distinction between two kinds of truth, logical and empirical, which is seldom if ever invoked in the 'rationalist' tradition that is Hume's supposed target. John Locke (who is normally classified as an 'empiricist' rather than a 'rationalist', but this merely shows the poverty of the conventional classification) does indeed assert that if we could inspect the minute constituents of matter we could know as much of the interactions between any two ordinary-sized bodies as we now know of the properties of squares or triangles; but the point he stresses is not, despite appearances, that there is a logical necessity in the connections between causes and effects. It would be a simple distortion to force his reasoning into the modern straitjacket of the 'logical' versus 'empirical' divide. Locke's point, rather, is (as he proceeds to explain) that if we knew enough about the minute mechanical

---

[13] David Pears, *Hume's System* (Oxford: Oxford University Press, 1990), 75.

[14] *Enquiry concerning Human Understanding*, sect. IV pt. 2, third paragraph, and pt. 1, second paragraph. The second of the passages quoted comes from Hume's discussion of another example, that of the sun rising tomorrow.

[15] 'the sciences of Geometry, Algebra and Arithmetic ... and in short any affirmation which is either intuitively or demonstratively certain'. Ibid. sect. IV pt. 1, opening paragraph.

[16] Ibid. sect. VII pt. 1.

structure of rhubarb or hemlock, we would understand their respective purgative or dormitive actions with the same transparency as a watchmaker understands the operations of a watch by inspecting the structure of its cogs and wheels.[17] Going back to Descartes, we again search in vain for any insistence on the supposed 'logical' necessity of links between causes and effects. Rather, what we get is a resolute explanatory reductionism: instead of invoking occult powers and hypotheses, we should attempt to explain phenomena observed at the macro level by investigating the 'infinite variety' of shapes and motions in the particles that make up the observed objects:

I considered what are the principal differences which can exist between the sizes, shapes and positions of bodies which are imperceptible merely because of their small size, and what observable effects would result from their various interactions. Later on, when I observed just such effects in perceptible objects, I judged that they in fact arose from just such an interaction of bodies that cannot be perceived.[18]

Granted, both Locke and Descartes, in the passages from which we have just quoted, draw strong comparisons between the potential certainty of good natural science and the actually achieved certainty of mathematics.[19] But again, it would be a distortion to see this as evidence for causal logicism. What the seventeenth-century revolution aimed at was scientific knowledge that could replace the obscurities and circularities of scholasticism with a systematic body of transparent mechanical explanations of observed phenomena. *Transparency* was the key: the explanations were supposed to be so simple and straightforward in mechanical terms that we could just see straight off how they worked. Our knowledge, as Locke put it, would be as certain as that which a smith has when he knows a given key will open a given lock.[20] The notion is not without its problems (and I shall come back

---

[17] An *Essay concerning Human Understanding* [1689], ed. P. Nidditch (Oxford: Clarendon, repr. 1984), bk. IV ch. 3 §25. [18] *Principles of Philosophy* [*Principia philosophiae*, 1644], pt. IV art. 203.

[19] Though the two philosophers differ in that Descartes believes he has actually produced certainty of the required kind in science, while Locke takes a far more sceptical line on its actual achievability.

[20] 'Did we know the Mechanical affections of the Particles of Rhubarb, Hemlock, Opium and a Man, as a Watchmaker does those of a watch ... we should be able to tell beforehand that Rhubarb will purge, Hemlock kill, and Opium make a Man sleep. [Such things] would be then perhaps no more difficult to know than it is to a Smith to understand why the turning of one key will open a Lock and not the turning of another' (*Essay*, loc. cit.). The word 'beforehand' (and Locke's earlier comment in the same section that if we knew the shape and texture of the minute parts of matter we could 'know without trial' how two bodies would behave) may seem to make him a more apt target for Hume.

to it later). But it is very far from the bizarre claim that an isolated causal explanation should be expected or required to exhibit the kind of a-priori logical necessity found in the statement that a triangle has three sides. The latter claim might make the Cartesian conception of science a nice easy target for Humean style strictures, but unfortunately it just does not correspond to anything that Descartes, or any other seventeenth-century rationalist, actually said.

3. Atomism and Holism

An objector might point out that there is a certain disingenuousness in the selection of passages so far cited. Other texts can be found where Descartes does seem to hold out the prospect that the scientist can achieve 'absolute' certainty, defined as the kind of certainty that belongs to 'mathematical demonstrations' and which arises 'when we believe that it is wholly impossible that something should be otherwise than we judge it to be'.[21] Is this not precisely the 'necessitarianism' which Hume and his successors love to hate? Not quite. For a look at the context of Descartes's claim reveals that his confidence in the certainty of his system derives from its systematic and unificatory structure. There is an 'unbroken chain' that links together seemingly diverse phenomena, such as light and heat, magnetism and fire, clouds and vapours, plants and animals; the 'long chains of reasoning' of the geometers are a model for the way in which 'all the items which fall within the scope of human knowledge are interconnected'.[22] The claim, in short, involves a holistic conception of knowledge: the system has to be evaluated as a whole. Is coherence an absolute guarantee of truth? In his cautious moments, Descartes backtracked from absolutist pretensions: in relation to the incomprehensible and absolute power of God, anything is possible.[23] What he did claim is that, in the light of the revealed interconnections

---

But since we have already acquitted Descartes of the charge of scientific apriorism, a fortiori Locke is surely in the clear. What he evidently means is that the relevant operations would be so transparent to us that, given our experience of locks and watches, we should know without *further* trial how the relevant bodies would interact.   [21] *Principles*, pt. IV art. 206.

[22] *Discourse*, Pt. Two: AT VI 19: CSM I 120.

[23] Compare *Principles*, pt. IV art. 205: some things may reasonably be considered as 'morally certain', that is certain for all practical purposes, even though 'they may be uncertain in relation to the absolute power of God'.

between all the items of the system, it 'seems scarcely possible' that there can be any alternative explanations to those he offered.[24] The claim is no doubt an arrogant one—perhaps laughably so in the light of the scientific developments that were to sweep away Cartesian physics so soon after its author's death. But it is not a claim self-evidently flawed on philosophical grounds, as the Humean critique would have it.

At this point the objector may respond with a brusque insistence that the Cartesian rationalist should be made to come clean on the precise logical status of any given causal explanation. Surely the connections posited must be interpreted either as analytic truths or as merely contingent 'brute' facts. And since the whole spirit of Cartesian rationalism is clearly hostile to allowing the existence of unaccommodated brute facts, the only alternative is that the connections, or the propositions asserting them, must be supposed to have analytic status—which makes an ideally apt target for Hume's demolition job. But the trouble with this rejoinder is that it begs the question in favour of Hume by interpreting the Cartesian conception through the distorting lens of a Humean account of knowledge.

From a late-twentieth-century standpoint there should be no excuse for this. Quine's critique of the dogmas of empiricism has taught us that the idea of trying to assess the truth of a proposition in isolation is a chimera. And the broader lesson is that the analytic/synthetic distinction itself is suspect, if it is taken to imply that there is a class of absolutely privileged propositions, forever immune to the possibility of revision.[25] If we accept, as there are powerful Quinean arguments for doing, the view that a body of knowledge has to be assessed as a whole, and that the 'analytic' truths are merely those that lie at the centre of the system—those whose revision would necessitate major structural readjustments everywhere else—then the Cartesian account of science emerges in tolerably good shape. Descartes offers a systematic corpus of interconnected explanations, with, at their core, certain very simple and general definitions of the nature of matter and motion; he is willing for the system to be assessed as a whole, and for its

---

[24] 'Caetera omnia, saltem generalia quae de Mundo et Terra scripsi, vix aliter quam a me explicata sunt, intelligi posse videntur.' (It seems that all the other phenomena, or at least the general features of the universe and the earth which I have described, can hardly be intelligibly explained except in the way I have suggested.) *Principles*, pt. IV art. 206. In this article Descartes in fact seems to shift rather uneasily between the notions of 'absolute' and 'virtual' certainty.

[25] W. V. O. Quine, 'Two Dogmas of Empiricism', in *From a Logical Point of View* (Cambridge Mass.: Harvard University Press, 1951).

acceptability to hinge on the fact that no coherent alternative is available. Against this background, the ability of a critic to extract a particular link [cause *A* yields effect *B*], isolate it from the rest of the system, and declare that there is no 'logical' contradiction in the conjunction [*A* and not *B*], is a wilfully perverse misunderstanding of the kind of claim that is being made.

4. Foundationalism

One feature, however, has so far been ignored in our exposition of the rationalist programme—its supposed 'foundationalist' character. Descartes, as is well known, aimed to sweep away the rubble of preconceived opinion from previous ages, and make a clean start; he sought an 'Archimedian point' which would serve as the self-evident starting point for a new and wholly reliable system of knowledge. Now this gives rise to the standard present-day objection to the rationalist project, that of 'bootstrapping'. No system, it seems clear, can be self-validating. The very tools of reason that Descartes uses to demolish previous beliefs and to construct a new system surely have to be taken on trust, in which case, despite the specious claim to be 'starting afresh', a good deal will have to be presupposed. On pain of circularity, reason cannot be expected to perform the task of validating itself.

The charge is not a new one,[26] but closely relates to the conundrum of the Cartesian circle, originally raised by Marin Mersenne and Antoine Arnauld: if the reliability of the reasoning needed to establish the existence of God and the other metaphysical foundations of the Cartesian system cannot be guaranteed until the existence of a non-deceiving God is established, then how, without circularity, can those foundations be guaranteed in the first place? Since I have elsewhere discussed Descartes's attempted reply to the problem of the Cartesian circle,[27] I shall here confine myself to

---

[26] Cf. Hume: 'much inculcated by Des Cartes … as a sovereign preservative against error [is a method proceeding] by a chain of reasoning, deduced from some original principle which cannot possibly be fallacious … But neither is there any such original principle, which has a prerogative above all others … or if there were, could we advance a step beyond it, but by the use of those very faculties of which we are already supposed to be diffident.' *Enquiry concerning Human Understanding*, sect. XII pt. 1 para. 3.   [27] Cottingham, *Descartes*, 66 ff.

the more general bootstrap charge. Descartes was perfectly clear that his metaphysical starting points could not be conjured into existence *ex nihilo*. When challenged about the primacy of his Archimedian point, the Cogito argument, he frankly admitted that in order even to get this far, a great deal of prior knowledge was required. To arrive at the certainty of his own existence, the meditator needs to have access to a whole apparatus of conceptual truths, for example the principle that 'it is impossible to think without existing'; further, even in order to apply those truths he needs to know at least what is meant by thought and existence.[28] To see the Cartesian meditator as engaged on the grotesque exercise of smashing up the entire vessel of reason and trying to rebuild it while still at sea thus runs afoul of the explicit account that Descartes himself gave of what he was attempting to do. The Cogito, he insisted, is 'primary' only in the sense that it is the first existential proposition the meditator arrives at. The project of the First Meditation is not to 'validate reason',[29] for such a project would be doomed to circularity by the very attempt to undertake it using the tools of reason. What the Cartesian meditator does do is to challenge preconceived opinions (based largely on inherited prejudice and the deliverances of the senses) about the nature and existence of the material world around us. Following a long tradition going back to Augustine and ultimately Plato, he 'directs the mind away from physical things', so that it can turn in on itself and let the natural light within each of us reveal the truths that cannot be doubted. The project is aptly summarized in the dramatic dialogue, the *Search for Truth*, which may have been composed about the same time as the *Meditations*. The job is not to conjure knowledge out of nothing, but to 'bring to light the true riches of our souls', so as to 'prepare the best and most solid materials' to serve as the foundations of a new edifice of knowledge (AT X 496, 509: CSM II 400, 407).

On this interpretation, the programme of Cartesian rationalism is a good deal less radical than is sometimes supposed. Despite the use by commentators of such labels as 'universal doubt', Descartes's enquiries operate within an accepted framework of reason; what he had earlier[30] called

---

[28] *Principles*, pt. 1 art. 10.

[29] Cf. Harry Frankfurt, *Demons, Dreamers and Madmen: The Defence of Reason in Descartes's Meditations* (New York: Bobbs Merrill, 1970).

[30] In the *Rules for the Direction of our Native Intelligence* [*Regulae ad directionem ingenii, c.1628*], AT X 418: CSM I 44.

the 'intellectual simple natures'—the basic building blocks of metaphysical reasoning—are left largely untouched in the sceptical exercise of the First Meditation. But this defence of Descartes is still vulnerable to at least three objections. The first is an internal objection: within the terms that Descartes has set himself, is he not being disingenuous or evasive about the limits of possible doubt? The second is external and Wittgensteinian in character: does not the fact that Cartesian meditation is necessarily conducted within a pre-existing conceptual and linguistic framework undermine the very project of reconstructing knowledge from a supposedly isolated and autocentric perspective? And the third is more general: if the thrust of Cartesian doubt is, after all, less radical than at first appears, does not rationalist metaphysics escape from the Scylla of circularity or bootstrapping only to fall into the Charybdis of bland and uncritical epistemological conservatism?

The first, internal, charge, that of evasiveness, relates to the radical scope of the deceiving God hypothesis of the First Meditation. The extreme level of doubt that Descartes himself raised there left open the possibility that the meditator might go astray 'every time [he adds] two and three or counts the sides of a square *or in some even simpler matter if that is imaginable*'. But if a deceiving God could pervert my intuitions regarding the simplest concepts of mathematics, why could he not also pervert my grasp of the fundamental concepts I need in order to reach the Cogito? How, in short, can I trust my basic intuitions of the 'intellectual simple natures' like the concepts of thought and of doubt, not to mention the 'common simple natures' (AT X 419: CSM I 45), which include the concept of existence and also the fundamental rules of logic that seem necessary for any thought process to get off the ground? In places Descartes seems to want to reply that such an extreme level of doubt is self-stultifying. There are limits on what even an omnipotent deceiver could do: 'let him deceive me as much as he may, he can never bring it about that I am nothing so long as I think I am something'.[31] But the trouble with this reply is that the notion of self-stultification seems itself to presuppose precisely those logical rules whose status was in question. At this point the only recourse for the Cartesian seems to be to retreat from an absolutist conception of epistemology to a more psychologically oriented, or 'naturalized' conception, and to stress (as

---

[31] Second Meditation, AT VII 25: CSM II 17.

Descartes does in many places) the irresistible subjective certainty of basic truths such as the Cogito. This manoeuvre involves complex considerations whose full implications there is no space to explore here; but there is a good case (I shall simply state this without arguing it) for presenting it as a sound and orderly strategic withdrawal rather than a confused rout. Rout it certainly is for those who wish to lumber the rationalist with the task of providing some 'absolute' external guarantee (this is sometimes expressed in the triumphant scorn with which critics of rationalism point to the impossibility of our 'stepping outside our conceptual scheme' and validating it from the outside). But the straw-man factory seems to be grinding away again here, for Descartes himself explicitly disavows such absolutist or 'externalist' ambitions:

> If a conviction is so firm that it is impossible for us ever to have any reason for doubting what we are convinced of, then there are no further questions for us to ask: we have everything that we could reasonably want. What is it to us that someone may make out that the perception whose truth we are so firmly convinced of may appear false to God or an angel, so that it is, absolutely speaking, false. Why should this alleged 'absolute certainty' bother us, since we neither believe in it nor have even the smallest suspicion of it? For the supposition which we are making here is of a conviction so firm that it is quite incapable of being destroyed; and such a conviction is clearly the same as the most perfect certainty.
>
> (Second Replies, AT VII 145; CSM II 103.)

The reply here is unequivocal enough, and seems much more in tune with the 'internalist' ambitions of much contemporary metaphysics[32] than with the caricature rationalism that we are too often invited to dismiss. The moral is, once again, that we need to identify the body before being satisfied about what we have buried. The triumphant modernist may, after all, be interring an empty coffin.

Our second objection, which we labelled 'Wittgensteinian', is too familiar to need detailed exposition; it is the challenge to the whole notion of 'Cartesian privacy'. If we grant that Wittgenstein's celebrated private language argument establishes that for a term in any language to have meaning, there must be public criteria for its application, then this result, if we apply it to the Cartesian meditator, seems to undermine his entire programme. For the programme requires the meditator to doubt the

---

32 Cf. Hilary Putnam, *Reason, Truth and History* (Cambridge: Cambridge University Press, 1981).

existence of everything and everyone apart from himself, in order to reach sure knowledge of his own existence. Yet if the very understanding of terms such as 'thought' and 'existence' presupposes a public realm of criteria determining their application, there is something inherently unstable about the private, autocentric perspective of the Cartesian quest for knowledge. If, as the Wittgensteinian argument seems to show, our grasp of concepts is an inescapably public, socially meditated, phenomenon, then the very ability of the meditator to employ concepts presupposes from the outset the existence of the real, extra-mental world which he is supposed to be doubting. From a modern perspective, in short, the very idea of the epistemic primacy of the subject is undercut.

There is, I think, no plausible way of denying the force of this challenge to the rationalist project in its Cartesian form.[33] When Descartes outlines his search for truth and describes the turn inwards—'I resolved one day to undertake my studies within myself'[34]—he embarks on a private retreat from which, ultimately, there can be no coherent escape. Rather than trying to defend this turn, it is best to notice that the autocentricity, the 'idiocy' (in the strict etymological sense) of the Cartesian perspective is a feature that is the personal stamp of René Descartes on metaphysics rather than an inescapable orientation for the rationalist project in general. There is, for example, little sign of it in Leibniz; and Spinozan metaphysics, for all its deep indebtedness to Cartesian categories of thought, is presented from the outset in a way that studiously avoids the picture of an isolated, first-personal quest for knowledge. If we move on to Kant, the vindication of reason seems to proceed in a way that explicitly disavows the possibility of autocentrist metaphysics. The 'tribunal which will assure to reason its lawful claims'[35] is from the start a public tribunal; modern philosophy comes of age as the Cartesian 'I' gives way to the Kantian 'we'. 'We cannot refrain from building a secure home, but we have to plan our building with the supplies we have been given.'[36] As an insightful contemporary commentator has put it, 'the plan must be one that can be followed by a plurality of workers'.[37]

[33] For a retraction of the view expressed in this paragraph, see Chs. 5 and 6, below, where it is argued that the 'privacy' of the Cartesian perspective is by no means as obvious as is often supposed.

[34] *Discourse*, Pt One: AT VI 10: CSM I 116.   [35] Kant, *Critique of Pure Reason*, A xi–xii.

[36] *Critique of Pure Reason*, A 707/B 735.

[37] See O'Neill, *Constructions of Reason*, 12 and throughout ch. 1 (in the course of which reference is made to all the passages cited above).

A grand verdict on the implications of all this is beyond the scope of this chapter. But this much can be said: the Kantian move involves not the overthrow of the Cartesian project, but its reworking. The Kantian agenda is still the authentically rationalist one of establishing a secure edifice of reliable human knowledge, using the tools of human reason. It is an agenda that could not have been conceived without the groundwork prepared by Descartes. In Kant's 'Copernican revolution' we see not so much a revolution as a progression: the inward turn that Descartes had initiated is pushed to its logical conclusion, not as an isolated introspective exercise, but as a publicly mediated enquiry that, nevertheless, attempts to ground our system of knowledge on the resources of the human mind. Kant does not discard the Cartesian legacy, but transforms it in a way that remains ultimately true to Descartes's ambition of 'bringing to light the riches of our souls'.

Our third and final objection to Cartesian foundationalism, that of escaping circularity at the cost of a bland conservatism about human knowledge, will require fuller treatment. It is time to recognize a crucial feature of Descartes's conception of what philosophical reason can do: Descartes's ambition patently goes beyond that of scrutinizing the existing structures of human thought and conserving its most coherent elements. The Cartesian method aims to discern *the truth*: it is the method 'for rightly conducting reason and reaching the truth in the sciences' (AT VI 1: CSM I 111). Despite the passage from the Second Replies quoted earlier which prefigures a modern 'internalist' conception of metaphysics, there can, it seems, be no avoiding Descartes's insistence on the power of the human mind to discern the workings of reality. The *lux rationis* gives us a self-evident and transparent cognition of the way in which God, or God in nature, has constructed the universe. It is this thesis above all, the transparency thesis as we may term it, that tempts us to dismiss Cartesian rationalism as preposterously ambitious, as irredeemably pre-modern. So it is to this thesis that we must now turn.

5. The Transparent Light of Reason

Visual metaphors for cognition abound in Descartes. Despite his claims to be an innovator, he draws heavily on the earlier rationalist tradition of Plato, Plotinus, and Augustine—a tradition that was, incidentally, still alive and well in the philosophical climate of the late Renaissance in which Descartes's teachers grew up.[38] But what exactly is the Cartesian claim: what is it that the 'natural light' or the 'light of reason' enables us to discern?

One aspect of the claim has already been noticed.[39] Descartes's micro-mechanical explanations of phenomena were supposed to be intellectually satisfying because they enabled us to discern what lay behind the seemingly mysterious unfolding of a whole range of celestial and terrestrial phenomena. When flame burns wood, to take one of Descartes's instances, the scholastics had been content to invoke the 'substantial form' of fire, or the 'real quality' of heat. Instead, Descartes offered the following: 'the body of the flame which acts on the wood is composed of minute parts which move about independently of one another with a very rapid and very violent motion. As they move about in this way they push against the parts of the bodies they are touching and move those which do not offer them too much resistance ... '[40] And so on. The revolutions of the planets, explained by reference to the way bits of flotsam are spun round in the eddying whirlpools or 'vortices' of a river is the most famous (or notorious) example of the strategy. Throughout Descartes's physics we have elementary push–pull and impact–reaction models whose operation is taken to be transparently obvious. There are, Descartes tells us, 'no properties of magnets and of fire which are so amazing ... no powers in stones or plants that are so mysterious, no marvels attributed to sympathetic or antipathetic influences that are so astonishing that they cannot be explained in this way'.[41]

Two things, at least, are wrong with this. The first is that what purports to be an exercise in transparent rationalism is constantly in danger of sliding into a naive empiricism.[42] The alleged transparency seems to boil

---

[38] Cf. for example the use of the term *lumen naturale* by the Spanish humanist Vives in his *De Disciplinis* [1531]. See further Francisco Sanches, *Quod nihil scitur* [1581], ed. E. Limbrick and D. Thomson (Cambridge: Cambridge University Press, 1988), 28–32. For more on this, see J. Cottingham, 'A New Start? Cartesian Metaphysics and the Emergence of Modern Philosophy', in T. Sorell (ed.), *The Rise of Modern Philosophy* (Oxford: Oxford University Press, 1992), repr. as Ch. 2, above.

[39] Another is the Cartesian view that we have transparent awareness of the nature and workings of our own minds. Although this view still commands some respect today even among those who would scornfully dismiss transparency claims in physical science, it seems to me one of Descartes's least plausible claims. Cf. Malebranche's critique, discussed in J. Cottingham, *The Rationalists* (Oxford: Oxford University Press, 1988), 149–55.   [40] *Le Monde* [c.1630], ch. 2, AT XI 8: CSM I 83.

[41] *Principles*, pt. IV art. 187.

[42] For this theme, see Desmond Clarke, *Descartes's Philosophy of Science* (Manchester: Manchester University Press, 1982).

down to no more than the fact that we are relatively familiar with how stones react on impact, or how twigs behave in whirlpools, and so we are lulled into thinking that confining science to such models would constitute a genuine explanatory advance. Advance in Occamist terms it is, since there is a spectacular reduction in the numbers of special entities introduced, and there also seems to be a pleasing avoidance of the need to invoke occult powers. But that in itself falls far short of entailing that what remains is genuinely self-evident or transparent to the intellect. Indeed (and here is the second worry), a close inspection of the allegedly translucent explanatory models reveals that they carry a considerable amount of metaphysical (in Leibniz's sense) baggage—notions, for example, such as 'force' and 'resistance'. Descartes, to do him justice, was aware of this and often struggled to eliminate all but 'purely geometrical' concepts from his explanations.[43] But the spectre of Hume is never far from the horizon: however far down into the micro level you go, nothing that could even in principle be observed could warrant anything more than the thin judgement of mere brute regularity. It may be an advance to subsume formerly disparate phenomena under a few general principles, but the gain in simplicity should not be mistaken for a gain in transparency: at the end of the day, the opacity which it is the rationalist goal to eliminate still remains.

A third concern is rather different, though it connects with the impression of a certain naivety in the seventeenth-century assumption of a neat clockwork world. Why should we assume that the universe everywhere and at all levels operates in a way that corresponds to our ordinary earthly conceptions of what is 'obvious'—conceptions, moreover, that seem to be based largely on what we are familiar with through everyday macro observations? Descartes is perfectly frank about his 'simplicist' assumption, as we may pejoratively, but quite legitimately, label it: 'la nature ne se sert que de moyens qui sont fort simples'.[44] But his confidence rings hollow

---

[43] See *Principles*, pt. III art. 56: 'When I say that the globules of the second element "strive" [*conari*] to move away from the centres around which they revolve, it should not be thought that I am implying that they have some thought from which this striving proceeds. I mean merely that they are positioned and pushed [*incitari*] into motion in such a way that they will in fact travel in that direction, unless they are prevented from some other cause.' The manoeuvre is shaky: Descartes avoids 'striving' by banishing 'thought' from matter, but he fails to eliminate the notion of 'push'.

[44] 'Nature only uses very simple means.' Letter to Huygens of 10 October 1642, AT II 797: CSMK 215.

in the light of what today's physics has taught us of the stupendous gulf between operations in the comfortable world of medium-sized hardware and the flickering and elusive interplay of energy exchanges at the micro level. Descartes's disarming frankness cannot rescue him from the charge of what appears from our modern perspective to be a blinkered optimism about the match between our ordinary human grasp of things and the ultimate workings of the cosmos.

At this point it is time to notice that Descartes's confidence in his rationalist programme for uncovering the secrets of the universe derives in large part from that other great pillar of his scientific methodology—not its mechanical modelling, or use of macro analogies, but its use of mathematics as the principal tool of physics.[45] Announcing this strategy in the *Discourse*, he wrote 'I noticed certain laws which God has so established in nature, and of which he has implanted such notions in our minds, that after adequate reflection we cannot doubt that they are exactly observed in everything which exists or occurs in the world.'[46] The thought is not unique to Descartes; in that other giant of the seventeenth-century revolution, Galileo, we find a similar assertion of the power of the mathematical intellect to discern the ultimate language in terms of which reality is structured.[47] This takes us straight down into the gulf that might seem to separate the aspirations of traditional rationalism from our modern worldview. For the rationalist, mathematics is a hotline to God himself; the human mind is illumined, by divine grace, with knowledge of those self-same patterns that inform the whole of creation. To the modern secular ear this claim may sound either preposterously arrogant, or else wildly anthropocentric. Against the background of such a claim, the whole of modern philosophy could be (and has been) seen as a struggle to escape from a model of knowledge based on access to the divine intellect, and to put in its place a more modest epistemological constructivism—a move from 'the mind of God' to 'the works of man'.[48]

---

[45] The two aspects should be clearly distinguished; the common use of the label 'mechanism' to describe Descartes's geometricization of science is not particularly helpful here. Cf. Anthony Kenny, *Descartes* (New York: Random House, 1968), ch. 9, where the label is used, but the relevant distinction is clearly made.   [46] *Discourse*, Pt. Five, AT VI 41: CSM I 131.

[47] 'The great book of the universe cannot be understood unless one first learns to comprehend the language and read the alphabet in which it is composed; it is written in the language of mathematics.' Galileo, *Il Saggiatore* [1623], in A Favaro (ed.), *Galileo, Le Opere* (Florence: Barberà, repr. 1968), vi. 232.

[48] See Edward Craig, *The Mind of God and the Works of Man* (Oxford: Oxford University Press, 1987).

But the charge of arrogance is misplaced. Descartes never claims that humans can achieve a complete insight into the nature of reality. Two Cartesian doctrines, which for the most part have curiously failed to percolate through to the standard picture of Cartesianism, rule this out. The first is the doctrine of the incomprehensibility of God. Descartes firmly and consistently distinguishes between knowing something, and fully grasping or comprehending it. Just as we can touch a mountain but not put our arms around it, so, Descartes asserts, 'we can know that God is infinite and all-powerful, even though our soul, being finite, cannot comprehend or conceive him'.[49] The second doctrine, again consistently asserted by Descartes throughout his writings, is the doctrine of the divine creation of the eternal verities (the truths of logic and mathematics). 'Since God is a cause whose power exceeds the bounds of human understanding, these truths are ... subject to the incomprehensible power of God.'[50] For humans, it is impossible to conceive of the radii of a circle being unequal, but this geometrical truth, like all others, is subject to the inscrutable will of God: he was 'just as free to make it not true that the radii of a circle were equal as he was free not to create the world' (AT I 152: CSMK 25). The upshot is that Cartesian rationalism does not claim that the human mind is an exact 'mirror of nature', a faithful reflection of the divine intellect. Indeed, the doctrines just outlined seem to entail quite the reverse. If the basis for the fundamental principles of logic is not ultimately accessible to human reason, but depends on the inscrutable will of God, then the very notion of ultimate truth, of something's being 'true for God', turns out to be beyond our grasp.[51]

Does this not launch the Cartesian into a nightmare of opacity, and threaten to attack the very heart of the rationalist project? The answer is no. We have seen earlier that Descartes resists the temptation to aim for an 'absolute' external validation of human reason. Risking an anachronism, we might say that his thought gropes towards the Kantian idea that the ultimate nature of reality 'in itself' is unknowable. But this does not lead to total opacity, since the human mind, though finite and imperfect, does have at its disposal clear and distinct mathematical perceptions that enable

---

[49] Letter to Mersenne of 27 May 1630, AT I 152; CSMK 25.

[50] Letter to Mersenne of 6 May 1630, AT I 149: CSMK 25.

[51] For this theme, see Stephen Gaukroger, *Cartesian Logic* (Oxford: Oxford University Press, 1989), ch. 2.

us to construct a model of such elegance and comprehensiveness as to unify all observed phenomena within a single explanatory framework. The mathematical laws are within our power to formulate; and understanding how they are instantiated in the behaviour of all material objects gives us all the scientific understanding that we could reasonably want. Descartes's mathematical physics was not, in actual fact, terribly good: it falls very far short indeed of the quantitative rigour and predictive power of the Newtonian system. But such rigour and power is precisely what his conception of science aims at. The fact that Descartes would have described the relevant laws as divinely decreed correlations emanating from the inscrutable will of God,[52] while Hume describes them as mere natural regularities, turns out, from this perspective, to matter little. What remains untouched is the irresistible appeal of the rationalist project for uncovering the relevant laws, and the evident capacity of the human mind to undertake it.

Honorific references to Newton in this connection may leave an uncomfortable taste in the mouth, since we have now, of course, discovered that Newton did not get it quite right. But that is a worry only if the rationalist is lumbered with the overambitious claim that the truth is wholly self-manifesting.[53] Descartes clearly believed he had got a lot of it right, and that the general outlines of his system represented an adequate framework for explaining the physical universe. But he explicitly warns us that, though we may hope that we in fact possess such adequate knowledge, a finite mind can never know that its knowledge is adequate and complete.[54] Even in his smuggest moments, Descartes is never complacent: the work that remained to be done was so vast that 'neither his dexterity nor his income, were it a thousand times greater than it is, could suffice for the task'.[55] The claim that the rationalist stakes out is not the bombastic and self-deluding one of purveying the last word on absolute truth; what is offered, rather, is the manifesto for a continuous and unending struggle to use the tools of reason

[52] For more on this 'occasionalist' strand in Descartes, which is particularly prominent in his philosophy of mind, see J. Cottingham, 'Descartes's Metaphysics and Philosophy of Mind', in *A History of Western Philosophy*, iv, ed. G. Parkinson (London: Routledge, 1993), ch. 6.

[53] Spinoza seems to claim this (e.g. at *Ethics*, pt. II prop. 43), but inspection of his holistic account of knowledge reveals that such self-manifestingness could only come as the ideal end-point of a complete and all-embracing account of the universe—something that even the most ambitious modern physicist is still very far from being able to articulate.

[54] For Descartes's account of adequate knowledge, see AT VII 140: CSM II 100. For the impossibility of a finite mind knowing that it has adequate knowledge, see AT VII 200: CSM II 155, and AT V 151.

[55] *Discourse*, Pt. Six, AT VI 65: CSM I 144.

to make our view of the world progressively clearer, more comprehensive, and more accurate.

The moral is that the rationalist project is the one on which we are still engaged. We could, of course, give up science and philosophy—cease, as we have recently been urged to do, to use such expressions as 'discovering the truth',[56] and retreat into the labyrinths of post-epistemological anarchism within which the physicist or philosopher has the status of a poet with inexplicable delusions about what he or she is trying to do. But handwaving remarks about the 'contingency' of the human predicament should not be mistaken for an exposure of inherent philosophical flaws in the language and goals of rationalism.[57] The other, more limited moral, which it has been the main aim of this chapter to articulate, is that much of what is called 'Cartesian rationalism' is a historiographer's fiction. The fiction is not a wholly arbitrary one—it takes its cue from Hume and Kant, who preferred to present themselves as exposing the errors of their predecessors rather than (as would have been expected in an earlier, more deferential age) preserving the best traditions of the past. If we look afresh at the Cartesian system, then although there is of course a great deal that seems naive or oversimplified, there is also much that points the way forward to subsequent and more sophisticated approaches to the philosophy of knowledge. In Descartes's struggle with the tension between the aspirations of reason and the limits of human capacity we see prefigured the major problematic of post-Kantian philosophy—the struggle to articulate a secure but non-absolutist conception of science. The thread from Descartes through Hume and Kant to the present day is part of a seamless web; we cannot write the obituary of Cartesian rationalism in its entirety unless we are prepared to declare that the philosophical enterprise itself is defunct.[58]

[56] See Richard Rorty, *Contingency, Irony and Solidarity* (Cambridge: Cambridge University Press, 1989), ch 1.

[57] Cf. Rorty, *Contingency*, ch. 3, where we are urged to discard the vocabulary of 'enlightenment rationalism' based on the notions of 'truth and rationality' and replace it with a vocabulary that 'revolves around the notions of metaphor and self-creation' (p. 44).

[58] I benefited from many helpful comments on earlier drafts of this chapter, especially from Jonathan Bennett, Julian Dodd, Hanjo Glock, and John Preston.

III

Mind and World

4

Descartes on Thought

1. Introduction

In a famous passage in the Second Meditation Descartes asks, 'What am I then? A thing that thinks. What is that? A thing that doubts, understands, affirms, denies, is willing, is unwilling, and also imagines and has sensory perceptions.'[1] On the face of it, the gloss Descartes offers on 'a thing that thinks' (*res cogitans*) is quite extraordinary. Doubting and understanding are evidently kinds of thinking. But it is far from obvious that affirming, denying and willing (*affirmans, negans, volens*) are to be classified in this way. And as for *sentiens* (which denotes 'feeling', 'sensing', 'having sensory perceptions'), this is, in any normal sense, something entirely different from thinking. In this short discussion I want to look at the reasons behind Descartes's startling employment of the term 'thought' (*cogitatio, la pensée*). I shall first reject some widely accepted accounts of it, and then propose an alternative solution.

2. A Commonly Accepted Explanation

A highly influential account of what is going on in the passage cited and other similar passages has been proposed, among others, by Alexandre Koyré: 'The term "thought"—*pensée, cogitatio*—had, in Descartes's time, a much wider meaning than it has now. It embraced not only "thought" as it is now understood, but all mental acts and data: will, feeling, judgement, perception, and so on.'[2]

---

[1] 'Sed quid igitur sum? Res cogitans. Quid est hoc? Nempe dubitans, intelligens, affirmans, negans, volens, nolens, imaginans quoque et sentiens' (*Meditations* [*Meditationes de prima philosophia*, 1641], AT VII 28: CSM II 19).

[2] A. Koyré, Introduction to *Descartes, Philosophical Writings, A Selection*, trans. and ed. E. Anscombe and P. T. Geach (London: Nelson, 1969), p. xxxvii.

Taking a similar line, Elizabeth Anscombe and Peter Geach warn that 'to use *think* and *thought* as the standard renderings for *cogitare* and *penser* and their derivatives gives Descartes's conception an intellectualistic cast that is not there in the original'.[3] Accordingly, they render *res cogitans* as 'conscious being', and frequently (though not always) use more general terms like 'experience' for Descartes's *cogitatio*. And indeed textbooks on Descartes routinely caution the student not to construe the term 'thought' in its normal, narrowly cognitive sense. Typical is the observation: 'In English such terms [as "thought"] are specially connected with … cognitive processes. For Descartes, however, a *cogitatio* or *pensée* is any sort of conscious state or activity whatsoever.'[4]

However, while it is clear that during and after Descartes's lifetime *cogitare* was widely used in this extended sense, it is quite possible that the principal force influencing such an extended usage was the Cartesian corpus itself. What is far from clear is that when Descartes first used *cogitare* and *pensée* in this way he was simply following established usage. Despite Anscombe and Geach's claim that '*cogitare* and its derivatives had long been used in a very wide sense in philosophical Latin',[5] the scholastic tradition makes a very clear distinction between the 'cognitive' and 'appetitive' parts of the mind: according to Eustachius (following the standard Thomist line), 'duae sunt praecipue facultates … quarum altera est cognoscitiva, altera appetitiva'.[6] So it is not at all clear that Aquinas and his disciples would have accepted it as self-evident that 'res cogitans' (a thing that thinks) implied 'res volens' (a thing that wills/is willing). With regard to Descartes's own contemporaries, moreover, we have the strongest possible evidence that Descartes's use of the term *pensée/cogitatio* was initially puzzling and confusing. Marin Mersenne wrote to Descartes in 1637 objecting that if the nature of man was simply to think, it would follow that he had no will. Descartes had to explain carefully in reply that he regarded willing, understanding, imagining, and feeling as 'various ways of thinking'.[7]

---

[3] Translator's Note to *Descartes, Philosophical Writings, A Selection*. p. xlvii.

[4] Bernard Williams, *Descartes: The Project of Pure Enquiry* (Harmondsworth: Penguin, 1978), 78.

[5] Anscombe and Geach (eds.), *Descartes, Philosophical Writings*, p. xlvii.

[6] 'There are two principal faculties [of the soul] of which the first is cognitive, the other appetitive.' Eustachius, *Summa philosophiae quadripartita* [1609], pt. II, second part, treatise 1. Cf. Aquinas, *Summa theologiae* [1266–73], pt. I qus. 75–89.

[7] 'Pour ce que vous inferez que, si la nature de l'homme n'est que de penser, il n'a donc point de volonté, je ne vois pas la consequence; car vouloir, entendre, imaginer, sentir etc. ne sont que des diverses façons de penser' (AT I 366: CSMK 56).

3. The Cartesian Context

Descartes's use of *cogitatio* then, was, if not downright innovative, at the very least somewhat curious. But there is something deeply unsatisfactory about simply leaving it there. When philosophers use central terms in an unusual way there is invariably an underlying philosophical rationale for it; compare 'perceive' in Berkeley, or 'pleasure' in J. S. Mill. What I want to suggest is that the 'intellectualistic' overtones of the terms *cogitatio* and *pensée*, so far from being misleading, or calling for special translation, are in an important sense meant to be there, for reasons which have their roots deep in Cartesian method and metaphysics. Let us start by going back to the context of our original quotation. Descartes asserts that he is a thinking thing. On what basis? Because the extremity of doubt—the malicious demon—failed to separate this attribute from his nature: 'What shall I now say that I am, when I am supposing that there is some supremely powerful and, if it is permissible to say so, malicious deceiver, who is deliberately trying to trick me ... Thought—at last I have discovered it—this alone is inseparable from me.'[8] Descartes's claim that 'thought' is inseparable from his nature is, like his discovery of the certainty of his existence, inextricably bound up with a strictly cognitive process—the method of doubt: 'it is easy for us to suppose that there is no God and no heaven and that there are no bodies, and even that we are ourselves have no hands or feet, or indeed any body at all. But we cannot for all that suppose that we, who are having such thoughts, are nothing.'[9] Or again:

from the mere fact that I thought of doubting the truth of other things it followed quite evidently and certainly that I existed. Whereas I if had merely ceased thinking, even if everything else I had imagined had been true, I should have had no reason to believe that I existed. From this I knew I was substance whose whole nature or essence is simply to think.[10]

The way in which 'cogito ergo sum' and 'sum res cogitans' are arrived at thus suggest a strictly intellectualistic interpretation of *cogitare*. Indeed, though it is sometimes claimed that 'any conscious process will do as a

---

[8] 'Quid autem nunc, ubi suppono deceptorem aliquem potentissimum ... ? Hic invenio: cogitatio est; haec sola a me divelli nequit' (AT VII 26–7: CSM II 18).

[9] *Principles of Philosophy* [*Principia philosophiae*, 1644], pt. I art. 7 (AT VIII 7: CSM I 194–5).

[10] *Discourse on the Method* [*Discours de la méthode*, 1637], Pt. Four (AT VI 32–3: CSM I 127).

premise for the Cogito', this seems inconsistent with Descartes's method. 'I want' is not indubitable in the sense in which 'I think' or 'I doubt' are. The demon could presumably deceive me into thinking I wanted an ice cream (though perhaps he could not deceive me about being aware of wanting one; I shall return to this point later). For the indubitability of 'I think' (unlike 'I want an ice cream') consists precisely in the fact that doubting it entails its truth. So far, then, the 'thinking being' of whose existence Descartes is apprised as his first step out of the morass of doubt is precisely that—a being that thinks, in the ordinary, strictly cognitive sense.

4. An Objection

Before going any further, it is time to face an obvious difficulty. What has so far been said appears to ignore the definition of 'thought' (*cogitatio*) that Descartes himself explicitly provides in the Second Replies:

> *Thought.* I use this term to include everything that is within us in such a way that we are immediately aware of it. Thus all the operations of the will, the intellect, the imagination and the senses are thoughts.[11]

A closely similar account is given in the *Principles*:

> By the term 'thought' I understand everything which we are aware of as happening within us, in so far as we have awareness of it (*quatenus eorum in nobis conscientia est*).[12]

Notice first, however, that both these passages have a somewhat idiosyncratic flavour. In the Second Replies, other definitions are introduced in the third person: 'such and such is called (*vocatur*) "substance"'; 'such and such is called "God"'. But in the passages just quoted we have 'in the term "thought" I include (*complector*)'; 'by the term "thought" I *understand* (*intelligo*)'. Yet—and here is the vital point—this is not simply a matter of arbitrary personal stipulation. Descartes does not simply say 'I am extending the denotation of the term *cogitatio*, and that is that'. On the contrary, the appropriateness of including acts of will and sensation under the label *cogitatio* appears to follow naturally, for Descartes, from a special feature

---

[11] 'Cogitationis nomine complector illud omne quod sic in nobis est, ut ejus immediate conscii simus. Ita omnes voluntatis, intellectus, imaginationis & sensuum operationes sunt cogitationes' (AT VII 160: CSM II 113). [12] *Principles*, pt. I art. 9 (AT VIII 7: CSM I 195).

of such acts—the mental awareness or *conscientia* involved. Thoughts are everything inside us *in such a way that we are aware (sic ut conscii simus)* of them, or 'in so far as we have awareness of them' (*quatenus eorum in nobis conscientia est*). The crucial terms *conscius* and *conscientia* are not defined in the Second Replies or Principles; but their original meaning (deriving from *scire*, to know) is inescapably cognitive and intellectualistic. And indeed when Descartes himself discussed the meaning of 'to be aware' (*conscius esse*) with Frans Burman, in a discussion held in 1648, he made it clear that what was involved was a reflective act of the mind.[13] Thus, so far from being a difficulty for the line taken in this chapter, Descartes's definitions of *cogitatio*, when properly understood, provide further support for the 'intellectualistic' interpretation. For it turns out that, for Descartes, acts of will, etc., are *cogitationes* not qua acts of will, etc., but qua objects of reflective awareness.

One further objection to this account needs to he dealt with here. Anscombe and Geach have argued that sensations, at least, cannot be thoughts qua objects of reflection, since 'Descartes ascribes *cogitationes* of pleasure, pain, warmth and cold to an unborn child, which he admits would be incapable of reflection.'[14] But the text that Anscombe and Geach rely on here (the letter to 'Hyperaspistes' of August 1641) says no such thing. In the letter, Descartes is concerned to defend his thesis that the mind or soul always thinks (*cogitare*); and he argues that the fact that we cannot now remember the thoughts of early infancy (including intra-uterine thoughts) is in itself no argument against his view.[15] Infants and the unborn do, then, think; and nowhere does Descartes say this thought is non-reflective in character. Descartes does deny that 'the mind of an infant meditates on metaphysics in its mother's womb'; but this is because 'the mind newly united to an infant's body is occupied wholly with a confused perception or sensation of the ideas of pain, pleasure, heat, cold and other similar ideas which arise from its union and intermingling with the body'.[16] I shall have

---

[13] AT V 149: CSMK 335. See J. Cottingham, *Descartes's Conversation with Burman* (Oxford: Clarendon, 1976), 7 and 61. In this passage, Burman raises the pertinent question (which there is no space to deal with here) of whether Descartes's account of *conscientia* may not involve an infinite regress.

[14] Anscombe and Geach (eds.), *Descartes, Philosophical Writings*, p. xlvii.

[15] AT III 423: CSMK 189.

[16] 'Mentem corpori infantis recenter unitam in solis ideis doloris, titillationis, caloris, frigoris et similibus, quae ex ista unione ac quasi permistione oriuntur, confuse percipiendis sive sentiendis occupari' (AT III 424: CSMK 190).

more to say about this 'confused perception' shortly, but for the moment it is sufficient to observe that nothing Descartes says rules out construing it as a reflective awareness of a purely cognitive kind.

It may seem strange to ascribe this kind of awareness to an infant, but then many things Descartes says about the infant mind are strange, including the whole doctrine of innate ideas (which is vigorously defended in the passage under discussion). I suppose we nowadays tend to think of foetal and early infant mental processes as simple sensations (of warmth, hunger, and the like) without any conceptual awareness; but we should not foist such a view on to Descartes. If Descartes was really saying that this sort of simple sensation was sufficient to count as a *cogitatio*, it would be puzzling to understand why he so adamantly denied the possibility of *cogitationes* in animals. Only a more restricted account of *cogitatio* will make full sense of what Descartes emphatically ascribes to infants and denies of animals.[17]

5. The 'Special Modes of Thinking'

It is now time to look more closely at exactly what Descartes means by the frequent inclusion of sense-perception and sensation as 'modes of thinking' (*modi cogitandi*). Perhaps the clearest indication of what is going on comes in Part I of the *Principles*, where Descartes discusses why 'video ergo sum' (I see therefore I am) might not do equally as well as 'cogito ergo sum'. Descartes in effect says that 'I see' is ambiguous. If understood 'de visione' (of vision) it is not a good premise for inferring one's existence (since, for one thing, it could then imply the existence of a body, which is subject to doubt). Alternatively, however, it may, says Descartes, be understood 'concerning the actual sense or awareness of seeing' (*de ipso sensu sive conscientia videndi*); here it is quite certain 'since it is in this case referred to the mind which alone feels or thinks it sees' (*quia tunc refertur ad mentem quae sola sentit sive cogitat se videre*).[18] Once again, in connection with Descartes's employment of *cogitare*, we are presented with the crucial term *conscientia* (self-awareness); and this makes it clear just how misleading it is to say *tout*

---

[17] See further J. Cottingham, 'A Brute to the Brutes? Descartes's Treatment of Animals', *Philosophy*, 53 (1978), 551–9; repr. as Ch. 8, below.   [18] *Principles*, pt. I art. 9 (AT VIII 7: CSM I 195).

court that *cogitatio* 'includes' sensations and feelings. The only sense in which seeing is a true *cogitatio* is the sense in which it may involve reflective mental awareness—the self-conscious perception of the mind that it is aware of seeing.[19]

The more one looks at what Descartes says about perceptual operations such as like seeing and hearing, as well as sensations such as feeling pain, the more one observes that he regards them as having a curious hybrid nature. Descartes often calls such sense-perception (e.g. seeing) a 'special mode of thinking';[20] and sensations (e.g. of heat) are frequently called 'confused modes of thinking'.[21] The 'special' nature or 'confusedness' turns out to be tied up with this: that such operations qualify as *cogitationes* at all only in a partial and restricted sense.

In a famous passage in the Sixth Meditation Descartes points out that when the body is damaged we do not merely notice the damage *puro intellectu*, purely intellectually, as a pilot observes damage to his ship; in addition we actually *feel* pain, because of the mysterious 'intermingling' of the mind with corporeal substance. What is seldom if ever asked about this much discussed passage is *why* Descartes should have put the matter in this way. Why should one ponder on the curious possibility of being aware of bodily damage in a purely cognitive way? Once one looks for a rationale behind Descartes's train of thought, the answer springs into focus: *because that is exactly how one would expect it to be for a res cogitans*. In a letter to Regius, Descartes discusses how an angel (a pure *res cogitans*) might experience things if he were in a human body: he would not feel (*sentire*) as we do, but would merely 'perceive the motions caused by external objects'. This is because sensations such as pain are not the pure thoughts (*purae cogitationes*) of a mind distinct from a body, but are rather the 'confused perceptions' that result from the real union 'with the body'.[22]

---

[19] Cf. a closely similar passage in the Second Meditation: 'Idem denique ego sum qui sentio ... videlicet iam lucem video ... Falsa haec sunt, dormio enim. At certe *videre videor* ... ' (Lastly it is the same 'I' who has sensory perceptions, or is aware of bodily things as it were through the senses. For example I am now seeing light ... But I am asleep, so all this is false. Yet certainly I *seem* to see ...) AT VII 29: CSM II 19, emphasis supplied.

[20] 'specialis modus cogitandi' (AT VII 78: CSM II 54). Cf. Cottingham (ed.), *Conversation with Burman*, 75.

[21] 'confusi modi cogitandi' (AT VII 81: CSM II 56). Cf. Descartes's description of the infant in the womb, occupied with 'confused perceptions or sensations of pleasure, pain, heat and cold, etc.' (AT III 424: CSMK 190).   [22] Letter of January 1642 (AT III 493; CSMK 206).

The picture that thus emerges is this. (1) A human being is not a pure *res cogitans*, he is a *res cogitans* mysteriously united with a body. (2) Much of his mental life none the less consists of pure *cogitationes*—the cognitive intellectual operations which a disembodied spirit might enjoy. (3) However, perceptions (seeing) and feelings (pain) are not *cogitationes simpliciter*, but 'confused perceptions'. This last category, I suggest, breaks down for Descartes into two elements. In the first place, there is the reflective awareness of the mind that it is being presented with a datum of some kind; this alone is what qualifies as a *cogitatio* proper. In the second place, there is a curious residual element, which might be called the 'qualitative feel' (e.g. the painfulness or 'hurtiness' of pain), that remains, in terms of Descartes's metaphysics, ultimately mysterious. Indeed, the proposition 'I am in pain' is not, contrary to what is sometimes suggested, something I can clearly and distinctly know. For to be clear and distinct a proposition must contain nothing but what is clear.[23] Yet on Descartes's own account our perception of being in pain is intrinsically 'confused'. We can have a clear and distinct awareness of 'being in pain' only if we, as it were, slice off the purely reflective element; provided, as Descartes puts it, 'we take great care not to include in our judgement anything more than that which is strictly contained in our perception'.[24]

6. Conclusion and Caveat

Let me draw the threads of the argument together. What I have argued is that Descartes's inclusion under the label *cogitatio* of willing, perceiving, feeling, etc., is a deliberate and idiosyncratic move. It is a move, moreover, that should not be baldly accepted as an arbitrary extension of usage, but as one that requires careful diagnosis. And the proper diagnosis reveals the philosophical reason for the labelling: the various operations listed are *cogitationes* only and precisely in so far as they include a reflective cognitive act—the mind's intellectual awareness of itself which Descartes

---

[23] *Principles*, pt. I art. 45 (AT VIII 22; CSM I 207).

[24] 'Si accurate caveamus ne quid amplius de iis judicemus quam id praecise quod in perceptione nostra continetur', *Principles*, pt. I art. 66 (AT VIII 32: CSM I 247).

terms *conscientia*. The upshot is that when Descartes calls himself *a res cogitans* there is an important and illuminating sense in which he means precisely that—a thing that *thinks*.

I must end with an important caveat. What has so far been said provides a kind of explanation of Descartes's procedure; but it is very far from providing a full justification of it. On the contrary, the diagnosis of Descartes's terminology reveals some important underlying philosophical confusions. I noted earlier that Descartes's discovery of himself as a thinking being is crucially bound up with an intellectual process—the method of doubt ('let [the demon] deceive me as much as he likes, he can never bring it about that I am nothing so long as I think that I am something').[25] 'Thinking' cannot be torn from my nature because the act of doubting it confirms it. But the incorrigibility of a judgement concerning this intellectual process does not *eo ipso* imply the incorrigibility of judgements concerning the other processes that Descartes proceeds to list in his gloss of *res cogitans*. There is no prima facie reason why the demon should not deceive me into thinking, for example, that I wanted or desired something. Descartes's reasoning at this point appears to be that even in these other cases we can slice off the reflective awareness of some datum (it still *seems* to me that I am wanting, or seeing), and there can be no mistake about *this*.[26] But this is a different and more perilous line of argument than the proof of 'sum' and 'sum res cogitans' by the method of doubt. The new line of argument rests on the (dubious) thesis of the 'perfect transparency of the mind': that the mind cannot but be clearly aware of its own data, in so far as these are objects of pure reflection. The method of doubt, by contrast, relied not on the supposed pellucid awareness of a mental datum, but on a logical guarantee concerning the content of the datum. Descartes does not simply argue—as he does for willing and feeling—that 'if I am thinking it at least seems to me that I am thinking'; rather he argues, much more powerfully, that 'I am thinking' is incorrigible because so long as I am thinking there is nothing the demon could do to bring it about that I am not thinking.

Descartes's *cogitatio*, then, is intellectualistic and cognitive: there is always a reflective mental act involved. But the fact that there is, for Descartes, an

---

[25] AT VII 25: CSM II 17.   [26] Cf. the passage quoted above, n. 19.

important common denominator to '*dubito*' (I doubt) on the one hand, and '*volo*', '*sentio*', etc. (I will, I feel) on the other, does not justify the move from 'sum res cogitans' to 'sum res volens, sentiens, etc.'. The most that Descartes's hyperbolical doubt could allow him to assert as essential to his nature is that—in the narrowest sense—he thinks.

5

'The only sure sign ...' Thought and Language in Descartes

1. Introduction

Some people like to think that the modern discipline of philosophy has little if anything to learn from the history of the subject, but in reality the philosophical enquiries of each generation always take shape against the background of an implicit dialogue with the actual or imagined ideas of past thinkers. Many of our current debates on the relationship between thought and language bear the imprint of what the 'father of modern philosophy' said, or is supposed to have said.

A basic presupposition of the 'Cartesian' metaphysical framework as normally interpreted is the idea of thought as something inner, hidden, private. We start, each of us, from the inside, from our own internal reflections and cogitations, and then by a problematic and circuitous route move outwards, to the public world of communication. The validity of the private perspective of the Cartesian meditator has had a curious dual fate in the twentieth century: the majority of philosophers (from Ryle and Wittgenstein onwards) have found it, in one way or another, deeply suspect; but for many non-philosophers it still strikes a responsive chord. Most people, unversed in philosophy, would probably respond favourably to the words of T. S. Eliot in *The Waste Land*: 'we think of the key, each in his prison'.[1] Words, on

I am most grateful to Max de Gaynesford, Hanjo Glock, and David Oderberg for stimulating discussions of an earlier version of this chapter. Thanks are also due to various participants at the Royal Institute of Philosophy conference on Thought and Language, held at the University of Reading in September 1996, for a number of helpful comments.

[1] 'We think of the key, each in his prison | Thinking of the key, each confirms a prison ...' *The Waste Land* [1922], pt. v lines 413–14, in T. S. Eliot, *Collected Poems 1909–1935* (London: Faber, 1963), 77.

this picture, are attempts to clothe the true inner core of thinking, private to each of us. 'Cartesian privacy', it seems, has not lost its popular hold.

Descartes himself, however (though this is often forgotten), devoted most of his career not to metaphysics but to science. There is strong evidence, for example, that much of the famous metaphysical argument in Part Four of the *Discourse* was cobbled together, in a fairly hasty fashion, and hurriedly inserted when the main scientific part of the work was ready for the press.[2] And I shall be suggesting later on that we best understand Descartes if we realize that scientific enquiry is the engine that drives much of his philosophy, even when he invokes such seemingly very metaphysical items as souls. At all events, when wearing his scientific hat, Descartes ended up with a quite different perspective on the relationship between language and thought from that which is implied by the model of the mind as a secret prison. In his scientific correspondence and in the *Discourse* (written as a preface to his first published collection of scientific essays), Descartes unequivocally advanced the claim that there is *no thought without language*; and in arguing for this claim he treats language, throughout, as an objective, interpersonally fixed, phenomenon, subject to firm 'external' criteria for what can count as its genuine instantiations. And hence he maintains that we are quite mistaken in attributing any kind of thought to non-human animals, given that they lack genuine language. The fate of *this* Cartesian thesis has been exactly the opposite of that which has befallen the doctrine of the privacy of the mental. This time, it is the philosophers who have tended to embrace it, while our non-philosophical culture has found it uncongenial. 'No thought without language' is a slogan that many philosophers, following the lead of Donald Davidson and others, have found highly persuasive.[3] But the 'lay public' tends to recoil at the restriction of thought to language-users: oysters and sponges, to be sure, don't think (some weirdos might be tempted, even here, to add 'probably'); but the cat scrabbling at the door of the fridge, then rubbing itself round its owner's legs, or the dog fetching its lead and depositing it by the

---

[2] Descartes wrote to a correspondent that the metaphysical section of the *Discourse* was 'the least worked out section in the whole book…I did not decide to include it until I had nearly completed the work and the publisher was becoming impatient' (letter to Vatier of 22 February 1638, AT I 560: CSMK 85–6).

[3] See Donald Davidson, 'Thought and Talk' [1975], repr. in Davidson, *Inquiries into Truth and Interpretation*, 2nd edn. (Oxford: Clarendon, 2001).

master's armchair, then staring mutely up into his face—these are instances which the prephilosophical intuitions of the great majority would classify as involving thought: Felix thinks there is cat-food in there, and is asking you to get it out; Fido has figured out how to get you to take him for a walk.

The two Cartesian claims so far mentioned—the privacy of thought and the linguisticity of thought—hardly look compatible. Or at any rate, if thought is entirely and essentially private, then there seems to be no conclusive reason for restricting it to language-users: for aught we know, cats and dogs might have an inner mental life. And conversely, if thought is analytically linked to linguistic competence, then language-use becomes a public criterion for the presence of thought, undermining the alleged essential privacy of the mental. We thus appear to have two pairs of opposed options, arising from the disagreements just sketched. In the first place, with regard to thought, its privacy can either be (1a) upheld, 'Cartesian'-style, or (1b) denied, in line with much contemporary philosophy. On view (1a) Descartes was on to something important, that there is a crucial sense in which thinking is, in part at least, a subjective, private phenomenon, in principle accessible only to the thinker; and our popular culture has correctly preserved elements of this fundamental Cartesian insight. On view (1b), Descartes fathered a monumental error, the fallacy of essentially private thought, which has deeply infected our popular culture, but which it is the task of modern philosophy of mind and language to eradicate. In the second place, with regard to language, we have two opposing positions: (2a) linguisticism—Descartes was right, and our contemporary lay culture wrong; thought is indeed confined to language-users; and, opposing this, (2b) a more 'generous' view, prevailing in our contemporary culture (and indeed going back to Montaigne in the Renaissance), but characteristically denied by many modern philosophers: that thought extends beyond the restricted domain of genuine language-users. The positions are set out for convenience in Table 5.1.

The strategy of this chapter is as follows. First, with respect to the first two rows in Table 5.1, I want to side with the 'philosophical' rather than the lay position, defending 1b. But I propose to offer a reinterpretation of the actual Descartes according to which he is not, in fact, lumbered with (1a). In other words, I will try to show that the label 'Cartesian privacy', despite its widespread use, is a highly misleading one, since it does not accurately correspond to what the actual historical Descartes held. Secondly,

TABLE 5.1

Thesis		'Cartesian' view	Prevailing view in modern philosophy	Prevailing 'lay' view
1a	privacy of thought	yes	no	yes
1b	publicity of thought	no	yes	no
2a	linguisticity of thought	yes	yes	no
2b	thought extends beyond language use	no	no	yes

with respect to the second two rows, I shall end up suggesting something closer to the 'lay' as opposed to the 'philosophical' position: thought may indeed extend beyond the domain of language. This will involve taking issue with some of Descartes's actual conclusions; but, paradoxically, I shall maintain that the arguments he deploys on this subject would, if developed more fully, have permitted him to take a more generous (and less counter-intuitive) view of the realm of thought.

2. The Myth of Cartesian Privacy

Why has Descartes's name been so automatically associated with the idea of the privacy of thought? The word 'private' is never used by Descartes in any of his discussions of mental phenomena. And to his seventeenth-century contemporaries it would, I think, have seemed quite bizarre to interpret him as some kind of introverted, subjectivist metaphysician, preoccupied with the supposedly internal domain of the mental. In the vast majority of his writings, Descartes approaches the phenomena of human experience from the perspective of a natural scientist, searching for perfectly objective 'external' schemas of explanation. In Descartes's early work on the nature of man, what strikes the reader is not the use made of a subjectively accessed 'soul', but the extent to which appeals to the soul are declared to be redundant. The *Traité de l'homme*, composed in the early 1630s, advances a wholesale mechanistic reductionism,[4] whereby a vast range of human activities is ascribed to the operations of a self-moving machine that, like a

---

[4] Though I cannot develop this here, Descartes's mechanism, in my view, should be construed as reductionist, but not, as is sometimes supposed, eliminativist; that is, he offers scientific explanations of

'clock or an artificial fountain or mill', has the power to operate purely in accordance with its own internal principles, depending solely on the disposition of the relevant organs (AT XI 120: CSM I 99). Descartes insists that it is not necessary to posit any 'sensitive or vegetative soul' (of the kind favoured by the scholastics), just as he refuses to acknowledge any principle of life apart from the internal fire of the heart—a fire which has the same nature as the fires to be found elsewhere in inanimate objects (AT XI 202; CSM I 108).

The list of functions to be explained in this way, without any reference to soul, is remarkably comprehensive:

digestion of food, the beating of the heart and arteries, the nourishment and growth of the limbs, respiration, waking and sleeping, the reception by the external sense organs of light, sounds, smells, tastes, heat and other such qualities, the imprinting of ideas of these qualities in the organ of the 'common' sense and the imagination, the retention or stamping of these ideas in the memory, the internal movements of the appetites and passions, and finally the external movements of all the limbs which aptly follow both the actions and objects presented to the senses and also the passions and impressions found in the memory. (AT XI 202; CSM I 108)

To those brought up on standard conceptions of 'Cartesian dualism' it will be something of a surprise to see how far the list extends beyond what we might think of as 'pure physiology'. What are declared to be capable of explanation without reference to any inner 'soul' are not just functions belonging to the autonomic nervous system such as respiration and heartbeat, but—on the face of it at least—'psychological' functions such as sense-perception and memory, passions and sensations such as fear and hunger, and even, apparently, voluntary actions such as running. When a sheep sees a wolf and runs away, Descartes was later incredulously asked, are we really supposed to believe that this can occur in the absence of any kind of 'sensitive soul'? His answer was unequivocal: yes. And he went on to insist that, *in the case of humans too,* a mechanistic explanation was quite sufficient to explain even such waking actions as walking and singing, when they occur 'without the mind attending to them'.[5]

---

phenomena such as animal sensation, but does not need to deny to animals the ascription of e.g pain. See further J. Cottingham, 'A Brute to the Brutes? Descartes's Treatment of Animals', *Philosophy,* 53 (1978), 551–9, repr. as Ch. 8, below, and see Ch. 1 sect. 3(d), above.

[5] *animo non advertente* (Fourth Replies, AT VII 230: CSM II 161). For more on this passage, and the significance of the final qualification, see J. Cottingham, 'Cartesian Dualism: Theology, Metaphysics and Science', in Cottingham (ed.), *Cambridge Companion to Descartes,* 236 ff.

In his first published psychological essay, *La Dioptrique* (1637), Descartes provides an explanation of vision which, despite what the modern use of the label 'Cartesian' might lead us to expect, systematically *attacks* the picture of a private soul contemplating images. 'We must take care not to assume, as some philosophers do, that in order to have sensory awareness the soul must contemplate certain images ... resembling external objects.'[6] Instead, vision is explicated in terms of a scientific model which can properly be called functionalist. When the blind man finds his way around using a pair of sticks, his awareness of shapes and distances has nothing to do with the contemplation of private images; rather, it is a matter of the sticks being 'caused to move in different ways, setting in motion the nerves in his hand and then the regions of his brain where these nerves originate' (AT VI 114: CSM I 166).

What is true for the blind person is true for the sighted person, except of course that the relevant molecular motions occur in the optic nerves and the brain, instead of in the nerves of the hands and the brain. You might say (again trying to foist the 'Cartesian' label on to Descartes): 'well, here he is talking merely of the physiological *causes* of vision, not vision

FIG. 5.1

---

[6] *La Dioptrique* [1637], AT VI 112: CSM I 165. There are complexities in Descartes's arguments, associated with his debate with the scholastics, which cannot be examined here. For more on the details of Descartes's attack on the 'pictorial' hypothesis, see the excellent discussion in J. Hyman, *The Objective Eye: Color, Form and Reality in the Theory of Art* (Chicago: University of Chicago Press, 2006), ch. 6.

itself—vision itself must be a matter of images displayed in the private domain of the mind'. But very little that Descartes says supports this kind of private theatre view. The crucial point about the blind man analogy is that it tries to move us *away* from the idea of the private theatre of images. Look at the information-processing system, Descartes is saying; observe the causal flow of the transmission of neural impulses, and you will see that talk of the reception of images is way off the mark—and once you have freed yourself from that misleading picture by reflecting on the blind person case, you will be ready to discard it in the sighted case as well.

Admittedly, Descartes is cryptic about precisely *how* the relevant modes of sensory awareness come about as a result of the operation of this functional processing. Coining an awkward phrase that generated decades of fruitless metaphysical theorizing after his death, he simply says that the brain events 'occasion' the soul to have sensory awareness, by a divine or 'natural' institution.[7] What exactly Descartes meant by this is a highly complex question. Interpreted one way it points forward to a Leibnizian-style conception of pre-established harmony between body and soul; interpreted another way, it takes us forward to the Malebranchian notion of divine monocausality. Descartes probably means neither, and is possibly doing no more than signalling that the relationship between the brain events and the mental events cannot be construed in terms of efficient causation—and in fairness to Descartes, we have to admit that this much, at least, is true. What Descartes is quite clear about is that sensory awareness is *not* a matter of images being transmitted to the soul. Even when he maintains, for physiological reasons, that images are formed (on the retina, or the pineal gland), he explicitly rejects the homunculus model, which would lead to an infinite regress of further sets of inner 'eyes'.[8] The brain (or the pineal gland) is emphatically *not* construed as a 'fax machine to the soul', in Daniel Dennett's delightfully scathing phrase;[9] that may be a just lampoon of the picture we have come to regard as 'Cartesian', but it is not the picture offered by Descartes himself.

---

[7] For the notion of 'occasioning', see AT XI 144: CSM I 103. Cf. also *Comments on a Certain Broadsheet* [1648], AT VIIIB 359: CSM I 304. For the idea of a 'natural' institution see *La Dioptrique*, AT VI 130: CSM I 167.

[8] 'We must not think that it is by means of resemblance [between image and external object] that the picture causes our sensory awareness of these objects, as if there were yet other eyes within our brain by means of which we could perceive it' (*La Dioptrique*, Discourse 6, AT VI 130: CSM I 167).

[9] D. Dennett, *Consciousness Explained* (Boston: Little Brown, 1991), 106.

Yet whatever the correct interpretation of Descartes's early scientific work may be, you might feel that once we come to the metaphysics of his mature period we are unavoidably confronted with a truly 'Cartesian' picture of thought as an essentially private, first-person-singular process. But the reality is by no means so straightforward. In the book that Descartes offered as the canonical presentation of his metaphysical views, and that he tried to get adopted as a university textbook, namely the *Principles of Philosophy* (1644), virtually the entire metaphysical argument is presented in the public, intersubjective domain. The narrative (though hardly any commentators, so far as I know, have even remarked on this) is conducted not in the first person singular, but the first person *plural*. 'Quoniam infantes nati sumus…', says the opening sentence: 'Since we began life as infants, and made various judgements concerning the things that can be perceived by the senses before we had the full use of our reason, there are many preconceived opinions that keep us from knowledge of the truth' (pt. I art. 1). Later on, to be sure, the famous Cogito argument makes its appearance, but it is introduced, again, in an interpersonal context: 'In rejecting, and even imagining to be false, everything which *we* can in any way doubt, it is easy for *us* to suppose that there is no God and no heaven, and there are no bodies, and even that *we ourselves* have no hands or feet, or any body at all. But *we* cannot for all that suppose that *we*, who are having such thoughts, are nothing' (art. 7).[10] Elsewhere, in the *Search For Truth* (composed sometime in the 1640s),[11] Descartes explores the Cogito in an even more overtly interpersonal mode—that of a two-way dialogue—and the relevant verbs occur not in the first but the second person: '*You* cannot deny that you have doubts', says Eudoxus to Polyander; 'rather it is certain you have them, so certain in fact that you cannot doubt your doubting. Therefore it is also true that *you who are doubting exist*' (AT X 515: CSM II 410, emphasis supplied). This is not, moreover, just a matter of how Descartes conjugates his verbs (though that, to be sure, is highly significant). For if Descartes really considered thought to be an essentially private domain,

---

[10] *Principles of Philosophy* [*Principia philosophiae*, 1644], pt. I art. 7 (emphasis supplied). Later in this passage, of course, the famous dictum *cogito ergo sum* is introduced (in the first person); but it is presented 'interpersonally', as it were, as 'the first and most certain piece of knowledge to occur to *anyone* who philosophizes in an orderly fashion' (AT VIIIA 7: CSM I 195, emphasis supplied).

[11] The date of the (unfinished) *Recherche de la vérité* is uncertain. It may have been written about the time of the *Meditations*, but may well have been composed during Descartes's ill-fated stay in Stockholm during 1649–50.

directly accessible only to the subject, one would surely have expected his reconstruction of the foundations of knowledge to have addressed the so-called problem of other minds: how can I be sure that others, apart from myself, really feel pain, or have genuine consciousness, in the way I do? Yet nowhere, in the entire Cartesian corpus, is that stock-in-trade of modern epistemology courses even remotely touched on, much less discussed.

Descartes was not, in fact, an 'epistemologist' at all, in the modern sense of one who tries to engage with that absurd philosopher's dummy, 'the sceptic'. 'No sane person', he brusquely observes at the Synopsis prefixed to the *Meditations*, 'has ever seriously doubted that there really is a world or that human beings have bodies' (AT VII 16: CSM II 11). Moreover, the *ordo essendi*, the order of reality that structures his system, is from first to last an objective, divinely guaranteed order, in which everything flows from the commands of the supreme being—the laws (to quote the *Discourse*) 'which God has established in nature and of which he has implanted notions in our hearts'.[12]

But what of the *Meditations*? *Solus secedo*, says Descartes in the opening paragraph: I am here quite alone. But withdrawing into solitude, something most of us do from time to time in order to philosophize, need not imply any radically solipsistic view of the essential privacy of thought. It is, of course, true, that the *Meditations* purport to follow not the *ordo essendi*, the objective order of reality that Descartes accepted, but rather to take the reader along an *ordo inveniendi*, an order of discovery, which starts from the self and proceeds on to God, and then to science and the external world. If this is supposed to provide a free-standing foundation for knowledge, then as countless commentators have eagerly pointed out, it does not and cannot work. My present purpose is not to defend Descartes on this old score, or to rehash the problems of circularity that were so ably uncovered by Arnauld and Descartes's other contemporary critics. But what is clear, even in the most apparently solipsistic mode of the First Meditation, is that despite what may be called the *epistemic* privacy of the scenario, Descartes does not, and cannot, subscribe to the notion of *semantic* privacy: his exercise could not even be formulated on the basis of the kind of private assignment of meanings that Wittgenstein famously attacks. 'Whether I am awake or asleep, two and three added together are five, and a square has no

---

[12] *Discourse on the Method*, pt. Five (AT VI 41: CSM I 131).

more than four sides.'[13] The objective constraints of language and meaning are in operation from the outset, and become ever more prominent as the argument of the *Meditations* develops.

The basic argumentative structure of the *Meditations* involves an invest-igation of the 'ideas' that the meditator finds within him. Now despite the frequently heard complaint that Descartes 'privatized' or 'psychologized' the mind and its objects, if we look at Descartes's own use of the term 'idea', we find instead that it has strong links with the classical and medieval usage, stemming ultimately from Plato, in which *idea* is a formal, not a psychological notion. In the Third Meditation, indeed, Descartes comes close to explicitly Platonic terminology, when he traces the source of our ideas to a primary idea associated with an archetype: 'although one idea may perhaps originate from another, there cannot be an infinite regress here, but eventually one must reach a primary idea, the cause of which will be like an archetype'.[14] When asked to provide a definition of the term 'idea', Descartes distinguishes an episode of thinking ('that which is within us in such a way that we are immediately aware of it') from an *idea*, which is 'the *form* of any given thought'.[15] Considered from a psychological point of view, the nature of an idea is 'such that of itself it requires no reality except what it derives from my thought of which it is a mode, i.e. a manner or way of thinking'.[16] But considered from a logical point of view, it has a certain representational content. 'Considered simply as modes of thought, there is no inequality among my ideas—they all appear to come from within me. But in so far as ideas are considered as representing different things, they differ widely'—in that some contain more 'objective reality' or representational content, than others.[17] It may be seen from passages like this that Cartesian ideas are in some respects much more like publicly accessible concepts than private psychological items. Since the occurrent modifications of my consciousness belong to me, rather than to you, you of course cannot have my thoughts, in this sense; but it is implicit in Descartes's whole project, and the route he offers to validate the foundations of knowledge, that two people can be

---

[13] The doubts subsequently raised by the introduction of the demon are, in my view, much weaker in scope than is often supposed. See J. Cottingham, 'The Role of the Malignant Demon', *Studia Leibnitiana*, 8 (1976), 257–64, repr. in G. Moyal (ed.), *Descartes: Critical Assessments* (London: Routledge, 1991), ii. 129 ff.   [14] Third Meditation, AT VII 42: CSM II 29.

[15] Second Replies, AT VII 160: CSM II 113.   [16] Third Meditation, AT VII 41: CSM II 28.

[17] Third Meditation, AT VII 40: CSM II 28.

said to have the same *idea* in so far as their thoughts have a common representational content.[18]

It is significant that Descartes links the possession of an idea to the ability to use a linguistic term correctly: 'whenever I express something in words, and understand what I am saying, this very fact makes it certain that I have an idea of what is signified by the words in question'.[19] He is thus careful to distinguish an idea, in his sense, from the scholastic notion of a phantasm in the corporeal imagination: 'it is not only the images depicted in the imagination which I call "ideas"; indeed, in so far as these images are in the corporeal imagination, that is are depicted in some part of the brain, I do not call them "ideas" at all; I call them "ideas" only in so far as they give *form* to the mind itself'.[20] Thus anyone who has a conception corresponding to the expressions 'God' and 'soul' must *eo ipso* know what is meant by the 'ideas' of God and the soul, 'namely nothing other than the conception he has'.[21] Thomas Hobbes, perhaps wilfully, misunderstood Descartes on this point—trying to assimilate Cartesian ideas to his own theory of corporeal images, or quasi-pictorial impressions—an interpretation that Descartes brusquely dismissed, in the Third Set of Replies printed with the Meditations.[22]

Ideas in Descartes have a publicly accessible structure; they are not dependent on the private vagaries of individual psychology, but relate to 'immutable and eternal essences which are not invented by me or dependent on my mind' (AT VII 64: CSM II 45). That is why Descartes's disciple Nicolas Malebranche, extrapolating from the master, but not departing from his model in any important respect, located ideas in the divine intellect: in Malebranche's slogan we 'see all things in God'. This was regarded by some of Malebranche's contemporaries as little more than a curiosity; in Locke's dismissive phrase, ' 'Tis an opinion that spreads not, and is like to die of itself or at least do no great harm'.[23] But Malebranche's development of the Cartesian model is in crucial respects an accurate development of Descartes's thinking, and it has the signal merit of resisting the later tendency

---

[18] These points will be taken up again in Ch. 6.   [19] Second Replies, AT VII 160: CSM II 113.

[20] Second Replies, AT VII 160–1: CSM II 113, emphasis supplied.

[21] Letter to Mersenne of July 1641, AT III 392: CSMK 185.

[22] Third Replies, AT VII 180–1: CSM II 126–7.

[23] A comment made by Locke some three days before his death; cited in N. Jolley, *The Light of the Soul* (Oxford: Clarendon, 1990), 81.

to privatize or psychologize all ideas.[24] At all events, as far as Descartes is concerned, the semantic privatization charge can be firmly rebutted. The reflections of the Cartesian meditator, properly understood, relate to ideas construed as objects in the public domain, objectively determined forms of thought whose structure is grounded in an independent reality, accessible to all. That reality, to be sure, is one we nowadays tend to think of as a social construct, evolving over time through the developing rules of language, whereas Descartes conceives it in more Platonic fashion as a set of immutable and eternal archetypes. But that difference, important though it is for understanding how our contemporary worldview has become more secularized, is irrelevant to the public, intersubjective status of our concepts. So far from wanting to privatize thought, Descartes confided to his friend and editor Mersenne that he had a dream of formulating a *mathesis universalis*—a public, formal language possessing the same kind of objective structure as a mathematical symbolism, whereby 'all possible thoughts might be arranged in order like the natural order of the numbers', thus enabling us to 'express all the other things which fall within the purview of the human mind'.[25] If we look at the argumentative structure of the *Meditations*, it is clear that the meditator's thoughts are supposed by Descartes to conform to just such objective patterns of meaning. They cannot, on pain of the incoherence of the whole project, belong in some kind of 'private semantic domain'; that very phrase, for good Wittgensteinian reasons, can be seen to be a contradiction in terms. Cartesian privacy, at least in respect of Descartes's views on the structure of thought, is a myth.

3. The Relation of Thought to Language: Philosophical Analysis and Scientific Evidence

I now turn to some of Descartes's scientifically driven work on the topics of thought and language, beginning with his views on the states and processes

---

[24] The seemingly bizarre theory of vision in God turns out, on Nicholas Jolley's suggestive interpretation, to be a corollary of his firm separation of the province of logic from that of psychology; 'to say that we directly perceive ideas in God is to say that we directly perceive items in logical space'. *The Light of the Soul*, 87.

[25] Letter of 20 November 1629, AT I 81: CSMK 12. The phrase *mathesis universalis* comes in Descartes's early treatise on method, the *Rules for the Direction of our Native Intelligence* [*Regulae ad directionem ingenii*, *c*.1628], Rule Four (AT X 378: CSM I 19).

attributable to animals. Descartes had an enduring scientific interest in non-human animals, dating from the days when he lived in Kalverstraat (the butchers' quarter) in Amsterdam, and regularly ordered veal carcasses to be bought to his house for dissection.[26] 'I cannot share the opinion of Montaigne and others', he subsequently wrote, 'who attribute thought to animals':

> I know that animals do many things better than we do, but this does not surprise me. It can even be used to prove that they act naturally and mechanically, like a clock which tells the time better than our judgement does. Doubtless when the swallows come in spring, they operate like clocks. The actions of honeybees are of the same nature; so also is the discipline of cranes in flight, and of apes in fighting, if it is true that they keep discipline. Their instinct to bury their dead is no stranger than that of dogs and cats who scratch the earth for the purpose of burying their excrement; they hardly ever actually bury it, which shows that they act only by instinct and without thinking.[27]

Later in this passage (from a letter to the Marquis of Newcastle) Descartes considers a possible argument of his opponents: since the bodies of animals are so like ours, might not some elementary kind of thought be 'attached to these organs'. Descartes rejects this argument on the grounds that if similarity of organs is a reason for allowing the possible presence of thought, then it would be a reason for assigning a rational soul to all animals: 'there is no reason to believe it of some animals without believing it of all, and many of them, such as oysters and sponges, are too imperfect for this to be credible'. This seems a bit of a muddle; Descartes's opponents could surely just deny that oysters and sponges are anatomically similar in the relevant respects, and thus resist the implied *reductio*. In fact Descartes is being a little mischievous, or at least brusque, here, since he was well aware of the difference between creatures with pineal glands, and those without; the latter operate merely in a reflex fashion, via the flow of the so-called animal spirits, while the

---

[26] Later on, working on the problem of the circulation of the blood, Descartes performed vivisections on dogs and rabbits; any possible ethical scruples supposedly allayed by his belief that the squeaks of the victims were of no more significance than the fact that a church organ makes a certain sound when you press one of the keys (cf. AT XI 165: CSM I 104). Descartes's stance on whether non-human animals have *feelings* or *passions* (as opposed to thoughts) is, however, complex and problematic; see Cottingham, 'A Brute to the Brutes?' (Ch. 8, below).

[27] Letter to Newcastle of 23 November 1646 (AT IV 573, 575–6: CSMK 302, 304). For Montaigne's views, see his 'Apology for Raymond Sebond', in *Essais* [1580], ii. 12; trans. M. A. Screech (Penguin: Harmondsworth, 1978).

former, as we have seen from the earlier quotation about animal memory, sensation, and purposive activity, are capable of far more complex kinds of behaviour. So he is being distinctly cavalier in lumbering his opponents with the position that once you attribute thought to a dog you may be committed to attributing it to an oyster. However that may be, his denial of genuine thought, that is intellection,[28] to all non-human animals, is clear (his position with respect to sensations and passions is a great deal more complicated).[29] As far as anatomical arguments are concerned, Descartes notoriously rejected the whole idea of a physical organ of thought, and this may partly explain his summary treatment of the Montaigne lobby in this passage. But to understand the rationale for his position, we need to look at a far more powerful argument he has in his armoury, one that hinges not on anatomical similarities and differences, but on functional output.

The stronger argument is developed in a letter to another Englishman, the Cambridge Platonist Henry More, written three years later:

In my opinion the main reason for holding that animals lack thought is the following. Within a single species some of them are more perfect than others, as humans are too. This can be seen in horses and dogs, some of which learn what they are taught much better than others; and all animals easily communicate to us, by voice or bodily movement, their natural impulses of anger, fear, hunger and so on. Yet in spite of all these facts, it has never been observed that any brute animal has attained the perfection of using real speech, that is to say, of indicating by word or sign something relating to thought alone and not to natural impulse. *Such speech is the only sure sign of thought hidden within a body.* All human beings use it, however stupid and insane they may be, even though they may have no tongue and organs of voice; but no animals do. Consequently this can be taken as a real specific difference between humans and animals.[30]

Why is speech so important? Descartes's reasoning strikingly anticipates the line taken in our own time by Noam Chomsky.[31] It hinges on the

---

[28] For Descartes's 'narrow' use of the term 'thought' (*pensée, cogitatio*), see Cottingham 'Descartes on Thought', *Philosophical Quarterly*, 28 (1991), 208–14, repr. as Ch. 4, above.

[29] See Ch. 8, below.   [30] Letter to More of 5 February 1649 (AT V 278: CSMK 366).

[31] Cf. N. Chomsky, *Language and Mind* (New York: Harcourt, Brace & World, 1968). Cf. Descartes: 'Since reason is a universal instrument which can be used in all kinds of situations, whereas [bodily] organs need some particular disposition for each particular action, it is morally impossible for a machine to have enough different organs to make it act in all the contingencies of life in the way in which our reason makes us act' (*Discourse*, Pt. Five, AT VI 57: CSM I 140). By 'morally impossible' Descartes means impossible for all practical purposes.

observation that a machine, or a *bête machine*, is essentially a stimulus–response device. You may be able to train a magpie to say 'bonjour', Descartes observed elsewhere, but each word will be a fixed response to an external stimulus causing a given change in the nervous system.[32] As Descartes put it in the *Discourse*:

> We can certainly conceive of a machine so constructed that it utters words ... corresponding to ... a change in its organs (e.g. if you touch it in one spot it asks what you want of it, and if you touch it in another spot it cries out that you are hurting it). But it is not conceivable that such a machine should produce arrangements of words so as to give an appropriately meaningful answer (*pour répondre au sens*) to whatever is said in its presence, as even the dullest of men can do.   (AT VI 56; CSM I 140)

In short, the human language-user has the capacity to respond appropriately to an indefinite range of situations, and this capacity seems generically distinct from anything that could be generated by a 'look-up tree' or finite table correlating inputs with outputs.

Descartes's language argument, properly construed, is *not* an argument about how linguistic competence provides plausible evidence for the occurrence of an essentially *private* process. It is based on an analysis of what it is to think—namely that it involves an indefinitely rich, stimulus-free capacity to respond to 'all the contingencies of life': it is based, on other words, on a gap between input and output, as observed 'from the outside'. Genuinely linguistic competence (*vera loquela*), the creation every day of new sentences, unlinked to specific behavioural stimuli, is something which could not in principle be produced by a purely mechanical automaton. There is nothing whatever in these arguments that invokes the picture of thought as a mysterious inner process accessible only to the subject.

But what of the phrase from the letter quoted a moment ago: 'speech is the only sure sign of thought hidden in a body' (*loquela est unicum cogitationis in corpore latentis signum certum*)? This could be read as implying a commitment to one form of 'Cartesian privacy'—the idea of thought as an essentially hidden process, of which speech is merely the outward sign. Whether this is right hinges on the exact meaning of the Latin participial

---

[32] Letter to Newcastle of 23 November 1646, AT IV 574: CSMK 303. Descartes does, however, add the curious comment that the word so produced will be the 'expression of one of the bird's passions, e.g. the hope of eating'. For Descartes's not entirely consistent stance on animal passions, see 'A Brute to the Brutes?' (Ch. 8, below) and J. Cottingham, *A Descartes Dictionary* (Oxford: Blackwell, 1993), s.v. 'animals'.

adjective 'hidden' (*latens*). We may be tempted to read it as indicating something in principle unobservable, and something accessible only to the subject. But that is by no means the only possible meaning of the term. The compelling idea of the scientist as an investigator of something 'hidden' (*latens*), had been presented some thirty years earlier by Francis Bacon (whom we know Descartes had read),[33] in his *Novum Organum* (1620). The true 'work and aim of human knowledge', wrote Bacon, is to investigate and uncover the *latens schematismus*—to search for the 'hidden schematisms', or micro processes and configurations of matter, that are responsible for the behaviour of all observed physical phenomena.[34] 'Latent' here does not imply anything occult or mysterious: the explanatory structures uncovered by empirical science are 'hidden' only in the sense that they are not readily observable at the macro level. What the scientist does, starting from careful observation of the phenomena, is to theorize about the possible fine structures that might be responsible for what is observed, with the eventual goal of bringing what is initially hidden into the light. This, of course, is precisely the aim of Descartes in all his scientific work. To explain magnetism, fire, the beating of the heart, growth, respiration, and (as we have seen) even vision, and purposive behaviour like the sheep's running away from the wolf, Descartes offered explanations in terms of the minute interactions of particles too small to be observed with the naked eye. The incredibly fast-moving jostlings of subtle matter, he reasoned, are the unobserved causes responsible for what we call light; the whirrings of tiny screw-shaped molecules are responsible for magnetism; the pneumatic pressures of animal spirits are responsible for reflex behaviour in humans and animals; the events in the nervous system and brain responsible for more purposive action.

In the case of reasoning and language, to be sure, Descartes saw no way forward for the physical scientist. He did at least consider (in the *Discourse*) the possibility of a corporeal 'instrument' (*instrument*) of reason. But what made a physical realization of such an instrument hard for him to envisage was, at least partly, a matter of *number and size*—of how many structures of the appropriate kind could be packed into a given part of the body. Descartes's anatomical dissections of the brain and nervous system had revealed the harmonious operation of tiny structures, which he believed

---

[33] Cf. letter to Mersenne of 10 May 1632, AT I 251: CSMK 38.
[34] Francis Bacon, *Novum Organum* [1620]. Bk. II §1, in *The Philosophical Works of Francis Bacon*, ed. J. M. Robertson (London: Routledge, 1905), 302.

had considerable explanatory power. But they had also, so he believed, established the essential underlying *simplicity* of those structures. Everything going on in the heart and brain, the nerves and muscles, and the 'animal spirits' worked by means of elementary 'push and pull operations', not in principle any different from the simple operations of cogs and levers and pumps and whirlpools that could be readily inspected in the ordinary macro world of 'medium-sized hardware'. Everything happened *according to the laws of mechanics*, the same laws that operated always and everywhere in the universe (AT VI 54; CSM I 139). And Descartes could not envisage the brain or nervous system as being capable of accommodating enough mechanisms of the requisite simplicity to generate sufficiently complex responses to constitute genuine thought or linguistic behaviour. So he was driven to suppose that the hidden schematism responsible for thought was something mysterious and incorporeal (a non-explanation, of course, since there is no reason to suppose the problem of *complexity* is somehow solved simply by positing an immaterial substance). Had he been alive today, then it is conceivable that he might have seen considerably less reason to propose an immaterialist account of the mind. For the language argument in the *Discourse* hinges on the practical impossibility of a physical mechanism possessing a *sufficiently large number of different parts* ('assez de divers organes') to facilitate the indefinite range of human responses to 'all the contingencies of life' (AT VI 57: CSM I 140). Could such an argument survive the modern discovery of the staggering structural richness of the microstructure of the cerebral cortex, composed as we now know, of over ten billion neural connections? Well, Descartes might still have maintained that a purely physical structure could not generate the relevant kind of plasticity and innovativeness necessary for genuine linguistic output; but his view of what matter might or might not do was coloured by a very crude conception of material stuff as pure geometrical extension, so there must be an element of speculation in trying to transfer his arguments to the context of our far richer contemporary physics. However that may be, Descartes's general quest, I am arguing, was for latent (in Bacon's benign sense) structure capable of explaining all behavioural phenomena; unable, in the case of thought, to conceive of a physical structure capable of doing the job, he was driven to posit a non-physical entity—the rational soul.

But there may seem to be a major obstacle to this line of interpretation: Descartes's rational soul, the *res cogitans* responsible for thought, is surely an entity that the reasoning of the *Meditations* shows to be entirely hidden in a more suspect sense, accessible only from the inside, through the subjective reflections of the individual meditator. And does not this take us right back to the idea of a 'latent' soul, not in the benign Baconian sense, but in the more problematic sense familiar from modern attacks on the mind as an essentially private theatre? Well, the term 'thought' is unquestionably used by Descartes to 'include everything that is within us in such a way that we are immediately aware of it' (Second Replies; note again, by the way, the first person plural—'us'). But this encapsulates a relatively harmless truth: that when we are conscious we are immediately aware of thoughts, feelings, and sensations—something not many even of the most materialistic philosophers have been tempted to deny.

You may, if you wish, describe this in terms of each individual's immediate transparent access to the contents of his or her mind; but even with this, though I cannot develop it here, there are complications. When we look at Descartes's later work on ethics and psychology, he departs significantly from the official dualism of the *Meditations*, and suggests that a proper understanding of our human nature involves recognition of the extent to which we are not just angelic minds inhabiting bodily mechanisms, but what he calls 'genuine human beings' (*veri homines*)[35]—creatures whose deepest and strongest feelings are intimately tied up with structures and events that are concealed from us as 'thinking beings'. This, moreover, is not just at matter of causes, but of the very character of those feelings. Descartes, the very thinker who is so often accused of having a naive theory of the perfect *transparency* of the mind,[36] is actually telling us in his later writings that our emotional life as embodied creatures, as human beings, is subject to a serious and pervasive *opacity*. Cartesian transparency, rather like Cartesian privacy, is a label that embodies very great oversimplifications.[37]

---

[35] See letter to Regius of January 1642, AT III 493: CSMK 206.

[36] It is fairly common, e.g., for commentators on the Freudian notion of the unconscious mind to say that Freud broke from the *Cartesian* thesis that mentality and consciousness are equivalent; cf. S. Gardner, *Irrationality and the Philosophy of Psychoanalysis* (Cambridge: Cambridge University Press, 1993), 207. Margaret Wilson attributes to Descartes 'the doctrine of epistemological transparency of thought or mind', though she does go on to discuss certain aspects of Descartes's philosophy of mind which are in potential conflict with that doctrine. M. Wilson, *Descartes* (London: Routledge, 1978), 50; cf. 164.

[37] For more on this issue, see J. Cottingham, 'Cartesian Ethics: Reason and the Passions', *Revue Internationale de Philosophie*, 196 (1996), 193–298, repr. as Ch. 11, below, and *Philosophy and the*

But even if we ignore Descartes's complicated theory of the human being, and restrict ourselves to his metaphysical conception of the pure mind, the *res cogitans*, the fact that our thoughts are transparently presented to consciousness does not entail that we have some kind of privileged access to our nature as thinking things. Admittedly Descartes, in a series of very shaky arguments in the Second Meditation, claims that mind is better known than body. But Malebranche, again seeing the implications of the master's work more clearly than perhaps Descartes always grasped them, astutely pointed out that these arguments established only the *existence* of thinking, not its underlying nature. 'Je ne suis que ténèbres à moi même.' (To myself I am but darkness, and my own substance seems something which is beyond my understanding.)[38] Yet even in Descartes, there is a realization that much of our mental activity involves far more than is transparently accessible to consciousness. He believed, for example, that the soul always thinks, even in sleep—yet had to admit that the evidence for this, in terms of subjective awareness, is very slight.[39] But the doctrine of continuous mental activity hints at the powerful idea, never properly developed by Descartes himself, of latent structures and processes whose operation qualifies as genuine thinking, even though it is not fully accessible to the subject. How often, on waking up in the morning, does the scientist find that a tightly knotted puzzle has begun to unravel, or the novelist that the 'blocked' final chapter has begun to take shape? Thinking, genuine creative thinking—it is hard to see how this could be reduced to mere mechanical crunching—surely goes on beneath the surface of what we consciously monitor.

Even if we confine ourselves to what happens when we are awake, it is clear that the thoughts traced out by our conscious intellect are 'produced' by a staggeringly complex process of whose workings, as we ponder and deliberate, we are largely unaware. Descartes himself, though he never developed the point, implicitly recognized that the simple nature he called a *res cogitans* was actually far too *thin and meagre* a conception to have genuine explanatory power in explaining what we are. In the Third Meditation, Descartes recognizes the utter weakness and dependency of

---

Good Life: Reason and the Passions in Greek, Cartesian and Psychoanalytic Ethics (Cambridge: Cambridge University Press, 1998), ch. 3.

[38] *Méditations chrétiennes et métaphysiques* [1683], ix. 15. See further J. Cottingham, *The Rationalists* (Oxford: Oxford University Press, 1988), 154–5 and 220 n. 67.

[39] Cf. *Conversation with Burman* [1648], AT V 150: CSMK 336.

the thinking ego: the Cartesian meditator, qua thinking thing, is forced to acknowledge that it depends on a power far greater than itself, so much so that it could not even continue to exist from moment to moment without being supported by the unseen substance that sustains and preserves it.[40] Descartes, of course, was referring to the supreme power of God, without which everything would slip out of existence. But there is a secular analogue. The rational thinking self, as it ponders and deliberates from moment to moment, is, as Descartes saw, something extraordinarily thin and fleeting—a series of isolated moments of cogitation: 'I am, I exist, that is certain. But for how long? For as long as I am thinking. For it could be that were I totally to cease from thinking, I should totally cease to exist.'[41] The fragility and momentariness of the Cogito requires divine conservation to give it an enduring identity. Translating this into a less metaphysical and more biological idiom, we might say nowadays that beneath the thinking episodes of which we are immediately aware, sustaining their continuity and grounding their identity, is an awesomely powerful nexus of psychophysical structures and processes; it is these that provide us with our enduring sense of self, with the memories and patterns of recognition that enable us to locate ourselves in a story with a history, with the imaginative and creative drives that urge us to recover our past, and take us forward to the future—in short with everything that makes us truly ourselves as thinking things.[42] Notice that this continuing activity is the very reverse of a private, immediately present, subjective process. For, in the first place, much of it (as Descartes sometimes glimpsed) is, in large part, not present to inner awareness at all; and in the second place the criterion for its occurrence is something public and intersubjectively accessible, the resulting, publicly expressed, output.

To conclude: I hope it is clear that I have not been attempting in this chapter to defend Descartes's theory of the mind, or even to suggest he has a consistent or finished theory, but rather to suggest that if we read him carefully we can see that he is groping towards a host of insights that are ignored if we focus exclusively on the official metaphysical doctrines that are so familiar from standard introductions to his thought. What emerges about the relation between language and thought? Descartes, as we have

---

[40] Third Meditation, AT VII 49: CSM II 33.   [41] Second Meditation, AT VII 27: CSM II 18.

[42] For a wider development of this theme, see Cottingham, *Philosophy and the Good Life*, ch. 4.

seen, came close to treating language as criterial for thought—as necessary and sufficient for its occurrence. He seems clearly correct in arguing that it is sufficient. *Loquela cogitationis certum signum*: the presence of genuine language is a sure sign of the presence of thought (perhaps, indeed, this comes near to being a tautology). But is it necessary? If I am right, and Descartes's more considered stance on these matters takes us *away* from the notion of thought as a hidden, occult process, inaccessible from the outside, then he ought to have allowed (as indeed he did allow in many of his writings) that whether cats and dogs can be said to think must be a function of the complexity of the output they produce—a function of whether such output can be reduced to a finitely determined, mechanical pattern of response. Whether cats and dogs do qualify as thinking in this sense remains far from settled. The examples I mentioned at the outset—those of the cat demanding its feed, or the dog requesting a walk—seem on reflection to involve an output far too thin, in relation to the relevant stimuli, to decide the matter. Such examples seem quite compatible with the judgement that attributing genuine thought to the pets in question is merely sentimental anthropomorphizing on the part of their owners. It might be possible to devise more subtle experiments, perhaps examples of the kind of inferential, hypothesis-testing behaviour allegedly observed in the case of Chrysippus' dog (which was supposedly observed at a three-way fork in the road, finding no scent after sniffing path *A* and *B*, and then immediately setting off on path *C*).[43] Such experiments (though they would have to be more controlled than in the Chrysippus example) might uncover the kind of output warranting the ascription of at least rudimentary thought. But this is an empirical issue, as the general thrust of Descartes's scientific arguments on this question unmistakably allow.

There are other cases nearer home, however, which seem clearly to show that linguistic output is not necessary for thinking. Consider the composer, trying out something on the piano, then flinging himself into an armchair,

---

[43] The famous example, attributed to the Stoic philosopher Chrysippus (3rd century BC), is summarized by Thomas Aquinas (though he goes on to dispute the conclusion that it indicates genuine rationality): 'For a hound in following a stag, on coming to a crossroad, tries by scent whether the stag has passed by the first or the second road: and if he find that the stag has not passed there, being thus assured, takes to the third road without trying the scent; as though he were reasoning by way of exclusion, arguing that the stag must have passed by this way, since he did not pass by the others, and there is no other road. Therefore it seems that irrational animals are able to choose.' *Summa theologiae* [1266–73], IaIIae (First Part of the Second Part), qu. 13 art. 2.

brow furrowed, his whole demeanour exuding intense concentration. After five minutes he rushes to the piano again, and modifies the melodic or harmonic sequence. I cannot imagine anyone but a philosopher denying that thinking is going on during such intervals. And it seems, moreover, to be thinking that operates in a manner entirely free from linguistic activity, from any kind of propositional conceptualizing. Perhaps a musicologist could give linguistic expression to what the composer is trying to do, or to 'say' (to use a dubious metaphor); but such musicological expressions, though themselves instances of thought, seem at several removes from the actual musical thinking that is going on. And plainly someone could be a brilliant composer while being musicologically speaking utterly inarticulate or illiterate (compare some of the great early jazz composers). In general terms, human composers are, of course, always language-users, and it may be contingently true that no one could be a composer unless they were an active participant in a genuine language-using community. But it seems logically possible to imagine inhabitants of a distant planet, sustained perhaps by an entirely benign and superabundantly nutritious environment, who lacked linguistic competence in the Descartes/Chomsky sense, yet produced musical compositions that we immediately recognized as far superior to those of Mozart or Wagner. I suggest it could not reasonably be denied of such beings that they engaged in highly complex forms of thinking.

The truth of the 'no thought without language' slogan thus remains open; but those, like Descartes, who assert it are on to something vitally important, that thinking is not something in principle inaccessible from the outside, but is essentially bound up with complexity of information processing, and signalled by complexity of output when measured against what is inputted. Our modern philosophical and scientific enquiries into the nature of thought clearly still have a long way to go before we develop a conceptual and empirical schema adequate to understanding, much less explaining, what is going on when thought occurs. But if we are to make progress in devising such a schema, we would do well to leave behind the 'Cartesian' paradigm, and be ready to learn more from the non-Cartesian legacy of René Descartes.

6

Intentionality or Phenomenology? Descartes and the Objects of Thought

1. Introduction

Descartes, according to a widespread conception, is seen as having set a distinctive stamp on the mind–body problem: by taking the mind to be something privately accessed by each individual, he made its relationship to the public world of science a matter for prolonged philosophical puzzlement. But for many late twentieth-century philosophers, the long tangle of problems stemming from the supposed 'privacy' of the mental is at last reaching its end, and the focus of debate has shifted back to a quite different aspect of the mind, discussed by philosophers long before Descartes,[1] and later made famous by Brentano,[2] namely its intentionality. Intentionality, that property of the mind in virtue of which it is *directed at*, or *about*, or *of*, certain objects,[3] is not normally thought of as a topic on which Descartes had much to say. In fact, the 'aboutness' or representative

I am most grateful to Max de Gaynesford, Hanjo Glock, James Handel, Brad Hooker, David Oderberg, and John Preston for helpful comments on an earlier draft of this chapter.

[1] The key figure for the medieval debates is Aquinas, who distinguished *esse naturale* (real existence in the world) from *esse intentionale* (roughly, existence as an object of thought). See *Summa theologiae*, Pt. I qu. 56 art. 3; Aquinas's views are discussed by Anthony Kenny in 'Aquinas: Intentionality', in T. Honderich (ed.), *Philosophy Through Its Past* (Harmondsworth: Penguin, 1984), 78–96.

[2] F. Brentano, *Psychology from an Empirical Standpoint* [*Psychologie vom empirischen Standpunkt*, 1874], trans. L. L. McAlister (London: Routledge, 1974), bk. II ch. 1.

[3] See John Searle, 'Intentionality', in S. Guttenplan (ed.), *A Companion to the Philosophy of Mind* (Oxford: Blackwell, 1994), 397. Searle defines intentionality in terms of the mind's being directed at 'objects and states of affairs in the world', though this could be misleading, since neither the medieval scholastic philosophers who first wrestled with intentionality, nor Franz Brentano, who later proposed it as the hallmark of the mental, were committed to supposing the objects of thought must be items

nature of mental states turns out to play a crucial role in his philosophy. I shall argue that it is central to his view of the mind, so central as to elbow to the edge the 'private' or subjective aspect that has long been taken to be the distinctive feature of the 'Cartesian' approach to the mental.

In this chapter, which falls into five parts, I shall start (in the first two, mainly exegetical, sections) by examining how Descartes characterizes the objects of thought from the epistemologically austere starting point of the *Meditations*; it will emerge that his account is by no means as immersed in subjectivity and privacy as often supposed. This result will be reinforced in the last three sections (which I hope will have some relevance to recent debates in philosophy of mind), where the main focus will be on the special problems posed by Descartes's account of sensory ideas. Some philosophers nowadays believe that our experience of colours and pains is characterized by a certain distinctive phenomenology, accessible only to the subject. Since this approach to an important subclass of mental phenomena is often labelled 'Cartesian', it is of some interest to see whether Descartes himself adopted it. I shall argue that despite intermittent tendencies towards a proto-Nagelian subjectivism, Descartes's dominant approach is firmly objectivist: some aspects of the relevant phenomena are dealt with by scientific reductionism, others by a conceptual or language-based approach in terms of intentional content.

2. Preliminaries: Ideas, Psychology, and Logic

The solitary perspective of the Cartesian meditator has given rise to some distorted conceptions of Descartes's view of the mind and its objects. The first is the complaint, often repeated in various guises, that Descartes 'privatized' or 'psychologized' the mind and its objects, paving the way for a suspect Lockean or Humean conception of ideas as psychological episodes of some kind. If, however, we look at Descartes's own use of the term 'idea', we find instead that he is frequently closer to Plato than to Locke: 'idea', as he employs the term, is often a formal rather than a psychological

---

in the world. It would be better, perhaps, to say that intentionality has to do with the *representational* powers of the mind, leaving open the ontological status of what is represented.

notion.[4] In defining the term, Descartes distinguishes a *thought* ('that which is within us in such a way that we are immediately aware of it') from an *idea*, which is 'the *form* of any given thought' (*forma cujuslibet cogitationis*, Second Replies, AT VII 160: CSM II 113). When I think of something (a triangle, say) my consciousness is, of course, modified in a certain way. According to Descartes this involves on the one hand a subjective psychological episode of some kind, but on the other hand it involves something more objective—an idea's *informing* or *giving form to* the mind (*mentem informare*, ibid.). There thus seems to be a tolerably clear distinction in Descartes between what we should nowadays call the psychological and the logical points of view. Considered from the psychological point of view, the nature of an idea is 'such that of itself it requires no reality except what it derives from my thought of which it is a mode, i. e. a manner or way of thinking' (Third Meditation, AT VII 41: CSM II 28). But considered from a logical point of view, it has a certain representational content: 'considered simply as modes of thought, there is no inequality among my ideas—they all appear to come from within me. But in so far as ideas are considered as representing different things, they differ widely [in that some contain more 'objective reality' or representational content, than others]' (AT VII 40: CSM II 28). Cartesian ideas are in some respects more like publicly accessible concepts than private psychological items: two people could not be said to have the same *thought,* since a thought is a (private) mental item or mode of consciousness; but they could be said to have the same *idea* in so far as their thoughts have a common representational content.[5]

As far as the ontological status of Cartesian 'ideas' is concerned, Descartes's position seems to allow him to take an attractive middle course between psychologizing ideas on the one hand, and reifying them

---

[4] The closest Descartes comes to explicitly Platonic terminology is in the Third Meditation, where he traces the source of ideas to a primary idea associated with an archetype: 'although one idea may perhaps originate from another, there cannot be an infinite regress here, but eventually one must reach a primary idea, the cause of which will be like an archetype' (AT VII 42: CSM II 29).

[5] Somewhat confusingly modern (post-Fregean) usage with respect to the terms 'idea' and 'thought' seems to be pretty much the opposite of Descartes's: people now tend to think of 'ideas' as psychological items, whereas they talk about 'the thought that *x*' when referring to the (public) content of a proposition. It is significant that Descartes links the possession of an *idea* to the ability to use a linguistic term correctly: 'whenever I express something in words, and understand what I am saying, this very fact makes it certain that I have an idea of what is signified by the words in question' (Second Replies, AT VII 160: CSM II 113).

on the other. On the one hand, an idea is not a simple private impression, or purely subjective modification of consciousness, since ideas, in virtue of their representationality or 'aboutness', may be said to have a certain content, and that content (though Descartes does not quite put it this way) is intersubjectively accessible. On the other hand, ideas are not made into wholly independent entities, in extreme Platonic style, since they turn out to be a way of talking about the formal or representational aspects of my thought.

This last point needs clarifying. In the centuries preceding Descartes, scholasticism had developed out of a continual three-cornered tension between Platonic, Aristotelian, and Christian thinking. Plato's notion of ideas as real, eternally existing objects had appealed to Christian writers seeking an eternal world beyond this transitory earthly life; but consistent with their monotheistic metaphysics they were reluctant to allow them independent status, and located them as eternally existing archetypes in the mind of God. This was the line taken by Augustine, and it also appears in Aquinas.[6] But Aquinas was also strongly influenced by the anti-Platonic arguments of Aristotle concerning universals; and this led him to resist construing an idea as an object really distinct from its instantiations. Thus for Aquinas the intellect has the power to abstract a universal concept from its particular manifestations, but the idea is the 'means of cognition' (*id quo intelligitur*) rather than a separate object of cognition (*id quod intelligitur*).[7] These tensions partly explain a certain fuzziness (deliberate or not) in Descartes's view of the ontological status of ideas—a legacy that led to the protracted and inconclusive debate between Arnauld and Malebranche later in the seventeenth century. Except among his fellow Oratorians, Malebranche's insistence on reverting to the Augustinian solution of placing ideas in the mind of God was widely regarded as little more than a curiosity; in Locke's scathing phrase, ''Tis an opinion that spreads not, and is like to die of itself or at least do no great harm.'[8] But Malebranche's development of the Cartesian model has distinct advantages as against the

    [6] Augustine, *De diversis quaestionibus* [388–96], lxxxiii. 46; Aquinas, *Commentary on the Sentences of Lombard* [*Scriptum super libros Sententiarum*, 1253–6], bk. I dist. 36 qu. 2 art. 1, and *Summa theologiae* [1266–73], pt. I qu. 15 art. 1.
    [7] Aquinas, *Summa theologiae*, pt. I qu. 85 art. 2. See also J. Cottingham, *A Descartes Dictionary* (Oxford: Blackwell, 1993), s.v. 'idea'.
    [8] A comment made by Locke some three days before his death; cited in N. Jolley, *The Light of the Soul* (Oxford: Clarendon, 1990), 81.

privatizing tendencies of its Lockean alternative.[9] I shall return to some further important aspects of the Malebranchian line later (in sect. 4).

3. What are Ideas About?

As we have seen, ideas in Descartes are associated with the representational powers of the mind. An idea is certainly not an image or picture,[10] but in one respect it is, says Descartes, *like* a certain sort of picture (*veluti quamdam imaginem*), since it is *of* something.[11] But of what? Descartes's typical answer, most notably in the Third Meditation, is that ideas are of things (*rerum*) or 'as it were of things' (*tanquam rerum*).[12] But the word 'thing' here emphatically does not mean an actually existing object in the world, as the famous presentation of the ontological argument in the Fifth Meditation makes crystal clear: I have innumerable ideas of things (*rerum*) which 'even if they perhaps exist nowhere outside me cannot be said to be nothing, since they have they own true and immutable natures' (AT VII 64: CSM II 45). When he was asked to comment on this passage in his interview with Frans Burman in 1648, Descartes is reported to have observed that everything that can be clearly and distinctly conceived is a true entity (*verum et reale ens*).[13] Thus the objects of mathematics are real and true entities, just as much as those of physics, even though they are not actualized. When we think about triangles, our thought is about divinely generated objects (albeit not actualized objects), the properties of and relations between which we clearly and distinctly

---

[9] The seemingly bizarre theory of vision in God turns out, on Jolley's interpretation, to be a corollary of his firm separation of the province of logic from that of psychology; 'to say that we directly perceive ideas in God is to say that we directly perceive items in logical space' (ibid. 87).

[10] Descartes rebuked Hobbes for failing to distinguish an idea, in his sense, from the scholastic notion of a phantasm in the corporeal imagination (AT VII 181: CSM II 127). Cf. Second Replies: 'it is not only the images depicted in the imagination which I call "ideas"; indeed, in so far as these images are in the corporeal imagination, that is are depicted in some part of the brain, I do not call them "ideas" at all' (AT VII 160–1: CSM II 113).

[11] Ideas are *veluti quasdam imagines* ('like images of a certain sort', AT VII 42 line 12: CSM II 29).

[12] *Nullae ideae nisi tanquam rerum esse possunt* ('There can be no ideas except as it were of things', AT VII 44: CSM II 30). Cf. also the phrases: *Quaedam ex [ideis] tanquam rerum imagines sunt* ('some ideas are as it were images of things', AT VII 37: CSM II 25); *una [idea] unam rem, alia aliam repraesentat* ('different ideas represent different things'; lit.: 'one idea represents one thing, another another', AT VII 40: CSM II 28).

[13] AT V 160: CSMK 343. Cf. J. Cottingham (ed.), *Descartes's Conversation with Burman* (Oxford: Clarendon, 1976), 23 and 90 ff.

perceive.[14] Ideas, in short, are objects of understanding that are independent of the vagaries of human psychology because they are grounded in the divine being or, as one might nowadays say, located in objective 'logical space'.[15]

Now for two interesting complications. The first is that representations may be clear or fuzzy. The great struggle for the Cartesian meditator is to render our ideas clear and distinct. Because of the imperfection of the human intellect, and the interference effects generated by our bodily condition, many of our ideas may be like photographs that are fuzzy, and include extraneous shadows and haloes which do not properly belong to the objects represented. The task is to lop off these indistinct and confused elements (often supplied by the confusing deliverances of the senses), until we are left with a representation that is distinct—that contains *only* what is clear and open to the attentive mind. The paradigm here is the famous discussion of the wax in the Second Meditation. We start from a confused and unsatisfactory representation, clouded by preconceived opinions and fluctuating sensory impressions. But by systematically eliminating this overlay of dross, and reducing our conception to what is detected by the scrutiny of the intellect alone (*solius mentis inspectio*, AT VII 31: CSM II 21), we can arrive at

---

[14] Nowadays, we may tend to construe the objects so referred to as belonging to the realm of logical necessity, or describing what is true in all possible worlds. But this (post-Leibnizian) way of thinking is largely alien to Descartes, who instead regards the verities of logic and mathematics, no less than the actually existing universe, as the inscrutable creations of the divine will. This view of the status of the objects of logical and mathematical thought generates a worm of contingency at the heart of the Cartesian system (cf. 'The Cartesian Legacy', *Proceedings of the Aristotelian Society*, Supp. 66 (1992), 1–21; repr. as Ch. 3, above). It is not just that such truths *must* be so, or that they are so in all possible worlds; it is just that they, as a brute fact (as far as our knowledge is concerned), are so. Indeed, it gets worse. If the items to which our thought is directed correspond to fiats of the divine will rather than objects of the divine intellect, this seems to call into question the truth-stating function of the relevant propositions. What we humans take to reflect truth and reality is grounded in something ultimately imperatival rather than indicative. So the famous Cartesian natural light, the divine light of reason which illuminates our souls, turns out in the end to be more like an external force that constrains our thinking than a searchlight that picks out real intellectual objects. A radical gulf thus opens up between human and divine cognition. From the human perspective, our ideas represent 'real and true entities': there is a correspondence-relation between our thought and what it refers to. But from the divine perspective, there is no such correspondence, but rather a kind of pure volitional activity—not a vision of truth, but a series of commands about how lesser creatures are to think. The metaphysics here becomes pretty murky, however, especially when we add in the Cartesian rider that the divine intellect and the divine will cannot really be distinguished: 'we must not think that God understands and wills as we do, by means of operations that are in a certain way distinct from one another; rather, there is always a single identical and perfectly simple act by means of which he simultaneously understands, wills, and brings about all things.' (*Principles of Philosophy*, Pt. I art. 23, AT VIIIA 14: CSM I 201).

[15] For this way of putting it, see Jolley, *Light of the Soul*, 87.

a representation of a pure extended object, mathematically describable. At the conclusion of this Cartesian process, our idea will conform properly to the thing—the true and immutable essence of extended substance.

The second complication is more troubling. Some of our ideas have what Descartes in the Third Meditation calls 'material falsity', and he defines this by saying that materially false ideas 'represent a non-thing as a thing' (*non-rem tanquam rem repraesentant*, AT VII 43). Sensory ideas (of heat and cold, for example) are like this. We might be tempted to construe this as a failure to refer to anything actually existing—like the bogus Victorian photos of fairies at the bottom of the garden, beloved of Lewis Carroll: the photo has a representational content, but there is nothing in the world that corresponds to the *representatum*. But this cannot be what Descartes means; actual external existence is not in question at this stage of the *Meditations*, and in any case, the 'reality' of the things represented by authentic ideas (e.g. of triangles) has nothing to do with actual existence. The problem about sensory ideas is, it seems, not just that there is nothing external corresponding to heat and cold, but that the ideas have *no genuine representational content at all*. In the scholastic jargon that Descartes employs, they lack 'objective' reality. But then Descartes's description of them, namely that 'they represent non-things as things', looks singularly inept: how can they have a representational *character* if there is no representational *content*? To say the least, the divorce between representative character and objective reality is (as Margaret Wilson once remarked) 'an embarrassment'.[16] Descartes's way of putting the matter is clearly not a very happy one. But perhaps what he is saying can be compared to something like this: I start with a set of photographic negatives. Some are fuzzy and indistinct, full of blotches, blemishes, and hazy overlays, but after suitable editing, lopping, and developing, they yield images with genuine objective reality or representational content. Such is my idea of the lump of wax. But others, though they at first sight may appear to have some sort of representational content, turn out, at the end of the developing process, to yield photographs that are entirely blank—there is just nothing represented.

Perhaps this is not an incoherent notion in itself. A linguistic analogue might be this: someone could advance a string of propositions which they

---

[16] M. Wilson, *Descartes* (London: Routledge, 1978), 111.

initially take to present an account of, say, causation, capable of truth or falsity. And as a result of philosophical analysis and argument, they might come to defend the theory as true, or discard it as false. But a third possibility is that they come on reflection to realize that the theory is so confused as to be wholly empty of content: they might end up admitting, 'I now just do not know what I was initially trying to say.' There is nothing to put in the album but a blank print. Even if it is internally coherent, however, this account does not cohere with what Descartes elsewhere wants to say about sensory ideas. For when he moves away from the pure metaphysics of the disembodied thinking self, and turns to the organic life of the embodied human being, he does, I believe, want and need to maintain that sensory ideas, so far from being quite blank, so far from being, as it were, 'about nothing', do indeed have a certain crucial sort of intentionality. It is to the Cartesian theory of sensory ideas, and its implications for his theory of the mind, that I turn in the remaining three sections of this chapter.

4. Sensory Ideas

In a letter to Mersenne written in 1641, Descartes distinguishes two classes of ideas, the ideas of pure mind (*idées de pur esprit*), and ideas which are 'phantasms' attributable to the senses and the imagination (AT III 395: CSMK 186). The latter are thoroughly confusing and misleading for the purposes of metaphysics and mathematical physics, but extremely beneficial for the health and safety of the human being, the mind–body composite (most of the Sixth Meditation is devoted to explaining this). All the ideas relating to what Locke was later to call 'sensible qualities' come into this latter category—the ideas relating to the external senses such as those of colour and taste and smell, and the ideas relating to the internal senses, e.g. of pain.

What sort of intentionality, if any, do these sensory ideas possess? As later developed by Malebranche, the answer seems to be: *none*. Malebranche firmly distinguishes between the mental phenomena he calls *sentiments*,[17] which are purely subjective and lack any intentionality (do not have representational content), and what he calls ideas in the strict sense; the

---

[17] The term embraces not only 'internal' sensations such as pain, but also mental phenomena such as colour perceptions. Cf. Jolley, *Light of the Soul*, 60.

latter involve objects of cognition—abstract items that exist over and above any subjective mode of consciousness. Please distinguish, Malebranche insists in the *Dialogues on Metaphysics* (1687), between knowledge and mere sensation: 'Je vous ai exhorté à vous accoutumer à reconnaître...la différence qu'il y a entre connaître et sentir, entre nos idées claires et nos sentiments toujours obscurs et confus.'[18]

A plausible rationale for the underlying thought here is that intentionality is closely associated with language: an idea in the strict sense (what Descartes calls an 'idea of pure mind') has a *linguistically expressible content,* and in virtue of this it enables us to arrive at a representation of real objects, including, for example, triangles and God—objects which fall under the rubric of extended or thinking substance. We can formulate propositions describing these substances, and characterizing their essential attributes and the various modes of those attributes. Sensory phantasms, by contrast, are mere internal sensations lacking anything that could be called propositional content. Both Malebranche and—sometimes—Descartes talk about them in a way that suggests they are characterized merely by a distinctive phenomenology: beyond that, any attempt to say what they are 'about' falters and tails off into mere gesturing. Compare, in the Sixth Meditation, Descartes's awkwardly hesitant and wholly non-cognitive talk of pain as that 'curious I know-not-what sensation' (*iste nescio-quod doloris sensus*). Note the so-called 'strong' demonstrative *iste,* rather than the more neutral *hic* or *ille*; in Latin this is often used as a kind of 'shuddering' or pejorative demonstrative (*non erit* iste *amicitia sed mercatura* says Cicero: '*that* [shuddering] will not be friendship but a commercial transaction').[19] Descartes goes on in the same passage to talk of hunger as a *nescio-quae vellicatio ventriculi*—an 'I-know-not-what tugging in the stomach'. The '*nescio-quae*' (*je ne sais quelle,* in French) conveys more than just imprecision: the sense is that there is something here that defies cognitive description, that eludes linguistic representation. It calls to mind (may even conceivably be the source for) Hegel's later account of 'sense-certainty' as a mere particular given, something too particular and unmediated to serve as a basis for anything that could be called knowledge, something that is *Das Unwahre, Unvernunftige,*

---

[18] 'I have encouraged you to accustom yourself to recognise the difference there is between knowledge and sense-perception, between our clear ideas and our invariably obscure and confused sensations.' *Entretiens sur la Métaphysique* [1687], Dialogue III §9.

[19] Cicero, *De natura deorum* [45 BC], bk. I, conclusion.

bloss Gemeinte ('untrue, irrational, simply gestured at'.)[20] What Hegel is suggesting (I think) is that though we may think we 'mean' something when we point to a sensory datum, there is nothing that can coherently be expressed in language.

All this impinges in a fairly crucial way on the famous thesis of Franz Brentano that intentionality is the hallmark of the mental. If sensory ideas lack intentionality, we would be forced to modify Brentano's thesis, or at least expand it to a disjunctive list, in the manner, for example, of Richard Rorty, who argues that for something to be classed as mental it must fall into one or other of *two* domains, the intentional or the phenomenological.[21] Mental states, on this view, include, on the one hand, propositional states such as beliefs and desires, which are about something, and, on the other hand, raw feels or sensations, which are mental in virtue of being present to consciousness in a certain characteristic way, despite the fact that (in some cases at least) they lack any intentional content.[22] It might seem from our analysis so far that Descartes's view of the mind corresponds pretty much to the schema canvassed by Rorty: on the one hand we have pure ideas (Malebranche's ideas proper), which have representational content, expressible in language, and are about something; on the other hand we have sensory ideas (Malebranche's *sentiments*), which have a characteristic phenomenology but are not about anything, and are not associated with any cognitive content expressible in language. Well, perhaps that is Descartes's view. But I want in the final two sections of this chapter to underline the philosophical problems that beset such a view, and to argue that Descartes is in a position to offer a different and arguably better account.

5. Beyond Phenomenology

One of philosophy's principal tasks, now as in the seventeenth century, is to explore how mental phenomena can be integrated into the rest of our conceptual scheme. But if sensations are characterized in raw

---

[20] G. W. F. Hegel, *Phänomenologie des Geistes* [1807], sect. 110.

[21] R. Rorty, *Philosophy and the Mirror of Nature* (Oxford: Blackwell, 1980).

[22] The dichotomy is not meant by Rorty to be an exclusive one: it allows for the possibility of mental states—for example being angry with someone—which have an intentional object as well as a phenomenological aspect.

phenomenological terms, unrelated on the one hand to our linguistic and cognitive capacities, yet on the other hand implying mental activity that goes beyond mere physiological and behavioural response, they risk becoming mysterious *sui-generis* items beyond the reach of scientific or philosophical understanding. From the scientific point of view, if they are accessible only from a subjective perspective, then either they turn out to be 'nomological danglers', detached from the objective laws of science, or—even if they can somehow be *correlated* with physiological or functional properties—their intrinsic character remains beyond the reach of scientific understanding. Moreover, there are also serious difficulties on the conceptual side: familiar Wittgensteinian arguments against private meaning pose intractable problems for the notion of sensory items as 'semantic danglers', detached from objective rules of meaning, and identifiable only by a mysterious process of internal baptism ('I name thee "Hunger" ').

Descartes himself was by instinct an integrator, and if we interpret the strange, seemingly isolated world of his metaphysical meditations in the light of the rest of his philosophy, we discover a far richer and more integrated account of the nature of sensations. In the essay on *Optics* (*La Dioptrique*) published with the *Discourse on the Method* in 1637, one of Descartes's targets is the popular construal of ideas as images, which inclines us to think that the representational powers of the mind must operate via the construction of something quasi-pictorial. The pictorial model might seem nice and simple, but it is not as straightforward as it looks. 'Engravings', says Descartes, 'consist simply of a little ink placed here and there on a piece of paper,' but manage thereby to 'represent to us forests, towns, people and even battles and storms'; and 'although they make us think of countless different qualities, it is only in the case of shape that there is any real resemblance'. But in any case, argues Descartes, representation can be achieved in the absence of anything that is remotely pictorial: 'we should recall that our mind can be stimulated by many things other than images—by signs and words, for example' (AT VI 112–13: CSM I 165). What Descartes is unmistakably telling us here is that *representation need not imply resemblance*; and this in turn allows room for the possibility that a mental item can have intentionality, can be about something, even though there is nothing in its intrinsic qualities to yield anything like a transparent match between *representans* and *representatum*. The problem, he notes in the *Optics*, is to discover how brain events can 'enable the soul to have sensory awareness of all the various qualities of the object to which they correspond, not to know how they can resemble those objects' (AT VI 113: CSM I 166).

Descartes, like Locke and many other early-modern philosophers, often stresses that our ideas of colour, say, do not resemble anything in external objects. But what the passages from the *Optics* show is that this need be no bar to their having intentional content. And the more closely one looks at what Descartes says about sensory ideas, the more it emerges that they are indeed representational. They involve something's being 'indicated to the mind' (*menti exhibere*, Sixth Meditation, AT VII 88 line 9). When the foot is damaged, there arises in the soul a sensory idea, which indicates that something untoward is happening in the foot, and which has the function of 'stimulating the mind to do its best to get rid of the cause of the pain' (ibid.). Now this kind of idea is not like the clear and distinct perceptions of the intellect. It does not represent certain patterns of extended substance—it does not, so to speak, give us a computer printout of the position and shape of all the affected particles in the environment and in the nervous system. But a moment's reflection reveals that, for creatures of finite intellect, such information would be useless to the point of dangerousness. An airline pilot who had to analyse a computer printout before being able to take evasive action would still be at work with his calculator and log tables when the crash occurred. Instead, he is alerted to the danger by various crude but effective devices—warning buzzers or flashing lights. These represent the relevant information very selectively, and in highly schematic and simplified form, but one that enables the necessary decisions to be taken quickly. This is exactly how it is with respect to human beings and their bodies. Sensory ideas are indeed about something: they convey information about the internal states of our bodies, and the relationship between our bodies and the environment. But the mode whereby such representation is effected is entirely unlike that which operates in the case of the mathematical ideas employed by the physicist: instead of a transparent presentation of configurations and properties as they obtain in the extended world, there is a kind of opacity. The structure of the relevant objects does not correspond to my sensory grasp of them; but the sensory grasp is adequate for survival purposes—indeed more effective for those purposes than a more transparent representation would be.

Is this consistent with Descartes's apparent talk elsewhere of the confused and indistinct nature of sensory awareness? I think it is; and to explain how, it may be useful to draw an analogy with Sigmund Freud's account of how things are represented in dreams. In the *Traumdeutung* (*The Interpretation of Dreams*, 1900), Freud introduces the notion of *representation in displaced form*:

> The ... species of displacement which occurs in dream formation ... results in a *colourless and abstract* expression ... being exchanged for a *pictorial and concrete* one. The advantage, and accordingly the purpose of such a change jumps to the eyes. A thing that is pictorial is, from the point of view of a dream, a thing that is capable of being represented: it can be introduced into a situation in which abstract expressions offer the same kind of difficulties of representation in dreams as a political leading article in a newspaper would offer to an illustrator ... The dream seeks to reduce the dispersed dream-thoughts to the most succinct and unified expression possible ...[23]

The analogy is a powerful one, irrespective of whether one buys the wider Freudian theory of the psychoanalytic significance of dream experience. The central point is that the dreaming mind is ill-equipped to cope with certain kinds of information except in a displaced and stylized form. And similarly, the Cartesian view is that the human being is ill-equipped for survival unless the realities of the extended universe (the 'colourless and abstract' molecular configurations in the environment and in our own bodies) are represented in a displaced and stylized form. From a cognitive point of view, sensory ideas are representationally inadequate; but from a functional point of view, they do the job of enabling us to take the appropriate actions to preserve the health of the mind–body composite.

The analogy can be pressed further. Just as, if Freud is correct, the symbols that appear in dreams need to be deciphered, via the psycho-analytic process, if we are to achieve a full understanding of what is really going on, so in Cartesian science, the deliverances of the senses need to be decoded if we are to achieve an adequate understanding of what the reality of the world is like.[24] 'If we say we see colour in an object,' says

---

[23] S. Freud, *The Interpretation of Dreams* [*Traumdeutung*, 1900], ch. 6; emphasis added. In *Standard Edition of Complete Works*, trans. J. Strachey, iv.

[24] Compare Jean-Luc Marion, *Sur la théologie blanche de Descartes* (Paris: Presses Universitaires de France, 1991).

Descartes, 'this amounts to saying that we see something there of which we are completely ignorant' (*Principles*, pt. I art. 68). Or again: 'when we say that we perceive colours in objects, this really must be the same as saying that we perceive something in the objects whose nature we do not know, but which produces in us a very vivid sensation which we call the sensation of colour' (art. 70). The Cartesian scientist, like the Freudian psychoanalyst, needs to 'crack the code'—not, of course, the code used by the mind in dreams, but the code encapsulated (whether naturally or by divine decree) in our sensory awareness. Visual sensations, says Descartes in his early treatise *Le Monde*, are 'signs established by nature'; what it is that is signified remains to be discovered.

6. The Boundaries of the Mental

If sensory ideas are like signs, if they do have intentionality (even though the mode of representation involves a certain sort of opacity), then Descartes's approach to mentality turns out to match Brentano's rather closely. Intentionality does indeed turn out to be the hallmark of the mental, and what is given in sensory awareness does not need to be classified separately, as pure, non-intentional phenomenology. Cartesian sensory ideas represent, crudely and schematically, certain states or events: 'something nasty is occurring to my left foot'; 'here is a flower of a distinctive visual hue'. There is clearly intentional content here: we are dealing with something much richer than mere 'natural meaning'—'those clouds mean rain'; 'those rings mean the tree is fifty years old'—since when I have a sensory idea this involves a directedness of thought towards my own internal condition, and/or the condition of the environment.[25]

Even if the claim just made is correct, the question nonetheless arises as to whether sensory states such as being in pain, or seeing a yellow colour, may not involve, and involve essentially, something *more* than just the presentation of ideas with a certain intentional content. Those who believe in this 'more', this raw, non-intentional residue, rely on what we

---

[25] Arguably, even when I am subject to a vague feeling e.g. of anxiety or euphoria (without any specific object of dread or elation), the feeling can still be said to be directed on something—myself. (See T. Crane, 'Intentionality', in E. Craig (ed.), *The Routledge Encyclopedia of Philosophy* (London: Routledge, 1998).)

nowadays think of as the Nagelian dimension: the subjective or qualitative aspect of a sensory idea, the *way it is* for the experiencing subject. And this is supposed to be a further fact, not captured by the intentional content of the sensory idea (nor indeed by the purely physical properties of its bodily counterpart).[26] In favour of this view is what seems to many to be an intuitively clear gulf between merely *believing* that, for example, one's foot is being damaged (plus desiring to remove it from the noxious source), and *feeling* that damage as a *painful* stimulus (though for functionalists, of course, the alleged gulf could be shown to disappear in the light of a correct analysis of the complex pattern of input–output relations involved). Against the view in question is the philosophical difficulty (already touched on) of giving a coherent account of such 'qualia', construed as items beyond the reach both of linguistic contents on the one side, and of even the fullest functional-cum-physiological account of the workings of our bodies on the other.

As far as Descartes was concerned, there are at least two pieces of evidence that he was from time to time (rightly or wrongly) drawn to the notion of sensory qualia in the sense just alluded to. The first is the fact, already noted, that he refers to sensations such as hunger and pain in a way that suggests they have an irreducible and indescribable phenomenology—the 'I know not what' aspect. The second piece of evidence is Descartes's assertion (which I have discussed elsewhere)[27] that God bestows kinds of sensation on his creatures in a fashion that Leibniz scathingly called *arbitrary*: God simply decrees, Descartes sometimes suggests, that sensations of such a kind, rather than of another kind, should 'arise' in our souls when our brains are stimulated in a certain way. Thus, talking of damage to the foot, and its associated nerve stimulations and brain events, Descartes suggests that 'God could have made the nature of man such that this particular motion generated an entirely different kind of sensation in the mind' (AT VII 88: CSM II 60). Now if sensations involve access to intrinsic qualities that can be arbitrarily bestowed or withheld at will by the Deity, then the secular analogue of this is that there is part of the

---

[26] Thus Crane (op. cit.) invokes qualia to suggest that pains have essential non-intentional *properties*. Though I cannot defend this here, I am myself inclined to the view that qualia talk is best analysed in terms of abilities and dispositions (of 'knowing how' rather than 'knowing that'), and hence that it is misguided to think that *properties* (and hence *facts*) are involved here.

[27] See J. Cottingham, 'Descartes on Colour', *Proceedings of the Aristotelian Society*, 90/3 (1989–90), 231–46; repr. as Ch. 7, below.

mental realm that has an intrinsic nature that lies beyond either intentional content on the one hand or physical reduction on the other. If this can indeed be laid at Descartes's door, then he is father to a long history of philosophical puzzles: Locke's bizarre suggestion that your violet could be my marigold, and the whole barrage of arguments—qualia swaps, inverted spectrums, and the like, which have bedevilled the philosophy of mind ever since.

The term 'bedevilled' is appropriate here for the reason that, if qualia are really as 'arbitrary' and 'free-floating' as this story suggests, then it seems they might belong to anything—chimpanzees, goldfish, even tomatoes. Without any scientific basis for connecting the occurrence of qualia with either propositional thoughts on the one hand, or physiological or behavioural states on the other, we appear to be plunged into a problem of other minds so acute that total scepticism threatens. Of course there are attempted replies to this, and clearly I do not have the space to launch into this vexed issue here (though I will briefly touch on one aspect of it in bringing this discussion to a close). The relevant point I want to pick out for the present purpose is that if Descartes really was a wholehearted qualia-merchant, then we might expect him to line up with the sceptics on what mental states could or could not be attributed to other creatures. But in fact he generally takes both a firm (non-sceptical, non-hesitant) and also an austere (that is to say, restrictive) line, adamantly refusing the attribution of mentality to non-human creatures. Let me conclude this survey of Descartes's account of the mind and its objects by focusing on the special problem posed by animal sensations.

Descartes has taken a lot of stick for characterizing animals as mechanical automata—a thesis that is taken to imply a denial that, for example, they can be in pain. The truth of the matter, I think, is that Descartes often adopts a *reductionist* stance about sensation (and for that matter, locomotion, nutrition, memory, and a lot of other faculties), but that his reductions are not *eliminativist*: he does not *deny* any of these faculties to animals, or indeed to the mechanical android described in the *Treatise on Man*; he merely attempts to explain their workings in micro-mechanical terms.[28] What he does deny is that these faculties and events are *mental*.

---

[28] See my 'Cartesian Dualism: Theology, Metaphysics and Science', in J. Cottingham (ed.), *The Cambridge Companion to Descartes* (Cambridge: Cambridge University Press, 1992), esp. 246 ff.

But (I hear you cry) if he denies mentality to animals, doesn't that mean they can't have sensations? It depends what you mean by mentality, and it depends what you mean by sensations. I have suggested that the dominant account of mental states in Descartes is that they are intentional states with a propositional content; this applies primarily to pure intellectual representations, but secondarily to sensory representations, which still have intentional content, albeit of a rather special and schematic kind. It fits in rather well with this that the famous discussion of animals in Part Five of the *Discourse* is almost entirely concerned with the refusal to attribute *linguistic* abilities to them—a refusal which (aside from the marginal and still debated case of chimpanzees) is surely entirely correct. So what is denied to animals by this reasoning? Not, as I have just explained, that they can be in pain, or be hungry, or see objects in the environment; all these statements remain true, and reductively explained. What is denied is that they have sensory *ideas*. But that, surely, is, once again, entirely correct. Given what I take it we agree, that animals have no access to propositional content, it is hard to see how one could defend the notion of their having ideas, in the sense of representational mental states. For in the light of the Cartesian analysis that I unfolded earlier, this would have to come out as—absurdly—the subjects' having access to 'signs' which they were wholly incapable, *even in principle*, of interpreting linguistically, let alone decoding into the language of mathematical science.

If the points made in the last two paragraphs are conceded, then Descartes's position with respect to the mental life of animals is neither suspect because he denies they can see or be in pain (for he does not deny that such properties, reductively explained, can be ascribed to them), nor because of his denial that they have representational states (since such a denial, if 'representational' is construed propositionally, is eminently defensible). So what remains to object to in his position? Presumably, that his view threatens to rob animals of 'qualia'—that it denies that animals are the subjects of raw phenomenological states of an entirely non-linguistic kind. Yet how, given the way qualia are supposed to be accessed, namely from an entirely subjective standpoint, can we possibly know whether such a denial is correct or incorrect? The worry whether we should tack access-to-qualia onto animals (or for that matter onto goldfish or tomatoes) seems entirely intractable. It is important to see, moreover, that this is not just an epistemological problem. In the absence of an account in terms of intentional linguistic content on the one hand, or the possibility of reductive explanation in terms of physiology and behaviour on the other, we are left entirely without any criteria for the attribution of such qualia-access to others. So the supposed problem of leaving no room for animal qualia can hardly, I suggest, be a decisive objection to the Cartesian position, for the simple reason that we are now in an area beyond the bounds of the sayable.

I want to end, however, with a concession. Though I think the Cartesian position is broadly defensible, suspicions may remain that it draws the boundaries of the mental too narrowly. Most people, one suspects, would be fairly happy to deny mentality to cockroaches and goldfish, but intuitively inclined to extend it to dogs. Do we not want to allow for some kind of mentation that falls short of the full propositional intentionality of the language-user, yet goes beyond the mere teleology of the wasp or the shark? I tend to agree that we do. When we see a group of chimpanzees chasing a monkey, gesturing, throwing stones, screaming with excitement, we are strongly inclined to maintain that the screams are 'about' something, albeit in a rudimentary way.

One way of understanding what is going on here is in terms of what Marcia Cavell has dubbed 'pre-intentionality' (a term she uses to describe the responses of infants at the pre-language stage). The behaviour in question can indeed be about something, in so far as it forms part of a complex interactive context in which X recognizes a mutuality in respect of its dealings with Y. The baby begins to learn that its smiling responses to the mother's smile elicit further complex maternal responses, and so on. In short, Cavellian 'pre-intentional' behaviour is intentional in a rudimentary sense, which can be cashed out, in a Wittgensteinian way, by focusing on a complex network of social practices: 'the path the child travels in learning to *mean* will be the same as that which teaches her something about the responses of another, about how to elicit those responses, and to know that something she has done is the reason why the other is responding as he is'.[29] I should add that it is hard not to agree that something similar is going on when the dog fetches its lead and lays it at the feet of the master—something that may or may not have been done to Descartes by his own pet dog, whom, significantly, he named 'Monsieur Grat'.[30]

---

[29] Marcia Cavell, The Psychoanalytic Mind: From Freud to Philosophy (Cambridge, Mass.: Harvard University Press, 1993), 122. See further my review of Cavell, in Philosophical Quarterly, 46/182 (Jan. 1996), 134–6.   [30] Adrien Baillet, La Vie de M. Des-Cartes [1691], ii. 455–6; see also AT V 133.

It is these genuine, if rudimentary, cases of intentionality that make us want to extend the boundaries of the mental to at least some animals. But if this is supposed to be a victory over Descartes, it is a Pyrrhic one. For the dominant Cartesian thesis (or the Descartes–Brentano thesis, as one may perhaps now be allowed to call it) is that intentionality exhausts the domain of the mental. The Cavellian strategy just canvassed either works or it does not (there is no space for me to evaluate it here). If it fails, then Descartes's restriction of mentality to humans is not threatened. If it succeeds, then mentality can be extended to animals, but only in so far as intentionality turns out to be stretchable a little way beyond the linguistic domain; and this would turn out to be a perfectly benign extension, since it can be cashed out in terms of the complex interactive patterns of mutually recognized purposes among relatively intelligent creatures. Such cases will remain, to be sure, on the borderline of the mental; but a grey area here is something that after Darwin we should accept, and indeed expect. Descartes's creaking ontology, of course, is something that does not support grey areas: you either have an immaterial soul or you don't. But if I am right, he nonetheless went a long way towards identifying, correctly, intentionality as the feature delimiting the boundary of the mental. And the identification of such a property remains a significant philosophical achievement despite the demise of the incorporeal substrate in which Descartes misguidedly insisted that any such property must inhere.

We can see in conclusion that Descartes's view of the mental is Janus-faced. He was sporadically attracted by ineffability, the mind as private theatre, the raw phenomenology of the 'I-know-not-what' inner feeling—the whole catalogue of tangles so often pejoratively labelled 'Cartesian'. But what I have called his dominant view was that when we have taken out all the aspects that can be fully explained physiologically and behaviourally, we are left with a residual realm of the mental that can adequately be characterized in terms of the capacities of language-users and the intentional content of ideas. It is an ambitious and in some ways revisionary view, which prefigures post-Kantian conceptualist accounts of the mental domain. And it may very well be correct.

7

Descartes on Colour

1. Introduction

'Philosophy scarcely ever advances a greater paradox in the eyes of the people than when it affirms that Snow is neither cold nor white: Fire neither hot nor red.' So wrote Hume on 4 July 1762; and he commented on the great 'pains' it had cost Malebranche and Locke to establish that 'the Sensible Qualities of Heat, Smell, Sound and Colour' are 'not really in Bodies'.[1] What Hume had in mind was Malebranche's vigorous attack on the 'error' whereby almost everyone believes that 'heat is in the fire ... and colours in coloured objects' (*Recherche de la vérité* [1674], bk. I ch. xi), and Locke's assault on the 'vulgar' way of talking 'as if Light and Heat were really something in the Fire more than a power to excite [certain] Ideas in us' (*Essay concerning Human Understanding* [1670], bk. II ch. xxxi §2). But Hume might have gone back further. For both Malebranche and, whether directly or indirectly, Locke, were powerfully influenced in their attitude to colour and other sensible qualities, by the arguments of René Descartes.[2] It is the contribution of Descartes to what we now know as the 'secondary qualities' tradition that will be the main theme of this chapter.

Hume's way of summarizing the tradition—as the affirmation that 'snow is not white nor fire red'—makes the tradition sound more paradoxical than perhaps it need. Descartes is sometimes more cautious, for example when he observes that 'in the bodies we call coloured, the colours are nothing

---

[1] Letter to Hugh Blair of 4 July 1762, printed in *Mind*, 95/380 (Oct. 1986), 411–16.

[2] Though Descartes is very far from being the founder of what we now call the 'secondary qualities' tradition. Among his immediate predecessors, the most important is Galileo who wrote in *Il Saggiatore* (1623) that colours are 'nothing but names for something that resides exclusively in our sensitive body, so that if the perceiving creature were removed, all such qualities would be annihilated from existence'. Trans. A. C. Danto, in A. Danto and S. Morganbesser (eds.), *Philosophy of Science* (New York: Meridian, 1960), 28. See further P. M. S. Hacker, *Appearance and Reality* (Oxford: Oxford University Press, 1988), ch. 1.

other than the various ways in which the bodies receive light and reflect it to our eyes'.[3] Clearly this does not deny that objects are coloured; it merely offers an explanatory account of what their being coloured consists in—an account that takes us beyond what is immediately perceived by the senses. On the whole, though the details of Descartes's explanatory account are widely erroneous when viewed from the perspective of modern scientific theory,[4] there seems to me to be little to object to here, from a purely philosophical point of view. (I shall come back to this at the end of the chapter.) But there is a second strand in Descartes's account of colours and other sensible qualities, which is not always clearly separated from the first: this involves the claim that there is a sense in which colours do not 'inhere in' or 'belong to' objects, or are not ascribable to objects 'in themselves'.

In the first half of this chapter I shall lay out what I take to be the fundamental rationale for Descartes's claim about the non-inherence of colour properties. In the second half I shall widen the focus and raise some critical questions about the coherence of Descartes's account of colour perception, which I hope will be of interest not merely to students of Descartes but to those concerned with perception and the philosophy of mind in general.

2. Descartes's Arguments for the Non-Inherence of Colour

In the *Meditations*, talking of the famous piece of wax, Descartes argues that the colour he sees does not belong (*pertinere*) to the wax, on the grounds that it changes when the wax is heated.[5] In the *Principles* he argues more sweepingly that 'body considered in general' (*corpus in universum spectatum*) cannot be coloured, since there are bodies so transparent as to lack all colour.[6] The conclusion we are invited to draw is that sensory perceptions like those of colour 'do not tell us except occasionally and accidentally what bodies are like in themselves' (*Principles*, pt. II art. 3). Those who

---

[3] *Optics* [*La Dioptrique*, written early 1630s; first pub. 1637], AT VI 85: CSM I 153.

[4] Cf. the bizarre account of the explanation for an object's appearing red or blue in the *Description of the Human Body* (AT XI 256: CSM I 323).

[5] *Meditations on First Philosophy* [*Meditationes de prima philosophia*, 1641], Second Meditation (AT VII 30: CSM II 20).

[6] *Principles of Philosophy* [*Principia philosophiae*, 1644], AT VIII 42 & 46: CSM I 224 & 227.

take a robustly 'common sense' or realistic view of colour properties are unlikely to be too impressed by this. Admittedly the apparent colour of an object may change if we vary the standard background conditions for colour ascription; admittedly some bodies have no colour at all. But none of this need overwhelm those who want to say that many things are really, essentially, coloured. Is not its characteristic blue hue an essential attribute of a sapphire? Descartes, of course, proposes to banish from science all properties that cannot be described in purely quantitative or geometrical terms (AT VIII 78: CSM I 247). But this allegiance to the Galilean programme for the 'mathematicization' of science hardly constitutes an independent argument for the non-inherence of colour properties. If the Cartesian declares, as a matter of method and policy, that he will employ only quantitative modes in describing the material world, and if someone then objects that this leaves out an important property of the material world, namely colour, then it is no reply to say 'I don't need to include colour, since it is not a quantitative mode.'

To see the underlying reasons why Descartes maintained that colours do not belong to objects 'in themselves' we need to look further afield, to his writings on physiology. In the *Optics* (*La Dioptrique*, 1637), he declares:

> Regarding light and colour ... we must suppose our soul to be of such a nature that what makes it have the sensation of light is the force of the movements taking place in the regions of the brain where the optic nerve-fibres originate, and what makes it have the sensation of colour is the manner of these movements ... But in all this there need be no resemblance between the idea which the soul conceives and the movements which cause these ideas.   (*Optics*, Discourse 6, AT VI 130: CSM I 167)

According to Descartes, what occurs in sense-perception, from a purely physical point of view, is that motions of matter in the external world impinge on the body and set up further motions there. As a result of this, certain ideas 'arise' in the soul; but there need be no resemblance between the ideas and their cause. In this connection Descartes employs the simile of a blind man probing the world with a pair of sticks. He is able to differentiate 'trees, rocks, water and similar things', but there is no reason to suppose any resemblance between 'the idea he forms' and 'the resistance or movement of the bodies, which is the sole cause of the sensations he has of them'.

What the blind man example seems designed to show is that our sensory apprehension of qualitative differences in things (hardness of rocks, fluidity of water) does not require the supposition that the objects themselves possess qualities resembling our ideas of them. There may be some philosophical muddles here linked to the notoriously problematic theory of 'ideas' as immediate objects of perception: how, for example, does Descartes know what the blind man's 'ideas' of hardness and fluidity are like? But the general point Descartes is making does not have to be couched in terms of the jargon of ideas. The blind man, we might say, has some sort of representation of the environment (he has beliefs and thoughts about the world around him); and Descartes now argues that *representation does not require resemblance.*[7] 'We should recall', he says elsewhere in the *Optics*, 'that our minds can be stimulated by many things other than by images—signs or words, for example, which in no way resemble the things they signify' (AT VI 112: CSM I 165). And so, even in the case of sighted people seeing colours, there is 'no need to suppose there is something in the objects which resembles the ideas we have of them' (AT VI 85: CSM I 153).

But although representation may not require resemblance, although the fact that we represent colours to ourselves in a certain qualitative fashion need not force us to attribute exactly corresponding qualities to the objects themselves, we still do not seem to have been offered any particular forceful reason why we should *not* do so. If the argument from physiology is simply designed to draw our attention to the fact that our sensory perception is not (as the scholastics thought) a matter of the transmission from object to observer of some sort of 'image' or 'form', but depends merely on transfers of matter in motion to our nervous systems, then this fact, true though it may be, still does not seem enough to rule out the notion that colours really inhere in objects. For our sensory perceptions of shape and size, no less than our perceptions of colour and taste, seem to depend on just such impingings of matter on our nervous systems; yet the resulting ideas of shape and size *do*, Descartes maintains, correspond to properties that can be attributed to the objects themselves. So the need, in describing the mechanism of sensory perception, to tell a complicated physiological story about movements of nerve fibres surely cannot, in and of itself, be sufficient to rule out any resemblance between idea and object.

---

[7] For the development of this thesis by Descartes's disciples such as Robert Desgabets in the latter seventeenth century, see R. Watson, *The Breakdown of Cartesian Metaphysics* (Atlantic Highlands: Humanities Press, 1987), ch. 6.

If we look deeper, it emerges that the underlying reason why Descartes rules out alleged 'real' qualities such as redness as inhering in objects has to do with his notion of causation. 'Nothing in the effect which was not in the cause' is a fundamental principle that Descartes claims in the Third Meditation to be manifest by the natural light (AT VII 40: CSM II 28). This suggests that there must be, for Descartes, some similarity between cause and effect—an interpretation supported by Descartes's reported allegiance to the sweeping and general maxim 'the effect is like the cause' (AT V 156: CSMK 339–40). Admittedly, the Third Meditation principle could be taken (as it is by some commentators)[8] to mean only that a cause must be as perfect as, or more perfect than, its effect—which would allow a cause to be quite unlike its effect, provided it satisfies the condition of being of a higher (or equally high) order of reality. Yet when Descartes introduces his causal maxim in the Third Meditation, he employs metaphors that strongly suggest that causal transactions must be a matter of the bestowing or handing on of features from cause to effect: 'where could the effect *get* its reality from if not from the cause; and how could the cause *give it* to the effect unless it possessed it?' (AT VII 40: CSM II 28, emphasis added).[9] And if we take the transfer model seriously, then a similarity relation is indeed required between the causes and effects: cause and effects cannot be utterly heterogeneous, since for any explanandum *Fa* (i.e. where we are required to explain *a*'s possession of some feature *F*), the cause must itself be the kind of thing to which *F*-ness can be attributed.

Given that Descartes is committed to a Causal Similarity Principle,[10] his refusal to allow colours as real properties inhering in objects becomes

---

[8] See e.g. L. E. Loeb, *Descartes to Hume* (Ithaca: Cornell University Press, 1981), 140–1. Loeb also takes the maxim 'the effect is like the cause' (which Descartes is reported as affirming in the *Conversation with Burman*) as implying only a 'degree of perfection' requirement: 'the effect must be like its total cause [only] in that both must be ... substance' (ibid. 142). But a closer reading of the Burman passage shows that Descartes consistently sees causation in terms of the cause bestowing attributes on the effect: 'Even stones have the image and likeness of God, albeit remotely and indistinctly. But as for me, God's creation has endowed me with a greater number of attributes, so his image is in me to a greater extent' (AT V 156–7: CSMK 340).

[9] Compare *Principles*, pt. II art. 40: motion is produced by being imparted or transferred from a body which is itself in motion.

[10] Some scholars have recently questioned whether Descartes in fact held to a causal similarity principle. See Loeb, *Descartes to Hume,* and R. C. Richardson, in 'The Scandal of Cartesian Interactionism', Mind 91/361 (1982), 20–37, who points out that in the letter to Clerselier of 12 January 1646 (AT IX 213: CSM II 275) Descartes appears to deny that the different nature of the soul and body is any obstacle to their interacting causally. But this passage has to be interpreted with caution. For, first, Descartes here readily concedes that he is not yet in a position to provide a satisfactory

readily intelligible. For suppose it were granted, for the sake of argument, that the quality of redness is indeed present in the rose. To explain how I am aware of this quality, it would have to be supposed that this quality has the power to set up motions of matter (since physiology tells us that all that actually reaches the brain when we perceive a rose is mere local motions in the nerve fibres). But how could a supposed 'real quality' such as redness have the power to set up something so different from itself? If it had such a power, we would have a casual chain of the following kind:

$$Q \ldots M$$

(where 'Q' stands for the supposed real quality of redness in objects and 'M' stands for the corporeal motions transmitted via the optic nerves). Yet the maxim 'the effect is like the cause' rules out such a causal chain, since there is no intelligible similarity between Q and M. Indeed, there would seem to be no intelligible relationship at all between Q and M—it would just be a brute fact that certain 'real qualities' set up certain corporeal motions. Descartes's rejection of occultism, and his rationalistic insistence that causal relationships be transparently perspicuous to the intellect, rule out such brute facts.[11] Here is how Descartes presents this causal argument in *Principles*, pt. IV art 198:

We understand very well how the different size, shape and motion of the particles of one body can produce various local motions in another body. But there is no way of understanding how these same attributes can produce something else whose *nature is quite different from their own*—like the ... real qualities which many

account of the mind–body relation; so he is far from asserting, *tout court*, that there is no problem whatever about causal interaction between items as heterogeneous as mind and body. Second, he goes on, somewhat ruefully it seems, to observe that his own account of mind–body causation (as it occurs in sense-perception) is no harder to accept than that of the scholastics—an account which, of course, he regards as quite unintelligible! Cf. a closely similar passage in the letter of 'Hyperaspistes' of August 1641 (AT III 424: CSMK 190), and see the comments of F. Alquié in his edition of Descartes, *Œuvres Philosophiques* (Paris: Garnier, 1963–73), ii. 362. For the strongest evidence that Descartes does insist on causal similarity, see the passage from *Principles*, pt. IV art. 198, to be quoted shortly.

[11] From a post-Humean perspective one may be inclined to ask what is wrong with brute facts, provided they are describable in terms of law-like regularities. From this perspective, insistence on causal similarity may appear to stem from a naive and outmoded view of causality. But, of course, not all modern philosophers of science are prepared to boil causation down to mere regularity; some see science as the search for explanatory mechanisms operating at the micro level (see e.g. R. Harré, *The Philosophies of Science* (Oxford: Oxford University Press, 1972). This mechanistic conception (which itself owes much to Descartes) seems to imply some meshing, some kind of interface, between the items that are causally related; and this in turn evidently implies that causal relata cannot be utterly heterogeneous. It may thus be too soon to write the obituary of the causal similarity principle.

philosophers suppose to inhere in things; and *we cannot understand how these qualities or forms could have the power to produce local motions in other bodies*... Not only is this unintelligible but ... we do not find that anything reaches the brain from the external sense organs except for local motions. In view of this we have every reason to conclude that the properties in external objects to which we apply the terms light, colour, smell, taste, sound, heat and cold, as well as the other tactile qualities ... are, so far as we can see, simply various dispositions in those objects which make them able to set up various kinds of motion in our nerves.

(AT VIII 322: CSM I 285; emphasis supplied)

For Descartes, then, nothing can be explained by attributing to objects a real quality of redness, for such a quality is incapable of figuring in a causal explanation of how our senses are affected by those objects. The only way in which it could so figure is if it were construed as a disposition of the rose (in virtue of the shape, size, and motions of its particles) to set up local motions in our nervous system. There is an unmistakably clear anticipation here of the Lockean notion of a secondary quality as a disposition possessed by an object to produce certain changes in virtue of its primary qualities. Incidentally, although Locke is sometimes misunderstood on this point, he is quite clear that secondary qualities are genuinely in objects, not in our minds;[12] and Descartes in the passage just quoted is also clear that a sensible property, such as redness, *construed as a disposition to set up certain types of motion*, may genuinely inhere in objects. What is denied is the inherence of redness qua redness—redness construed as a certain sort of *sui-generis* quality supposed to inhere in objects in a way that exactly matches our sensory awareness of it.

3. Cartesian Occasionalism and the Arbitrariness of Qualia

Having uncovered the rationale for Descartes's refusal to allow that colours, qua 'real qualities', inhere in objects, I want now to widen the focus and ask, in the light of the principles Descartes is committed to, whether he is in a position to give a coherent explanation of colour perception. We have seen that the Causal Similarity Principle prohibits a causal chain of the

---

[12] See P. Alexander, *Ideas, Qualities and Corpuscles* (Cambridge: Cambridge University Press, 1985), ch. 8.

form $Q \ldots M$ (where Q is the supposed 'real quality' of redness, and M the motion set up in the nervous system when someone views a rose). From this it appears that the Cartesian will insist on some kind of reductionistic analysis, whereby $Q \ldots M$ is ultimately replaced by

$$M_1 \ldots M_2$$

where M_1 represents the corporeal motions to be found in the rose, and M_2 the subsequent motions eventually set up in the nervous system. Colours can appear in causal chains only if they are reduced to descriptions in terms of matter in motion. But what then would a full Cartesian account of colour perception look like? The short answer is that it would have to look something like this:

$$M_1 \ldots M_2 \ldots S$$

where S is the sensation of redness finally arising in the soul as a result of the various corporeal events first in the environment and second in the nervous system. But this in turn raises a crucial problem for Descartes. How can it be, given his own allegiance to the Causal Similarity Principle, that S appears at the end of a causal chain composed of purely corporeal events? A sensation of redness, on Descartes's own account, has no resemblance at all to the corporeal events going on in the external world and in the nerve fibres; so how can such a sensation 'arise as a result of' or 'be produced by' those events? The answer Descartes sometimes gives is that it is 'ordained by nature' that certain corporeal motions should produce certain sensations or feelings in the soul (*Passions*, pt. I art. 36, AT XI 357: CSM I 342). By this, however, he cannot, given his allegiance to the Causal Similarity Principle, mean that there is some discoverable law of nature of the kind to be found within Cartesian physics, relating corporeal motions to sensations. When Descartes uses the phrase 'ordained by nature' in this type of context, he is equating nature with God; indeed, as is perhaps still not sufficiently widely known, the famous phrase 'God or nature', so often credited to Spinoza, actually occurs in Descartes's *Principles* (pt. I art. 28).[13] What Descartes has in mind by an ordinance of nature is a divine fiat—an arrangement specially instituted by the Creator:

I maintain that when God unites a rational soul to this machine [of the body] ... he will place its principal seat in the brain, and will make its nature such that the soul

---

[13] See further J. Cottingham, *The Rationalists* (Oxford: Oxford University Press), 92 ff.

will have different sensations corresponding to the different ways in which the entrances to the pores in the internal surface of the brain are opened by means of the nerves.   (*Treatise on Man*, AT XI 143: CSM I 102).

In creating the human soul, God has simply decreed that a range of 'qualia', or qualitative sensations of a distinctive kind, should arise in it whenever the brain to which it is joined is stimulated in various ways. What we have here is not causation proper, but rather a divinely decreed correlation—a notion that brings Descartes remarkably close to the occasionalism developed some forty years later by Malebranche. As Descartes puts it in his critique of Regius, the *Comments on a Certain Broadsheet*, the stimulation of our nervous systems is 'the occasion of our mind's forming certain ideas by means of the faculty innate to it' (AT VIIIA 359: CSM I 304).[14]

An interesting implication of Descartes's theory (and one ultimately independent of his theological commitments) is the claim that the correlations between brain events and qualia are, so to speak, arbitrary. This aspect of arbitrariness was something that Leibniz acutely picked up in his *New Essays* (*c*.1704):

The Cartesians conceive of the perception we have of these qualities (such as colour, heat and so on) as being arbitrary, that is to say, as if God had given them to the soul at his good pleasure without any regard to any essential relation between perceptions and their objects—an opinion which surprises me, and seems to me hardly worthy of the wisdom of the author of things, who does nothing without order and reason.[15]

A distant modern analogy that might be helpful in illustrating the thesis of the arbitrariness of qualia is that of a computer display of, for example, a meteorological chart, where the programmers have arranged things in such a way that areas of, say, low pressure show up as red patches on the monitor screen. The choice of red as the display colour is completely arbitrary: there is no natural, law-like correlation between the colour red

---

[14] See also *Traité de l'Homme*, AT XI 144: CSM I 103. This schematic account, developed in one possible direction, leads to the occasionalism of Malebranche (where the only cause of sensations, strictly speaking, is God); developed in another possible direction by taking seriously the notion of an innate predisposition in the soul to come up with certain kinds of sensation at certain times, it leads to the Leibnizian notion of pre-established harmony.

[15] G. W. Leibniz, *New Essays on Human Understanding* [*Nouveaux essais sur l'entendement humain*, *c*.1704; first pub. 1765], trans. P. Remnant and J. Bennett (Cambridge: Cambridge University Press, 1981), 56.

and the low barometric pressure. The programmers have decided to flag low pressure areas by using red, but they could equally well have chosen green, or yellow, or black dots, or grey stripes. This is precisely the kind of thing that Descartes takes to be true of the qualia that arise in the soul when the brain is stimulated in certain ways. God, the programmer of the human soul, has chosen that certain corporeal events should be 'flagged' for us in certain ways; but he could have chosen a completely different flagging system. This is how Descartes expresses it when discussing pain arising from damage to the foot:

When the nerves of the foot are set in motion in a violent and unusual manner, this motion, by way of the spinal chord, reaches the inner parts of the brain and thereby gives the mind its signal for having a certain sensation ... God could have made the nature of man such that this particular motion in the brain indicated something else in the mind. It might for example have made the mind aware of the actual motion occurring in the brain, or in the foot, or in any of the intermediate regions, or it might have indicated something else entirely.   (Sixth Meditation: AT VII 88: CSM II 60)

There is, for Descartes, no scientific explanation (that is, no explanation in terms of rationally intelligible causal connections) of the flagging system that actually obtains.

The only kind of explanation Descartes regards as appropriate in such cases (a kind of explanation that elsewhere he resolutely avoids) is one in terms of final causes or purposes: God wants to give us sensations of a kind conducive to the preservation of life and health (AT VII 87: CSM II 60). From a present-day perspective it seems promising to suggest that natural selection can play the beneficent role in this system that Descartes assigns to God. Thus any being for whom serious damage to the foot did not give rise to a highly urgent and intrusive sensation of an unwelcome kind would not survive long. So there would seem to be considerable selective pressure in favour of the emergence of certain kinds of qualia; and this in turn would seem to offer the hope, ruled out by Descartes, of integrating the realm of subjective sensation into the rest of our scientific account of the world.

It might be objected, however, that this evolutionary approach cannot explain all the distinctive qualitative aspects of our sensations. Compare a remark of Malebranche: 'since the senses were given us for the preservation of our body, it is to our advantage ... given that pain and heat can injure our limbs, that we should be warned when they assail us, in order to avoid being hurt. But such is not the case with colours ... '(*Recherche*, bk. I ch. xii, final two paragraphs). The thought here seems to be, to put it in modern dress, that even if there is likely to be a selective advantage in developing a system of visual perception that is sensitive to variations in spectral wavelength, nevertheless the way in which these differences appear to the subject—the 'mode of presentation' as Colin McGinn has termed it[16]—might be arranged in a variety of different ways. Consider the much discussed notion of 'qualia inversion' or 'qualia variation' apparently first invoked by Locke when he raised the possibility that 'the Idea that a Violet produces in one Man's mind' might be the same as 'that which a Marigold produces in another Man's' (*Essay*, bk. II ch. xxxii §15). If this notion makes sense, and if, more generally, the notion of different possible 'modes of presentation' makes sense, this would support the Cartesian notion that there is a degree of 'arbitrariness' about the subjective character of our sensations.[17] However that may be, it seems that as far as Descartes's own views on colour qualia are concerned, there is one major flaw in his position which cannot be avoided. If we draw the threads of Descartes's account together, his argument is this:

1. All that reaches the brain from the outside world is a certain pattern of matter in motion;
2. what we are aware of is a colour sensation of a distinctive kind;
3. there can be no causal relation between a pattern of matter in motion and a sensation of colour; therefore
4. the relation between the material events and the colour sensations is arbitrary (and the relevant correlations must have been ordained by God).

---

[16] Cf. C. McGinn, *The Subjective View* (Oxford: Oxford University Press, 1983), ch. 5.

[17] For my own part (though I cannot discuss this here) I am sceptical about whether the notion of qualia inversion does make sense. If we postulate a flagging system that serves to mark out the whole complex family of resemblances and differences associated with our colour perceptions—if, in short, we imagine a being whose internal mapping enables him to match us point for point in all the discriminations we make—then the suggestion that his flagging system could be 'qualitatively' different from ours seems to me to lose its grip. Scenarios of qualia inversion seem to get what plausibility they have from artificially *isolating* colour perceptions: we are invited to imagine a 'swap' between violet and marigold without pausing to think about the radical changes in a whole range of similarity and difference judgements ('shade x is closer to y than z') that such a swap would imply. As for the notion of a complete inversion of the entire spectrum, I have yet to see a plausible account that manages to preserve all similarity and difference judgements intact (including, for example, judgements about relative luminosity).

The picture which is covertly implied by this argument is one which I and my conscious experiences have to mesh, at some point, with the micro events in the brain and the nervous system that give rise to my sensations. And since the Causal Similarity Principle rules out the possibility of a genuine causal meshing here, God is brought in to close the gap. But it seems clear that Descartes has here crossed two distinct levels of description. What we have at the macro level is a human being seeing a red rose. What we have at the micro level is a configuration of plant molecules, a flow of electromagnetic radiation, and a set of changes in the brain (or, in Descartes's terms, some jostlings of particles and a flow of animal spirits). Now as long as we remain at the micro level, focusing on such things as the firing of neurons (or the flow of animal spirits), then it is indeed hard to see how we can find a place for my colour sensations as individual items in this particular causal chain. Yet it does not follow that the only recourse in the face of this puzzle is to invoke a *deus ex machina* to bridge the two levels of description and ordain the occurrence of sensations when neurons fire or animal spirits flow. One available alternative, for example, is that which Spinoza was in effect to put forward—namely to say that sensations are not *generated* but *constituted* by brain events: there is one single set of events or processes 'expressed' or described in two ways. I do not propose to defend the 'Spinozistic' approach here, or claim that it can solve all the problems associated with the 'qualitative' aspects of perceptual experience. But at the very least it does not lead to the explanatory impasse that confronts the Cartesian theory, when it attempts to tack sensations onto the end of causal chain consisting of nervous impulses and brain events.

4. Coda: The 'Opacity' of Sensory Qualities

Let me end, however, on a note which is more favourable to Descartes—a note that brings us back to the first of the two 'strands' in Descartes's account of colour that I referred to at the beginning of the chapter. At the end of the day, despite his confused and often excoriated theory of the mind, Descartes does, I think, manage to say something interesting and true about colour perception What he is at pains to stress, throughout his discussions of our perception of sensible qualities, is that when we apprehend such qualities via the senses, we perceive, as it were, through a glass darkly. We monitor what is going on in the world, but the monitoring system provided by the senses gives us only very imperfect and limited access to what is actually occurring. It is as if (to take up a suggestion made by the French Cartesian scholar Jean-Luc Marion)[18] the senses provide *coded* information that has to be deciphered. A visual sensation, for example of redness, indicates (under normal observing conditions) the presence of some property of the external object, but tells us little or nothing about the nature of that property; we need, as it were, to crack the code and discover what the property in question consists in. Though Descartes himself does not talk of codes, he does remark in his early treatise, *Le Monde*, that visual sensations (e.g. of light and colour) are 'signs established by nature' (AT XI 4: CSM I 81); what it is that is signified remains to be discovered.

The implication here is that anyone who supposed that the nature of the significatum (the property in question) could be revealed by reflecting on the sign (the sensation of colour) would be like a Latin-less reader who thought that the meaning of the sentence 'Cave canem' could be found by scrutinizing these Latin words. But of course until the code is cracked, until he can look the words up in a dictionary and work out what they mean, the words remain, to him, no more than a set of mysterious symbols. So, if he walks up the driveway and says 'I know what is going on here; this is a case of *cave canem*,' although he has read the symbols with perfect clarity, he remains in a state of crucial ignorance as to what is really happening—namely, that he is about to be attacked by a large dog. There is an exact analogy here, Descartes wants to say, with the pre-philosophical man's judgements about colour. Although he may have a perfectly clear visual sensation of redness, 'if he says he sees the colour in the object', says Descartes, 'this amounts to his saying that he sees something there of which he is completely ignorant' (*Principles*, pt. I art. 68). Or again: 'when we say that we perceive colours in objects, this is really just the same as saying that we perceive something in the objects whose nature we do not know, but which produces in us a very vivid and clear sensation which we call the sensation of colour' (ibid. art. 70).

Descartes's claim, then, is that even when our colour judgements are true, they are in need of 'decoding', so that we can appreciate exactly what it is that we are attributing to objects when we say, for example, 'this is

---

[18] See J. L. Marion, *Sur la théologie blanche de Descartes* (Paris: Presses Universitaires de France, 1981).

red'. No doubt there are various philosophers today (particularly those of a Wittgensteinian bent) who may be inclined to reject this as a piece of needless mystification. Why should we suppose, they may ask, that there is any asymmetry between, for example, our perceptions of shape and our perceptions of colour? Are there not, in each case, perfectly clear and straightforward rules of language for an object's counting as round, or as red; and do we not in each case know perfectly well what we mean by saying 'this is round' or 'this is red'? Although I think the linguistic point is perfectly correct, it still seems to me that there is a crucial asymmetry between shape and colour. For when we see the sun and judge that it is round, what we are apprised of, what figures as part of the content of our judgement, is that all the points on the circumference are (roughly) equidistant from the centre. And the explanation of our perceiving it that way is that the object in question does indeed have a surface such that all the points on its circumference are roughly equidistant from the centre. In discerning the shape, then, we have what may be called a transparent perception of the property of the object that is responsible for our perceiving in the way we do.[19] But this is not so with colour. For the content of our judgement, when we perceive that the sun is yellow, is simply that it has a hue of a certain distinctive kind; and though it could be said that we are indeed aware of the property of the sun that causes us to see it as yellow, namely its yellowness, nevertheless we are quite unaware, until enlightened by the scientist, that what this yellowness consists in is, for example, a disposition to radiate light of a certain wavelength. And that property was not part of the content of our judgement (or at least not under that description), whereas the property of having all the points on the surface equidistant from the centre was part of the content of our judgement as to its roundness. Put at its simplest, then, Descartes's claim is that there is an opacity about our colour judgements that is not the

---

[19] To avoid any possible misunderstanding: I do not of course mean that our judgements about shape are somehow epistemically privileged over, or less likely to be in error than, our judgements about colour. As Berkeley rightly observed, distortions and errors are just as possible in the case of judgements about primary qualities as they are in the case of judgements about secondary qualities (*Principles of Human Knowledge* [1710], pt. I §14). My point is a quite different one, which concerns not the greater reliability of our judgements about shape but their greater transparency of content. I may be right or wrong about an object's being spherical but at least I know what sphericity is. Whereas, as Descartes puts it in the Third Meditation, my ideas of qualities such as colours contain so little clarity and distinctness that they do not enable me to tell what kind of real quality, if any, I am supposed to be attributing to an object when I say, for example, that it is yellow (AT VII 43–4: CSM II 30).

case with our judgements about, for example, shape. This should not lead us to say that objects are not really coloured (as Hume ineptly put it) or that colours do not inhere in objects (as Descartes was from time to time tempted to say). Hume was wrong to disparage the beliefs of the 'vulgar' about colour; what Malebranche superciliously calls the 'peasant' is quite correct in believing that roses are really red. What Descartes's approach invites us to notice, however, is that in our perceptions of colour there is something indistinct: that in the case of colour, unlike shape, the nature of what we are attributing to the object goes beyond what is 'present and open to the attentive mind'. And *this* Cartesian thesis is one that it seems to me we have every reason to accept.

8

'A Brute to the Brutes?':
Descartes's Treatment of Animals

1. Introduction

To be able to believe that a dog with a broken paw is not really in pain when it whimpers is a quite extraordinary achievement even for a philosopher. Yet according to the standard interpretation, this is just what Descartes did believe. He held, we are informed, the 'monstrous' thesis that 'animals are without feeling or awareness of any kind'.[1] The standard view has been reiterated in a recent collection on animal rights, which casts Descartes as the villain of the piece for his alleged view that animals merely behave 'as if they feel pain when they are, say, kicked or stabbed'.[2] The basis for this widely accepted interpretation is Descartes's famous doctrine of the 'animal machine' (bête-machine); a doctrine that one critic condemns as 'a grim foretaste of a mechanically minded age' which 'brutally violates the old kindly fellowship of living things'.[3]

But if we look at what Descartes actually says about animals it is by no means clear that he holds the monstrous view that all the commentators attribute to him. In fact the traditional rubric 'Descartes's doctrine of the bête-machine' is vague and ambiguous; it needs to be broken down into a number of distinct propositions if we are to sort out what Descartes said, and what he is implicitly committed to, from what he neither said nor implied.

I am indebted to Professor Antony Flew, whose questions about Descartes's position stimulated me to pursue the line of enquiry developed in this chapter.

[1] N. Kemp Smith, *New Studies in the Philosophy of Descartes* (London: Macmillan, 1952), 136 and 140.

[2] T. Regan and P. Singer (eds.), *Animal Rights and Human Obligations* (Englewood Cliffs, NJ: Prentice Hall, 1976), 4.   [3] A. Boyce Gibson, *The Philosophy of Descartes* (London: Methuen, 1932), 214.

Consider, then, the following assertions:

(1) Animals are machines.
(2) Animals are automata.
(3) Animals do not think.
(4) Animals have no language.
(5) Animals have no self-consciousness.
(6) Animals have no consciousness.
(7) Animals are totally without feeling.

Proposition (7) is the 'monstrous thesis' with which Descartes is so often credited. I shall argue that Descartes held theses (1) to (5), but that there is no evidence that he held (7), and even some positive evidence that he regarded (7) as false; however, fuzziness about (6) and its distinction from (5) (together with certain general features of his metaphysics) laid him open to be interpreted as committed to (7).

2. Machines and Automata

Thesis (1) is not explicitly asserted by Descartes in this form, but he commits himself to it in so many words in the famous passage on animals in Part Five of the *Discourse on the Method*, where he says the body may be regarded 'comme une machine qui, ayant été faite des mains de Dieu, est incomparablement mieux ordonnée … qu'aucune de celles … inventées par les hommes.'[4] Thesis (1) in fact forms part of Descartes's general scientific 'mechanism', and, roughly translated, means that all animal behaviour is subsumable under physiological laws, which, for Descartes, are ultimately derivable from mathematical principles. Essentially, when Descartes says that 'all the motions of animals originate from the corporeal and mechanical principle',[5] he is concerned to promulgate a scientific animal physiology that seeks explanations in terms of efficient rather than final causes.[6] Now from none of all this does it follow that when Descartes calls something

---

[4] 'as a machine which, having been made by the hand of God, is incomparable better ordered … than any of those … invented by human beings' (*Discours de la méthode* [1637], Part Five, AT VI 56: CSM I 139).

[5] Letter to More of 5 February 1649, AT V 276: CSMK 365.

[6] *Principles of Philosophy* [*Principia philosophiae*, 1644], pt. I art. 28 (AT VIII 15: CSM I 202). See further AT V 158: CSMK 341, and J. Cottingham (ed.), *Descartes' Conversation with Burman* (Oxford: Clarendon, 1976), 85–6.

a 'mechanism' or 'machine' he is automatically ruling out the presence of sensations or feelings; Boyce Gibson's claim that Descartes 'uses the term [mechanism] explicitly to exclude ... feeling' is not supported by any evidence.[7] In fact it is important to notice that the human body is, for Descartes, a machine in exactly the same sense as the animal body: 'God made our body like a machine, and he wanted it to function like a universal instrument, which would always operate in the same way in accordance with its own laws.'[8] The phrase *bête-machine* can thus be rather misleading, since the mechanical physiology Descartes has in mind operates equally in the case of homo sapiens. Of course it is true that in the human, but not the animal, case there is the extra dimension of a 'soul' (I shall come back to this); but this is a separate point. To deny that X has a soul is a separate claim from the claim that X's movements can be explained by mechanical principles, and is not strictly entailed by it.

Proposition (2) is implied frequently by Descartes, and is stated explicitly in a letter to Henry More of 5 February 1649: 'it seems reasonable since art copies nature, and men can make various automata which move without thought, that nature should produce its own automata much more splendid than the artificial ones. These natural automata are the animals.'[9] It is Descartes's use of the term 'automaton' more than any other that has led critics to convict him of holding the monstrous thesis (thus, Kemp Smith speaks of the Cartesian view that animals are 'mere automata... incapable of experiencing the feelings of well-being or the reverse, hunger or thirst').[10] But the inference from 'X is an automaton' to 'X is incapable of feeling' is a mistaken one. Webster's dictionary gives the primary meaning of 'automaton' as simply 'a machine that is relatively self-operating'; and neither this nor the subsidiary meaning ('creature who acts in a mechanical fashion') automatically implies the absence of feeling.[11] Even today, then, to regard total insensibility as part of the meaning of 'automaton' would seem to be an error; and this seems to have been even more true in the seventeenth century, where 'automaton' probably carried

---

[7] Nor does Gibson cite any; see Gibson, *The Philosophy of Descartes*, 211.

[8] AT V 163–4: CSMK 346; cf. Cottingham (ed.), *Descartes' Conversation with Burman*, 29.

[9] 'deinde quia rationi consentaneum videtur, cum ars sit naturae imitatrix, possintque homines varia fabricare automata, in quibus sine ulla cogitatione est motus, ut natura etiam sua automata, sed artefactis longe praestantiora, nempe bruta omnia, producat' (AT V 277: CSMK 366). This is a development of material found in *Discourse*, Pt. Five (AT VI 56: CSM I 139). [10] *The Philosophy of Descartes*, 135.

[11] *Webster's Seventh New Collegiate Dictionary* (Springfield, Mass.: Merriam, 1963).

no more than its strict Greek meaning of 'self-moving thing'. Thus Leibniz, defending his claim that we possess 'freedom of spontaneity' speaks of the human soul as 'a kind of spiritual automaton', meaning no more than that its action-generating impulses arise solely *ab interno*, from within, and produce their effects without the intervention of any external cause.[12] What fascinated Descartes's generation about machines ranging from clocks to the elaborately contrived moving statues to be found in some of the royal fountains was simply this: the complex sequences of movements which to primitive (or medieval) man might have appeared as certain proof of some kind of inner motive 'force' or 'spirit', could all be explained quite simply by reference to internal mechanical structure—cogs, levers, and the like (Descartes mentions as an example a statue of Neptune which would threaten with his trident the approaching onlooker who had unwittingly stepped on a button).[13] The point Descartes is concerned to make over and over again about the behaviour of 'natural automata' such as dogs and monkeys is that the mere complexity of their movements is no more a bar to explanation in terms of inner mechanical structure than is the case with the responses of the trident-brandishing 'Neptune'.[14]

3. The Language Argument

So far then, I maintain that Descartes's characterization of animals as 'machines' and 'automata' is of itself quite insufficient to allow us to conclude that he thinks that animals lack feelings. When we get on to the remaining propositions in our list, things are not so simple.

It is, Descartes asserts, in principle possible to mistake a cleverly contrived artificial automaton for an animal. But we could never mistake an automaton, however ingenious, for a man. Why not? Because, says Descartes, an automaton could never talk: it could not 'produce different arrangements of words so as to give an appropriately meaningful answer to whatever is

---

[12] Leibniz, *Theodicy* [*Essais de théodicée*, 1710], pt. I §52.

[13] Descartes, *Treatise on Man* [*Traité de l'homme*, written early 1630s, first pub. 1677], AT XI 130–2: CSM I 100–1. Cf. E. Gilson (ed.), *René Descartes, Discours de la Méthode* (Paris: Vrin, 1925), 420 ff.

[14] Descartes compares the plants in this connection, 'que [la nature] remplit d'une infinité de petits conduits imperceptibles à la vue' ('which nature has packed with an infinity of tiny ducts invisible to the naked eye'); letter to Reneri of April 1638 (AT II 40: CSMK 100).

said in its presence'.[15] This for Descartes indicates the crucial difference between animals and man—animals do not think. They do not *penser* or *cogitare*; they are not endowed with a mind (*mens; esprit*); they lack reason (*raison*); they do not have a rational soul (*âme raisonnable*).[16]

Descartes is thus explicitly committed to thesis (3), and holds, moreover, that it is entailed by (or at least strongly evidenced by)[17] thesis (4). Descartes was of course aware that parrots can be made to 'talk' and that dogs make noises which might be analogous to speech; but he has strong and, since Noam Chomsky's updating of them, widely admired arguments against construing such utterances as genuine speech. The talking of parrots is dismissed because it is not 'relevant to the topic';[18] but the most important point Descartes has to make is that the utterances of dogs, cats, etc., are never, to use the Chomskian phrase, 'stimulus-free'; they are always, says Descartes, geared to and elicited by a particular 'natural impulse'.[19]

I shall come back to these arguments, but first an obvious objection must be faced. In admitting that Descartes held thesis (3) (that animals de not think), have I not thereby conceded that he must have held the 'monstrous thesis' (7) (that animals do not feel)? For does not Descartes's special sense of 'think' (*cogitare, penser*) include feelings and sensations? Well, it is certainly true that Descartes deliberately extended the normal use of *cogitatio* or *pensée*. In answer to a misunderstanding of Mersenne (that if man was purely *res cogitans* he must lack will), Descartes states that willing is a way of thinking (*façon de penser*); he further explains that *la pensée* includes 'not only meditations and acts of the will' but 'all the operations of the soul' (*toutes les operations de l'âme*).[20] This is generally taken to include

---

[15] *Discourse*, Pt. Five (AT VI 56–7: CSM I 140).

[16] *Discourse*, ibid. Cf. letter to More of 5 February 1649 (AT V 278: CSMK 366): 'speech is the only sure sign of thought hidden in the body' ('loquela unicum est cogitationis in corpore latentis signum certum').

[17] Descartes at one point observes that 'although I regard it as established that we cannot prove that there is no thought in animals, I do not think it can be proved that there is none, since the human mind does not reach into their hearts' ('quamvis ... pro demonstrato habeam, probari non posse aliquam esse in brutis cogitationem, non ideo puto posse demonstrari nullam esse, quia mens humana illorum corda non pervadit'). AT V 276–7: CSMK 365.

[18] To Newcastle, 23 November 1646 (AT IV 574: CSMK 303).

[19] See the letters to More and to Newcastle already cited, and N. Chomsky, *Language and Mind* (New York: Harcourt Brace & World, 1968), ch. 1.

[20] For willing (along with understanding, imagining, and sense-perception) as a *façon de penser* see letter to Mersenne of May 1637 (AT I 366: CSMK 56); for *la pensée* as including all the operations of the soul, see letter to Reneri of April 1638 (AT II 36: CSMK 97). Cf. A. Kenny, *Descartes* (New York: Random House, 1968), pp. 68 ff.

sensations and feelings—indeed, seeing and hearing are explicitly included by Descartes in the list of 'operations de l'âme' just mentioned.

Further analysis, however, makes it clear that the matter is not as straightforward as this, and that translators who render *cogitatio* or *pensée* as simply 'experience' are moving much too swiftly.[21] When discussing whether *video ergo sum* (I see therefore I am) might not do as well as *cogito ergo sum* (I think therefore I am), Descartes says that 'I see' is ambiguous. If understood as *de visione* (of vision) it is not a good premise for inferring one's existence; but if understood 'concerning the actual sense or awareness of seeing' (*de ipso sensu sive conscientia videndi*) it is quite certain, since it is in this case referred to the mind which alone feels or thinks it sees (*quae sola sentit sive cogitat se videre*).[22] From this we can see that it is misleading to say, *tout court*, that *cogitatio* 'includes' sensations and feelings. The only sense in which a sensation such as seeing is a true *cogitatio* is the sense in which it may involve the reflective mental awareness that Descartes calls *conscientia*—the self-conscious apprehension of the mind that it is aware of seeing.[23]

The upshot is that Descartes's assertion of proposition (3) (that animals do not think) need not commit him to denying any feeling or sensation to animals—for example a level of feeling or sensation that falls short of reflective mental awareness. Notice, moreover, how the language argument fits into all this. In pointing out that animals have no genuine language, Descartes clearly thinks that he has a powerful case for concluding that they do not think. Yet for Descartes to regard this argument, 'non loquitur ergo non cogitat' ('he does not speak, therefore he does not think'),[24] as having such evident force, *cogitat* (think) here must evidently be used in the fairly restrictive sense just described above. If Descartes were using *cogitat* in the alleged very wide sense, he would be offering us an argument of the form *non loquitur ergo non sentit* (he does not speak therefore does not feel). It is

---

[21] See E. Anscombe and P. Geach, *Descartes, Philosophical Writings* (London: Nelson, 1969), pp. xlvii–xlviii, and J. Cottingham, 'Descartes on Thought', *Philosophical Quarterly*, 28 (1978), repr. as Ch. 4, above.   [22] *Principles*, pt. I art. 9 (AT VIII 7–8: CSM I 195).

[23] *Conscientia* is defined in the Conversation with Burman: 'conscium esse est ... cogitare et reflectere supra suam cogitationem' ('to be aware is to think and to reflect on one's thought'; AT V 149: CSMK 333); cf. Cottingham (ed.), *Conversation with Burman*, 7 and 61.

[24] Strictly, the argument must be of the form 'he does not speak and has no capacity for language acquisition, therefore he does not think'; for Descartes says that infants think (AT VII 246: CSM II 171–2)—though only after a fashion (AT V 149–50: CSMK 336).

inconceivable that Descartes could have proudly produced this argument to his correspondents as self-evidently clinching.

4. Animal Passions

Our conclusion so far is that neither in calling animals machines or automata, nor in denying they have thought or language, does Descartes commit himself to the monstrous thesis that they have no feelings or sensations. It is now time to look at some positive evidence that he actually regarded the monstrous thesis as false. The strongest evidence, to which those who credit Descartes with the monstrous thesis seem strangely blind, comes from the famous letters already cited where Descartes denies speech to the animals. Writing to More, Descartes says that the sounds made by horses, dogs, etc., are not genuine language, but are ways of 'communicating to us ... their natural impulses of anger, fear, hunger and so on'.[25] Similarly, Descartes wrote to Newcastle that:

If you teach a magpie to say good-day to its mistress when it sees her coming, all you can possibly have done is to make the emitting of this word the expression of one of its feelings. For instance it will be an expression of the hope of eating, if you have habitually given it a titbit when it says the word. Similarly, all the things which dogs, horses, and monkeys are made to do are merely expressions of their fear, their hope, or their joy; and consequently, they can do these things without any thought.[26]

'Impulses of anger, fear, hunger'; 'expression of one of its feelings'; 'expressions of fear, hope and joy'. These are quite extraordinary phrases to use for a man who is supposed to believe animals are 'without feeling or awareness of any kind'. Is it possible that Descartes is here speaking loosely or metaphorically? This seems strange in letters that are explicitly and painstakingly devoted to clarifying the Cartesian position on animals. If

---

[25] 'impetus suos naturales ut iras metus famem et similia ... significant' (AT V 278: CSMK 366).

[26] 'Si on apprend à une pie à dire bonjour à sa maîtresse, lorsqu'elle la voit arriver, ce ne peut être qu'en faisant que la prolation de cette parole devienne le mouvement de quelqu'une de se passions; à savoir, ce sera un mouvement de l'espérance qu'elle a de manger, si l'on a toujours accoutumé de lui donner quelque friandise lorsqu'elle l'a dit; ainsi toutes les choses qu'on fait faire aux chiens, aux chevaux et aux singes ne sont que des mouvements de leur crainte, de leur espérance ou de leur joie, en sorte qu'ils les peuvent faire sans aucune pensée' (AT IV 574: CSMK 303).

this were not enough, in the letter to More, Descartes specifically separates *cogitatio* (thought) from *sensus* (sensation), and states that he denies the former, but not the latter, to animals: 'I should like to stress that I am talking of thought, not of ... sensation; for ... I deny sensation to no animal, in so far as it depends on a bodily organ.'[27]

5. Dualistic Complications

The last quotation might make a pleasing and neat vindication of Descartes's kindly fellowship with the beasts: he denied that animals think, but not that they feel. But philosophy is seldom as tidy as this, and we must conclude by discussing a major difficulty that has been put off until now. The difficulty, in a nutshell, is that the monstrous thesis fits in with, and the pleasing vindication clashes with, Descartes's dualism.

If substance is divided exclusively and exhaustively into *res cogitans* and *res extensa,* what room is there for animal sensations? Since an animal is not a *res cogitans,* has no mind or soul, it follows that it must belong wholly in the extended divisible world of jostling Cartesian shapes. And this means that what we call (and, evidently, Descartes himself called) 'animal hunger' cannot be anything more than a set of internal muscle contractions leading to the jerking of certain limbs, or whatever. This then must be the authentic Cartesian position—a position summed up when Descartes quotes with approval the passage in Deuteronomy which says that the soul of animals is simply their blood;[28] or when he says that animal life is no more than 'the heat of the heart'.[29]

No doubt this is where a pure Cartesian, a consistent Cartesian, would stop. But we have seen that Descartes, dualist or no, undoubtedly and explicitly attributes such feelings as anger, hope, and joy to animals. I think the only explanation of this is that Descartes, either inadvertently or wilfully, failed to eradicate a certain fuzziness from his thinking about consciousness and self-consciousness. To say that X is in pain (angry, joyful)

---

[27] 'velim notari me loqui de cogitatione, non de vita vel sensu; vitam enim nulli animali denego, utpote quam in solo cordis calore consistere statuo; nec denego etiam sensum quatenus ab organo corporeo dependet' (AT V 278: CSMK 366).

[28] Deuteronomy 12: 23; see Descartes's letter to Plempius of 3 October 1637 (AT I 415: CSMK 62–3).

[29] Letter to More of 5 February 1649 (AT V 276: CSMK 365).

is certainly to attribute a conscious state to X; but this need not amount to the full-blooded reflective awareness of pain that is involved in the term *cogitatio*. To be dogmatic for a moment, I should certainly say that cats feel pain, but not that they have the kind of full mental awareness of pain that is needed for it to count as a *cogitatio* (i.e. the sort needed to support the premise of a Cogito-type argument *patior ergo sum* (I am suffering/I am in pain, therefore I am). Descartes is certainly committed to thesis (5), that animals do not have self-consciousness; but when as a result he consigns animals to the realm of *res extensa*, he simply does not seem to bother that terms such as pain, anger, etc., which he uses of animals, clearly imply some degree of conscious (though perhaps not 'self-conscious') awareness.

6. Concluding Reflections

It is important to notice, in conclusion, that this strange fuzziness is not simply the result of a blind spot that Descartes had when dealing with animals, but connects with a fundamental and unresolved difficulty in Cartesian metaphysics. There is a fascinating article in part IV of the *Principles* dealing with human sensations (*sensus*) and feelings (*affectus*). 'When we hear a piece of good news', says Descartes, we feel 'intellectual joy' (*gaudium intellectuale*); this is the sort of *pura cogitatio* that, presumably, God and the angels experience. But when the news is grasped by the imagination, the 'animal spirits' flow from the brain to the heart muscles, which in turn transmit more 'movements' to the brain, with the result that we experience a feeling of 'animal joy' (*laetitia animalis*).[30] It is evident that Descartes is in a philosophical mess here. One might expect that joy would be regarded as a purely mental state and thus confined firmly to the realm of *res cogitans*. But here is Descartes distinguishing between the pure intellectual apprehension of joyful news, on the one hand, and, on the other, a *feeling* of joy. This latter is the bizarre item called 'animal joy', which is somehow bound up with heart muscles and brain commotions. The choice of the phrase *laetitia animalis* here is no accident. Descartes clearly wants to say that the joy of dogs and cats is analysable into just such physiological events. But what he seems to forget is that as a strict dualist he

---

[30] *Principles*, pt. IV art. 190 (AT VIII 317: CSM I 281).

should not be using the word 'laetitia' at all in this case. For a true dualist, if something is *laetitia* (an inescapably 'mental' predicate) it cannot be *animalis* (part of *res extensa*); and conversely, if it is *animalis* it cannot be *laetitia*.

The truth, perhaps, is that Descartes was never completely comfortable with strict dualism, however emphatically he affirmed it. As the contortions in the Sixth Meditation show, feelings or sensations (like those of hunger or thirst) are an insoluble worry for him. We do not merely 'notice' that we are in pain, as a pilot observes that his ship is damaged, we actually feel it; and this shows that there is a 'conjoining and as it were intermixing'[31] between mind and body—a mysterious 'intermingling' of what are, remember, logically distinct and incompatible substances. This 'substantial union' is the uncuttable knot in the centre of Cartesian metaphysics. Descartes once wrote to a correspondent that if an angel (a pure *res cogitans*) were in a human body, he would not feel like us; he would merely observe the changes in his nervous system. This shows, Descartes observed, that feelings like that of pain are not the *purae cogitationes* of a mind distinct from body, but rather are the 'confused perceptions which result from a real union with the body'.[32] Feelings, in other words, are an inexplicable result of the animal side of our nature, our mysterious intermingling with *res extensa*. If this is what Descartes says about human feelings, it is not surprising that he never got animal feelings properly sorted out. Strict dualism makes nonsense of Descartes's common-sense attribution of feelings such as hunger to the animals; but then Descartes is unable to extract from dualism any clear account of the awkwardly undeniable experience of *human* hunger. At the end of the day, Descartes may not have been completely consistent, but at least he was not altogether beastly to the beasts.

[31] I am 'very closely conjoined and as it were intermixed' ('arctissime conjunctum & quasi permixtum') with the body (AT VII 81 line 3: CSM II 56). Or, ten lines later, there is a 'union and as it were intermingling' ('unio & quasi permixtio').

[32] 'sensus doloris, aliosque omnes, non esse puras cogitationes mentis a corpore distinctas, sed confusas illius realiter unitae perceptiones' (to Regius, January 1642, AT III 493: CSMK 206).

9

Cartesian Trialism

1. Introduction

Why does Descartes's mind–body dualism have so little appeal for most philosophers nowadays? There are many problematic aspects of the theory, but two seem especially troublesome. (1) The first may be labelled the 'noncorporeality dogma': by insisting on the essential non-corporeality of the mind, Cartesian dualism is committed to a thesis that modern advances in neurophysiology have made less and less plausible. The claim, made by Descartes, that an act of thinking or doubting 'does not require any place or depend on any material thing'[1] (e.g. requires no brain) seems in the light of today's knowledge to be simply a non-starter. (2) The second troublesome aspect of dualism may be labelled the 'mental or physical?' dilemma. By insisting that all attributes be regarded either as modes of thought or as modes of extension, Cartesian dualism seems to lumber itself with an impossible choice when it comes to complex psychophysical phenomena such as sensations. Descartes's attempts to deal with the dilemma led him to the bizarre position that, in the case of humans, having a sensation is a kind of thinking, while in the case of animals there are no proper sensations at all but mere motions of matter.[2]

Rather than harp on Descartes's failures, however, I want to look at some of his little-recognized successes. An examination of Descartes's writings reveals that he has many fascinating things to say about the mind that do not obviously square with his official dualistic doctrines, and—perhaps for this very reason—are often ignored by commentators. Consider, in particular, the two troublesome features of dualism mentioned above.

---

[1] *Discourse on the Method* [*Discours de la méthode*, 1637], Pt. Four (AT VI 33: CSM I 127).

[2] This last point needs some qualification: cf. J. Cottingham, 'A Brute to the Brutes? Descartes's Treatment of Animals', *Philosophy* 53 (1978); repr. as Ch. 8, above.

(1) The noncorporeality dogma: although Descartes stubbornly adheres to this when discussing intellection and volition, he nonetheless insists, throughout his writings, that some mental activities require a body and, more specifically, a brain. These activities involve what may be called the 'hybrid' faculties of imagination and sensation. (2) With regard to the 'mental or physical?' dilemma, again despite the official rigidly exclusive dichotomy, there are places where a different approach emerges. In the correspondence with Elizabeth, for example, Descartes speaks of certain primitive categories or 'notions' in terms of which we think about the world ('models on which all our other knowledge is patterned'),[3] and what emerges in the case of our ways of thinking about human beings is not a dualism but a grouping of three notions—what may be called a 'trialism'. It turns out that there are features that belong to the mind alone, features that belong to the body alone, and what may be called hybrid features—features that belong to man qua embodied being.

The plan of this chapter is as follows. In the first half, I want to take a detailed look at Descartes's treatment of the 'hybrid' faculties of imagination and sensation; and I shall suggest that even on Descartes's own account of these faculties, they do not fit happily within the confines of his official dualistic schema. In the second half, which I hope will have something to say not just to students of Descartes's philosophy but to those interested in the philosophy of mind in general, I shall try to develop an account of what I call 'Cartesian trialism' and its implications for what it is to be a human being.

2. Sensation and Imagination

Let us begin, then, with the faculties of sensation and imagination. This pair makes its appearance early on in the Second Meditation, where Descartes, having established *that* he exists, ponders on his nature, on *what* he is: 'But what then am I? A thing that thinks. What is that? A thing that doubts, understands, affirms, denies, is willing, is unwilling... (*dubitans, intelligens,*

---

[3] 'Certaines notions primitives qui sont comme des originaux sur le patron desquels nous formons toutes nos autres connaissances.' Letter of 21 May 1643, AT III 665: CSMK 218. This passage is discussed in more detail in sect. 3 of this chapter.

affirmans, negans, volens, nolens).'[4] So far so good; all the activities listed are straightforward acts of intellection or volition of the kind which Descartes will later classify as modifications of a *res cogitans*, a thinking thing. But now two unexpected verbs make their appearance: ' ... and also which imagines and has sensory perceptions (*imaginans quoque et sentiens*).'[5] Now in the context of the Second Meditation, Descartes is, of course, not prepared to commit himself to the real extra-mental existence of any of the objects of sense-perception or imagination. It follows that the verbs *sentire* and *imaginare* can here be used only in a very 'thin' sense, to refer to what the subject is indubitably aware of even if no extra-mental objects exist. This is made clear in the *Principles of Philosophy*, where (in what is virtually a commentary on this part of the *Meditations*) Descartes says that if we take a sensory act like seeing to apply not to vision as involving bodies but merely to the awareness or the thought that one is seeing, then this will be something that pertains to the mind alone.[6]

But even though Descartes is here employing *sentire* and *imaginare* in a very restricted sense, he reveals a certain reluctance to lump them with the other modes of thinking. There is a faint shift of emphasis between the first six members of the list and the last two, a shift signalled in the original text by the Latin particle *quoque* (also). A thinking thing is a thing that doubts, understands, affirms, denies, is willing, is unwilling—*and also* imagines and has sensory experiences. The last two verbs are paired together and tacked on to the rest of the list almost as an afterthought. Why should this be?

A possible reason is that Descartes knows that when he is eventually able to examine the true nature of sensation and imagination, he will discover

---

[4] *Meditations on First Philosophy* [*Meditationes de prima philosophia*, 1641], AT VII 28; CSM II 19.

[5] The Latin verb *sentire* (French *sentir*) is a major headache for translators of Descartes. In dealing with Descartes's phrase *res sentiens*, the rendering that is etymologically closest to the Latin is 'a thing which ... senses'; but *sense* in modern English has the wrong flavour (of an intuitive hunch). Haldane and Ross have 'feels'; but *sentire* can refer to e.g. visual sensations as well as internal feelings such as hunger. Veitch has 'perceives', but this risks confusion with the Latin verb *percipere*, which Descartes reserves for purely intellectual forms of cognition. The paraphrase 'perceives through the senses' will normally do for *sentire*; but the present context requires not an achievement-verb but some expression compatible with the possibility of dreaming and universal deception. Hence the somewhat cumbersome but unavoidable paraphrase 'has sensory perceptions'. For alternatives quoted above see D. A. Cress (ed.), *René Descartes, Meditations on First Philosophy* (Indianapolis: Hackett, 1979), 19; E. S. Haldane and G. T. R. Ross (eds.), *The Philosophical Works of Descartes* (Cambridge: Cambridge University Press, 1911), i. 153; J. Veitch, *Descartes, Discourse on Method, Meditations and Principles* (London: Dent, 1912), ad loc.

[6] *Principles of Philosophy* [*Principia philosophiae*, 1644], pt. I art. 9 (AT VIII 7–8: CSM I 195).

that they have special features that set them apart from the other members of the list. This point cannot be developed in the Second Meditation, but has to wait until the Sixth, when the existence of a non-deceiving God has been established, and the way is open for re-establishing the belief in the existence of bodies in general and one's own body in particular. Descartes is then able to give a much fuller treatment of sensation and imagination, and though these activities are still classified as types of thinking, they are singled out for distinctive treatment: the faculties of sensation and imagination are, says Descartes, 'faculties for certain special modes of thinking'.[7] When Frans Burman interviewed Descartes in April 1648, he asked the philosopher about this phrase, and Descartes (reportedly) gave the following account of what he meant by a 'special mode of thinking':

When external objects act on my senses, they print on them an idea, or rather a figure of themselves. And when the mind attends to these images imprinted on the gland [i.e. on the pineal gland] in this way it is said to have sense-perception (sentire). When, on the other hand, the images on the gland are imprinted not by external objects but by the mind itself, which fashions and shapes them in the brain in the absence of external objects, then we have imagination. The difference between sense-perception and imagination is really just this, that in sense-perception the images are imprinted on the brain by external objects which are actually present, while in the case of imagination the images are imprinted by the mind without any external objects, and with the windows shut, as it were.[8]

These remarks suggest that the 'specialness' of both imagination and sense-perception consists in the fact that their exercise requires physiological activity. The point is not such a straightforward one as may at first appear. Obviously, seeing and hearing require eyes and ears; this is an analytic truth. Furthermore, these activities require the possession of optic and auditory nerves—facts that seventeenth-century investigators were beginning to investigate properly for the first time. Descartes was of course very interested in these facts, but they are not the reason for his insistence here that the faculty of sense-perception involves physiological activity; for his claim covers imagination as well as sense-perception, and yet there are

---

[7] facultates specialibus quibusdam modis cogitandi (AT VII 78: CSM II 54).

[8] AT V 162–3: CSMK 334–5. Cf. J. Cottingham (ed.), *Descartes's Conversation with Burman* (Oxford; Clarendon, 1976), 27 and 74 ff.

no obvious 'organs' or 'nerves' of imagination.[9] The kind of physiological activity Descartes has in mind in this context is not activity of specialized organs or nerve-fibres, but brain activity—movements in the pineal gland at the centre of the brain.

At this point the modern reader may feel inclined to interject: '*Of course* sense-perception and imagination require the occurrence of brain activity. Descartes may have got the details wrong—he may have talked of movements in the pineal gland rather than electro-chemical changes in the cerebral cortex—but what is so remarkable about his having recognized the principle?' The answer is highly instructive. For we must remember that Descartes, the same Descartes who insists that sense-perception and imagination require the occurrence of physiological events, is quite satisfied—indeed convinced—that doubting, understanding, affirming, denying, and willing can often occur as 'pure actions of the soul'; that is, they can occur without any physiological events whatsoever taking place.[10] We thus have a philosophical puzzle on our hands and one that is, as far as I know, seldom if ever discussed in the Cartesian literature: what convinced Descartes that sensory experience and imagination involve brain activity, when he was quite happy with analysing doubting, willing, and understanding as utterly non-corporeal?

Part of the answer to this lies in some remarkable things that Descartes has to say about the phenomenology of imagination. He notes in the Sixth Meditation that the exercise of the imagination is not at all like that of the pure intellect. When I think of a thousand-sided figure, there are certain properties I can know with absolute clarity and distinctness that it possesses. (For example, I can demonstrate that it has a thousand angles, and I can prove that this is as true and self-evident as that a triangle has three angles.) But if it is a question not of pure intellection but of imagination, things are very different. Imagination, Descartes notes, requires a 'peculiar effort of mind'.[11] This is apparent from experience. We can discuss and demonstrate

---

[9] The Aristotelians, it is true, talked of a 'common' sensorium which was the organ of the imagination but they were pretty hazy about its structure and location. Cf. Aristotle, *De Anima* [c.325 BC], bk. III ch. 3.

[10] Willing, it is true, may terminate in a bodily movement (e.g. in the case of a volition to raise the arm). But, says Descartes, some volitions (e.g. the desire to love God) terminate in the soul, in which case they are, from start to finish, non-corporeal. Cf. *Passions of the Soul* [*Les Passions de l'âme*, 1649], pt. I art. 18 (AT XI 343: CSM I 335).

[11] *peculiaris animi contentio* (AT VII 73: CSM II 51).

properties of the dodecahedron with just as much ease as we can discuss and demonstrate properties of a triangle; but imagining a dodecahedron is beyond most of us. Most people can get up to a pentagon or a hexagon, but then it starts to get harder and harder.

It is important not to misunderstand Descartes here. He is not, I think, suggesting that purely intellectual acts are always easy and imaginative acts are always hard. Some purely intellectual activities—for example, those involved in higher mathematics—are no doubt extremely demanding; while some imaginative acts—imagining a dog, for example, or a circle—are no doubt easy enough. What Descartes is appealing to is the inner, phenomenological quality or 'flavour' of an act of imagination: as we picture the pentagon, and then the hexagon, and continue on up to the larger figures, we are conscious each time of a curious 'gap' between our purely intellectual cognition of the figure in question, and our ability to image or visualize it. This strange sensation of having to wait until the figure 'comes' is, Descartes considers, evidence that what is involved is not a pure, non-corporeal act of the soul: what is happening is that in order for us to form an image, complicated physical events have to occur in the brain—events that, without practice and effort, we often find it hard to bring about at will. And so this strange sensation of effort we experience when trying to imagine a complex geometrical figure is cited as good evidence that we are not pure *res cogitantes* (thinking things) but that we are somehow united to a sometimes recalcitrant collection of matter—the body: 'When I give more attentive consideration to what imagination is, it seems to be nothing else but an application of the cognitive faculty to a body which is intimately present to it.' This is how Descartes puts it in the Sixth Meditation. The rather more detailed story in the *Conversation with Burman* tells us that imagining involves the mind attempting to fashion actual images in the brain; a similar story appears in the *Passions of the Soul*.[12]

It is interesting that Descartes offers us a precisely similar argument—one based on phenomenological considerations—when he discusses the faculty of sensory awareness (*sentire*) later on in the Sixth Meditation. On this occasion he focuses not on the 'external senses'—vision, hearing, etc.—but on the 'internal senses' such as hunger and thirst. The passage is one of

---

[12] Sixth Meditation, AT VII 71–2: CSM II 50. *Conversation with Burman*, 27 and 74 ff. (AT V 162: CSMK 345); *Passions of the Soul*, pt. I art. 43 (AT XI 361: CSM I 340).

the best known in Descartes: 'Nature teaches me by these sensations of pain hunger and thirst...that I am not merely present in my body as a sailor is present in a ship, but that I am very closely joined, and as it were, intermingled with it, so that I and the body form a unit.'[13] Commentators on Descartes's theory of the mind generally end the quotation at this point and go on to say something about how dualism cannot cope with causal interactions between mind and body. But if we complete the quotation, it becomes clear that the point of the passage is to draw our attention to the peculiar phenomenology of sensation—a phenomenology that Descartes regards as evidence for the fact that sensory awareness, like imagination, does not belong to us qua incorporeal 'thinking things', but attaches to us qua embodied beings:

If this were not so [i.e. if I and the body did not form a unit] I who am nothing but a thinking thing would not *feel pain* when the body was hurt, but would *perceive the damage purely by the intellect*, just as a sailor perceives by sight if anything in his ship is broken. Similarly, when the body needed food or drink, I should have an explicit understanding of the fact, instead of having confused sensations of hunger and thirst. For these sensations of hunger, thirst, pain and so on, are nothing but confused modes of thinking which arise from the union and as it were intermingling of the mind with the body.[14]

It is worth asking here, what things would be like, phenomenologically, for a pure thinking thing (e.g. a spirit or an angel), to which God had temporarily attached a body. This may seem to be a bizarre excursus into speculative medieval theology, but its point, I hope, will emerge in a moment. The answer that Descartes would appear to offer, on the basis of the passage just quoted, is that the awareness such a being had of his bodily condition would lack any phenomenological dimension; it would lack any 'colour' or 'flavour'. There would simply be purely intellectual judgements of the kind 'this body needs food', or 'this body is damaged'. Now of course we human beings make such judgements too: when educated diabetics take a blood sample and analyse it, they know, intellectually, that they require sugar; when I accidentally put my hand on a hot stove, and then inspect the result, I know, intellectually, that tissue damage has occurred. But of course this is not the whole story. The diabetic feels a funny dizzy feeling when

---

[13] AT VII 81: CSM II 56.   [14] Ibid., emphasis supplied.

his blood sugar is low; I feel a characteristically sickening flash of pain when my hand touches the stove. These sensations cannot, Descartes insists, be clearly and distinctly conceived: sensations like that 'curious tugging of the stomach' (*nescio quae vellicatio ventriculi*, literally the 'I-know-not-what tugging')[15] that I call 'hunger' are inherently 'confused', like the strange feeling of effort we have when we try to picture a dodecahedron. The reason for the gap between, on the one hand, understanding, doubting, affirming, denying, and willing and, on the other hand, imagining and having sensory experiences, now begins to emerge. The last two are not the transparently clear cognitive faculties of a thinking being; they have an inherently confused, indefinable, subjective quality—a quality that betrays the fact that what is involved is not the pure mental activity of an incorporeal mind, but the activity of a hybrid unit, a human being.

The results of our analysis of Descartes's account of imagination and sensation thus show that these faculties are not, for Descartes, straightforwardly 'mental' (after the fashion of e.g. understanding). For (1) their exercise always requires the occurrence of physiological activity in the brain; and (2) their characteristic phenomenology ('what it is like' for us to exercise these faculties) suggests that they belong to us not qua minds, but qua embodied beings. The upshot is that there is an important sense in which these faculties cannot properly be accommodated within Descartes's official dualistic schema. They are not readily assignable either to a *res cogitans* or to a *res extensa*.

3. Dualism versus Trialism

What has emerged so far is that the very account of sensation and imagination that Descartes himself provides puts his official dualism under considerable pressure. In the remainder of this chapter, I want to follow up this point by exploring the emergence in Descartes's writings, alongside his official dualism, of a more flexible trialistic pattern.

I referred, at the beginning of the chapter, to a passage in the correspondence with Elizabeth where Descartes classifies human attributes in terms not of a dualistic but of a threefold or trialistic pattern. He speaks of three

---

[15] Sixth Meditation, AT VII 76 line 9: CSM II 53.

'primitive notions': that of extension (comprising shape and motion), which is assignable to the body alone; that of thought (comprising understanding and volition), which is assignable to the mind alone; and finally the notion of the 'union' of mind and body (comprising the results of psychophysical interactions such as 'sensations and passions').[16] Commentators, it must be said, have expressed some irritation with this passage: how, it is asked, can a notion be called 'primitive' if it is dependent on a union of two elements? A mule can hardly be called a 'primitive' species if it comes from the union of a horse and an ass. Descartes has perhaps not expressed himself too helpfully here. But something of what he is getting at may become a little clearer in the light of our earlier discussion of the 'hybrid' faculties of sensation and imagination. If sensory experience and imagination cannot properly be treated either as modes of extension or as modes of thought, then a separate category is required. To pursue the mule analogy a little further: this hybrid animal may be the result of a union of two more primitive species, but for all that it has genuine, distinctive properties of its own which cannot satisfactorily be classified either as equine properties or as asinine properties. Thus what Descartes may be moving towards is the idea that, though the subject of sensations and feelings may not be a primitive substance, the *attributes* of sensation and feeling nonetheless fall into a distinct and irreducible category of their own. We shall return to this point later.

The trialistic grid that appears in the correspondence with Elizabeth is no isolated aberration, but often recurs when Descartes has to confront the phenomenon of sensory experience. In the Sixth Set of Replies, when prodded by Mersenne and others, Descartes provides an extended discussion of the faculty of sense-perception; and he produces an analysis in terms of not two but three 'grades' of sensory response (*tres gradus in sensu*):

The first is limited to the immediate stimulation of the bodily organs by external objects; this can consist in nothing but the motion of the particles of the organs and any change of shape and position resulting from this motion. The second grade comprises all the immediate effects produced in the mind as a result of its being united with a bodily organ which is affected in this way; such effects include

---

[16] Letter to Elizabeth of 21 May 1643, AT III 665: CSMK 218; cf. letter to Elizabeth of 28 June 1643 (AT III 692: CSMK 227). To be strictly accurate, Descartes speaks in both these passages of the soul (*l'âme*) rather than the mind (*l'esprit*); but for him the two terms are, in this kind of context, virtually interchangeable.

the perceptions of pain, pleasure, thirst, hunger, colours, sound, taste, smell and the like, which arise from the union and as it were intermingling of the mind and body, as I explained in the Sixth Meditation. The third grade includes all the judgements about things outside us which we have been accustomed to make from our earliest years.[17]

Later on, Descartes provides more detail. Suppose we are looking at some physical object—say a stick. The first grade of sensory response comprises motion in the optic nerves and the brain, which, says Descartes, is common to us and the brutes. The second grade extends to the 'mere perception of the colour and light reflected by the stick' and arises from the fact that the mind is intimately conjoined with the body; 'nothing further should be referred to the sensory faculty (*sensus*)', if we wish to distinguish it carefully from the intellect. Lastly, the third grade of sensory response comprises rational judgements about the properties of the stick, for example its size, shape, and distance from the observer; this, despite the common view, should not be attributed to the sensory faculty but 'depends on the intellect alone'.[18]

What exactly is going on here, and why are we offered this curious threefold pattern instead of (as one might have expected), a simple dualistic analysis of sense-perception into (1) the physical events involved and (2) the mental events involved? To answer this it will help to go back to the instructive example of hunger. The standard 'dualistic' conception analyses hunger in terms of two sets of events—those involving modifications of extension and those involving modifications of thought. But in fact there are not two but *three* aspects to hunger. First there are the 'purely physical' events—the fall in blood sugar, the contraction of the stomach, and so on; these are purely physical in the sense that they could occur in a completely anaesthetized or comatose patient.[19] Secondly, there are the 'purely intellectual' events that Descartes attributes to the soul. These are completely 'colourless' and dispassionate judgements, such as 'my body needs food';[20] to these may be added dispassionate volitions, such as the

---

[17] Sixth Replies, AT VII 436–7: CSM II 294–5.   [18] Sixth Replies, AT VII 437–8: CSM II 295.

[19] Cf. Descartes's description of digestion and nutrition in an artificially constructed android: *Traité de l'homme* [c.1633], AT XI 120 ff: CSM I 99 ff.

[20] Strictly speaking Descartes attributes only pure cognition or mental perception to the intellect; judgement is ascribed to the will (cf. Fourth Meditation). When speaking more loosely, however, Descartes uses the term 'intellectual' to cover both volitions and mental perceptions (cf. AT VII 438: CSM II 295).

calm formation of the intention to take food. Thirdly, and quite distinct from the first two, there is that indefinable 'I-know-not-what tugging' sensation that we call the feeling of hunger.

I say it is quite distinct from the first two notions for the following reasons: (1a) It could occur in the absence of a fall in blood sugar and a contraction of the stomach; someone, for example, might be hypnotized, or diseased,[21] in such a way that he honestly reported that he felt hungry, even though his blood sugar was high and his stomach full. (1b) Conversely, the bodily events—fall in blood sugar and contraction of stomach—could occur without the sensation, as in the case of an anaesthetized patient. So the sensation is neither a sufficient nor a necessary condition for the occurrence of the bodily events mentioned.

What is more, it is neither a sufficient nor a necessary condition for the occurrence of the 'purely intellectual' events (the judgements and volitions described earlier). For (2a) one could have the sensation without forming the belief that the body needed food, and without forming an intention to eat. You might, for example, believe that the sensation had been implanted by the devil, to tempt you into taking food when your body did not require it. A more interesting (though controversial) example is that of a young child of about 3 years old who, as mealtimes approach, will sometimes say things like 'my tummy hurts' or 'my tummy feels funny'; it seems a reasonable hypothesis that what the child is having is precisely that indefinable sensation which, if it occurred in an older child or an adult, would lead to the judgement 'I need food'. (2b) Conversely, one could form the belief that one needed food, and the intention to eat, without the sensation of hunger. One might, for example, be deprived of that sensation, perhaps as a result of a stroke, and have to rely on some expedient such as taking blood-sugar analyses every few hours, in order to make sure that the body got enough food.

The three notions involved in the analysis of hunger are thus quite genuinely distinct in the way just explicated. Those who need more convincing are invited to ponder on one of those perplexing but strangely illuminating Kripkean questions that begin 'what would God have to do...?'[22] What would God have to do to create a being that was hungry in the way in which normal adult human beings are hungry? Well, he would have to

---

[21] Cf. Descartes's dropsical patient, AT VII 84: CSM II 58 (Sixth Meditation).
[22] Cf. S. Kripke, *Naming and Necessity* [1972] rev. 2nd edn., (Oxford: Blackwell, 1980), pt. III.

do three things. (1) He would have to create a being with a body whose nutrient levels sometimes fell below a desirable minimum for health and activity; (2) he would have to create in that being an intellectual awareness of when its bodily condition was such that it was necessary to replenish those nutritional levels; and (3) he would have to bring it about that when the nutritional levels fell, the being had an unpleasant sensation of a characteristic kind—the kind we refer to when we talk about 'feeling hungry'. It seems clear that God could do any one, or any two, of these things, without doing the other(s). If he did (1) alone he would have created an automaton, or perhaps an amoeba (assuming these creatures have no sensations of hunger). If he did (1) plus (2), then he would have created an automaton hooked up to a pure intellect—for example a mechanical body controlled by an angel, or perhaps (to move from angelology to the even more controversial field of artificial intelligence) a robot hooked up to a sophisticated language-using computer that had no sensations, but was able to form intentions and make the judgement that it needed to top up its nutritional levels or its energy reserves.[23] Finally, if he did (1) plus (3) he would have made something like a dog or a cat, that is, a being that sometimes has an empty stomach plus a sensation of hunger, but which has no language or concepts, and hence cannot make the judgement that it requires food.

To avoid possible misunderstanding: the above scenarios are not meant to beg any questions against physicalist theories of the mind. If physicalism is correct, then creating intellectual and sensory awareness does not require God to bring about non-physical events. Having created a non-conscious body, he will simply have to go on to endow it with further complex electrical and chemical properties, and in so doing he will *eo ipso* have endowed it with intellectual and sensory awareness.[24]

At this point, it may be helpful to provide two illustrative tables incorporating some of our results so far. If we follow Descartes's official dualistic classification, we have only two available categories, extension and thought; the logically possible permutations of these give us a four-line table (Table 9.1).

---

[23] The example is controversial because Searle and others have argued that it is quite wrong to attribute intentional states to even the most sophisticated AI devices. See J. Searle, 'Minds, Brains, and Programs' in D. Hofstadter and D. Dennett (eds.), *The Mind's I* (Harmondsworth: Penguin, 1982).

[24] For this view see B. Williams, *Descartes: The Project of Pure Enquiry* (Harmondsworth: Penguin, 1978), 296: 'If we conceive a world determined just as ours is with regard to all the physical facts, then surely we have already included the facts of persons having pains and thoughts and being in other conscious states?'

TABLE 9.1

Extension	Thought	Item
yes	yes	human being
yes	no	animal; plant; stone
no	yes	spirit (angel; God)
no	no	[nothingness]

Notice several unsatisfactory features of this schema. First, there is no proper place for animals: they are dumped into the non-conscious inanimate world of mere extension. Second, the phenomenon of sensation is, even in the case of man, left out of the picture, unexplained. As we saw in the first half of the chapter, it does not belong in any straightforward way under the category of thinking; nor is it a purely physiological phenomenon, such as, for example, kidney filtration. It just 'arises', inexplicably, when an extended object is 'intermingled' with a thinking being.

Now let us see how the picture looks if sensation is treated as a third category, distinct from extension and thought. We now have not four but eight possibilities (see Table 9.2). Since sensation is treated as a separate category, this allows for the possibility of thought without sensation and vice versa. That is, it allows for the (not entirely fanciful) possibility of beings with intellect but no sensations or feelings; and it also allows for the possibility that we know to be actualized on this planet, namely that of beings with feelings and sensations but no thought. Descartes's official dualistic schema of course rules out this last possibility: the official line is that there are no non-thinking but sentient creatures; animals are mere mechanical automata. But it is interesting that in several places Descartes acknowledges the possibility that sensation might occur without thought. The soulless non-thinking manikin described in the 1633 *Treatise on Man* is characterized as having a sensory faculty and an imagination by means of which the ideas of 'colours, sounds, tastes and other such qualities' are impressed on the 'common' sense to be subsequently stored in the memory. And elsewhere, even in much later writings, Descartes speaks of animals such as dogs, monkeys, and birds as having sensations and feelings (e.g. visual sensations and internal feelings such as hunger).[25]

---

[25] *Traité de l'homme*, AT XI 202: CSM I 108; letter to Newcastle of 23 November 1646 (AT IV 569 ff.: CSMK 302 ff. See also Cottingham, 'A Brute to the Brutes?' (Ch. 8, above).

TABLE 9.2

Extension	Thought	Sensation	Item
yes	yes	yes	human being
yes	yes	no	embodied angel (or ?robot controlled by AI device)
yes	no	yes	animal
yes	no	no	plant; stone
no	yes	yes	[no examples]
no	yes	no	spirit (angel; God)
no	no	yes	[no examples]
no	no	no	[nothingness]

To call the model sketched in Table 9.2 'Cartesian' may be misleading; Descartes of course never formulates the threefold distinction involved in such a schematic way. But the table is nonetheless consistent with Descartes's frequent recognition of the special character of sensation, and its recalcitrance to straightforward classification under the categories of extension or thought. One important caveat should, however, be entered with regard to this 'trialistic' schema. Although the three categories listed are distinct in the way explicated earlier, nothing that Descartes says, even in his most trialistic moments, suggests that there are three distinct ontological categories involved here. That is, Descartes never suggests that the world might contain, in addition to a *res extensa* and a *res cogitans*, a *res sentiens* or 'sensing thing', i.e. a separate substance that could have sensations without having any physical properties. Not only are there no examples of such beings (as the right-hand column in lines 5 and 7 of Table 9.2 indicates), but there is every indication that Descartes would have regarded the idea of a non-physical *res sentiens* as ridiculous. A non-corporeal being (e.g. God) does not, Descartes firmly insists in the *Principles*, have the form of awareness we call sensation or sense-perception; sensory experience is by its very nature a property of embodied beings.[26] It seems, then, that at least one of the categories or notions involved in the trialistic scheme is to be construed attributively rather than substantivally. It corresponds to a distinct aspect of a thing's nature, not to a distinct type of thing.

[26] *Principles*, pt. I art. 23 (AT VIII 13: CSM I 200–1.). An interesting question, never directly raised by Descartes, is whether God could not endow a non-corporeal being with conscious states that were qualitatively identical to human sensory experiences. The argument from diabolic deception in the First Meditation implies that this is at least a possibility.

In so far as Descartes recognizes a third category or 'notion' alongside thought and extension without proceeding to reify it as a separate substance, this may be regarded as a significant philosophical improvement on his approach when formulating his initial dualistic distinction. For in distinguishing between thought and extension, Descartes invariably insists on reifying the notion of thought in such a way as to create a separate non-corporeal substance; yet while thought is a distinct and in many ways still mysterious aspect of our nature, what seems overwhelmingly clear to us nowadays is that it cannot subsist on its own, but must somehow be a property of a physical system, or be somehow grounded in a physical substrate.

But even if everything in the universe is ultimately physical, it remains true that there are three quite distinct ways in which we can think about ourselves as human beings, three quite distinct aspects of our humanity. First, there are those countless vitally important events going on inside our bodies that do not presuppose or require any form of consciousness; secondly, there are all the thoughts, beliefs, desires, and intentions which are true of us qua *res cogitantes*—thinking, language-using beings; and thirdly, there are those many curious sensations produced by the effects of the external world and the condition of our own bodies—sensations that we can label, but cannot properly define or explicate in language. A grasp of this trialistic distinction, which Descartes articulates—or comes close to articulating—on several occasions, seems to be an essential step towards achieving a true understanding of our nature. For our nature comprises what we have in common with primitive non-conscious organisms that have a physiology but no sensory experience; what we have in common with more complex animals with whom we share 'confused' and indefinable sensations such as hunger and thirst; and finally, comprises those concept-dependent activities of the intellect and will that set us apart from all other known living things.

IV

Ethics and Religion

10

The Intellect, the Will, and the Passions: Spinoza's Critique of Descartes

1. Introduction

This chapter examines (in sect. 1) Descartes's theory of judgement and (in sect. 2) Spinoza's well-known criticisms of it. I argue (in sect. 3) that, despite some important differences, there are many ways in which Spinoza's views, so far from being anti-Cartesian, can be seen as a natural development of those of Descartes. I then go on to argue (in sect. 4) that Spinoza's general critique of the Cartesian theory of the will does not take sufficient account of what Descartes actually claimed, and that if the Cartesian concept of freedom is properly understood, Spinoza is closer to it than he himself recognized. Finally (in sect. 5) I say a brief word about the relation between the will and the passions, and suggest that here again Spinoza tended to misinterpret Descartes's true position, and as a result exaggerated the difference between his own views and those of Descartes. I hope that it will emerge by the end of the chapter that for all Spinoza's anti-Cartesian flourishes, his views on the will are much closer to those of Descartes than is often supposed.

2. Descartes's Theory of Judgement

Within the general category of conscious thought (*cogitatio*), one may, according to Descartes, distinguish two principal modes of operation: perception, or the operation of the intellect (comprising sensory perception, imagination, and pure intellection), and volition, or the operation of the will (comprising desire, aversion, assertion, denial, and doubt; *Principles*, pt. I art. 32). This distinction is important for many reasons. In the *Passions of the Soul*, for example, it is suggested that perception is a passive faculty of the mind, while volition is active, and this notion seems to have influenced many later thinkers.[1] But in Descartes, the most important application of the distinction concerns the diagnosis of error in our judgements.

Descartes sees the problem of error as a theological problem, rather like the traditional problem of evil. Instead of having to explain away moral or metaphysical evil, Descartes feels himself called upon to explain away intellectual error; but the reasons why an explanation seems called for are closely parallel. Just as, if God is good and the omnipotent Creator of all, it seems odd that there should be evil in the world, similarly, if God is good and the source of all truth, it seems odd that there should be error. More specifically, if God created me and gave me a mind that is, in principle, a reliable instrument for the perception of truth,[2] how does it happen that I often go astray in my judgements?

A standard theological move in coping with the problem of evil was to put the blame on man's exercise of his free will; and Descartes makes the selfsame move in explaining away error. His first premise is that judgement is an act that involves the will as well as the intellect: 'In order to make a judgement, the intellect is of course required [since otherwise nothing would be perceived—there would be no content to the judgement] ... but the will is also required so that, when something is perceived, our assent may then be given' (*Principles*, pt. I art. 34). Descartes's second premise is the celebrated Cartesian thesis that the will extends further than the intellect: *latius patet voluntas quam intellectus*. 'The perception of the intellect extends only to the few objects presented to it and is always extremely limited. The will on the other hand can in a certain sense be called infinite, since we observe that its scope extends to anything' (ibid. 35). Given these two premises, the explanation for error is quite straightforward: 'It is easy for us to extend our will beyond what we clearly perceive; and

---

[1] *Passions of the Soul* [*Passions de l'âme*, 1649], pt. I art. 17 (AT XI 342: CSM I 335). For the active/passive distinction cf. the letter to Regius of May 1641 (AT III 372: CSMK 182); for this distinction in later writers, see George Berkeley, *Philosophical Commentaries* [1707–8], Notebook A, §643, in M. R. Ayers (ed.), *George Berkeley, Philosophical Works* (London: Dent, 1975), 343.

[2] 'My mind does not deceive me, since it is a reliable instrument which I received from God' (AT V 148: CSMK 334). See J. Cottingham (ed.), *Descartes' Conversation with Burman* (Oxford: Clarendon, 1976), 5.

when we do this it is no wonder that we may happen to go wrong' (ibid.).

To complete the theodicy, Descartes adds some further considerations (the most detailed presentation is in the Fourth Meditation). God cannot be blamed for giving us an infinitely extended will; in this he has allowed men to share in one of his divine perfections. Nor can he be blamed for giving us a finite intellect, since if he is going to create at all, he must create creatures less endowed than himself.[3] Moreover, though our intellectual perception is limited, it is, as far as it goes, completely accurate. Whatever we do perceive clearly is true: that is guaranteed by God's goodness. But where we do not perceive something clearly, it is hardly God's fault if we jump in and rashly give our assent where we should have suspended judgement.[4]

How original was Descartes's approach here? According to Anthony Kenny, it was quite new to construe judgement as falling under a conative or appetitive, rather than a cognitive faculty: the doctrine that judgement is an act of the will has, he claims, no precedent in medieval or scholastic philosophy.[5] However that may be, Descartes's formal account in the *Principles* makes it clear that whenever judgement occurs, both the intellect and the will are always involved; intellectual perception and voluntary assent are both necessary conditions for the occurrence of a judgement (ibid. art. 34). And in broad outlines at least, this follows the traditional account of judgement. As Kenny himself notes, Aquinas makes a clear distinction between, on the one hand, apprehending (*apprehendere*) some fact (which happens willy nilly *per virtutem luminis naturalis*, through the power of the natural light), and, on the other hand, assenting (*assentire*) to what is apprehended, which is 'in our power and falls under the command of the will'.[6] This Thomist distinction, which Descartes broadly accepts,

---

[3] *Meditations on First Philosophy* [*Meditationes de prima philosophia*, 1641], Fourth Meditation: 'It is in the nature of a finite intellect to lack understanding of many things, and it is in the nature of a created intellect to be finite' (AT VII 60: CSM II 42). The thought that created items must necessarily have some imperfection is developed in Leibniz; see G. W. Leibniz, *Theodicy: Essays on the Goodness of God, the Liberty of Man and the Origin of Evil* [*Essais de théodicée sur la bonté de Dieu, la liberté de l'homme et l'origine du mal*, 1710], pt. I §20; trans. E. M. Huggard (London: Routledge, 1951), 40.

[4] Fourth Meditation, loc. cit.; cf. *Principles of Philosophy* [*Principia philosophiae*, 1644], pt. I art. 38 (AT VIII 19: CSM I 205).

[5] A. Kenny, 'Descartes on the Will', in R. J. Butler (ed.), *Cartesian Studies* (Oxford: Blackwell, 1972), ch. 1.

[6] Thomas Aquinas, *Summa theologiae* [1266–73], IaIIae (First Part of the Second Part), qu.17 art. 6; cited in Kenny, 'Descartes on the Will', 2–3. On the question of innovation, Kenny argues that

has an obvious and straightforward basis in common sense: there seems a clear intuitive difference between entertaining some proposition—being apprised of its content, as it were—and actually asserting it or assenting to its truth. (Take, for example, the proposition that there is life on other worlds; this is a proposition whose content we all understand, though we may be divided, as the scientific community in fact is at present, between those who believe it is true, those who are sceptical, and those who are agnostic).

3. Spinoza's Critique

In his exposition of Descartes's *Principles* (*Principia Philosophiae Renati Descartes*, 1663), Spinoza gives a full account of the Cartesian diagnosis of the causes of error and its remedy. (The account is tolerably accurate, though there are some oversimplifications to which we shall return later.) 'Error depends entirely on the use of the freedom of the will. Since the will is free to determine itself, it follows that we do have the power to contain our faculty of assenting within the limits of the intellect, and so can bring it about that we do not fall into error' (G I 174: C 258).[7] But Spinoza's own view of the matter is strongly at odds with this, as is explicitly recorded in the Preface to the work penned by his friend Lodewijk Meyer: 'Although the author felt himself to be obliged not to depart a hair's breadth from Descartes's opinion … let no one think that he is teaching here either his own opinions or only those he approves of … An example of this is what is said concerning the freedom of the will. For he [Spinoza] does not think that the will is distinct from the intellect, much less endowed with such freedom' (G I 131: C 229).

First, the will is not distinct from the intellect; secondly, the will is not endowed with the kind of freedom that Descartes postulated. Both these points of difference were developed fully by Spinoza in the *Ethics*. I shall leave the second till sect. 5 and concentrate here and in the next section on the first.

Descartes's thesis that judgement is not just commanded by the will, but is itself an act of will, is new and requires explanation.

[7] 'G' refers by volume and page number to Spinoza, *Opera*, ed. C. Gebhardt (Heidelberg: Winters, 1925). 'C' designates *The Collected Works of Spinoza*, trans. E. Curley (Princeton: Princeton University, 1985), i.

In *Ethics*, pt. II prop. 49 cor.,[8] Spinoza asserts that the will and the intellect are one and the same: 'voluntas et intellectus sunt unum et idem'. This uncompromising departure from Cartesian orthodoxy is perhaps initially a little surprising given that Spinoza fully accepts Descartes's definition of the will as 'a faculty of affirming or denying' (pt. II prop. 48). For in order to affirm X, one might have supposed, we must first understand the content of X: the faculty of affirming can only begin to operate, it might seem, once the faculty of understanding has done its work. As Descartes puts it: 'When we direct our will towards something, we must always have some sort of understanding of it' (AT VII 377; CSM II 259). Spinoza, however, makes it clear that he regards the notions of a faculty of understanding and a separate faculty of willing as 'fictions'.[9] And at *Ethics* pt. II prop. 49, he proceeds to provide a demonstration that the will and the intellect are identical, taking as an illustration the proposition that a triangle has angles equal to two right angles. Spinoza argues (1) that the affirmation or judgement that this property holds is inseparable from the concept or idea of the triangle—the affirmation cannot be conceived without the idea. Then he goes on to argue the converse, (2) that the idea cannot be conceived without the affirmation. Presumably this is because to understand that X is a triangle is inseparable from affirming that X's angles equal two right angles. Thus, the affirmation cannot be conceived without the idea, nor the idea without the affirmation; and if X cannot be conceived without Y nor vice versa, then (by Definition Two at the start of *Ethics*, pt. II) there is no essential difference between X and Y (X belongs to the essence of Y, says Definition Two, if X cannot be conceived without Y and vice versa). Spinoza concludes that so far from being distinct from intellection, will is 'something universal which is predicated of all ideas' (universale quid quod de omnibus ideis predicatur).[10]

The first premise of this argument (namely, that the affirmation of X is inseparable from the idea of X) is clearly correct. Evidently, one cannot affirm a proposition without perceiving its content. But what of

---

[8] *Ethics* [*Ethica more geometrico demonstrata, c.*1665]. References are to part and proposition numbers, which are common to all editions; the suffixes 'cor.' and 'schol.' refer respectively to a corollary or scholium annexed to a given proposition.

[9] For a discussion of Spinoza's somewhat obscure support for this claim at *Ethics*, pt. II prop. 48 schol., see E. M. Curley, 'Descartes, Spinoza and the Ethics of Belief', in E. Freeman and M. Mandelbaum (eds.), *Spinoza: Essays in Interpretation* (La Salle, Ill.: Open Court, 1975), 167.

[10] G II 135 line 3: C 489.

the converse (premise 2)? Recent commentators have on the whole been very sympathetic to Spinoza's refusal here to separate perception from affirmation. Thus R. J. Delahunty applauds Spinoza for having grasped an important insight: so far from its being true that judgement consists of an act of will that supervenes on the entertaining of a proposition, judgement is, says Delahunty (following Bell), 'phenomenologically basic'.[11] Well, if this means that introspection reveals that a judgement cannot be separated into a perceptual and a volitional component, I am not at all clear how introspection does, or indeed could, reveal any such thing. Delahunty, however, goes on to develop his argument in support of Spinoza, by reference to logico-grammatical considerations. 'The occurrence of an unembedded thought', he tells us, 'is naturally or inherently assertoric'; and this, he claims, shows that Spinoza is right in refusing to analyse judgement as a compound of (1) the entertaining of an idea and (2) the giving of assent. This argument seems to me to illustrate the dangers of approaching seventeenth-century philosophy from a modern, post-Fregean interpretative standpoint. It is, of course, correct that an indicative sentence is conventionally taken to be assertoric unless this assertive or assertoric force is nullified by the context, or by the scope of some special operator (e.g. inverted commas, or the prefix 'once upon a time'); but it is surely a mistake to transfer these truths about the grammar of declarative utterances to the realm of individual thoughts. The context in which Descartes and Spinoza are operating is not that of public discourse but of private thought. The paradigm we should keep in front of our minds is not that of A's making a statement to B, but that of an idea's arising in A's consciousness. And when I have an idea, I am not (at least not typically) uttering or conveying a proposition to someone else. So whether or not Spinoza's position on the inseparability of idea and assertion is correct, it seems to me that it cannot plausibly be supported simply by reference to the logical grammar of declarative utterances.

The distinction between public discourse and private thought is clearly recognized by E. M. Curley in an illuminating defence of Spinoza's theory of judgement. Curley notes that in the realm of public discourse there is often a gap, as it were, between the declarations of a speaker and his judgement as to the truth; but in the realm of private thought such a gap

---

[11] R. J. Delahunty, *Spinoza* (London: Routledge, 1985), 35.

is impossible: 'It is nonsense to speak of someone as saying-in-his-heart or judging what he does not believe to be true.'[12] In short, to say (publicly) that P and to judge that P is true are different; but to say (privately) that P *is* to judge that P is true. This is undoubtedly correct; but it is not clear that it closes the gap between intellectual perception and voluntary assent. For it seems that one may 'entertain' (in one's heart) a proposition, while nevertheless withholding assent or denial. Is not the 'suspending of judgement' required by the Cartesian programme just this? Curley is well aware of the possibility of this sort of reply, and he meets it by providing a rival, Spinozistic, analysis of what it is to suspend judgement. It will be convenient, however, to postpone discussion of this until the next section.

Another commentator who sees merit in Spinoza's view of judgement is Jonathan Bennett. Most of us, says Bennett in his book on the *Ethics*, would agree with Spinoza as against Descartes that belief is not a 'voluntary intellectual act that we choose to perform on a given proposition'.[13] 'We cannot', says Bennett, 'switch beliefs on and off at will'; this he suggests (though without fully defending the suggestion) may be a 'conceptual truth stemming from the structure of the concept of belief'.[14] Bennett is clearly right to point out that belief is not something we switch on and off at will (though what appears to be involved here is a plausible generalization rather than a conceptual truth, for it does seem that sometimes at least we can decide what to believe—or certainly what not to believe). In general though it is true that we do not go around deciding what to believe. But to suppose that this fact is fatal to Descartes's position is to miss, or to misrepresent, what Descartes is saying about the relation between the intellect and the will. The fact is that Descartes is quite prepared to allow that there are many cases where believing a proposition is not something entirely within the control of the will—and interestingly such cases would include the very type of case that Spinoza takes as his illustration: a judgement concerning the elementary properties of a triangle. As several commentators have recognized,[15] Descartes maintains that in the case of

---

[12] Curley, 'Descartes, Spinoza, and the Ethics of Belief', 177.

[13] J. Bennett, *A Study of Spinoza's Ethics* (Cambridge: Cambridge University Press, 1984), 162.

[14] Ibid. 160.

[15] Kenny, 'Descartes on the Will', 21; Curley, 'Descartes, Spinoza and the Ethics of Belief', 165. See also the earlier comments in F. Alquié (ed.), *Œuvres Philosophiques de Descartes* (Paris: Garnier, 1967), ii. 461.

clearly and distinctly perceived propositions, I do not have the two-way power to assent or dissent. On the contrary, it is asserted in the Fourth Meditation that 'ex magna luce in intellectu magna consequitur propensio in voluntate' ('a great light in the intellect gives rise to a great propensity in the will'). 'I cannot but judge', says Descartes, 'that what I understand so clearly is true' ('non possum non judicare id quod tam clare intelligo verum esse').[16]

In the case of clearly and distinctly perceived propositions, then, Spinoza's account of the relation between the intellect and the will, so far from being radically opposed to Descartes's account, has some striking affinities with what Descartes himself says when he argues that clear and distinct perception is inseparable from assent. Of course, to say that X is inseparable from Y, or follows automatically on Y, is not to say that X is identical with Y, so we are still short of the Spinozan claim that the intellect and the will are 'one and the same'. But as we have seen, Spinoza argues for the essential identity of X and Y on the basis that it is impossible to conceive of X without Y and vice versa. So if it were to turn out that one's perceptual state always necessarily fixed one's belief states, so that it was inconceivable for the latter to change without a change in the former, then we would at least be partly on the way to the Spinozan position that there is no real distinction between intellect and will.

4. Suspension of Assent and Inadequacy of Perception

But despite the convergence between Spinoza and Descartes over the psychology of clear and distinct perception, there remains a crucial point on which their views appear to be in headlong conflict, namely the question of what happens when a proposition is *not* clearly and distinctly perceived. In such cases, Descartes tells us, we can *either* jump in and rashly give our assent, *or*, more prudently (following the Cartesian recipe for the avoidance of error), we can decide to withhold assent (AT VII 62: CSM II 43). Here the

---

[16] AT VII 58–9: CSM II 41 (tense altered from past to present). There are many other passages where Descartes asserts the thesis of the irresistibility of the clear and distinct perceptions of the intellect; lack of assent is possible only when there is lack of attention. See the letter to Mersenne of end of May 1637 (AT I 366: CSMK 56) and the letter to Mesland of 2 May 1644 (AT IV 117: CSMK 234), discussed in Kenny, 'Descartes on the Will', 21 ff.

will seems to be presented as a wholly separate and independent faculty that operates at one remove, as it were, from the perceptions of the intellect.

On this issue, it is the Cartesian position that appears to harmonize with our common-sense beliefs about what happens when we do not perceive something clearly, and Spinoza himself recognizes this: 'It can be objected that experience seems to teach nothing more clearly than that we can suspend our judgement so as not to assent to things we perceive. For example, someone who imagines (*fingit*) a winged horse does not on that account grant that there is a winged horse ... Therefore experience seems to teach that the will or faculty of assenting is free and different from the faculty of understanding' (*Ethics*, pt. II prop. 49 schol.).[17] Having, apparently, devised a rod for his own back (in fact the example of the winged horse was one that Spinoza himself had earlier employed, in his exposition of Descartes's *Principles*, to illustrate the plausibility of the Cartesian approach),[18] Spinoza now attempts to nullify its impact: 'I deny that a man affirms nothing in so far as he perceives. For what is perceiving a winged horse other than affirming wings of the horse?'[19]

What Spinoza seems to be saying here is that the mere idea of a winged horse involves what might be called 'affirmatory predication'. The object referred to, or depicted by the idea, namely *equus*, has ascribed to it the predicate *alatus*. One could debate whether there is any merit in adopting this distinctly attenuated sense of 'affirmatory' (which would entail that a composite idea of the form RA where R is a referring expression and A an attribute would automatically count as 'affirmatory'). But however that may be, Spinoza's strategy seems to involve a gross *ignoratio elenchi*. For the objection originally raised was that one can have an idea of a winged horse without affirming its existence. And Spinoza's point about the 'affirmatory' nature of the predicate 'winged' leaves this quite untouched.

What Spinoza goes on to say, however, is much more promising:

If the Mind perceived nothing else except the winged horse, it would regard it as present to itself, and would not have any cause of doubting its existence, or any faculty of dissenting, unless either the imagination of the winged horse were joined to an idea which excluded the existence of the same horse, or the mind perceived that its idea of a winged horse was inadequate. And then either it will necessarily deny the horse's existence, or it will necessarily doubt it.[20]

<hr />

[17] G II 133: C 487.   [18] G I 173: C 257.   [19] G II 134: C 489.   [20] Ibid.

This offers us a trichotomy. For any object represented by an idea, there are, as it were, three modes of presentation. Either the object is presented as actually existing, or (as in the case of a round square) as excluding existence, or, thirdly, the idea manifests itself as inadequate—that is, it contains insufficient information from which to deduce the existence or non-existence of its object. But in this third case, it is not a matter of our having to decide to suspend assent; rather assent is already ruled out by the manifest inadequacy of the perception. As Spinoza himself puts it a little earlier, 'when we say that someone suspends judgement, we are saying merely that he sees that he does not perceive the thing adequately. Suspension of judgement therefore is really a perception, not [a separate act of] free will.'

This position has considerable attractions. E. M. Curley has supported it as follows:

I cannot doubt whether *p* unless I already have some existing tendency to believe *not-p*, unless it already seems to me in some measure that *p* is false. These conflicting tendencies are necessary conditions for doubt, and insofar as I am aware of them and find them to be of approximately equal strength, they are sufficient. Suspending judgement…is not an action I take as a consequence of finding the arguments pro and con are pretty evenly balanced. It is simply the state itself of finding them to be so.[21]

The central point here, I take it, is that abstaining from judgement is not, so to speak, an arbitrary act of will, detached from the perceptions of the intellect; rather it is a perceived equilibrium in the reasons for or against a given proposition. This seems right; but it is interesting to note how close it comes to what Descartes himself says in the First Meditation about the suspension of assent. The meditator who wishes to find indubitable foundations for knowledge cannot simply 'decide' to suspend his previous beliefs. For the *praejudicia* or 'preconceived opinions' thoughtlessly acquired since his childhood are like an army of occupation. They 'capture his belief' (*occupant credulitatem*); his belief is chained (*devincta*) to them by 'long use and the law of custom' (*usus et ius familiaritatis*). His prejudices are like crushing weights (*pondera*) and no progress can be made in freeing oneself from these encumbrances, until some line of thought can be devised whereby the weights are 'counterbalanced' (*aequatis utrimque praejudiciorum ponderibus*).[22]

[21] Curley, 'Descartes, Spinoza, and the Ethics of Belief', 175.   [22] AT VII 22: CSM II 15.

The suspension of assent on Descartes's view is thus not just a mental fiat; it occurs when meditative reflection has thrown up reasons for mistrusting previously held beliefs. The senses have been found to be unreliable in the past; I may now be dreaming; it is even conceivable, for all I know here and now, that the entire external world is a sham. The celebrated Cartesian technique of calling everything into doubt is thus not the exercise of a sovereign will acting 'at one remove' from intellectual perception. It is a technique of rational reflection on the adequacy (or lack of it) of one's basis for belief. It is true that Descartes speaks in the First Meditation of 'turning his will in the opposite direction [from previous beliefs]' (*voluntate plane in contrarium versa*); but the will is employed not in 'suspending assent' *tout court*, but on the decision to explore arguments that provide reasons for doubt. This comes out with particular force in the Sixth Meditation when Descartes provides a kind of résumé of his earlier train of thought (in the three paragraphs beginning *Primo... Postea vero... Nunc autem...*).[23] What Descartes rehearses is not a series of independent decisions of a sovereign will concerning his beliefs, but a series of reflections about the basis of his previous beliefs, the reasons for doubting them, and the foundation for his present confidence in at least some of his judgements. Throughout this résumé, belief is represented as flowing not from volitional decision but from perceptual apprehension of reasons and causes. (Compare the phrasing that introduces this long passage: 'To begin with I shall go back over all the things I previously ... reckoned to be true, and my reasons for thinking this. Next, I will set out my reasons for subsequently calling these things into doubt ... ')[24] It is true that Descartes frequently stresses the single-mindedness and determination needed to pursue his meditations resolutely ('I shall stubbornly persist in this meditation ...'),[25] but his exercise of will is not supposed to exert a direct control on his beliefs. These are always generated by the preponderance of reasons and causes pro or con. One could put the point by saying that we do not, according to Descartes, achieve suspension of assent by a direct act of will. Instead, we decide to follow up a certain line of argument that reveals the inadequacy of

---

[23] AT VII 74–8: CSM II 51–4.

[24] 'Primo repetam quaenam illa sunt quae antehac ... vera esse putavi et quas ob causas id putavi; deinde causes expendam propter quas eadem postea in dubiam revocavi...' (AT VII 74 lines 11 ff.: CSM II 51).   [25] 'Manebo obstinate in hac meditatione defixus' (AT VII 23: CSM II 15).

the grounds for our previously held beliefs, and it is the (intellectual) recognition of this inadequacy that brings suspension of assent. Again, though not exactly what Spinoza says, this is much closer to the Spinozan picture than at first appeared. The Cartesian meditator suspends assent in terms very close to those described by Spinoza: he 'comes to see that he does not perceive the thing adequately' (*Ethics*, pt. II prop. 49 schol).

5. Spinoza and 'Cartesian Freedom'

In Spinoza's critique of Descartes's account of the relation between intellect and will there seem to be two main strands. The first, which we have already examined (at least in part), hinges on Spinoza's theory of judgement and his thesis of the inseparability, in judgement, of the intellect and the will. The second strand relates to a more pervasive and general feature of Spinoza's philosophy—his thoroughgoing determinism. As his contemporary Lodewijk Meyer put it, Spinoza 'does not think that the will is distinct from the intellect, nor that it is endowed with the kind of freedom [that Descartes postulates]'.[26] As Jonathan Bennett has recently put it, 'Spinoza would not use a concept of freedom radical enough to conflict with strict determinism.'[27] And as Spinoza himself put it at *Ethics*, pt. II prop. 48, in the section that leads into the critique of Descartes we have just examined, there is 'no absolute or free will' [sc. of the kind Descartes supposed]: 'nulla est absoluta sive libera voluntas'. Cartesian freedom, Spinoza insists, is a kind of illusion. Men think themselves free because they are conscious of their volitions, but not the causes thereof (*Ethics*, pt. I, appendix). This is, incidentally, one central area of metaphysics where Leibniz aligns himself with Spinoza against Descartes (though the details of his account of freedom are very different from Spinoza's). 'Monsieur Descartes,' writes Leibniz, 'requires a freedom for which there is no need when he insists that the actions of the will of man are entirely undetermined—a thing which never happens'.[28]

For both Spinoza and Leibniz, the non-freedom of the will (in what they take to be the 'absolute' Cartesian sense) follows from the particular

---

[26] G I 131–2: C 229.   [27] Bennett, *A Study of Spinoza's Ethics*, 159.
[28] Leibniz, *Theodicy: Preliminary Discourse*, §69.

brand of rationalism that each of them espouses. The term 'rationalism', like charity, covers a multitude of sins; but in Leibniz's case the denial of 'absolute' freedom flows from his commitment to what Jonathan Bennett has called 'explanatory' rationalism—the refusal to allow the existence of unexplained 'brute facts'.[29] In a universe in which there is a sufficient reason for everything that occurs, there can be no human two-way power such that, when all antecedent conditions are fixed, it is still possible for the agent to decide to X or not to X. For if such a power existed, then the actual decision would be undetermined by the antecedent conditions, so that it would be impossible, even in principle, to have predicted that the decision would go one way rather than the other—a clear violation of the principle of sufficient reason. In the case of Spinoza, the denial of absolute freedom flows from what is often called his 'necessitarianism'—a doctrine expressed most concisely in the *Metaphysical Thoughts*: 'If men clearly understood the whole of nature, they would find everything just as necessary as the things treated of in mathematics; but since this is beyond human understanding, we regard certain things as contingent.'[30] The precise sense in which all things are 'necessary' for Spinoza has been the subject of debate: it is possible, as E. M. Curley has suggested, that he is prepared to allow that individual truths are not absolutely, but only 'relatively' necessary (i.e. they are entailed by antecedent conditions plus nomological statements).[31] But however we construe Spinoza's necessitarianism, a two-way contra-causal power of the will is ruled out. For if I decide to X, then my X-ing is either necessary in some absolute sense, or 'relatively' necessary in the sense that given the total set of antecedent conditions, and the causal laws that govern the universe, it was impossible for me not to have X-ed.

But did Descartes in fact postulate the existence of an absolute, contra-causal freedom of the kind that Spinoza and Leibniz denied? I shall argue that Spinoza (and Leibniz too for that matter) misinterpreted Descartes on this point; the position they take to be the Cartesian one does not

---

[29] Bennett, *A Study of Spinoza's Ethics*, 29.

[30] In the *Metaphysical Thoughts* [*Cogitationes Metaphysicae*, 1663, published as an Appendix to Spinoza's *Exposition of Descartes's Principles*], ch. IX §2 (G 1 266: C 332). In this passage Spinoza explicitly cites a human act (Josiah's burning of the idolaters' bones on Jeroboam's altar) as an example of something that we may mistakenly suppose to be contingent, although it is in fact necessary. Cf. also *Ethics*, pt. I prop. 35.

[31] E. M. Curley, *Spinoza's Metaphysics: An Essay in Interpretation* (Cambridge, Mass.: Harvard University Press, 1969), ch. 3.

correspond to the stance that Descartes centrally and characteristically adopts in his discussions of freedom. The central Cartesian position on freedom, I shall suggest, is much closer to that of Spinoza; indeed there is a sense in which Spinoza's views, so far from being in radical conflict with Descartes's, can be seen as a natural development of those of his predecessor.

To describe Spinoza as having 'misinterpreted' Descartes at once needs qualifying. The absolutist position he attributes to Descartes is one for which some support can be found in the Cartesian texts. Unfortunately, the way Descartes expresses himself concerning the freedom of the will is often confusing; frequently his remarks seem open to an indeterministic interpretation (indeed, when I wrote my introduction to *Descartes' Conversation with Burman* I was persuaded that he was committed to an indeterministic view of the kind Spinoza attributes to him).[32]

Both Leibniz and Spinoza took Descartes's *Principles of Philosophy* as the main source for their view of Descartes on the subject of freedom. We know, of course, that Spinoza took the *Principles* as his text for his detailed exposition of Descartes's views in 1663, and (as already noted) the question of free will is explicitly mentioned in the Preface as one issue where Spinoza's views differ from those of Descartes. As for Leibniz, the phrase 'entirely undetermined', which he uses to describe what he takes to be the Cartesian position on freedom, is lifted directly from the French version of *Principles*, pt I art. 41: 'La toute puissance de Dieu ... laisse les actions des hommes entièrement ... indéterminées' (the supreme power of God ... leaves the actions of human beings entirely ... undetermined).

But there are important respects in which this particular section of the *Principles* is unrepresentative and potentially misleading in the picture it gives of Descartes's views. This is particularly true of the 1647 French version, which was done not by Descartes but by the Abbé Picot. Picot's phrasing talks of human actions being left 'entièrement libres et indéterminées', adding the emphasizer 'entirely' which is not present in the original; furthermore, by conjoining 'free' and 'undetermined' so closely, it almost suggests that being free is, for Descartes, practically equivalent to being undetermined (a highly misleading suggestion, as will appear). But in any case, and irrespective of whether one looks at the French or the original Latin, article 41 is dangerous ground on which to build an interpretation of

---

[32] Cf. Cottingham (ed.), *Descartes' Conversation with Burman*, pp. xxxvi–xl.

Descartes's notion of freedom. For the article does not purport to contain any information about the precise respect in which we are free, or about the way in which, according to Descartes, we exercise our freedom, nor does it touch on the all-important question of how our powers of willing are related to our intellectual perceptions. Instead, it is designed to steer the reader past the notorious theological puzzle of how to reconcile human freedom with divine preordination. As is well known, Descartes was always hesitant and evasive when dealing with areas that might embroil him in ecclesiastical controversy and this is particularly true of the *Principles*—a book he hoped would be approved and adopted as a university text. So what he says on this theological puzzle should be treated with great caution, rather than as a key text for unravelling his account of freedom. What he does say, in any case, is precious little: we cannot grasp how divine power and human freedom are reconcilable, but since we have inner awareness of our freedom, and since the nature of God cannot be grasped by us, it is best not to trouble ourselves with doubts on the matter.

Although Spinoza may have been influenced by the language of *Principles* here at pt. I art. 41, the article he explicitly mentions in his exposition of Descartes's views on freedom[33] is article 39—a passage that at first sight might again be taken as evidence for an indeterministic view, since it appears to identify freedom with a two-way power. Freedom is defined in terms of the ability we have 'to assent or not assent at will in many cases' ('multis ad arbitrium vel assentiri vel non assentiri'). But as Anthony Kenny has noted,[34] it is important to stress that Descartes says *multis*, not *omnibus*: in many cases, not in all cases. It is soon made clear that our power to withhold assent is limited to those matters that are 'not quite certain or fully examined'.[35] In the case of truths clearly and distinctly perceived, it is explained in a later article, we are quite unable to resist giving our assent: 'quoties aliquid clare percipimus, ei sponte assentimur et nullo modo possumus dubitare quin sit verum'.[36]

Now on an 'absolutist' or indeterministic conception, such inability to avoid assenting would negate freedom. Yet Descartes explicitly states in the *Meditations* that we are perfectly free when our will is determined, and our

---

[33] *Principia Philosophiae Renati Descartes*, G I 175: C 258.
[34] Kenny, 'Descartes on the Will', 21.   [35] AT VIII 20 line 5: CSM I 206.
[36] 'whenever we perceive something clearly, we spontaneously give our assent to it and are quite unable to doubt its truth'. *Principles*, pt. I art. 43 (AT VIII 21: CSM I 207).

assent necessitated, by our intellectual perception: 'The more I incline in one direction, either because I clearly understand that reasons of goodness and truth point that way, or because of a divinely produced disposition of my inmost thought, the freer is my choice.'[37] Cartesian freedom here is certainly not an absolute contra-causal power. On the contrary, it is the spontaneous assent that is irresistibly determined by the clear and distinct perception of the intellect. In putting forward this conception of liberty—*liberté éclairée* or 'liberty of enlightenment', as Alquié has aptly termed it[38]—Descartes seems much closer to the compatibilist conception of Spinoza and Leibniz than is suggested by their attacks on 'absolute' Cartesian freedom.

It is clear from Spinoza's exposition of Descartes that he was well aware of these important passages in the Fourth Meditation.[39] How then was he able, at the end of the day, to characterize the Cartesian position on freedom as an absolutist one? Part of the reason for this may perhaps be found in the language Descartes uses, not just in the passages from the *Principles* already mentioned, but also elsewhere in the Fourth Meditation, to describe human liberty. In the Fourth Meditation great stress is laid on the 'perfection' of the will; and Descartes asserts that 'my freedom of choice is so great that the idea of any greater faculty is beyond my grasp; so much so that it is above all in virtue of the will that I understand myself to bear the image and likeness of God'.[40] This talk of a perfect will that is comparable to that of God himself might well suggest that Descartes is committed to an independent contra-causal conception of the will. But aside from the general impression left by Descartes's honorific language regarding the will, there is a more specific reason that may have led Spinoza to construe Cartesian freedom in absolutist terms, namely, what Descartes has to say about 'freedom of indifference'. The connotations of this phrase, as traditionally used, were highly favourable: what the partisans of freedom of indifference believed in was an autonomous and sovereign power of the will—its unrestricted and total freedom. It is in this sense that God is said, in the *Conversation with Burman*, to be acting with 'maximum indifference'.[41]

Now Descartes does speak, in the Fourth Meditation, of the 'indifference' of the will. But scrutiny of the text reveals that what he means by this

---

[37] AT VII 58: CSM II 40.
[38] F. Alquié (ed.), *Descartes, Œuvres Philosophiques* (Paris: Garnier, 1963–73), ii. 461.
[39] G I 174 lines 20–5: C 258.   [40] AT VII 57: CSM II 40.   [41] AT V 166: CSMK 348.

should be sharply distinguished from the autonomous sovereign power of the will such as God enjoys. The indifference referred to in the Fourth Meditation is described as evidence of a 'defect in knowledge' or a 'kind of negation' ('defectus in cognitione sive negatio quaedam'): 'The indifference I feel when there is no reason pushing me in one direction rather than the other is the lowest grade of freedom; it is evidence not of any perfection of freedom but rather of a defect in knowledge.'[42] The situation Descartes has in mind here is one where the reasons for and against a certain proposition (or course of action) are equally balanced. In such cases Descartes does imply that we can, by exercising our will, select one alternative rather than the other. But he goes on to contrast such 'low-grade' freedom with true liberty—the 'liberty of enlightenment' discussed above. True freedom, *liberté éclairée*, is in inverse proportion to freedom of indifference: 'tanto magis sponte et libere credidi quanto minus fui indifferens'.[43] The point about situations of evenly balanced evidence, Descartes seems to want to say, is that although I can theoretically say to myself of a given proposition 'Yes, it's true,' or 'No, it isn't,' such a move will be wholly arbitrary and empty.[44] For all I know the judgement might be quite wrong; but even if it happens to be true, this will be a pure accident (*casu incidam in veritatem*) and I will still be at fault (*non culpa carebo*).[45] The fact that we can be in such a situation at all flows, according to Descartes, from a 'privation' in our nature (AT VII 60–1). In short, though Descartes does acknowledge a two-way power of choice in conditions of equilibrium, he is very far from extolling it as the model of true human liberty.

Spinoza, both in the *Cogitationes Metaphysicae* and later in the *Ethics*, discusses this case of 'indifference', which he takes (mistakenly, as I hope it will now be emerging) to hold pride of place in Descartes's account of human freedom. The example he employs is the celebrated case of Buridan's ass, who is equally hungry and thirsty and equidistant from hay

---

[42] AT VII 58: CSM II 40.

[43] 'I believed all the more spontaneously and freely in proportion to my lack of indifference.' AT VII 59 line 3: CSM II 40 (quotation abridged).

[44] One may go further here and ask whether Descartes has not already gone too far in allowing that such behaviour (exercising the will in conditions of total equilibrium) is even feasible. Could one really judge in such cases? Or would the 'Yes, it's true' be no more than a mere *flatus vocis*, an empty gesture or grunt? Cf. Curley's illuminating discussion of whether one could assent to the proposition 'It rained three hours ago on Jupiter' (Curley, 'Descartes, Spinoza and the Ethics of Belief', 178).

[45] AT VII 60 line 3; CSM II 41.

and water.[46] In the *Cogitationes Metaphysicae*, the imaginary Cartesian argues that a man in such a situation would clearly not perish from hunger and thirst; and hence (it is implied) man must have a contra-causal power of the will: he can just decide to go for either the food or the drink.[47] In the *Ethics*, we find Spinoza's own response to this supposed major Cartesian defence of contra-causal freedom: biting the bullet, Spinoza insists that the Buridanian man would indeed perish of hunger and thirst. The reasoning appears to be this: if the premise is that there is absolutely nothing impinging on the man's perception but the feelings of hunger and thirst and the equally distant food and drink, then on this assumption there will indeed be no decision. But Spinoza goes on: 'If you ask me whether such a man should be thought an ass rather than a man, I do not know.'[48] The point, I take it, is that a being whose perceptions were limited strictly to these immediate stimuli and nothing else would not be anything recognizable as a human being in the sense of a normal rational agent.

Recent investigation of how primitive creatures such as ants and wasps behave in response to environmental stimuli suggests that it might be possible to devise an experiment in which there would indeed be a kind of indefinite paralysis or suspension of action in an insect confronted with equal and opposite stimuli. But this hardly answers the question of what would occur in the more complex human case. For it does seem possible to imagine a situation where a given individual is ignorant of the considerations that would settle which of two alternatives X and Y is superior, and who, because of that ignorance, finds the arguments in favour of X and of Y to be evenly balanced. In this type of case it appears that Spinoza would deny the Cartesian thesis that when reasons appear evenly balanced we can, by mere exercise of will, effect a decision. Spinoza's comments do seem to be a good argument against the existence of the kind of pure libertarian free will conceived of by some philosophers (e.g. some existentialists). In such a situation of equilibrium, a pure exercise of will, *ex nihilo*, would not seem to be a rational decision at all. Yet once again, if this is supposed to constitute a decisive critique of the Cartesian account of free

---

[46] Curley (C 487) notes (without expressing a view) that the historical author of the example may not be Jean Buridan. In fact, Aristotle, in the *De Caelo* [*c*.325 BC], 2. 13, refers to the case of a man remaining unmoved when he is equally hungry and thirsty, and standing at an equal distance from food and drink.   [47] G I 277: C 343.

[48] G II 135: C 490.

action, it seems to miss the target. For although Descartes does allow that we have the power to exercise the will in cases of indifference, he is, as we have seen, very far from holding up such a defective and arbitrary decision, taken in the absence of clearly perceived reasons on one side or the other, as a paradigm of human freedom. True freedom, for Descartes, is to be achieved first by rational reflection that leads to the complete suspension of judgement, and then by the search for a perception that is so clear and distinct that the two proposed alternatives cease, and cease dramatically, to be equally attractive: the equilibrium is shattered and one of the two alternatives simply compels our assent.

In short, Descartes did not make the notion of a two-way contra-causal power central to his account of freedom (except in the case of God);[49] and the kind of human liberty he extols is certainly not illustrated by the Buridanian type of case where choice is undetermined by reasons. In Descartes's view, the type of liberty we should aim for is not *liberté Buridanienne* but *liberté éclairée*; the truly free agent is one for whom the 'determination of the will' is always linked to the 'prior perception of the intellect'.[50] The conclusions Spinoza reaches about the will, though expressed in rather different terms, are by no means dissimilar from this.

6. Concluding Note on the Passions

A discussion of the Spinozan account of the passions and its relation to the work of Descartes would require a separate (and lengthy) chapter in its own right. All I shall do in this brief final section is to call attention to how Spinoza's remarks on the passions illustrate his general tendency to see himself as breaking with the Cartesian account of freedom when in fact he is quite close to it.

In the Preface to *Ethics*, part V, Spinoza refers disparagingly to the Stoic view that we have 'absolute dominion' over the passions—that they 'depend entirely on our will and that we can control them absolutely'.[51] He then goes on to criticize Descartes for holding that 'there is no soul so weak that it cannot—when it is well directed—acquire an absolute

---

[49] For God's absolute liberty, see letter to Mersenne of 15 April 1630 (AT I 145–6: CSMK 23).
[50] AT VII 60: CSM II 45.   [51] G II 277; C 595.

power over its passions'.[52] To some commentators on this passage Spinoza's condemnation of Descartes seems entirely justified. Thus Delahunty writes: 'The Stoic-Cartesian view that we have, or can have, absolute control over our passions seemed to Spinoza quite laughably naive; and he was right.'[53]

That the 'absolute control' view is laughably naive certainly seems correct, as any air passenger who has experienced that exquisite modern form of torture known as an emergency landing will testify. As the plane circles around and around jettisoning its fuel, and the fire engines and ambulances form up below, one may exhort oneself to 'calm down' but the abject fear and its physiological accompaniments (rapid pulse, sweating) persist in a way that appears wholly resistant to the commands of the will. But, once again, it is far from clear that Spinoza is right in naming Descartes as the representative of the absolutist view he wishes to combat.

In the *Passions of the Soul*, Descartes addresses the topic that was later to form the subject of Spinoza's *Ethics*, parts IV and V—the origin of the passions and the way to come to terms with them. But although Descartes does speak of 'absolute' mastery in the passage from article 50 that Spinoza quotes in the *Ethics*, he is very far from supposing that the will exercises a direct and immediate control over the passions. This is made explicit in *Passions*, article 45: 'our passions cannot be directly aroused or suppressed by the action of our will ... For example, in order to arouse boldness and suppress fear in ourselves, it is not sufficient to have the volition to do so.'

In the following article Descartes offers an explanation for our lack of direct voluntary control over the passions. The passions are 'caused, maintained and strengthened' by physiological events—disturbances in the heart, blood, and animal spirits; and physiological events of this sort are not under the direct control of the will (*Passions*, art. 46). Descartes points out, however, that it is possible by careful training to set up habitual associations between certain thoughts and certain movements in the pineal gland, which will in turn generate certain movements of the animal spirits; and once these networks are laid down, we will possess an indirect control over our passions.

Spinoza shows by what he says in the preface to *Ethics*, part Five, that he was well aware of these passages. But his main strategy in attacking Descartes

---

[52] G II 279: C 595. Spinoza is here quoting the title of art. 50 of *The Passions of the Soul*.
[53] Delahunty, *Spinoza*, 190.

is to pour scorn on the dualistic theory of psychophysical interaction to which he is committed. 'I should very much like to know,' observes Spinoza acidly, 'how many degrees of motion the Mind can give to that pineal gland and how great a force is required to hold it in suspense.'[54] The scenario of volitions pushing against the pineal gland from one side while animal spirits push against it from another does indeed seem a prime example of the 'ghost in the machine' at its most implausible; and I would certainly not want to defend everything Descartes says either about volitions or psychophysical interactions in general. But in the particular case of the control of the passions, Spinoza seems to have underestimated the subtlety of Descartes's position. The point is not that the animal spirits generating fear are bubbling up on one side, and the volition to be brave is exerting pressure on the other side. As we have already seen, it is no use, according to Descartes, to just directly 'will' that the passion of fear should abate. I cannot directly will that the agitation of the animal spirits should cease (in modern terms, I cannot directly will that my pulse should slow or that my adrenalin levels should go down). What I can do, according to Descartes, is to set up a habitual response whereby some mental performance that *is* under my control will trigger some automatic reduction in the agitation of the spirits (adrenalin levels, or whatever).

An interesting illustration Descartes offers of the kind of point he is making is the way in which the decision to pronounce a word will automatically produce certain muscle contractions in the tongue that it would have been difficult or impossible to produce directly by the command of the will. Again, 'dilate your pupils' is a command we cannot obey directly; but we can manage to comply indirectly by deciding to look at a distant object (*Passions*, art. 47; Descartes goes on to make a comparison with the way in which animals are trained: art. 50).[55] Thus, returning for a moment to the plight of our modern hapless aircraft passenger, the Cartesian technique would not be just to try and will the fear to subside; rather one should have trained oneself in such a way that some voluntary act (perhaps the repeating of a mantra) will automatically have the desired effect. Notice

---

[54] G II 180: C 569.

[55] Remarkably, Spinoza expressly notices these examples at *Ethics*, pt. V, Preface; but his remarks here (G II 27 lines 10–15: C 596) suggest that he takes Descartes to be saying that a simple act of will suffices to 'join to any volition any motion of the gland (and consequently any motion of the spirits)'. Yet to leave the matter there does not do sufficient justice to what Descartes says about the role of careful training and habit.

that the inherent plausibility of this account is not affected by the question of whether the mind–body dualism that Spinoza so bitterly criticizes is tenable. For whatever the status of volitions (i.e. whether they are wholly incorporeal events, or whether they are physiological events 'conceived of under the attribute of thought'), it undoubtedly remains true that one cannot directly will passions such as fear to subside, yet one can decide to train oneself in such a way that a passion subsides or is reduced automatically by the performance of certain actions that are within voluntary control.

This is no space here to discuss Spinoza's own account of the passions and how to control them (the general description and classification of the passions owes much to Descartes, though the recipe for control relies not on the type of technique envisaged by Descartes but rather on the role of the understanding in achieving a complete perception of what is inadequately or confusedly grasped by one who is passively in the grip of his passions).[56] The main point of this brief excursion into Descartes's theory of the passions has been to reinforce our earlier claim that Spinoza tended to exaggerate the kind of freedom that Descartes postulated. In the case of the passions, as in the case of the intellect, Descartes does not, *pace* Spinoza, make the notion of an absolute, contra-causal power central to his account of what it is to be free. 'The chief use of our wisdom,' wrote Descartes at the end of the *Passions de l'âme,* 'lies in its teaching us to be masters of our passions,' a sentiment with which Spinoza would surely have concurred. But such mastery was not for Descartes, any more than for Spinoza, a matter of standing wholly outside the world of natural causes, still less of simply deciding to override them by an arbitrary exercise of will. If there is a general lesson to be learned from this chapter it is that care is needed in evaluating Spinoza's claims to be departing from Cartesian orthodoxy. The methods and modes of argument of the two philosophers are radically different. But their philosophical positions, despite initial appearances, are often surprisingly close.

[56] See *Ethics,* pt. V prop. 4; for a critical discussion of Spinoza's strategy see Bennett, *A Study of Spinoza's Ethics,* 332.

11

Descartes and the Voluntariness of Belief

1. Introduction: Choosing to Believe

In a much admired paper Bernard Williams once observed that 'there is not much room for deciding to believe'. This is because beliefs are 'things which we, as it were, *find we have*', though of course we can decide whether to express them or not.[1] That we cannot decide to believe something on command is not, Williams goes on to say, just a brute empirical fact about our makeup: it is not a mere contingent aspect of our nature, like, for example, our inability to blush just by willing it. The fact that we cannot decide to believe something, just like that, depends, rather, on a feature that is analytically connected to the very concept of belief, namely that beliefs *aim at truth*. So if I could acquire a belief at will, presumably I could decide to acquire it, as it were, whether it was true or not. 'If, in full consciousness, I could will to acquire a "belief" irrespective of its truth, it is unclear that before the event I could seriously think of it as a belief, i.e. as something purporting to represent reality'.[2]

Though Williams does not explicitly discuss it, it seems not unlikely that one target he might have had in mind in criticizing the notion of

Earlier versions of this chapter were delivered at the Colloquium on 'Cartesian Philosophy in the Seventeenth Century' held at the University of Utrecht in October 2000, and to the Philosophy Seminar at Rutgers University in March 2001. I am most grateful for helpful discussions on both occasions, and especially to Theo Verbeek at Utrecht and Jerry Fodor at Rutgers. Thanks are also due to N. M. L. Nathan for valuable comments on an earlier draft of the chapter, and to Ward Jones, Andrew Gleeson, Veli Mitova, and Dylan Futter for helpful feedback received during the final reviewing process.

[1] Bernard Williams, 'Deciding to Believe', in *Problems of the Self* (Cambridge: Cambridge University Press, 1973), ch. 9 p. 147 (original quotation changed to *oratio recta*, and emphasis supplied).

[2] Ibid. 148.

belief-at-will is that of religious belief (at least as conceived of in certain traditions). The New Testament, particularly in the Epistles of Paul, is full of injunctions to believe, with the implication that this is a meritorious thing to do—which in turn implies it depends at least partly on the will. Thus the doctrine of the 'new circumcision', articulated in Paul's letter to the Romans, proclaims the idea of a new covenant, entered into not (like the old covenant) by the act of physical circumcision, but rather by the Christian believer's voluntary inner response to Jesus Christ—what Paul calls a 'circumcision of the heart'.[3] This looks very like a willed act of belief (though the exact sense of the Greek term *pistis* (belief, faith, trust), and the degree of voluntariness involved, given the role of divine grace in faith, are all matters of extensive scholarly dispute). Clearer perhaps is the command put by St John into the mouth of the risen Christ when he addresses the doubting Thomas: 'Be not faithless, but believing!'[4] Christians are *commanded* to believe—and if the relevant propositions seem difficult, they are simply to exercise their will, put away their doubts, as Thomas eventually did in the Gospel story, and firmly resolve to believe. By the time we reach the seventeenth century, the list of notions to which such willed assent is required has grown considerably: in the Anglican Baptism service in the 1662 *Book of Common Prayer*, the Minister asks each of the Godparents 'Dost thou believe in the Holy Ghost; the holy Catholick Church; the Communion of Saints; the Remission of sins; the Resurrection of the flesh; and everlasting life after death?', to which they are required to answer 'All this I steadfastly believe'.[5] 'Steadfastly' here surely implies some kind of act of will—a determination of the spirit, a decision to assent to the prescribed doctrines 'just like that', in Bernard Williams's phrase—or perhaps with a bit more struggle, perhaps with a certain sort of inner mental straining or grunt of cognitive effort.

We seem to have a *prima facie* tension here between belief as essentially truth-aimed or truth-centred, so that a necessary condition of a belief's being appropriately formed is (to put it rather grandly) that it should reflect

---

[3] Letter to the Romans [c.AD 50] 2: 29, 'peritome kardias en pneumati, ou grammati' ('circumcision of the heart, in the spirit and not in the letter').

[4] 'kai me ginou apistos, alla pistos'. Gospel according to John [c.AD 100] 20: 27.

[5] *Book of Common Prayer* [1662], The Ministration of Publick Baptism of Infants; 1662 is the date of the finally approved version, though most of the formulations date from the previous century, owing much to Thomas Cranmer (1489–1556).

reality; and on the other hand the notion of religious dogma as that which *ought* to be believed, or that which the adherent of the Church is *required* to believe. For the idea that *S* is obligated or required to *f* logically implies that *S* can *f* if he chooses; so if the Christian ought to believe a given proposition, it follows that he can believe it if he chooses; yet the notion of belief as achievable by an effort of will in this way evidently clashes with the idea (highlighted by Williams) that what makes a given belief adoptable is (in part at least) determined by what is actually the case independently of the believer's desires,[6] and hence cannot be within the scope of the believer's will in the manner supposed.

Now we might expect this tension to be particularly apparent in the philosophy of Descartes. For Descartes, of all philosophers, was perhaps most preoccupied with the search for truth: in the *Discourse* he defined his method as the right way of 'conducting one's reason and *seeking the truth* in the sciences'.[7] Yet he was also as a devout Catholic committed to the idea of articles of faith that ought to be believed—articles that it is required, and perhaps even meritorious, to accept. What I aim to do in this chapter is to explore how far Descartes's theory of belief is affected by the tension between the idea of correct belief as something that is determined by the truth, and the idea of belief as something that is within our voluntary control. I shall suggest that the Cartesian account does a tolerably good job of resolving this tension. And along the way I shall draw some comparisons and contrasts with the earlier views of Plato and the later views of Hume.

2. Models of Belief

It will be useful to begin by deploying the old distinction between rationalist and empiricist models of cognition—a distinction that, despite the onslaught that has been unleashed on it in recent years, remains in many respects a serviceable historiographical tool. In the case of belief, what we might call the rationalist model is exemplified by Plato in the *Republic*. Essentially it is a two-part model, which provides in the first

---

[6] Except perhaps in the limiting case where the belief is about one's desires.

[7] *Discours de la méthode pour bien conduire sa raison et chercher la vérité dans les sciences.* From the *Discourse* [1637], title page (AT VI 1: CSM I 111).

place a diagnosis of false belief (namely the reliance on inherently suspect modes of cognition, namely those based on sensory data), and goes on in the second place to give an account of epistemically sound belief as a direct response to appropriately perceived reality. The aspiring philosopher, emerging from the murkiness of the cave, where all is shifting and unstable, comes out into the clear upper world where he can contemplate the eternal forms shining above him.[8] Notice that the model is normative through and through: it tells us not so much how we actually operate as human beings, or how the mechanisms of belief actually arise from a psychological point of view, but rather what standards our cognition ought to conform to if it is to be awarded an epistemic accolade—if we are to count as having passed from darkness into light. Contrast the empiricist account offered by Hume, which shifts the attention from normative epistemology to empirical psychology. Belief is analysed as a natural phenomenon that occurs in a certain manner—something that, so to speak, 'happens to us'.[9] And Hume is concerned not so much to lay down standards for how belief could count as knowledge as to provide an explanation for how human belief arises: it arises from experience, and (to quote from the *Treatise*) 'is explained to be nothing but a peculiar sentiment, or lively conception, produced by habit'.[10]

Among the many interesting points of contrast between the Platonic and the Humean approaches is the fact that Plato's account puts the human cognizer *in charge*, in a way Hume's picture seems implicitly to reject. Sound belief is for Plato something *achieved*, the result of a philosophical struggle to escape from the imprisoning world of delusion and to attain a perspective from which we can grasp things as they really are. Hume's picture by contrast prefigures in a certain sense the kind of naturalistic or 'scientific' approach to mental phenomena more familiar from modern times—an approach that tends towards viewing humans as laboratory subjects rather than epistemic agents. It is almost as if the Humean takes up the white coat of the cognitive scientist, and records the experimental results: the plain fact is that if the subjects are exposed to certain experiential stimuli, they

---

[8] *Republic* [c.380 BC], bk. 4.   [9] Williams, 'Deciding to Believe', 148.

[10] David Hume, Abstract of *A Treatise of Human Nature* [1739–40], para. 27, in the edition of D. F. Norton and M. J. Norton (Oxford: Oxford University Press, 2000), 413–14. The Norton edition gives marginal paragraph numbering that facilitates identification of passages even for those using different editions.

will develop certain cognitive states. Developing this theme, John Biro has cast Hume as the founder, or at least early herald, of the modern discipline of cognitive science: the Humean recommendation is to 'replace endless and fruitless "cogitating" in an attempt to give a philosophical justification of our beliefs, with an attempt to find a scientific explanation of their origin'.[11] An important feature of both Humean and modern naturalizing approaches, according to Biro, is the view that the processes postulated to explain beliefs (or other mental functions) operate at a sub-doxastic level, 'below the threshold of the cognizer's consciousness'.[12] This closely connects, so it seems to me, with the notion of belief as something that 'happens to us': it turns out to be irresistible in somewhat the same way as the perception of an object such as a chair or a table is irresistible; although it is 'I' who am said to be the subject of the perception, or the belief, I do not, as it were, actively decide to perceive, or to believe, this or that; rather, the mechanisms of the mind do it for me. These facts (if they are facts) make it appropriate to use the language of passivity—belief as something that happens to me.

There may (to digress very briefly) seem to be a clash between this aspect of the Humean programme and the interpretation found in some commentators that Hume takes the mind to be 'complex, dynamic, ever changing', an 'active agent', with the 'constant activity of this mind' 'dominating' Hume's account of human psychology, both in the cognitive and the moral domains.[13] This latter activist picture certainly chimes in with many of the things Hume says (most famously his talk, which indirectly inspired Kant, of the mind's tendency to 'spread itself on external objects').[14] Talk of the mind's activity in this sense can, however, be misleading, unless two caveats are observed. (1) First, we need to be quite clear that the mind which is active in this sense is *not* the person who is believing or perceiving: the person is no more active vis-à-vis this sub-personal processing than I am active when I digest my meal. (2) Second, we need to remember that the 'activity' in question, even at the sub-personal level, is presumably (if we accept the naturalism implicit in the scientific programme) itself to be ultimately analysed in terms of functions and processes of a primitive and entirely automatic kind; so we need to be careful not to be misled

---

[11] John Biro, 'Hume's New Science of the Mind', in D. F. Norton (ed.), *The Cambridge Companion to Hume* (Cambridge: Cambridge University Press, 1993), 33–63, at 44.   [12] Ibid. 45.

[13] Ibid. 40–1.   [14] *A Treatise of Human Nature*, bk. I pt. 3 sect. 14 para. 25.

by the ordinary connotations of calling a mental process 'active'. At the level where the activity is going on, nothing and no one is 'in charge'; the mechanisms just tick away automatically.

To return to our main contrast between the Platonic view of the human epistemic agent as in charge, and the Humean account of belief formation as a passive process, it seems to me that, suggestive though this contrast is, it would be a mistake to suppose that we are required to make an exclusive choice between one or other of the models on offer here. On the one hand, any account that reduces belief to something that merely *happens* to us will run afoul of our undoubted ability as rational agents to adopt a critical stance vis-à-vis our belief states: we plainly do have, uniquely among our fellow creatures on this planet, the power to stand back from (given subsets of) the beliefs we 'find' ourselves having, and to enquire whether they are justified, with a view to modifying them in the light of further evidence or comparison with other parts of our belief system. There are complex epistemic procedures and normative principles involved here; by no stretch of the imagination can what is going on when we arrive at the beliefs that make up our outlook on the world be reduced to a set of automatic natural responses to the data of experience. Our epistemic life as humans, 'the examined life', as Socrates called it, must be more than a series of animal habits. Yet on the other hand, the loftier Platonic picture of epistemic states as states that we *achieve* as autonomous rational agents should not be allowed to foreclose all causal questions about how our beliefs are generated. This of course touches on highly vexed questions in the philosophy of mind; but it seems to me Williams is again right here when he observes 'the fact that there is a rational connexion between p and q does not mean that there is not a causal connexion between A's believing p and his believing q.'[15] Unless we want to relegate human knowledge to a noumenal realm that is wholly insulated from the causal nexus within which we live our lives, it seems hard to resist the suggestion that our rational adoption of certain beliefs, based on rational grounds, must involve certain mental states being not just inferentially but also causally related to other mental states: the believing that q which supports A's belief that p is also causally instrumental in A's believing that P.[16] It is a remarkable, and in my view insufficiently praised, feature of Descartes's account of belief-formation that he succeeds

---

[15] Williams, 'Deciding to Believe', 142.   [16] Ibid. 143.

in doing justice to both the rational and the causal aspects of our human cognitive faculties.

3. Cartesian Belief and the Will

Descartes's epistemic journey is in many ways like Plato's: it is a journey from darkness to light, from the *inextricabiles tenebrae*, the 'inextricable darkness' at the end of the First Meditation, to the *immensi luminis pulchritudo*, 'the beauty of the immense light' that dawns at the end of the Third.[17] It is not just a similarity of metaphor, with Descartes's God shining in the intellectual firmament with the same radiance as Plato's Form of the Good. There is a closely parallel story in each philosopher of the escape of the soul from confusion, a confusion in both cases arising largely from the unstable and unreliable deliverances of the senses; and there is the same ideal destination: the human epistemic agent confronting the truth with a direct gaze that leaves no room for doubt. But notwithstanding the rational credentials of the epistemic state so achieved—Plato's *logos* becomes the Cartesian *lux rationis*, the light of reason—we find in Descartes a readiness to entertain, indeed underline, the idea that such illumination also involves a *causally operative mechanism of belief*. In a sense, that could perhaps be seen as implicit in Plato's original visual metaphor: the sun that is the Form of the Good plays a causal role in tandem with its epistemic role—as well as functioning as the source of truth, its light-giving action actually *brings about* the right sort of vision of the Forms for the philosophers emerging from the cave.[18] But in Descartes there is a much more explicit link between epistemology and psychology; or perhaps it would be better to say that the logico–epistemic and the causal aspects are presented as running in parallel. The intellectual illumination generated by the divine light of reason immediately and directly produces a powerful mental inclination to believe—and the latter is characterized, in a way that might almost seem to prefigure Hume, as a *natural propensity*: 'ex magna luce in intellectu magna consequitur propensio in voluntate' (from a great light in the intellect there follows a great inclination in the will).[19] This, Descartes appears to

---

[17] *Meditationes de prima philosophiae* [1641], First Meditation, AT VII 23: CSM II 15, and Third Meditation, AT VII 52: CSM II 36.   [18] Cf. *Republic*, 515c.

[19] AT VII 59: CSM II 41 (original changed from past to present form).

be saying, is just the way we are, the way we are made: the *lux rationis*, the light of reason, is also called the *lumen naturale*, the *natural* light; and its operation within the human psyche is quite appropriately described in causal terms, as determining our belief.[20]

An obvious worry about this Humean reading of Descartes might now seem to arise. Natural propensities may be all very well for a radical sceptic such as Hume, but they seem dangerous territory for his French predecessor, the self-proclaimed defeater of scepticism. Descartes proudly announces the possibility of 'full and certain knowledge of countless matters, both concerning God and intellectual natures, and also concerning the whole of corporeal nature comprised within pure mathematics'.[21] Hume, by contrast, flags his account of belief with a frank admission that 'the reader will easily perceive that the philosophy contain'd in this book is very sceptical, and tends to give us a notion of the imperfections and narrow limits of human understanding'.[22] The differences between the two philosophers are best explained, however, not in terms of any clash of views about the importance of natural propensities in the realm of human cognition, but rather in their divergent conceptions of the essential character of the *Nature* under whose domain our minds operate. For Hume, nature is ultimately a set of brute facts, whose underlying rational principle, if there is any, is forever 'totally shut up from human curiosity and enquiry'.[23] For Descartes, by contrast, the term 'Nature', considered in its general aspect, means 'nothing other than God himself, or the ordered system of created things established by God', while 'my own nature' means 'the totality of things bestowed on me by God'.[24] This does not, of course, mean that we never go astray: Descartes underlines that because of human weakness, and the limitations imposed by our embodied status, we are often subject to all sorts of preconceptions and errors. But perhaps the most important aim of the *Meditations*, in essence a work of theodicy, is to show how such human liability to prejudice and error is compatible with the

---

[20] The notion of *lux rationis* or 'the light of reason', found in the *Regulae* [*c*.1628] (AT X 368: CSM I 14), becomes, in the *Meditations*, *lumen naturale*, 'the natural light' (e.g. AT VII 40: CSM II 28).

[21] Fifth Meditation, AT VII 71: CSM II 49.

[22] Abstract of *A Treatise of Human Nature*, bk. I pt. 3 sect. 14 para. 27.

[23] David Hume, *An Enquiry concerning Human Understanding* [1748], sect. IV pt. I para. 12, ed. T. Beauchamp (Oxford: Oxford University Press, 1999). The Beauchamp edition provides numbered paragraphs within each part, allowing references to be located by those using other editions.

[24] Sixth Meditation, AT VII 80: CSM I 56.

divine authorship of our minds. And the central claim runs like a clear thread through the whole of Cartesian metaphysics and epistemology: all of Nature, the nature manifest in the material universe, and the nature manifest in the workings of our own minds, owes its source and origin to a supremely perfect benevolent God, who 'cannot be a deceiver on pain of contradiction'.[25]

How far, then, is belief voluntary, in Descartes's scheme of things? It might be thought that the picture of a powerful natural (i.e. God-given) propensity to assent to certain truths somehow undermines the idea of the autonomous epistemic agent who is 'in charge' of searching for the truth on the basis of critical rational reflection. But this would be a mistake. Though doing full justice to the causality which makes true belief a fully determined process, Descartes also manages to allow genuine freedom and autonomy to the human epistemic enquirer.

The first part of the Cartesian solution is presented quite explicitly in the Fourth Meditation. Here we find a strongly compatibilist account of human freedom—one that is more than a little reminiscent of the 'reconciling project' later developed by Hume to defuse the apparent tension between freedom and necessity.[26] Hume, borrowing some traditional scholastic terminology, distinguished *liberty of indifference* 'which means a negation of necessity and causes', and *liberty of spontaneity,* which is simply the absence of external constraint.[27] The former is threatened by universal causation, while the latter is not, since it need not imply any contra-causal power, but merely the 'hypothetical' liberty to do something if we so chose—something that is 'universally allowed to belong to every one who is not a prisoner and in chains'.[28] And if this distinction, which 'few are capable' of observing, is carefully maintained, then the supposed clash between freedom and necessity disappears.

Prefiguring this Humean solution, Descartes explicitly denies the need for human freedom to be grounded in some supposed contra-causal power.

[25] Fourth Meditation, AT VII 62: CSM II 43. For more on the concept of 'nature' in Descartes, see sect. 3 of J. Cottingham, 'The External World, "Nature" and Human Experience', in G. Vesey (ed.), *Philosophers Ancient and Modern.* Royal Institute of Philosophy 20 (Cambridge: Cambridge University Press, 1986), 73–89. Reprinted in V. Chappell (ed.), *Descartes's Meditations, Critical Essays* (Lanham, Md.: Rowman & Littlefield, 1977), 207–24.

[26] *Enquiry concerning Human Understanding,* sect. VIII pt. I para 25.

[27] *Treatise of Human Nature,* bk. II pt. 3 sect. 2, opening para.

[28] *Enquiry Concerning Human Understanding,* sect. VIII pt. I para. 23.

'In order for me to be free', he asserts in the Fourth Meditation, 'there is no need for me to be capable of moving in each of two directions: on the contrary, the more I incline in one direction—either because I clearly understand that reasons of truth and goodness point that way, or because of a divinely produced disposition of my inmost thoughts—the freer is my choice'.[29] God has bestowed on me an irresistible inclination to assent to the truth of certain propositions once I understand them clearly and distinctly;[30] but that does not undermine my freedom. On the contrary (and Descartes is surely right here), what could be freer than assenting to the truth of 'two plus two makes four' on the basis that I understand with the utmost clarity what the symbols mean and why the proposition must therefore be correct? Or what could be freer that selecting x over y on the basis that I transparently perceive it to be the better option? The spontaneous assent of the will in such cases is not some kind of impediment to freedom, but on the contrary is a manifestation that our beliefs are operating entirely as they should, as well as we could possibly wish in our most ideally rational moments. Being determined to believe what is true when the intellect has perceived fully adequate support for those truths represents the ideal state for the epistemic agent; it is not *this* kind of state that is threatening to our conception of ourselves as free, but rather the vacillating state when we are unable to perceive the evidence clearly. In the latter case, the residual power to plump arbitrarily for one alternative rather than another, without rational justification, could aptly be called, as Descartes did in fact call it, 'the lowest grade of freedom'. 'The indifference I feel when there is no reason pushing me in one direction rather than another is the lowest grade of freedom (*infimus gradus libertatis*); it is evidence not of any perfection of freedom, but rather of a defect in knowledge or a kind of negation.'[31]

The suspicion may remain, despite the elegance of Descartes's presenta-tion, that the kind of freedom he extols (to assent spontaneously to manifest truth) does not quite match up to the ideal of the autonomous epistemic

---

[29] AT VII 57–8: CSM II 40.

[30] The notion of a naturally/divinely implanted mental propensity to assent to what is clear has a long ancestry. Cicero, following the teaching of the Academic philosopher Antiochus (1st century BC) notes that 'as a scale in a balance is necessarily depressed by the weights that are placed on it, so the mind necessarily yields to things that are clear; for as no animal cannot seek after that which appears adapted to its nature (in Greek, *oikeion*), so [the mind] cannot not approve a clear thing brought before it'. *Academica* [45 BC], 2. 13. 38; quoted in S. Menn, *Descartes and Augustine* (Cambridge: Cambridge University Press, 1998), 314.   [31] AT VII 58: CSM II 40.

agent. That our beliefs should be determined by a divinely bestowed disposition of the mind to assent to clear and distinct truths may in one sense appear a wonderful boon, but might also seem to carry the cost of making us more like divinely constructed epistemic robots than free enquirers. Further reflection suggests, however, that the Cartesian doctrine of the divine architecture of our minds should not be construed in a way that makes us helpless epistemic pawns of a cosmic Creator. God is not determining our beliefs in the manner that Daniel Dennett's malevolent hypnotist,[32] or Descartes own *malin génie*, might go for—the kind of determination that fails to track the truth, either by making us believe falsehoods, or (perhaps the more interesting case) by making our assent to the relevant propositions independent of their rational grounding, so that we would assent to them anyway, even if the supporting arguments were invalid. (This latter case would be the scenario of what one might call a 'benevolent hypnotist'—one who matches our assent to the truth, but in a way that bypasses any grasp of the justification for the proposition in question.)[33] The situation as analysed by Descartes, by contrast, is one in which my intellect clearly perceives the rational basis for a proposition, and my spontaneous assent irresistibly follows; and the 'follows' here (Descartes's *sequitur*) is surely not a mere arbitrary *post hoc*, but rather a matter of the assent following *in virtue of* what my intellect has perceived. The Cartesian point could in fact be put in entirely secularized terms: the emergence of rational creatures on the evolutionary scene is simply the emergence of creatures in whom an important subset of their beliefs (including, for example, their beliefs in validly derived geometrical theorems) are directly caused by their intellectual grasp of the reasons that in fact support those beliefs.[34]

4. Freedom and Belief

For those who remain unsatisfied that the 'freedom of spontaneity' just described could be enough to establish genuine epistemic autonomy,

[32] D. Dennett, *Elbow Room* (Oxford: Oxford University Press, 1984).

[33] I owe this thought to Ward Jones. Such 'benevolence' might in fact turn out to be illusory, since if our propensity to assent to the truth was of this kind, it would be unrelated to *understanding*, with potentially damaging long-term results that are not hard to visualize.

[34] Cf. Williams, 'Deciding to Believe', 143.

Descartes's position as unfolded in the *Meditations* does in fact provide the basis for seeing our doxastic processes as autonomous in a richer and fuller sense than that so far canvassed. What a sound epistemology might be thought to require is not that we can decide what to believe—since, for the reasons given by Williams, such a power to determine our beliefs at will would not be compatible with the idea of enquiry as a truth-aimed process—but rather that as enquirers we should have some degree of control over the circumstances in which our beliefs are adopted. To put this rather vague suggestion a little more precisely, what we want is not just that we should be passively led to the truth, but that we should play an active role in searching for that truth, in scrutinizing the candidates for truth, in devising procedures for eliminating the faulty candidates and establishing why the sound candidates are reliable. In short, we want a methodology of enquiry that is within our control as epistemic agents.

Such genuine epistemic agency is precisely what Descartes offers us. The true role of the will in the search for truth lies not in liberty of indifference with respect to clear and distinct perceptions—in some supposed weird contra-causal power to accept or reject that two plus two make four (for, of course, once they are seen, such propositions can only be accepted); it lies rather in what Descartes called the *directio ingenii*—the voluntary and autonomous decision to direct the mind in ways that will allow its natural rational powers to operate properly and productively.[35] We can see a vivid description of this process operating in Descartes's dramatic narrative in the First Meditation: the mind needs to be freed from the preconceived opinions uncritically adopted in childhood, or based on potentially misleading sensory information; and in order to facilitate this a series of voluntary mental exercises is proposed. My mind is besieged (*occupare*) by preconceived opinions which have taken over my belief-system (*credulitas*); very well, in that case I will deliberately 'turn my will in the opposite direction' (*voluntate plane in contrarium versa*) and deceive myself (*me ipsum fallam*), by entertaining the scenario of the malicious demon, until the weight of preconceived opinion is counter-balanced (*aequatis utrimque praejudiciorum ponderibus*) and the distorting force of habit, the *prava consuetudo*, which stops me seeing things as they truly are, is neutralized.[36]

---

[35] This is the goal of Descartes's *Regulae ad directionem ingenii*, the 'Rules for the Direction of our Native Intelligence'.   [36] First Meditation, AT VII 22: CSM II 15.

The phrase *prava consuetudo*, bad habituation, might almost have been written to expose the problems with the account of belief Hume was to develop a century later—the picture of belief as a 'peculiar sentiment produced by habit'. If belief is construed as *nothing more* than something that 'happens to us' in virtue of a kind of natural habituation, then (as, to do him justice, Hume himself readily admitted) there can ultimately be no escape from a destructive scepticism; the epistemic project as traditionally conceived by philosophers from Plato onwards collapses into a set of depressing brute facts about the doxastic mechanisms that govern the human mind, with no prospect of converting the resulting *doxa* into *episteme*.[37] But if humans have the power (which it seems hard to deny they do),[38] to stand back from a given subset of their beliefs, temporarily to suspend judgement (fortified if necessary by the kinds of ingenious philosophical exercise in thought-experiment that Descartes devises for us in the First Meditation), then the prospect opens up for a systematic evaluative procedure for sifting, comparing, discarding, grounding, reinforcing beliefs—in short for a critical epistemic methodology.

But can Descartes be consistent here? Can the thesis in the First Meditation about the possibility, indeed the necessity, of standing back from beliefs and suspending judgement be compatible with the Fourth Meditation thesis of doxastic determinism?

Recently, a distinction has been drawn between positive and negative control over our beliefs: perhaps we have the latter but not the former, that is, one may hold that belief-formation is involuntary, while at the same time maintaining that we can deliberately prevent it or suppress it. For example, twitching is involuntary, but we can perhaps learn to suppress it at will.[39] This suggestion is an interesting one, and invokes the possibility of a certain kind of indirect control which, as we shall see in a moment, is highly

---

[37] For an interesting attempt to give a more upbeat assessment of Hume's position, see D. Garrett, *Cognition and Commitment in Hume's Philosophy* (New York: Oxford University Press, 1997), ch. 10. For the ancient idea of the superiority of *episteme* (knowledge, understanding) over mere *doxa* (belief) see e.g, Plato, *Meno* [*Menon*, *c*.385 BC], 98a 1–5, and *Republic* [*Politeia*, *c*.380 BC], bk. 5, 474b–483e.

[38] At least for large chunks of belief. Descartes's 'method of doubt' in the First Meditation implies that such suspension is possible even for deeply ingrained belief patterns (AT VII 22–3: CSM II 15). The case is different when it comes to clear and distinct perceptions, where our doxastic determinations are such that only a kind of indirect or second-order suspension is possible: 'when I turn to the truths themselves', I cannot but assent (Third Meditation, AT VII 36: CSM II 25).

[39] R. Audi, 'Doxastic Voluntarism and the Ethics of Belief', *Facta Philosophica* (1999), 87–109, at 89.

relevant to Descartes's position. Nevertheless, the strategy that Descartes himself develops to establish the consistency of his doxastic determinism with his method of doubt relies not on a distinction between positive and negative control, but rather on the temporal dimension of belief.

The central text for understanding the key role of temporal indexing in Descartes's account of the causality of belief comes in paragraph 4 of the Third Meditation. Recapitulating the doubts of the First Meditation—might not God bring it about that I go wrong even in the simplest matters (even adding two and three or counting the sides of a square)?—Descartes makes a crucial distinction between what can happen at one remove, as it were, and what can happen 'whenever I turn to the truths themselves'.[40] When I actually focus on 'two plus three equals five', then the God-given propensity of the mind to assent to clear and distinct truths kicks in, and I cannot but spontaneously and immediately accept the truth of the proposition. The time-dimension is crucial: just as the certainty of the Cogito in the Second Meditation lasts only 'as long as it is put forward by me and conceived in my mind' ('quoties profertur vel mente concipitur'),[41] so the determination of the will to assent to the clear deliverances of the intellect lasts only so long as I am focused on the relevant propositions ('quoties ad ipsas res...me converto').[42] And since that focusing is an act of the will, it emerges that human beings are more than doxastic robots, led by the nose, or determined by the architecture of their divinely structured intellects. They are truly in control of the circumstances of their search for the truth, since the irresistibility of the natural light will always be contingent on their own free choice as to how far they keep the light focused.[43]

It follows from this that, despite his doxastic involuntarism, Descartes's position does allow for an 'ethics of belief'. To use a physical analogy, I cannot decide to contract the pupils of my eyes at will, but I can bring it about that they contract by deciding to look at a light source; and this means that there is a perfectly good sense in which I can be told (for example

---

[40] AT VII 36: CSM II 25.   [41] AT VII 25: CSM II 17.   [42] Third Meditation, AT VII 36: CSM II 25.

[43] Andrew Gleeson has it put to me that although the focusing is an act of will (and in this sense voluntary), nevertheless, since what ensues (once the mind's eye is focused) is a determination of the will (by the natural light), what is important for reaching the truth is a kind of 'resignation or surrender' rather than an assertion of the will. This way of putting the matter seems to me illuminating, provided one adds that assent as passive and involuntary response to the truth occurs within a context of active enquiry whose conditions of operation are subject to voluntary control.

by an ophthalmologist) that I need to contract my pupils, and be praised for complying. And what holds for eye-contraction can hold for belief. Descartes, it seems to me, would have been sympathetic to the position recently outlined by Robert Audi, who maintains that 'we [can] picture ourselves as agents of belief formation when what we have really done is create (or enter) circumstances in which [belief] occurs as a non-voluntary response to a pattern of evidence'.[44] Although the kind of voluntary control envisaged here is in a certain sense indirect (because what is under voluntary control is not the adoption of the belief itself, but the actions leading to its adoption), this is quite compatible with the idea that there are standards of belief, and indeed of rationality, that we can be praised or blamed for conforming to, or falling short of. As Audi puts it, in a way that seems to me to be strikingly in line with Cartesian insistence on the importance of mental focus as I have just interpreted it, 'an ethics of belief is possible ... for those who reject doxastic voluntarism ... [since it] could turn out that our epistemic obligations are, in broad terms, to be properly attentive both to logic (broadly conceived) and the evidences of our senses ...'[45]

The upshot, for Descartes, is that despite the truth of doxastic involuntarism with respect to clearly perceived truths, humans enjoy a genuine, and indeed robust, kind of responsibility for their beliefs.[46] But the key to this responsibility—the dependency of the infallibly truth-obedient propensity of the mind on the capriciously attentive power of the will—means that the freedom which God or Nature gave us was bestowed at a price—the price of allowing the possibility of evil, whether epistemic error or moral transgression, into the world. Men preferred the darkness to the light, says the Fourth Evangelist,[47] implying what is undeniably (and often tragically) obvious, that humans always have the ability to turn away from the good and the true. What Descartes adds to this ancient theme is that this can happen with regard to clearly perceived truths only, as it were, when we fail to attend, or relax the attention, letting the relevant propositions slip out of focus.[48]

---

[44] Audi, 'Doxastic Voluntarism and the Ethics of Belief', 94.   [45] Ibid. 105.

[46] One might put the point (as Ward Jones has suggested to me) by saying that Descartes is a voluntarist about (our control over) the processes leading to belief, but an involuntarist about believing itself.   [47] 'ēgapēsen hoi anthropoi mallon to skotos ē to phōs.' John 3: 19.

[48] When we move from metaphysics to morals, there is a much more complex story to be told about the distorting influence of the passions; for this see J. Cottingham, *Philosophy and the Good Life* (Cambridge: Cambridge University Press, 1998), ch. 3.

5. Coda: Religious Belief

Mention of sin brings us back, in conclusion, to the point raised at the outset of this chapter, the question of religious faith and the duty to believe in order to be saved. Descartes's position on the voluntariness of belief turns out to be remarkably well adapted to solve the knotty problem for the theologian of how belief can be meritorious. There is no need to quarrel with Williams's persuasive point that the notion of belief as truth-centred seems to allow little room for the idea of choosing to believe. But belief, for Descartes, nonetheless remains within our control in so far as we have the power to attend to, or to distract ourselves from, the deliverances of the natural light.

The position seems straightforward enough with regard to the truths about God's nature and existence that Descartes believed to be clearly and distinctly perceived. But what of the more specific doctrines of the Christian faith (such as the Incarnation or the Resurrection), that are (on the standard doctrine that Descartes accepted) a matter of revelation rather than reason? These might seem to pose a problem for Descartes; for if such doctrines fall short, logically speaking, of the kind of clarity and distinctness we find in 'two plus three equals five', are we to suppose that Descartes thought we could just plump for accepting them, in the absence of clear and distinct perception, exercising the 'lowest grade of freedom' that he so often flagged as a source of error? Would this not be a gross violation of the principle that is the founding maxim of the whole of Cartesian metaphysics: assent *only* to what you clearly and distinctly perceive?

Part of the answer is that Descartes believed—and there is no good reason to doubt his sincerity—that there was another source of clarity and transparency besides the natural light. In the Second Set of Replies, he articulates the idea of a 'double source' of clarity or transparency (*duplex claritas sive perspicuitas*), one coming from the natural light, the other from divine grace.[49] The latter, the *lumen supernaturale*,[50] gives rise, no less than the natural light, to the irresistible assent of the intellect. Indeed, the phrasing in the Fourth Meditation which we quoted earlier can now be understood better: irresistible assent can be produced *either* by 'clearly

---

[49] AT VII 147–8: CSM II 105.   [50] Second Replies, AT VII 148 line 27: CSM II 106.

perceived reasons of truth and goodness' (the natural light) *or* by a 'divinely produced disposition of my thought' (the supernatural light).[51]

So why (one might feel inclined to ask Descartes) does not everyone exposed to the Christian doctrines become a believer, given the irresistibility of the supernatural light? Perhaps, for quasi-Calvinist reasons, because God has predestined some not to receive such celestially sourced illumination.[52] Or alternatively for something close to the characteristically Cartesian reason already given: humans have the power not to reject clearly illuminated truths while they are perceiving them, but to avoid focusing on them, and so evading the assent which would otherwise follow. Men prefer the darkness to the light, as the Gospel says, but they can do so not because the light is not irresistible, but because they wilfully turn away from it. If this is right, Descartes's position here comes close to that of St Thomas Aquinas, who had argued that faith is a gift bestowed by God, but that men nonetheless deserve some merit for their belief by freely co-operating with the divine grace.[53]

Yet despite the Cartesian view of our responsibility for attending to or turning away from the revealed truths of religion, a problem remains about the epistemic credentials of such truths. For despite all the talk of 'illumination', the assent produced by divine grace in such cases is not assent in virtue of the clear and distinct perceptions of the intellect, but would appear to come down to some kind of supernaturally induced subjective certainty. To put the problem slightly differently, someone taking the Cartesian line seems to face the challenge of showing how submitting oneself to the supernatural light in the first place can be rationally defensible, given that the objects of faith are, *ex hypothesi*, not

---

[51] AT VII 58 lines 1–2: CSM II 40.

[52] Descartes's position with regard to the fierce controversies over divine preordination that followed the death of Calvin is ambiguous and hard to determine. For a discussion of the relevant texts, see J. Cottingham (ed.), *Descartes' Conversation with Burman* (Oxford: Clarendon, 1976), pp. xxxvii ff.

[53] There are in fact several points of difference between Aquinas and Descartes on the nature of faith, which are beyond the scope of this chapter. Faith is defined by Aquinas as the assent of the intellect determined by an act of will (as opposed to by the cogency of the object itself). (*Summa theologiae*, IIaIIae (Second Part of the Second Part), qus. 1 and 2). He argues that 'believing (*credere*) is an act of the intellect assenting to the divine truth on the basis of a command of the will moved by God through grace, and so it is subject to free choice of the will in its being ordered toward God. That is why the act of faith can be meritorious' (ibid. qu, 2 art. 9). Aquinas holds, moreover, that the act of will that appropriately directs one's belief towards God is an act of *love* (ibid.), and hence the belief that Christianity is true is a meritorious act of faith only if freely brought about by an act of will out of love of God.

susceptible of confirmation by the light of reason. This is a complex issue that cannot be properly evaluated here; but a plausible interpretation of Descartes's position is suggested by Stephen Menn, who argues that for Descartes 'faith or confidence in divine revelation is prudent for the same reason that the faith or confidence that one's food is not poisoned is prudent'.[54] In questions of religion, as with ordinary prudence in the daily conduct of life, our needs as human beings require us to proceed with some degree of trust, without waiting for conclusive epistemic credentials to be supplied; and this point applies as much to matters relating to spiritual health as it does in those concerned with bodily health and survival.

If this is Descartes's position, it would make his attitude to religious faith not too dissimilar from that of his contemporary Blaise Pascal: the emphasis, at least in the case of revealed truths, would be on the utility of religious belief, rather than its rational demonstrability.[55] If it is hard to achieve a final clarification of Descartes's views here, this is hardly surprising, given his notorious reluctance to pronounce on matters that might be held against him by the theologians.[56] Yet none of this, of course, undermines the clarity and consistency of his position on the voluntariness of belief with respect to knowledge of a more mundane kind.

[54] Menn, *Descartes and Augustine*, 332.
[55] Cf. Blaise Pascal, *Pensées* [1670], ed. L. Lafuma (Paris: Seuil, 1962), no. 418.
[56] Cf. AT V 176: CSMK 351, and Cottingham (ed.), *Descartes' Conversation with Burman*, 115.

12

Cartesian Ethics: Reason and the Passions

1. Introduction

One of the chief aspirations of philosophy as traditionally conceived was to help humans to lead happy and worthwhile lives. In the words of Descartes's scholastic predecessor Eustachius, 'universae philosophiae finis est humana felicitas'—the goal of a complete philosophical system is human happiness.[1] Despite his radically new approach to philosophy, Descartes was determined to show that his system was no less fertile than those of his predecessors from the moral and felicific point of view. As he resoundingly declared in the preface to the French edition of the his magnum opus, the *Principles of Philosophy*, the construction of a perfect moral system—'la plus parfaite morale'—was to be the crowning aim of his philosophy. The metaphysical roots and the physical trunk were established; now he could turn to the practical branches, including morality, which would yield the fruit:

[Par la morale] j'entends la plus haute et la plus parfaite morale, qui présupposant une entière connaissance des autres sciences, est le dernier degré de la sagesse. Or, comme ce n'est pas des racines ni du tronc des arbres qu'on cueille les fruits, mais seulement des extrémités de leurs branches, ainsi la principale utilité de la philosophie dépend de celles de ses parties qu'on ne peut apprendre que les dernières.[2]

But evocative though it may be, the arboreal metaphor leaves it very vague just how morality is supposed to relate to the rest of philosophy.

---

[1] Eustachius e Sancto Paulo, *Summa philosophiae quadripartita* [1609], Preface to pt. II.

[2] 'By "morals" I understand the highest and most perfect moral system, which presupposes a complete knowledge of the other sciences and is the ultimate level of wisdom. Now just as it is not the roots or the trunk of a tree from which one gathers the fruit, but only the ends of the branches, so the principal benefit of philosophy depends on those parts of it which can only be learned last of all' (Preface to the 1647 French translation of the *Principles of Philosophy*, AT IXB 14–15: CSM I 186).

As far as Descartes's own work is concerned, how exactly does the moral philosophizing of his later years connect up with the other parts of his system? Does it, indeed, connect up at all, or should we dismiss as mere propaganda his talk of philosophy as an organically unified structure encompassing all aspects of human understanding, including the ethical? In this chapter I shall argue that there are indeed genuine and important links between Cartesian science and Cartesian ethics, and I shall indicate some of the ways in which Descartes's innovations in the former area produce a distinctive approach to the latter. In sect. 2, I shall prepare the ground by uncovering some of the connections between scientific and ethical concerns that are to be seen even in Descartes's earlier writings. This will lead on to a brief account (in sect. 3) of Descartes's theory of human nature, which will set the scene for a discussion (in sect. 4) of Descartes's account of the relationship between reason and the passions. This oldest of topics in moral philosophy is at the centre of Descartes's later ethical writings, and the way he tackles it turns out to be the key for understanding why he considered his conclusions as a moral philosopher to be organically connected to his wider scientific and philosophical concerns.

2. Morality and the New Method

Nowadays Descartes is not widely regarded as a moral philosopher; indeed, in the anglophone philosophical tradition he is still often seen as first and foremost an 'epistemological' theorist, preoccupied with the conquest of scepticism and establishing the foundations for reliable knowledge. This narrow view of Descartes's philosophical interests—owing much to the specialized concerns of the our modern academic curriculum—cannot survive scrutiny of the voluminous writings on ethics and psychology that occupied Descartes's later years. But it turns out to be seriously misleading even with respect to his first published work, the *Discours de la Méthode* (1637) in which he announced his philosophical aims to the public.

A principal theme of the *Discourse on the Method* is the practical application of Descartes's scientific work: the famous purple passage in Part Six insists that the new science is not to be merely speculative, but is designed to yield real benefits for mankind.[3] Yet the context in which morality first makes its appearance, in Part Three, appears at first to give it a merely peripheral or incidental importance: in order for metaphysics to proceed, it will be necessary to articulate a 'provisional moral code' designed to keep the meditator out of trouble while he withdraws from the world in order to establish foundations for the new science. The first of the four maxims that constitute the *code provisoire* is timidly conservative in tone: the author records a resolution to 'obey the laws and customs of my country, holding constantly to the religion in which by God's grace I had been instructed from my childhood, and governing myself in all other matters according to the most moderate and least extreme opinions—the opinions commonly accepted in practice by the most sensible of those I should have to live with'.[4] The implied reluctance to enter the arena of public controversy certainly corresponds to an enduring element in Descartes's outlook. He aimed throughout his career to be 'a spectator rather than an actor in the comedy of life',[5] and seems to have been quite sincere when he later wrote to a correspondent who had asked about his 'views on morals' that he was reluctant to publish his opinions, since 'it is the proper function of sovereigns and those authorised by them, to concern themselves with regulating the behaviour of others'.[6] Descartes's moralizing in this part of the *Discourse* seems purely instrumental: his aim is to foreclose the possibility of malicious attacks of his method of doubt by critics who might have presented the Cartesian 'truth rule' ('Accept only what cannot be doubted') as subversive of public order. Hence he proceeds, in the second rule of

---

[3] '[Ces notions générales touchant la physique] m'ont fait voir qu'il est possible à parvenir à des connaissances qui soient fort utiles à la vie, et qu'au lieu de cette philosophie spéculative, qu'on enseigne dans les écoles, on en peut trouver une pratique, par laquelle, connaissant la force et les actions … de tous les … corps qui nos environnent, aussi distinctement que nous connaissons les divers métiers de nos artisans, nous les pourrions employer en même façon à tous les usages auxquels ils sont propres, et ainsi nous rendre comme maîtres et possesseurs de la nature.' ('[These general notions concerning physics] made me see that it is possible to arrive at knowledge that will be very useful for life, and that instead of the speculative philosophy taught in the schools, we may discover a practical philosophy whereby we could know the force and actions of … all the … bodies in our environment as distinctly as we know the various crafts of our artisans, and use this knowledge in a similar way for all the purposes for which it is appropriate, so as to make ourselves as it were the masters and possessors of nature.') (*Discourse*, Part Six, AT VI 61–2: CSM I 142–3).   [4] *Discourse*, Part Three, AT VI 23: CSM I 122.

[5] AT VI 28: CSM I 125. In an earlier letter to his friend Marin Mersenne, written soon after he had withdrawn his *Le Monde* from publication on hearing of the condemnation of Galileo, Descartes wrote, 'I desire to live in peace and to continue the life I have begun under the motto *Bene vixit qui bene latuit* [a good life is one which is lived to the end without attracting untoward attention]' (April 1634, AT I 286: CSMK 43).   [6] To Chanut, 20 November 1647, AT V 87: CSMK 326.

his 'provisional code', to make a clear distinction between intellectual judgement (where the suspension of belief is recommended wherever there is the mere possibility of doubt), and the sphere of ordinary practical life, where it is appropriate to follow prevailing opinion. In a letter written soon after the publication of the *Discourse*, Descartes showed himself sensitive to the criticism that 'universal doubt may produce great indecision and even moral chaos';[7] and he later commented in an interview that he had inserted the *code provisoire* in the *Discourse* specifically to avoid the charge that his new philosophy was such as to 'undermine religion and the faith'.[8]

Despite this caution, Descartes allows us, when he reaches the penultimate maxim of his code, a glimpse of the wider ethical concerns that were to form an integral part of his eventual project of constructing a complete moral system. 'My third maxim was always to try to master myself rather than fortune, and to change my desires rather than the order of the world.'[9] The scope of this third maxim, with the remarks that follow it, seems to go well beyond the need to devise a temporary set of rules for living while metaphysical speculation is in progress. Though still avoiding issues of public and social morality (where he was consistently reluctant to lay down the law),[10] Descartes now launches into the question of determining the conditions for individual happiness. The discussion takes us, in other words, to the central aspiration of philosophy as traditionally conceived, that of articulating a plan for the good life; and it becomes clear that Descartes wishes to make his own philosophy as enlightening in this respect as anything that the classical authors had to offer.

That Descartes sees himself as inheriting the traditional mantle of the moral philosopher is underlined both in the tone and the content of this part of the *Discourse*, where we find the argument couched in terms that would have been readily accessible to the thinkers of the ancient Hellenistic world. 'In general, I would [by following the third maxim]

---

[7] Letter of April or May 1638, AT II 35: CSMK 97.

[8] 'The author does not like writing on ethics, but he was compelled to include these rules because of people like the schoolmen who would else have said that he was a man without any religion or faith and that he intended to use his method to subvert them.' *Conversation with Burman* [1648], AT V 178: CSMK 352–3.   [9] AT VI 25: CSM I 123.

[10] The nearest Descartes gets to discussing our duties in the public arena is in the letter to Elizabeth of 15 September 1645—though even here the starting point is that 'each of us is a person distinct from others whose interests are accordingly in some way different from those of the rest of the world' (AT IV 293: CSMK 266).

become accustomed to believing that nothing lies entirely within our power except our thoughts, so that after doing our best in dealing with things external to us, whatever we fail to achieve is absolutely impossible so far as we are concerned... In this, I believe, lay the secret of those philosophers who in earlier times were able to escape from the dominion of fortune and, despite suffering and poverty, rival the gods in happiness.'[11] The allusion here is unmistakably to the Stoics, who had diagnosed one of the root causes of unhappiness as a tension between the inner world of our aspirations and the outer world of external circumstances.[12] To live well, on the Stoic account, is to live 'in accordance with nature'; and since the external world was, for the inhabitants of the classical age, largely something unalterable that one has to accept as it is, the Stoics reasoned that fulfilment must consist in a state of inner detachment and acceptance of what cannot be changed. Descartes returned to discuss this ancient theme in his correspondence with Princess Elizabeth of Bohemia in the mid 1640s, when he proposed as a text for discussion the *De vita beata* ('The Blessed Life') of the celebrated Roman Stoic, Lucius Seneca. Expounding Seneca's ideas to the Princess, Descartes commented that 'the things which can give us supreme contentment can be divided into two classes: those which depend on us, like virtue and wisdom, and those which do not, like honours and riches'. Everyone can 'make himself content without any external circumstance' provided he bears in mind that 'all the good things one does not possess are equally outside one's power, and hence becomes accustomed not to desire them'.[13]

The initial impression that emerges from some of these texts might suggest that Cartesian ethics consists merely in a kind of Stoic addendum that Descartes tacked on as an afterthought to the main body of his

---

[11] *Discourse*, Part Three, AT VI 25–6: CSM I 124.

[12] The sixteenth century had seen a powerful renaissance of Stoic thought. L. Zarka, who provides a thorough account of some of the key figures in this movement, points out that though certain elements in Stoic ethics chimed in well with Christian doctrine, the neo-Stoic movement could nevertheless be seen as potentially subversive of religious faith: 'le stoicisme, avec son culte exclusif de la raison, ouvrait la porte à la morale laïque, à la religion naturelle... Le néo-stoïcisme est en définitive un rationalisme chrétien, dans lequel le christianisme n'apparaît pas toujours comme essentiel, mais plutôt comme surajouté.' *La Renaissance du stoïcisme au xvie siècle* (Paris: Champion, 1914), 334, 337.

[13] Letter of 4 August 1645, AT IV 265: CSMK 257–8. There are other provisos in the letter, notably the requirement that we 'maintain a firm and constant resolution to carry out whatever reason recommends'; this corresponds to what will become a central emphasis in Cartesian ethics, its stress on the power of the will. I discuss the implications of this in my 'Partiality and the Virtues', in R. Crisp (ed.), *How Should One Live?* (Oxford: Oxford University Press, 1996), 57–76.

philosophy.[14] But to take seriously Descartes's insistence that his philosophy is a unified system requires us to dig deeper. If the 'perfect moral system' envisaged by Descartes is, as he claims, an organic outgrowth from the new physics, then its structure can be expected to differ in crucial respects from that of ethical systems that rested on wholly different foundations. That this is indeed so begins to come out in the fourth and final maxim of Descartes's *code provisoire*, where he touches on the question of which occupation is the most worthy of choice, and resolves to 'devote the whole of [his] life to the cultivation of reason'.[15] For the Stoics, the exercise of reason is the key to living in accordance with nature, and the calm acceptance of our place in the cosmos is one of the signal fruits of properly conducted philosophy.[16] But for Descartes, the right use of reason is intimately linked with his new method for 'reaching the truth in the sciences'—a connection explicitly made in the very title of the *Discourse*.[17] The projected results of this method go far beyond the passive and accepting contemplation of an unalterable providential order of nature.

In the first place physical nature is, in Descartes's conception, crucially different from the accessible pattern of providential design that had impressed the Stoics: Cartesian science reveals the world as an austere configuration of mechanical particle interactions, whose essential structure man confronts as something alien to his own nature as a thinking being.[18] And in the second place, the new scientific understanding of that mechanical universe is of a kind that promises far more than mere submissive acceptance. The list of the fruits of the new science which Descartes himself sketches out in the later sections of the *Discourse* opens the door to the possibility of wide-ranging technical manipulation and control: armed with Cartesian physics, man can learn how to produce new compounds, such as glass;[19]

---

[14] Though (as we shall see later on) Descartes is by no means always sympathetic to the Stoics; see further J. Cottingham, *A Descartes Dictionary* (Oxford: Blackwell, 1993) s.v. 'passions', and the introduction by G. Rodis-Lewis to Descartes's *Passions of the Soul*, trans. Stephen Voss (Indianapolis: Hackett, 1989).   [15] AT VI 27: CSM I 124.

[16] 'The world soul is rational or intelligent through and through [and] this doctrine provides the physical foundation for the ethical injunction that human beings, as parts of the whole, should conform themselves to universal nature by perfecting their rationality.' A. A. Long and D. N. Sedley, *The Hellenistic Philosophers* (Cambridge: Cambridge University Press, 1987), 319.

[17] *Discours de la méthode pour bien conduire sa raison et chercher la vérité dans les sciences* ('Discourse on the method needed for the good conduct of reason and for reaching the truth in the sciences'), AT VI 1: CSM I 111.

[18] See J. Cottingham, 'The Self and the Body: Alienation and Integration in Cartesian Ethics', *Seventeenth-Century French Studies*, 17 (1995), 1–13.   [19] Part Five, AT VI 44–5: CSM I 133.

how to understand the physiological processes in the human body, such as the circulation of the blood;[20] how to use the results of this knowledge in the development of a new medical science capable of 'freeing us from innumerable diseases and perhaps even from the infirmity of old age';[21] how, in short, to develop a systematic experimental technology enabling us to become 'lords and masters of nature'.[22] Descartes, no less than his Stoic predecessors, has a 'synoptic' conception of philosophy in which the recipe for the good life is integrally linked to an underlying cosmology, a theory of knowledge, and a characteristic vision of mankind's place in the world; but precisely because all the ingredients are now worked out differently, the resulting conception of how we should live turns out to be crucially different.

This is not to deny that Descartes has in common with the Stoics the objective of leading a contented life; and in common with them, he will advocate calm acceptance of what cannot be altered. But precisely because his new conception of science is progress-driven (the word 'progress' makes a conspicuous appearance in the very first sentence of the *Discourse*),[23] the extension class of what can be altered has undergone a momentous and irreversible expansion. It may be true that it is 'only our thoughts that are *entirely* within our power',[24] but nevertheless the indirect power humans can now aspire to have over the mechanical world and the mechanisms of the body is vastly increased. And the effects of this expansion make themselves felt not just in the areas of physics and physiology, but in the very subject matter of ethics itself. Like the Stoics, Descartes addresses the age-old task of helping mankind to live a rationally ordered life, and to come to terms with the often problematic relation between reason and the passions. But he will now bring to bear on that project a different analysis of the nature of mankind, a different notion of the role of the body in that nature, and a different account of the structure of the passions, and how they can be controlled.

---

[20] Part Five, AT VI 47 ff: CSM I 134 ff.   [21] Part Six, AT VI 62: CSM I 143.

[22] Ibid., quoted at n. 3 above. For the experimental emphasis in Descartes's scientific methodology, see AT VI 64–5: CSM I 144, and J. Cottingham, *A Descartes Dictionary*, s.v. 'experience'.

[23] The opening synopsis announces Descartes's aim of '*making further progress* in the investigation of nature than has hitherto been achieved' (*aller plus avant* en la recherche de la nature qu'il n'y a été); emphasis supplied.

[24] 'Il n'y a rien qui soit *entièrement* en notre pouvoir que nos pensées.' (AT VI 25: CSM I 123, emphasis supplied).

3. Human Nature

Notwithstanding his scientific programme for control of the environment and of the machine of the body, and despite his official dualistic metaphysics, Descartes became increasing preoccupied, when he came to develop the details of his ethical system, with the need for a genuine 'anthropology'—one which would do justice to the inescapable fact that we are not *merely* incorporeal minds inhabiting an alien mechanism, but creatures whose welfare is, in a special and intimate way, bound up with the operations of the body, and with the feelings, sensations, and passions that arise from our embodied state. The subject matter of Cartesian ethics becomes inescapably embroiled with what came to be the major task of Descartes's closing years, the task of coming to terms with—and trying to mitigate the harsher effects of—that alienation of man from nature which his own dualistic metaphysics and mechanistic science had threatened to generate.

The starting point for this project is Descartes's frequent insistence on the *special status* of human beings. Writing to Regius in 1642, Descartes observed:

Si angelus corpori humano inesset, non sentiret ut nos, sed tantum perciperet motus qui causarentur ab objectis externis, & per hoc a vero homine distingueretur. (If an angel were in a human body, it would not have sensations as we do, but would simply perceive the motions which are caused by external objects, and in this way would differ from a real human being.)[25]

A genuine human (*verus homo*): the phrase is a striking one, and it echoes the earlier French phrase that Descartes had employed in the *Discourse* several years earlier. To make a real human being, more is needed than the 'lodging' of a soul in the machine of the body: 'il est besoin qu'elle soit jointe et unie plus étroitement avec lui pour avoir ... des sentiments et des appétits semblables aux nôtres, et ainsi composer *un vrai homme*'.[26]

---

[25] Letter to Regius, January 1642 (AT III 493: CSMK 206).

[26] 'Next [after describing the machine of the body] I described the rational soul, and showed that, unlike the other things of which I had spoken, it cannot be derived in any way from the potentiality of matter, but must be specially created. And I showed how it is not sufficient for it to be lodged in the human body like a helmsman in his ship, except perhaps to move its limbs, but that it must be more closely joined and united with the body in order to have, besides this power of movement, feelings and appetites like ours, and so to constitute *a real human being*.' *Discourse*, Part Five, AT VI 59: CSM I 141, emphasis supplied. Descartes is here referring back to his earlier work in the *Traité de l'homme*.

A human is no mere soul making use of a body, no mere pilot lodged in the corporeal ship, but a genuine entity in its own right. It is an entity, moreover, with properties (sensory states, emotions, and passions) that are not reducible either to modes of extension, or to pure modes of thought.[27]

The special nature of human beings has obvious and immediate implications for ethics. Previous ethical systems developed by the Greeks tended to take on a 'ratiocentric' bias, which led to problems about applying a rationally devised life-plan to the awkwardly recalcitrant realm of human feeling and emotion.[28] The Cartesian model for science seems at first to be even more ratiocentric, viewing the world as an abstract, mathematically ordered system of 'extended matter in motion', and construing the human contemplators of that system as pure thinking things, detached from the world of extension, and alienated even from the physical mechanisms of their own bodies. But Descartes's attempt to develop a distinctive 'anthropology' puts all this in a rather different focus. Although the deliverances of reason reveal a rigidly dualistic world of extended matter plus incorporeal consciousness, our own daily experience as human beings provides a very different kind of awareness—one coloured by intimate and urgent feeling and emotion, one that projects us into the very centre of a 'substantial union' of mind and body, where, so far from operating as cognitive pilots of an alien bodily machine, each of us finds the operations of the body that is in a special and intimate sense his *own* giving rise to a rich and vivid sensory and emotional life. This is not to say that the Cartesian doctrine of man as 'substantial union' is free from problems; as Descartes himself had to admit, the way in which soul is united to body was beyond the power of philosophical reason to explicate fully, and has to be grasped on the level of our inner experience.[29] But what does emerge is a new

[27] For more on this irreducibility, see ch. 5 of J. Cottingham, *Descartes* (Oxford: Blackwell, 1986), and Ch. 9 above.

[28] The problems have their origins in Plato, but pervade the ethical thinking of many later writers, notably the Stoics. Compare Stobaeus [*c.*5th cent. AD], 2. 88–90: 'Every passion is overpowering, since people in states of passion, though they frequently see that it is not suitable to do something, are carried away by the intensity, as though by a disobedient horse, and induced to do it … In states of passion, even if people realize … that one should not feel distress or fear or be in any state of passion, they still do not give these up, but are brought into a position of being controlled by their tyranny.' Cited in Long and Sedley, *The Hellenistic Philosophers*, no. 65A.

[29] 'What belongs to the union of the soul and the body is known only obscurely by the intellect … but it is known very clearly by the senses … Metaphysical thoughts, which exercise the pure intellect, help to familiarise us with the notion of the soul; the study of mathematics … accustoms us to form very

account of the subject matter of ethics. The 'most perfect moral system' that Descartes envisaged as the crown of his philosophical enterprise would, to be sure, presuppose a fully developed physics of matter in motion, an understanding of the mechanical operations of extended matter. And it would also require an understanding that our own nature as thinking beings is distinct from, and irreducible to, the operations of the material world. The picture so far is of a predatory Cartesian ego, manipulating the alien material environment to its own purposes. But for all that, ethics will have its own distinct subject matter—a subject matter that is irreducible in the sense that it cannot be fully understood either in terms of the mathematical descriptions of physics, or of the purely intellectual and volitional operations of the mind. To understand what makes us most fully and distinctively human, we need to go beyond the categories of thought and extension, and focus on the affective dimension of which we are vividly and immediately aware in our daily experience as creatures of flesh and blood.

In his final work, Les Passions de l'âme, Descartes wrote that 'those whom the passions can move most deeply are capable of enjoying the sweetest pleasures of this life'.[30] The work is largely concerned with a detailed examination of the physiological basis for the occurrence of human emotions. But Descartes also insists on the subjective dimension—the way in which the passions affect the conscious subject who, as he had earlier put it, is 'not merely lodged in the body but closely intermingled with it'.[31] Descartes saw the passions as crucial for the ethical quality of our lives. And what matters from the ethical point of view is not just the physiological events (vital though these are for understanding how we work), but the way in which such events are presented to consciousness as fear, hope, anxiety, confidence, despair, jealousy, pity, anger, pride, shame, cheerfulness, and love. Here Descartes offers the hope that by careful training, and the resolute exercise of our will, we can become not the slaves but the masters of our biological inheritance: 'ceux même qui ont les plus faibles âmes pourraient acquérir un empire très absolu sur toutes leurs passions, si on employait assez

---

distinct notions of body. But it is the ordinary course of life and conversation, and abstention from meditation ... that teaches us how to conceive the union of the soul and body.' Letter to Elizabeth of 28 June 1643, AT III 691–2: CSMK 227.   [30] *Passions of the Soul*, art. 212 (AT XI 488: CSM I 404).

[31] Sixth Meditation, AT VII 81: CSM II 56.

d'industrie à les dresser et à les conduire.'[32] But the result of this will be a life not of confined and curtailed passions, but of passions properly channelled, a life where humans can experience emotional richness and joy.[33]

Descartes clearly saw that a complete philosophical system must find space for the affective dimension of our existence, for the significance of sensation, emotion, and feeling in the way in which we understand ourselves, and conduct our lives. The 'perfect moral system', in short, would be an organic outgrowth from Descartes's 'anthropology',[34] and would rest on the fullest possible understanding of the workings of the passions in human life.

4. The Role of the Passions

The conclusions of the previous section have underlined the special status of human beings, and the correspondingly special subject matter of ethics. But it might be supposed that this very specialness isolates Descartes's ethics from the rest of the Cartesian system, rather than integrating into the organically unified structure of his philosophy. How is such an integration possible?

Descartes wrote to a correspondent in 1646 that his results in physics had been 'a great help in establishing sure foundations in moral philosophy';[35] and when he finally published his treatise on the passions he distinguished his approach from that of many of his predecessors by stressing his goal of explaining the passions *en physicien*—from the point of view of a physical

---

[32] 'Even those who have the weakest souls could acquire a very absolute control over the passions, if enough work were expended on training and guiding them.' *Passions of the Soul*, art. 50 (AT XI 370: CSM I 348).

[33] 'La philosophie que je cultive n'est pas si barbare ni si farouche qu'elle rejette l'usage des passions; au contraire, c'est en lui seul que je mets toute la douceur et la félicité de cette vie.' ('The philosophy I cultivate is not so savage or grim as to outlaw the operation of the passions; on the contrary, it is here, in my view, that the entire sweetness and joy of this life is to be found.') Letter to ?Silhon, March or April 1648: AT V 135.

[34] Descartes's work on the passions is aptly described by Geneviève Rodis-Lewis as 'a ground-breaking study concerning a modality specific to the union between soul and body.' (Introduction to S. Voss (ed.), *Descartes: The Passions of the Soul*, p. xv.) Many of the issues raised in this chapter are brilliantly illuminated by Rodis-Lewis in her *L'Anthropologie cartésienne* (Paris: Presses Universitaires de France, 1990), Introduction and ch. 1.

[35] '...la notion telle quelle de la Physique, que j'ai tâché d'acquérir, m'a grandement servi pour établir des fondements certains en la Morale' (to Chanut, 15 June 1646, AT IV 441: CSMK 289).

scientist.[36] The etymology of the term 'passion' (derived from the Latin verb for 'to suffer'),[37] suggests something contrasted with an action—something that *happens* to a person, as opposed to that which he initiates. Hence Descartes observes that in the broadest sense anything that is not an active volition of the soul may be called a passion; but he reserves the term in its more restricted sense for those mental happenings that are the result of the soul's *union with the body*: 'those perceptions, sensations or emotions of the soul which … are caused, maintained and strengthened by some movement of the [animal] spirits'.[38] The passions, for Descartes, are but one group of phenomena whose operation depends on the transmission of neural impulses. According to Descartes, what we are aware of as sensations (such as those of heat or cold), feelings (such as those of hunger and thirst), and emotions or passions (such as joy and sadness) are all caused, on the material level, by various physiological disturbances (for example in the heart, the blood, and the surface of the skin); these disturbances excite movements of the 'animal spirits' that are in turn transmitted, via the nervous system, to the brain.[39]

What mediates the resulting brain events and the ensuing awareness in the soul is the tiny gland in the centre of the brain that, notoriously, Descartes identified as the 'principal seat of the soul'.[40] It is here that the minute fluctuations in the animal spirits produce a distinctive pattern of

[36] AT XI 326: CSM I 327. The idea that the passions involve both physiological and psychological aspects was an ancient one, going back to Aristotle. The sixteenth-century Coimbrian commentators on Aristotle had classified the passions as 'affects of the soul in common with the body' (affectus communes animae cum corpore): *Commentarii de anima*, I. 1, cited in E. Gilson, *Index Scolastico-Cartésien* (Paris: Alcan, 1913; 2nd edn., Paris: Vrin, 1979), no. 322. The scholastic philosopher Eustachius, Descartes's near-contemporary whom he had studied as a schoolboy, defines a passion as 'a movement of the sensitive appetite arising from the apprehension of some good or evil, accompanied with some unnatural bodily change'—'unnatural' here denoting an abnormal or excessive physiological response, such as increased heart-rate (Eustachius, *Summa philosophiae*, pt. II, third part, tr. 2, disc. 1, qu. 2, cited in Gilson, *Index*, no. 321). It is, of course, a matter of common-sense observation and personal experience that many emotions are accompanied by physiological changes (for example, embarrassment by flushing). Descartes, however, will bring the details of his mechanistic physiology to bear on a new account of how the passions may be controlled and modified.

[37] Descartes's use of the French *passion* corresponds to the standard scholastic Latin term *passio*, (from the verb *patior*, to suffer), which in turn corresponds to Aristotle's term *pathos*, similarly derived from the ordinary Greek verb for 'to suffer'. For standard definitions of the term in scholastic philosophy, see preceding note.   [38] *Passions of the Soul*, art. 27 (AT XI 349: CSM I 339).

[39] Compare the list in the *Principles of Philosophy*, pt. I art. 48. Descartes distinguishes the passions from other kinds of sensory and appetitive states by the fact that the passions are 'referred to the soul', while other items in the list (such as 'smells, sounds and colours') are 'referred to external objects', and others again (such as 'hunger, thirst and pain') are 'referred to our own body' (*Passions*, art. 29).

[40] *Passions*, art. 32. See Cottingham, *A Descartes Dictionary*, s.v. 'pineal gland'.

movement that causes the soul to have a particular mode of sensory or emotional awareness (and conversely, it is in the gland that the volitions of the soul are translated into movements that subsequently generate, via the nerves, appropriate muscle contractions for the performance of bodily movements such as walking or speaking).[41] The positing of a kind of cerebral 'fax machine to the soul' (in Daniel Dennett's scathing phrase)[42] has not impressed subsequent critics; those exercised with the problem of psychophysical causation (how an immaterial soul can be stimulated by, and cause movements in, the machine of the body) are hardly likely to have their worries allayed by being told that the soul interacts, not with the body as a whole, but with a particular gland in the brain. But it is important not to be sidetracked by Descartes's bizarre choice of a specific organ to be the 'seat of the soul'. For all its awkwardness, Descartes's theory does succeed in pointing up a crucial feature about the nature of human emotional and sensory awareness, namely that the various modes of such awareness are intimately linked with physiologically determined processes of which in our ordinary lives we are, for the most part, quite ignorant. This central point is quite independent of the truth or falsity of Descartes's official dualistic theory of an incorporeal mind. And it is also unaffected by the fine detail of the physiological story involved: Descartes's 'pneumatic' theory of the nervous system supposes the brain is stimulated by the rapid movements of a fine gas along the hollow pipes of the nerves; nowadays, we have at our disposal a vastly more sophisticated electrochemical explanatory apparatus. But in our ordinary lives, unless we are neuroanatomists or biochemists, we are more or less ignorant of what is going on at this level. And even if we do happen to know about it, such knowledge plays no role in the immediate and direct awareness we generally have of our sensory and emotional states. What is crucial for ethics, however, and it is this that Descartes is about to explore with illuminating effect, is that the operation and functioning of those affective modes (such as joy, excitement, and distress), despite the direct awareness we have of them, is nonetheless not under direct conscious control. For the causal genesis of those states, at the physiological level, is largely opaque to the conscious subject.

[41] Cf. *Traité de l'homme*, AT XI 176–7: CSM I 106–7.; *La Dioptrique*, AT VI 141–2: CSM I 172–3.

[42] Cf. D. Dennett, *Consciousness Explained* (Harmondsworth: Allen Lane, 1992), 106.

It is here that Cartesian anthropology, Descartes's insistence on our essentially embodied nature as human beings, yields a rich harvest. The traditional project of Greek ethics involved the goal of achieving the kind of rational mastery, or at least guidance, of the emotions and passions that would enable humans to lead a good and fulfilling life. And Descartes subscribes to this ancient aspiration: herein, he declares, lies the 'chief use' of philosophical wisdom.[43] But because of our embodied nature we cannot, by the mere exercise of our will, generate the desired patterns of emotional response, since we cannot directly control the relevant physiological changes in our bodies—any more than we can directly control any other events in the physical universe. The natural (or divinely ordained)[44] correlations between physiological events and psychological states are not within our power to set up from scratch; they were laid down, as part of our human nature, long before we came on the scene, so to speak—long before we emerged, either evolutionarily, as a species, or in our individual journey to adult life, as thinking beings.[45] But although human beings are not self-creating, although they are, as it were, lumbered with genetically and environmentally laid down patterns of psychophysical response, they are nonetheless in the unique position of being able to investigate, reflect on, and to a considerable extent modify, the relevant responses. It is here that Descartes makes a crucial contribution to the age-old debate over the relation between reason and the passions, by pioneering what we now know as the theory of the conditioned response.

Descartes's starting point is that even animals, who lack rational awareness, can be trained in such a way as to modify pre-existing patterns of physiological and behavioural response. As early as 1630 he had reflected on the possibility that 'if you whipped a dog five or six times to the sound of a violin, it would begin to howl and run away as soon as it

[43] *Passions*, art. 212.

[44] The two notions come down to the same thing for Descartes; cf. Sixth Meditation (AT VII 88: CSM II 60–1).

[45] The term 'evolution' is not entirely anachronistic when applied to Descartes, since he clearly subscribes to a gradualist view of the origins of the universe, and of living things (cf. *Le Monde*, AT XI 34: CSM I 91). However, Descartes's account of the human species invokes a special creative act whereby the Creator implants a rational soul in the body (cf. *Discourse*, Part Five, AT VI 59: CSM I 141). But the significance of the fact that we are lumbered with predetermined patterns of psychophysical response is unaffected by the question of whether those patterns evolved over time, or were specially ordained by God.

heard that music again'.[46] A more detailed canine example is given in the *Passions*:

When a dog sees a partridge it is naturally disposed to run towards it; and when it hears a gun fired, the noise naturally impels it to run away. Nevertheless, setters are commonly trained so that the sight of partridge makes them stop, and the noise they hear afterwards, when someone fires at the bird, makes them run towards it. These things are worth noting in order to encourage each of us to make a point of controlling our passions. For since we are able, with a little effort, to change the movements of the brain in animals devoid of reason, it is evident that we can do so still more effectively in the case of human beings. [47]

In adapting the example of animal training to the human sphere, Descartes retains the central idea of the conditioned response as the key to how the innately predetermined mechanisms of the body can be modified to our advantage. The idea that the good life requires training and habituation had, of course, been explored by Aristotle: virtue depends, in the Aristotelian account, on our having acquired the right habits of feeling and action, on our possession not just of 'right reason', but of the appropriate kinds of ingrained dispositions to feel and behave in the right ways.[48] What Descartes now adds to this story is the perspective of the behavioural and physiological scientist who is able to investigate the physical causes of our emotional patterns of response, and in time learn to manipulate and 'reprogram' them.

A memorable example that Descartes provides from his own personal experience has direct implications for ethics:

The objects which strike our senses by mean of the nerves move certain parts of our brain and there make certain folds...[and] the place where the folds were made has a tendency to be folded again in the same manner by another object resembling even incompletely the original. When I was a child, I loved a girl of my own age who had a slight squint (*une fille de mon âge qui était un peu louche*). The impression made by sight in my brain when I looked at her cross-eyes became so closely connected to the simultaneous impression which aroused in me the passion of love that for a long time afterwards when I saw persons with a squint I felt

---

[46] To Mersenne, 18 March 1630 (AT I 134: CSMK 20). Descartes's reflections in this regard were partly stimulated by the writings of some of his Renaissance predecessors. In art. 127 of the *Passions* he refers to the work of the sixteenth-century scholar Juan Luis Vives, who had cited an example of a morbid condition in which laughter was aroused by certain foods.   [47] *Passions*, art. 50.

[48] Aristotle, *Nicomachean Ethics* [*c*.325 BC], bk. 2.

a special inclination to love them simply because they had that defect; yet I had no idea myself that this was why it was. However, as soon as I reflected on it, and recognized that it was a defect, I ceased to be affected by it. So when we are inclined to love someone without knowing the reason, we may believe that this is because they have some similarity to something in an earlier object of our love, though we may not be able to identify it.[49]

There are two points of immediate importance here. The first is the notion of a physiological genesis for the passions: as a result of sensory stimulation, a 'fold' (or neural pathway, as we might now say) is set up in the brain that predisposes us to react in similar ways to future stimuli of a like kind. Second, there is the idea that an investigation of the circumstances of the original stimulus (backed up by an informed physiological theory) can enable us to stand back, as it were, from the causal nexus (in a way animals are unable to do), and consider the possibility of modifying our future responses.

But there is a third, underlying, insight that has special significance for the role of the passions in the good life. Traditional 'logocentric' models had assumed a kind of transparency about the operation of the passions: we are aware of what we ought rationally to do, and we are also aware of emotions that often pull us in the opposite direction. Ethically correct conduct consists, on this model, in devising some way to bring the passions into line with reason, but we are offered precious little guidance as to how this desired outcome is to be achieved; more striking still, on the traditional model, it is something of a mystery that the 'greater good', once perceived by reason is not automatically chosen. This left the classical moral philosophers signally ill-equipped to understand the phenomenon of weakness or *akrasia*—the plain fact that, as a result of the passions, human beings often just fail to select what is clearly perceived as the better of two options. To tackle this problem, Descartes now offers a strikingly original insight: *the causal genesis and subsequent occurrence of the passions is intimately linked to corporeal events in ways that often make the force of the resultant emotion opaque to reason.* What so often threatens to overwhelm us when we are in the grip of a potentially damaging passion is precisely the fact that

---

[49] Letter to Chanut of 6 June 1647 (AT V 57: CSMK 323). For the notion of 'folds in the brain' (a kind of crude mechanical anticipation of the modern notion of neural pathways) see *Conversation with Burman*, AT V 150: CSMK 336.

something is happening to us whose basis, in our physiological makeup, and our past psychological history, we only dimly understand, if at all. And realizing this in turn offers for the first time the hope that humans may be able to achieve successful 'management' of the passions. 'As soon as I reflected on [the causes]', says Descartes about his infatuation with cross-eyed women, 'I ceased to be affected by it.' Here there emerges the idea of a genuine 'therapy' for the passions that offers a completely new route from the old Stoic and Epicurean ideas of suppression and avoidance, on the one hand, or the purely cognitive exercise of eliminating false beliefs on the other.[50] Examining the passions *en physicien*, from the point of view of a natural scientist, reveals the full extent to which their influence depends on factors below the threshold of consciousness. We now have a striking paradox: Descartes, the very thinker who is so often accused of having a naive theory of the perfect *transparency* of the mind,[51] is actually telling us that our emotional life as embodied creatures, as human beings, is subject to a serious and pervasive *opacity*. A proper understanding of our human nature involves recognition of the extent to which we are not just angelic minds inhabiting bodily mechanisms, but creatures whose deepest and strongest feelings are intimately tied up with structures and events that are concealed from us as 'thinking beings'. Coming to terms with the essential opacity to the conscious mind of the operation of the passions now becomes the chief task of what might be called Descartes's 'anthropologically informed' ethics.

In what is, in some respects at least, a striking anticipation of the Freudian line, Descartes links his new approach to the passions with an analysis of the way in which the structure of our emotional lives is influenced by the forgotten events and pre-rational experiences of early childhood. In 1647, Queen Christina of Sweden, with blithely regal authority, had commanded the French resident in Stockholm to obtain Descartes's answer to the

---

[50] For a more 'therapeutic' view of the Epicurean approach, see Martha Nussbaum, 'Words Not Arms', in her edited collection *The Poetics of Therapy* (Edmonton: Academic Publishing, 1990).

[51] It is fairly common, for example, for commentators on the Freudian notion of the unconscious mind to say that Freud broke from the *Cartesian* thesis that mentality and consciousness are equivalent; cf. S. Gardner, *Irrationality and the Philosophy of Psychoanalysis* (Cambridge: Cambridge University Press, 1993), 207. Margaret Wilson in her *Descartes* (London: Routledge, 1978) attributes to Descartes 'the doctrine of epistemological transparency of thought or mind' (p. 50), though she does go on to discuss certain aspects of Descartes's philosophy of mind that are in potential conflict with that doctrine (cf. p. 164).

momentous question 'What is love?'[52] In his reply, Descartes made an important distinction between 'purely intellectual or rational love' and 'the love which is a passion'. The former consists simply in the calm volition of the soul to 'join itself' to some rationally perceived good. This is the kind of love, presumably, that a pure intellectual being such as an angel might enjoy, and which human beings experience when they pursue, rationally and without disturbance, those goods that their reason adjudges worthy to be obtained. But things are very different when, as so often happens, we desire something in an emotionally charged way, when, as we say, we feel 'churned up' about someone or something. What complicates the picture here is, on the physiological level, the powerful patterns of bodily response that have been laid down in the past, and, on the psychological level, the compelling, though often obscure and confused, emotions we experience without fully understanding their causes. In such cases, 'the rational thoughts involved are accompanied by the confused feelings of our childhood which remain joined to them'. A full explanation of the passions, in short, involves a detailed examination of the history of our early lives, going right back, says Descartes, to 'when we first came into the world'; 'it is this which makes the nature of love hard for us to understand'.[53]

Descartes's theory of the passions thus offers us the hope that by an informed understanding of their psycho–physiological causes we may be able to lead enriched lives, free from the feeling that we are dominated by forces outside our control. It might seem at first that this would lead his ethics back in a broadly Platonic or Stoic direction, towards the thought that the source of our human problems is an essentially cognitive one,

---

[52] The resident was one of Descartes's important correspondents in his later years, Hector-Pierre Chanut (later to become French ambassador to Sweden).

[53] By the phrase 'when we first came into the world', Descartes has in mind the soul's first union with the body; hence he traces the causes of the passions back even prior to birth, to the experiences undergone inside the womb: '...d'autant que l'amour n'était causée, avant la naissance, que par un aliment convenable qui, entrant abondamment dans le foie, dans le cœur et dans le poumon, y excitait plus de chaleur que de coutume, de là vient que maintenant cette chaleur accompagne toujours l'amour, encore qu'il vienne d'autres causes fort differentes' ('Before birth, love was caused only by suitable nourishment which, entering in abundance into the liver, heart and lungs, produced an unusual increase of heat, which is the reason why similar heat still always accompanies love, even though produced by very different causes.') The general moral is then drawn: 'Ce sont ces sentiments confus de notre enfance, qui, demeurant jointes avec les pensées raisonnables par lesquelles nous aimons ce que nous en jugeons digne, sont cause que la nature de l'amour nous est difficile à connaître.' ('It is because of the confused feelings of our childhood, which remain joined to the rational thoughts by which we love what we judge worthy of love, that the nature of love is hard for us to understand.') Letter to Chanut of 1 February 1647, AT IV 606: CSMK 308.

and that a purified understanding would leave us free to pursue the goods that are revealed by reason to be most worthy of attainment. There are certainly places where Descartes appears attracted by the Platonic idea that all weakness is due to ignorance. In the *Discourse on the Method* he remarks that 'to act well it is sufficient to judge well' ('il suffit de bien juger pour bien faire'); defending this claim to a correspondent he quotes with apparent approval the maxim 'omnis peccans est ignorans' (whoever sins does so in ignorance), an echo of the Platonic doctrine that no one intentionally chooses the lesser good.[54] An intellectualist approach to the ethics of reason and the passions is perhaps most prominent in a letter to Elizabeth written in 1645:

Often passion makes us believe certain things to be much better and more desirable than they are; then, when we have taken much trouble to acquire them, and in the process lost the chance of possessing other more genuine goods, possession of them brings home to us their defects; and thence arise dissatisfaction, regret and remorse. And so the true function of reason is to examine the just value of all the goods whose acquisition seems to depend in some way on our conduct, so that we never fail to devote all our efforts to trying to secure those which are in fact the more desirable.[55]

But although Descartes clearly shares with Plato and the Stoics a firm belief in the importance of an informed rational evaluation of the options open to us, he nonetheless goes on to resist the kind of austere intellectualism that rejects the operation of the passions as harmful to the good life. The Stoic ideal of *apatheia*, the transcendence of the normal human passions, is one he had implicitly condemned as early as the *Discourse*: the supposed virtues of the Stoic heroes, Cato and Brutus, are in his eyes, examples of insensitivity, pride, and despair.[56] Taking up the theme with a correspondent ten years

---

[54] Cf. Plato, *Protagoras* [c.390 BC], 345e1. In the *Conversation with Burman* (AT V 159: CSMK 342), Descartes is reported as asserting that 'no one can pursue evil qua evil', a direct echo of Plato's claim 'oudeis bouletai ta kaka' (*Meno* [c.385 BC], 78b1).

[55] Letter of 1 September 1645 (AT IV 284–5: CSMK 264). Descartes goes on to say that the passions often 'represent the goods to which they tend with greater splendour than they deserve and they make us imagine pleasure to be much greater before we possess them than our subsequent experiences show them to be.' The letter concludes with the observation that 'the true function of reason in the conduct of life is to examine and consider without passion the value of all the perfections, both of the body and of the soul, which can be acquired by our conduct, so that since we are commonly obliged to deprive ourselves of some good in order to acquire others, we shall always choose the better'.

[56] AT VI 8: CSM I 114. See further the comments by G. Rodis-Lewis in S. Voss (ed.), *Descartes, Passions of the Soul*, p. xvi, and in J. Cottingham (ed.), *The Cambridge Companion to Descartes*

later, he insisted not only that the passions were not to be suppressed, but also that some of them were a positive good, indeed the sole source of our greatest human joys.[57]

Here once more Cartesian 'anthropology' exerts its influence; for the 'substantial union' of soul and body that constitutes a human being requires, for its survival and well-being, not just intellection and volition, but the whole range of sensory and affective states. All sensory states, as we have seen, are attributable to us not qua pure 'thinking things', but qua embodied creatures—human beings. And it is clear that many of the psychophysical correlations involved are crucial for our survival, both as individuals and as a species: that we feel a characteristic kind of discomfort when the stomach is empty and the blood sugar low has obvious survival value in impelling us to eat (and thus relieving the feeling of hunger); that I feel pain when I tread on a thorn has evident utility in encouraging me to avoid such noxious stimuli in future. Nowadays, Darwinian explanations are available to account for the origin of this kind of beneficial sensory monitoring of our bodily states; Descartes, in more metaphysical terms, but with the same implicit functional thesis in mind, invokes the benevolence of God in providing human beings with 'information about what is beneficial or harmful for the [human] mind–body composite'.[58] The upshot, in the case of the passions, is that we are dealing with a psychophysical system whose operation has a signal utility for our life and health as human

(Cambridge: Cambridge University Press, 1992), 27–8. Cf. the following analysis by Zarka: 'Du stoïcisme, [Descartes] n'accepte point la théorie fondamentale de l'apathe, c'est-à-dire la suppression complète de toute passion. La passion, pour Descartes, participe de l'optimisme stoïcien; elle est par conséquent bonne, elle n'est nuisible que dans ses excès. Elle est bonne si l'on sait en faire un bon usage, c'est-à-dire, si la volonté sait s'en servir, et c'est alors que nous retrouvons le stoïcien. Descartes, lui aussi, ne voit dans l'âme qu'entendement et volonté; il sacrifie la sensibilité (La Renaissance du stoïcisme au xvie siècle, 337–8). Much of this analysis seems sound, except for the final clause: as will be clear from much of the discussion of 'Cartesian anthropology' in this chapter, I would fundamentally reject the notion that the domain of the sensible is 'sacrificed' in Descartes's philosophical psychology.

[57] See passage quoted above, n. 33. Descartes goes on to observe that 'although some of the passions can be vicious when carried to excess, others are such that the more extreme they are, the better they are'. (AT V 135).

[58] Sixth Meditation, AT VII 83: CSM II 57. The question arises of why animals, too, would not benefit from such apparatus; Descartes seems to believe that their avoidance of noxious stimuli arises purely from a mechanical response system, but there are clearly problems with this notion (which seems to make dogs too much like insects); for some of the difficulties, see J. Cottingham, A Descartes Dictionary, s.v. 'animal'. For a detailed discussion of Descartes's views on the epistemological and functional role of sensory experience, see Ann Wilbur MacKenzie, 'The Reconfiguration of Sensory Experience', in J. Cottingham (ed.), Reason, Will and Sensation : Studies in Descartes's Metaphysics (Oxford: Oxford University Press, 1994), 251–72.

beings; thus, 'the principal effect of all the human passions is that they move and dispose the soul to want the things for which they prepare the body—for example, the feeling of fear moves the soul to want to flee, and that of courage to want to fight, and similarly with the other passions'.[59]

If the good life is to be a life for human beings, the passions are to be embraced, since their operation is intimately related to our human welfare. This is not to say that they are always and uncontroversially good. Because of the relatively rigid way innate physiological mechanisms and environmentally conditioned responses operate, we may become locked into behaviour that leads to distress, misery, or harm. The dropsical man feels a strong desire to drink, even when fluid is the last thing his health requires; the young Descartes feels strongly attracted to cross-eyed women irrespective of how far they are worthy of his affection. But the appropriate way to cope with such irrational impulses is not to retreat to an austere intellectualism, nor to suppress the passions, but rather to use the resources of science and experience to try to understand what has caused things to go awry, and then to attempt to reprogram our responses so that the direction in which we are led by the passions corresponds to what our reason perceives as the best option. Despite the alienation of man from nature that Cartesian science often threatens to bring about, Descartes's underlying vision of the human condition is pervaded by a deep optimism. Awkwardly hybrid creatures of pure mind compounded with mechanical body, we are nonetheless, at the level of our ordinary daily experience, intimately aware of a whole range of sensory and emotional responses whose operation, in general and in the long run, is designed to conduce to human fulfilment.[60] This is why Descartes insists that 'the pleasures of the body should not be despised, nor should one free oneself altogether from the passions'.[61] The Christianized Platonist in Descartes acknowledges that 'the soul can have pleasures of its own'; but, that said, he immediately

---

[59] *Passions*, art. 40. Descartes's reflections on the functional role of the passions led him to some interesting reflections on the psychosomatic causes of illness and sound health; cf. letter to Elizabeth of May or June 1645 (AT IV 218–21: CSMK 250).

[60] For the qualifications 'in general' and 'in the long run', cf. the discussion in the Sixth Meditation, AT VII 87–90: CSM II 60–2.

[61] Letter to Elizabeth of 1 September 1645 (AT IV 287: CSMK 265). Contrast the antihedonistic orientation of the Stoics: 'vera voluptas voluptatum contemptio' (True pleasure is to despise the pleasures). Seneca, *De vita beata* [c.AD 58], 4. 2.

moves to a ringing endorsement of the affective dimension that arises from the inescapably corporeal side to our humanity:

The pleasures common to soul and body depend entirely on the passions, so that persons whom the passions can move most deeply are capable of enjoying the sweetest pleasures of this life. It is true that they may also experience the most bitterness when they do not know how to put these passions to good use, and when fortune works against them. But the chief use of wisdom lies in teaching us to be masters of our passions and to control them with such skill that the evils which they cause are quite bearable, and even become a source of joy.[62]

The message is one of reconciliation and integration. And the personal integration that is the goal of Descartes's moral teachings is paralleled by the philosophical integration that joins his moral theory to the rest of his system, as branch to stem. By understanding our special human nature, and coming to see how its workings relate both to the operation of the bodily machine and to our rational goals as thinking beings, we can achieve courage to endure, and hope of joy.

---

[62] *Passions*, art. 212.

13

The Role of God in Descartes's Philosophy

1. Introduction: The Cartesian Image

Each age tends to reinterpret or refashion the ideas of the great canonical philosophers for its own purposes, and the ideas of Descartes have not been exempt from this process. Indeed, perhaps more than any other major thinker, Descartes has become a kind of philosophical icon, displayed in the textbooks and commentaries of the last hundred years or so in a confusing variety of guises. In a version of the history of ideas that was widely promoted some decades ago, he figured as the archetypal 'rationalist' metaphysician, attempting to spin out a whole deductive system of philosophy and science a priori, from premises derived entirely from inner reflection. In the 'linguistic' phase that gripped philosophy in the wake of Wittgenstein, he was pilloried as the supposed advocate of the fallacy that language and thought can occur within a wholly subjective or private domain. And in the 'naturalistic' turn that has characterized much of the more recent philosophical past, he is routinely lambasted as the champion of a dualistic theory of the mind—the view that consciousness is a wholly immaterial phenomenon, entirely attributable to a non-physical soul.

These images of Descartes are all questionable, but that has not prevented their gaining a secure place in the set of default assumptions that condition how students and scholars use the label 'Cartesian'. In reality, the 'rationalist' image is belied by the importance Descartes himself gave to experimentation, and to empirical hypotheses tested against experience;[1]

---

[1] See D. Clarke, *Descartes' Philosophy of Science* (University Park: Pennsylvania State University Press, 1982), and J. Cottingham, 'The Cartesian Legacy', *Proceedings of the Aristotelian Society*, Supp. 66 (1992), 1–21, repr. as Ch. 2, above.

the image of Descartes's philosophy as starting from a domain of private or subjective ideas is belied by his belief in an objective realm of meaning;[2] and the 'dualist' label, though containing undeniable elements of truth, needs much qualifying when we start to look at Descartes's own insistence on the embodied nature of much of our human experience, in particular our feelings and emotions.[3]

Alongside these specific interpretations and counter-interpretations of various aspects of Descartes's philosophy, there is an interesting general question that all who approach the thought of 'the father of modern philosophy' must sooner or later confront: what exactly did Descartes himself chiefly take himself to be doing—what was his self-image as a philosopher? For many modern generations of students brought up on standard Introduction to Philosophy courses, the answer is obvious: he is primarily an 'epistemologist'—that is, he wanted to establish what, if anything, can be *known* for certain. On this view, the most important questions in Cartesian philosophy are such questions as 'Are the senses reliable?', 'Can I really know whether I am awake or asleep?', 'Are judgements such as "two plus two makes four" immune from error?', and 'Can I be certain of the existence of an external world?' More recently, the image of Descartes the epistemologist has partly given way to that of Descartes the scientist: the puzzles in the *Meditations* about illusions and dreaming, and the malicious demon bent on deceiving us, are (on this view) simply a preliminary to the building of a new scientific system, offering a complete set of explanations of the nature of the universe, and everything within it.[4]

These general accounts of the Cartesian project have much to tell us, though they also need to be treated with caution if they are supposed to give us 'the key' to Descartes's philosophy. René Descartes was one of those very few philosophical giants—perhaps two or three emerge each century, if we are lucky—whose genius defies easy classification, and whose

---

[2] See J. Cottingham, ' "The only sure sign..." Descartes on Thought and Language', in J. M. Preston (ed.), *Thought and Language* (Cambridge: Cambridge University Press), 29–50, reprinted as Ch. 5, above.

[3] See J. Cottingham, *Philosophy and the Good Life: Reason and the Passions in Greek, Cartesian and Psychoanalytic Ethics* (Cambridge: Cambridge University Press, 1998), or Ch. 12, above.

[4] See M. D. Wilson, *Descartes* (London: Routledge, 1978); D. Garber, *Descartes' Metaphysical Physics* (Chicago: Chicago University, 1992), and D. Clarke, *Descartes's Theory of the Mind* (Oxford: Clarendon, 2003).

thought is sufficiently original and challenging to resist boiling down to a simple set of aims and objectives. For the purposes of the present chapter, however, I want not so much to criticize any of the above interpretative accounts as to draw attention to something that is curiously absent from all the iconic images of Descartes so far mentioned.

Someone casting an eye over the various images sketched above might be forgiven for supposing that Descartes, however interpreted, is above all a *secular* philosopher. An a-priori system-builder, advocate of 'Cartesian privacy', philosopher of mind, epistemologist, proto-scientist—all these images fit, for the most part, as models or as targets, within the agendas of the modern anglophone philosophical academy. But if readers who are new to Descartes pick up any one of his great masterpieces, the *Discourse*, the *Meditations*, or the *Principles*, they will be surprised to find that what has pride of place in the construction of his philosophical system is something that is almost never found in today's typical research agendas—an appeal to God. Within contemporary philosophy departments there are still, of course, a considerable number of academics who discuss arguments for God's existence and other topics concerned with religious belief; but their work, for the most part, occurs within the confines of a specialized branch of philosophy called 'philosophy of religion', and as a general rule it tends not to spill over into the content of the 'mainstream' arguments and debates that preoccupy those working in the rest of the subject. For Descartes, by contrast, the nature and existence of the Deity is something that lies at the very heart of his entire philosophical system—something without which it would be entirely unrecognizable.

2. The Eclipse of God in Conceptions of Cartesianism

How is it, then, that something so central to Descartes's philosophy has faded, to a greater or lesser extent, from our contemporary images of his work? One answer has already indirectly been alluded to, and is connected with the 'naturalistic revolution which has swept anglophone philosophy over the last three decades'—a revolution inspired by the vision that philosophers should 'either … adopt and emulate the method of successful sciences, or … operate in tandem with the sciences, as their abstract and reflective branch'.[5] The considerable number of present-day philosophers who subscribe to this scientistic vision of how philosophy should proceed may (in so far as they pay any attention to the history of their subject) have some interest in Descartes's views on scientific method, or the criteria for knowledge, or his discussions on, for example, the relation between human and animal capacities and faculties; but his arguments and assertions about God are elements they are inclined to ignore, either as irrelevant to the central core of modern mainstream philosophy, or, perhaps, as what they take to be an embarrassing hangover from the medieval worldview that still conditioned the way Descartes was brought up.

Alongside this 'modern' secularist motive for sidelining the religious elements of Descartes's philosophy, there has been, from the other side as it were, a considerable resistance to accepting him as the devoutly religious philosopher that his frequent and often reverential references to God would suggest him to be. Historically, the Catholic Church, of which Descartes was all his life a member, has been highly suspicious of Cartesian philosophy, regarding it as unorthodox and potentially subversive of the faith. Soon after his death, Descartes's writings were placed by the Church on the 'Index' of prohibited books; and in the succeeding centuries 'the image of Descartes as an anti-clerical and indeed anti-religious force', even though 'deeply contrary to his actual disposition',[6] was to prove remarkably resilient. The factors behind this erroneous ecclesiastical view of Descartes as a danger to religion are many. In the first place, he was associated with Galileo as a supporter of the 'new', Sun-centred cosmology that was prima facie in conflict with biblical statements apparently implying a fixed and central Earth; and although Descartes prudently refrained from publishing his treatise on 'The Universe' (*Le Monde*) following the condemnation of Galileo by the Inquisition in 1633, and despite the fact that he concluded his eventually published major textbook *The Principles of Philosophy* [*Principia philosophiae*, 1644] with a statement of submission to the authority of the Church, his manoeuvres could not entirely shield him from suspicion in the tense and confrontational religious climate of the seventeenth century.

---

[5] B. Leiter (ed.), *The Future for Philosophy* (Oxford: Clarendon, 2004), 2–3.

[6] Bernard Williams, *Descartes: The Project of Pure Enquiry* (Harmondsworth: Penguin, 1978; repr. London: Routledge, 2005).

A more technical dogmatic issue that was to embroil Descartes during his own lifetime was that of transubstantiation (the doctrine that the bread and wine of the Eucharist is changed into the body and blood of Christ). The problem here was that Descartes aimed to replace the traditional Aristotelian philosophy of physics, which had dominated medieval thought, with a new geometrical conception of matter as consisting simply of extension in length, breadth, and depth. The Church had used the standard Aristotelian concepts to explain how the 'substance' of the bread changes into the body of Christ, while the 'accidents' (the colour, smell, taste, etc.) remain unaltered, and it was wary of allowing a new schema of physics that might sweep all this away. Descartes protested that his new physics was quite compatible with the divine 'miracle of transubstantiation' (AT VII 254: CSM II 177), but the controversy continued to grind on throughout the remainder of the century.[7]

Nowadays, of course, the Church has no problem with a Sun-centred planetary system, nor would it regard the mathematicization of physics as threatening the doctrine of the Eucharist; but, for all that, the received ecclesiastical image of Descartes remains, in many quarters, distinctly nega-tive. In a set of reflections published in the year of his death, Karol Wojtyla, the late Pope John Paul II, pointed to a period of moral disintegration that had characterized much of the twentieth century, with first the rise of totalitarianism, and later the erosion of traditional family values; and, perhaps surprisingly, he went on to trace the philosophical roots of this moral collapse to some of the central ideas put forward by Descartes. The rot started, he argued, with the way Descartes constructed his philosophy, basing it on the foundation of individual self-awareness, the famous *Cogito ergo sum* (I am thinking, therefore I exist):

The *Cogito ergo sum* radically changed the way of doing philosophy. In the pre-Cartesian period, philosophy, that is to say the *Cogito* ('I am thinking') or rather *Cognosco* ('I acquire knowledge') was subordinate to *esse* [being], which was considered primary. For Descartes, by contrast, *esse* appeared secondary, while he viewed the Cogito as primary. This...marked the decisive abandonment of what philosophy had been hitherto, particularly that of St Thomas Aquinas ... [For Aquinas] God as fully self-sufficient being (*Ens subsistens*) was considered as the indispensable support for every *ens non subsistens*, for every *ens participatum*, that

[7] See S. Gaukroger, *Descartes: An Intellectual Biography* (Oxford: Clarendon, 1992), 357.

is to say, for every created being, and hence for man. The *cogito ergo sum* carried within it a rupture with this line of thought. The *ens cogitans* (thinking being) thus becomes primary. After Descartes, philosophy became a science of pure thought: all that is *being*—the created world, and even the Creator, is situated within the ambit of the Cogito, as contents of human consciousness. Philosophy is concerned with beings as contained in consciousness, and not as existing independently of it.[8]

The orientation alluded to here, centred on the contents of personal consciousness rather than an independent external reality, is indeed one prominent strand in twentieth-century philosophical thought, found most notably in the school of 'phenomenology' founded by Edmund Husserl, whose *Cartesian Meditations* (1931) had argued that 'By my living, by my experiencing and acting, I can enter no world other than the one that gets its sense [*Sinn*] and validity [*Geltung*] *in and from me, myself*.'[9] Such an autocentric vision may indeed be seen as sinister, if it is taken to give primacy to individual consciousness in a way that threatens the existence of objective value and meaning; but a careful reading shows that it is anachronistic to retroject this conception back onto Descartes himself.

Descartes, to be sure, did begin his search for truth by establishing the indubitable certainty of his own existence. As he puts it in Part Four of his intellectual autobiography, the *Discourse on the Method*, 'seeing that this truth, *I am thinking therefore I exist*, was so firm and sure that even the most extravagant suppositions of the sceptics were incapable of shaking it, I decided that I could accept it without scruple as the first principle of the philosophy I was seeking' (AT VI 32: CSM I 127). Yet it simply does not follow that the 'I' so discovered is 'primary' for Descartes, in the sense that it no longer needs the support of a self-subsistent Creator, on which traditional theology had insisted. On the contrary, whenever Descartes discusses his 'Cogito' argument, he stresses the frail, temporary nature of his self-awareness: 'I am, I exist—that is certain. But for how long? For as long as I am thinking. For it could be that were I totally to cease from thinking, I should totally cease to exist' (AT VII 27: CSM II 18). Not only is such self-awareness a tiny flickering candle of certainty that could be

---

[8] John Paul II, *Memory and Identity* (London: Orion, 2005), 9.

[9] Edmund Husserl, *Cartesian Meditations* [*Kartesianische Meditationen*, 1931] trans. D. Cairns (Dordrecht: Kluwer, 1988), ch. 1 §8.

extinguished at any minute, but Descartes soon proceeds to use this very fragility of his thinking as a decisive indicator of his complete dependence on a power greater than himself:

A lifespan can be divided into countless parts, each completely independent of the others, so that it does not follow from the fact that I existed a little while ago that I must exist now, unless there is some cause which as it were creates me afresh at this moment—that is, which preserves me. For it is quite clear to anyone who attentively considers the nature of time that the same power and action are needed to preserve anything at each individual moment of its duration as would be required to create that thing anew if it were not yet in existence.   (Third Meditation, AT VII 49: CSM II 33)

For Descartes, my own existence may be the first thing I come to know, but as soon as I reflect on it I see that I could at any moment slip out of existence were there not an independent sustaining force to preserve me. I owe my being to God, the infinite Creator of all things; and indeed Descartes argues that the initial act of creation is only verbally or conceptually distinct from the same eternal and perpetual divine action whereby I am 'preserved' in every single moment of my existence.

To guard against the pervasive, but profoundly mistaken, 'subjectivizing' interpretation of Cartesian philosophy, we need to observe a crucial distinction that Descartes himself insisted on, in an interview he gave to a young Dutch disciple, Frans Burman, in 1648: 'the method and order of discovery is one thing, that of exposition is another' (AT V 153: CSMK 338). A similar distinction is made in a much earlier work, the *Regulae* or *Rules for the Direction of our Native Intelligence* (c.1628), between 'considering things in accordance with the way that corresponds to our knowledge of them', and 'considering things in accordance with how they exist in reality' (AT X 418: CSM I 44). In his metaphysical masterpiece, the *Meditations*, Descartes expects the reader to follow him along a subjective path of discovery: he begins his meditations 'quite alone' (AT VII 18: CSM II 12), asks what if anything he can be certain of, arrives at the indubitable Cogito, and then proceeds to acknowledge the existence of his Creator. As he put it earlier in the *Regulae*, 'Sum, ergo Deus est' ('I am, therefore God exists'; AT X 422: CSM I 46). But the priority of the self over God is simply an *epistemic* priority. Descartes, as St Augustine had done many centuries before, descends into his own interior self in order to discover his Creator; but none of this denies the genuine priority of God in the 'order of exposition'—that is, the order one would follow in expounding things in accordance with their status in reality. So far from initiating a 'rupture' with tradition, Descartes is here following a traditional line, going back to Aristotle, and further articulated by the great Christian philosopher Thomas Aquinas in the thirteenth century, when he distinguished matters that were 'prior from our point of view' (*priora quoad nos*) from those that were 'prior in themselves' (*priora simpliciter*).[10] Epistemically, the route may be from knowledge of self to knowledge of God (though even here the transition to God is, for Descartes, swift and inevitable); ontologically, by contrast, God retains absolutely primacy. As Descartes makes clear in the Third Meditation, the infinite substance that is God has 'more reality' than a mere finite substance such as myself. My very recognition of my own imperfection (which may come first in my order of discovery) already presupposes the ontological priority of this greater and more perfect reality:

I clearly understand that there is more reality in an infinite substance than in a finite one, and hence that my perception of the infinite, that is God, is in some way prior to my perception of the finite, that is myself. For how could I understand that I doubted or desired—that is lacked something—and that I was not wholly perfect, unless there were in me some idea of a more perfect being which enabled me to recognize my own defects by comparison?   (Third Meditation, AT VII 46: CSM II 31)

But what, to conclude this section, shall we say of John Paul II's remark, quoted above, that in Descartes's philosophy even the Creator is situated 'within the ambit of the Cogito'? Epistemically, perhaps, that is right, in so far as the Cartesian meditator reviews the ideas he finds within himself, and isolates one, the idea of God, for special enquiry. But Descartes's method in the Third Meditation is precisely to focus on the content of that idea as demonstrating that it could *not* have been constructed from his own resources as a thinking ego, but requires the real existence of a self-sufficient author, who 'in creating me, placed this idea in me to be, as it were, the mark of the craftsman stamped on his work' (AT VII 51: CSM II 35). The whole procedure is explained by Descartes with great precision in his later

---

[10] Thomas Aquinas, *Summa theologiae* [1266–73], pt. I qu. 2 art. 2.

work, the *Principles of Philosophy*, where the ontological primacy of God is made crystal clear:

There is a great advantage in proving the existence of God by this method, that is to say, by means of the idea of God. For the method enables us at the same time to come to know the nature of God, in so far as the feebleness of our nature allows. For when we reflect on the idea of God which we were born with, we see that he is eternal, omniscient, omnipotent, the source of all goodness and truth, the creator of all things, and finally, that he possesses within him everything in which we can clearly recognize some perfection that is infinite or unlimited by any imperfection.   (*Principles*, pt. I art. 22, AT VIIIA 13: CSM I 200)

3. The Fountain of Science

The Cartesian argument just referred to, sometimes known as the 'trade-mark argument', is Descartes's principal tool for moving from self-awareness to knowledge of God. His idea of infinite being has a certain representational content, he reasons, which cannot be explained as the production of his own finite and limited mind: the cause of the idea must have as much perfection as is found represented in the content of the idea, and hence that cause must indeed be an 'infinite, eternal, immutable, independent, supremely intelligent, supremely powerful substance, by whom all things were created' (AT VII 45: CSM II 31). Complex in its fine detail, and involving some controversial assumptions about causality, this argument has been subjected to a barrage of criticism by commentators.[11] But even if not so transparent as to command universal assent, 'even among the Turks', as Descartes hoped his arguments would do (AT V 159: CSMK 342), it nevertheless points to a fascinating aspect of our human conception of that infinitude that is called 'God': the infinite is a concept that we both clearly understand, and yet at the same time recognize as being 'beyond us'—as eluding our full mental grasp. As Descartes put it, 'it does not matter that I do not grasp (*comprehendere*) the infinite, or that there are countless additional attributes of God which ... perhaps I cannot even reach in my thought' (AT VII 46: CSM II 32); it is enough that I understand

---

[11] See e.g. A. Kenny, *Descartes* (New York: Random House, 1968), ch. 6, and B. Williams, *Descartes*, ch. 5.

it—just as I can touch a mountain, without being able to grasp it, or put my arms round it (AT I 152: CSMK 25). Our human conception of God, as is recognized in a long tradition going back to St Bonaventure in the thirteenth century, and beyond, is a conception of something infinitely beyond us, the understanding of which is intimately linked to awareness of our own weakness and finitude.[12]

One way in which we aspire to transcend that finitude is by using the faculty of reason that differentiates our species, that gift which Descartes, again following a long tradition, regarded as a 'light' shining in each human soul (the *lumen naturale*, or *lux rationis*, the divinely bestowed 'natural light' or 'light of reason'). Yet Descartes's ambitious project of founding a new philosophical and scientific system will not be satisfied with isolated flashes of rational illumination such as 'if I am doubting, then I must exist'. His aim is to use such flickering intuitions to light a whole blazing bonfire that will 'bring to light the true riches of our souls, opening up to each of us the means whereby we can find … all the knowledge we may need for the conduct of life', and 'the means of using it in order to acquire all the most abstruse items of knowledge that human reasoning is capable of possessing' (AT X 496: CSM II 400).

Such a project, as Descartes himself acknowledged, might seem so grandiose as to forfeit all credibility (ibid.). But here again the appeal to God emerges as the key to progress. For after reaching an awareness of God, and having 'gazed with wonder and adoration on the beauty of this immense light, in so far as the eye of my darkened intellect can bear it' (Third Meditation, AT VII 52: CSM II 36), the Cartesian meditator announces that 'from the contemplation of the true God, in whom all the treasures of wisdom and the sciences lie hidden', he thinks he can see a way forward to the knowledge of other things (AT VII 53: CSM II 37).

The phrase just quoted, from the opening paragraph of the Fourth Meditation, is, in the Latin wording of Descartes's original text, an almost exact citation from the Bible. In his letter to the Colossians (2: 3), St Paul had talked of 'the mystery of God and of the Father and of Christ, *in whom are hid all the treasures of wisdom and knowledge*' ('in quo sunt omnes thesauri sapientiae et scientiae absconditi'). Descartes, many of whose

---

[12] Bonaventure, *Itinerarium mentis in Deum* [1259] ('Journey of the Mind towards God'), in *Opera Omnia* (Quarachhi: Collegium S. Bonaventurae, 1891), pt. III §3.

contemporary readers would have instantly recognized the reference to the Vulgate (the standard Latin text of the Bible), subtly changes the singular *scientiae* ('knowledge') to the plural *scientiarum* ('sciences'). For St Paul, God (in Christ) is the mysterious source of all wisdom; for Descartes, reaching knowledge of God opens the path to 'the sciences'—to true scientific understanding.

'The Sciences' is something of a catchphrase in Descartes's thought. In his early notebooks, written about the time of his travels in Germany as a young man, when a day's meditations in a 'stove-heated room', followed by a night of disturbed dreams, had given him the conviction that he was destined to found a new philosophical and scientific system, Descartes wrote that the 'the sciences are at present masked, but if the masks were taken off, they would be revealed in all their beauty' (AT X 215: CSM I 3). Later, he entitled his first published work 'Discourse on the method of rightly conducting reason and reaching the truth in the sciences' (AT VI 1: CSM I 111). The 'masking' that Descartes refers to was, in his view, the distorting encumbrance of the old Aristotelian categories of explanation, which invoked such items as 'substantial forms' and 'real qualities'. Stones fell to earth, for example, because they possessed the quality of 'heaviness' (*gravitas*), this in turn being explained as a defining property possessed by things that had the form or essence of terrestrial matter. Yet such an apparatus, Descartes complained, was more obscure than the items it was supposed to explain (AT II 506: CSMK 208). To reach the truth, the sciences had to throw off these masks, and turn instead to the precise quantifiable notions of mathematics, disclosed to each soul by the light of reason. As Descartes puts it in the *Discourse*: 'I noticed certain laws which God has so established in nature, and of which he has implanted such notions in our minds, that after adequate reflection we cannot doubt that they are exactly observed in everything which exists or occurs in the world' (AT VI 41: CSM I 131).

Modern readers, however, may be inclined to step back at this point and ask if the theistic note here is really necessary. In replacing the vague qualitative notions of medieval science with laws expressible in quantitative terms, Descartes (together with his illustrious contemporary Galileo) might, to be sure, have taken a great leap forward: but does this seventeenth-century shift in our understanding of how to describe and predict the physical world really have any connection with the Cartesian metaphysical claims about God?

To answer this question, we need perhaps to recover a sense of just how revolutionary was the new scientific method of the seventeenth century—a sense that has perhaps been lost by familiarity. That the great book of the universe should, as Galileo put it, be written in the language of mathematics, is on any showing a remarkable fact—one that we perhaps have still not fully assimilated. The universe appears to operate in accordance with precise mathematical equations—equations that enable us, when we plug in the appropriate values for the relevant variables, to deliver predictions of extraordinary accuracy. (This is true, by the way, even of the mathematics of modern quantum physics, which, despite its 'indeterminacy principle' at the individual micro level, yields amazingly accurate predictive and explanatory results at a macro level.) Descartes's own formulations (in his work on physics) may have been flawed, but with the achievements of his successors, Newton and then Einstein, and on down to the present, we appear to be getting closer: our mathematical intuitions, intricately elaborated and fed into hypotheses that can be checked against careful observation, do indeed appear to be capable of mirroring the workings of nature. Descartes's picture of all this—that our finite human minds, though limited in scope, are in principle capable of reflecting the mathematical and logical structures laid down by our Creator in the workings of the universe—may admittedly not be the only possible picture of our relationship to the cosmos, but it is one whose coherence and power certainly cannot be dismissed out of hand.

To grasp this point further, it is important to see that the role of God in Descartes's system is not simply that of a mysterious 'prime mover' or 'first cause', of the kind envisaged by Aristotle, and subsequently developed in the first two of the five 'ways' or proofs of God offered by Thomas Aquinas. Certainly, that is part of the story: God is described in Descartes's *Principles* as 'the primary cause of motion' in so far as 'in the beginning he created matter, along with its motion and rest' (pt. II art. 36, AT VIII 61: CSM I 240). But the Cartesian universe is a corpuscular universe operating strictly in accordance with certain mathematically expressed laws—the law of conservation of motion, the law of rectilinear motion, and the law of impact—and the results of these laws are worked out in terms of seven rules for calculating the speed and direction of motion of bodies following impact (art. 37–52). What God does, in Descartes's cosmology, is, as it were, to write the equations governing the behaviour of all the particles out of which the cosmos is composed—to determine the values of the mathematical constants that give our world its rhythm and shape and order. Moreover, because God's action is immutable, and he 'always operates in a manner that is utterly constant and changeless' (art. 36), the universe is perpetually held in being and conserved without any change in the overarching laws. The Cartesian God is thus far from the caricature that his contemporary Blaise Pascal accused Descartes of leaving us with—that of the initial mover who 'flicks' the universe into motion and then leaves it to its own devices;[13] rather, God is the sole perpetual dynamic force in a cosmos that would otherwise, being simply 'extended matter', be as devoid of activity as a mere set of geometrical shapes.

Divine power and intelligence thus emerges, in Descartes's system, as the true source of all reality—both of everything there is, and of all human knowledge of everything there is. This creative power and intelligence brings the universe into being out of nothing; it decrees the laws of logic and mathematics governing the universe by no less free an act of will than that by which the universe itself is created (AT I 152: CSMK 25); and it implants in the finite minds of its creatures a limited but in principle perfectly accurate grasp of those laws (AT VII 61–2: CSM II 42–3). The resounding peroration where Descartes concludes his exposition of these matters in the *Meditations* is thus no vaguely pious afterthought, but an essential expression of the absolute centrality of God for his entire metaphysical and physical system of philosophy:

I thus see plainly that the certainty and truth of all knowledge depends uniquely on my awareness of the true God, to such an extent that I was incapable of perfect knowledge about anything else until I became aware of him. And now it is possible for me to achieve full and certain knowledge of countless matters, both concerning God himself and other things whose nature is intellectual and also concerning the whole of that corporeal nature which is the subject-matter of pure mathematics.   (AT VII 71: CSM II 49).

4. The Ethical Dimension

From what has so far been said, it might seem that the divine role is chiefly invoked by Descartes as a necessary structural support for his scientific

---

[13] Blaise Pascal, *Pensées* [1660], ed. L. Lafuma (Paris: Seuil, 1962), no. 1001.

system. That is true enough, provided we construe the label 'scientific' in a very broad sense—much broader than is now found in current English usage. Nowadays, even if the distinction between 'facts' and 'values' has recently come under increasing philosophical scrutiny, we nevertheless tend to think of science as concerned with the description and explanation of the natural world, while ethical questions about how we should live, or about the nature of goodness and justice, are taken to fall within a quite distinct area of human enquiry. For Descartes, things were very different. He would not have described himself as a 'scientist' (that notion had not yet been invented in the seventeenth century), but rather as a philosopher. But a 'philosopher' meant not (as it now so often does) someone working on a specialized theoretical topic within a tightly defined academic subject, but rather someone engaged in developing a systematic and comprehensive understanding of the whole of reality, including both 'natural philosophy' (more or less what we now call 'science') and also moral philosophy. One of the textbooks Descartes had studied as a schoolboy was the *Compendium of Philosophy in Four Parts* (the parts being Logic, Ethics, Physics, and Metaphysics), which had proclaimed that 'the goal of a complete philosophical system is human happiness'.[14] Descartes's plans for his own system were no less ambitious, and indeed he used a famous organic metaphor to emphasize the unified nature of his thought:

The whole of philosophy is like a tree. The roots are metaphysics, the trunk is physics, and the branches emerging from the trunk are all the other sciences, which may be reduce to three principal ones, namely medicine, mechanics and morals. By 'morals' I understand the highest and most perfect moral system which presupposes a complete knowledge of the other sciences, and is the ultimate level of wisdom.   (AT IXB 14: CSM I 186).

Morals could emerge as one of the most important branches of the philosophical system because of the theistic metaphysics in which the system was rooted. The God who is for Descartes the source of the physical creation is also the source of goodness; and the 'light of reason' enabling humans to intuit the mathematical structures underlying the universe also allows us to perceive the good. This again may seem somewhat strange

---

[14] Eustachius a Sancto Paulo, *Summa philosophiae quadripartita* [1609], Preface to pt. II. Translated extracts may be found in R. Ariew, J. Cottingham, and T. Sorell (eds.), *Descartes' Meditations: Background Source Materials* (Cambridge: Cambridge University Press, 1998), 68–96.

to the modern reader, since we tend to think of goodness and truth as quite distinct domains; but Descartes is more than a little influenced by the Platonic model according to which the good and the true are aspects of a single underlying reality. In the *Fourth Meditation*, we are told that when the mind focuses on an object with perfect clarity, the assent of the will automatically follows: that is, when you see that there is a clear reason for the truth of some proposition (for example, that two plus two makes four), what happens is not simply a passive intellectual perception, but a spontaneous judgement of assent—'Yes: it's true!' But in precisely the same way, according to Descartes's model, when you clearly focus on some action and see there is a clear reason why it is good, then again, you automatically and spontaneously judge—'Yes: it should be done!' The will is the faculty of affirming or denying a truth, and of pursuing a good (or avoiding its opposite). As Descartes puts it: 'The more I incline in one direction … because I clearly understand that reasons of truth and goodness point that way … the freer is my choice' (AT VII 57–8: CSM II 40).[15]

The flavour of the passage, with its overtones of something like religious submission (compare AT VII 52: CSM II 36), is significant, because we tend to think of the 'modern age' that Descartes inaugurated as championing the independent, critical, and autonomous power of humanity to determine the truth for itself. Descartes was certainly a critical thinker, resistant to relying on the authority of established wisdom, and insisting that each of us should follow for themselves the disciplines of reflective enquiry (see *Discourse*, Pt. One, AT VI 1 ff.: CSM I 111 ff.). But the destination of the journey is for Descartes not some supposedly quite independent and wholly self-determining state, but rather an awareness of the divine light that, once perceived, leaves us no choice but to assent. Just as the ancient prayer had affirmed that 'to serve God is perfect freedom', so Descartes's model of the free human intellect is of an intellect that is so gripped by the clarity of the divinely ordained truth and goodness it perceives that no other option is possible than to align oneself towards it.

This harmonious, theistically inspired vision may appear starkly at odds with the ordinary realities of human struggle, error, and failure; but Descartes is in fact acutely aware of the weakness of our nature, and spends a great deal of effort endeavouring to explain it in a manner consistent

---

[15] For more on this, see Ch. 11, above.

with his belief in a divine Creator who is the source of goodness and truth. Theologians for many centuries prior to Descartes had wrestled (as they have subsequently continued to do) with the so-called 'problem of evil'—the existence of so much wrongdoing and suffering in a world supposedly produced by a surpassingly good Creator; and St Augustine in the fourth century had offered a 'theodicy' (a vindication of God's justice) that laid great emphasis on the faulty human use of our free will. Descartes, strongly influenced by Augustine,[16] takes a very similar line in his own theodicy in the Fourth Meditation. If our minds are illuminated by the divine light, how come we make false judgements, or choose the bad, or a lesser good, when the greater good is staring us in the face? Descartes, as we have seen, maintains that while we focus on the truths disclosed by the light we cannot but assent; but because our intellects are *finite in scope*, there are many truths we do not clearly perceive. In such cases, we ought to withhold our assent, but instead we often rashly jump in and make a judgement—and 'in this incorrect use of free will' is to be found 'the essence of error' (AT VII 60: CSM II 41).

On the purely theoretical plane, this recipe for the avoidance of error ('Withhold judgement when the truth is not clear') may have much to commend it; but on the level of practical morality, Descartes has to admit that we do not always have the luxury of such aloof abstention from commitment (AT VI 22: CSM I 122). Choices often have to be made even when the evidence is not conclusive; people need to eat, without waiting for a full chemical analysis of the bread in front of them. The problem is compounded by the fact that much of our ordinary human life is not concerned with abstract intellectual judgement, but is inextricably bound up with bodily sensations, and more complex emotions—a whole range of affective states from hunger and thirst and pleasure and pain to hope, fear, anger, love, joy, sadness, and so on. The belief in a benevolent Creator faces a direct challenge here, one that Descartes must confront, for several reasons.

In the first place, our sensory states do not always seem to be reliable indicators of what is good for us: 'Those who are ill may desire food or drink that will shortly afterwards turn out to be bad for them' (AT VII 84: CSM II 58). Descartes here (in a further phase of his project of theodicy, this time in the

---

[16] See S. Menn, *Descartes and Augustine* (Cambridge: Cambridge University Press, 1998).

Sixth Meditation) replies that the mind–body complex is designed by God to work in accordance with fixed principles: certain physiological states (e.g. a shortage of fluid in the body) will produce certain psychological signals (e.g. a feeling of dryness in the throat). And although there may be some conditions, such as dropsy, where drinking when thirsty is not advisable, nevertheless 'the best system that could be devised is that [a given state of the nervous system and the brain] should produce the one sensation which, of all possible sensations, is most especially and most frequently conducive to the preservation of the healthy human being' (AT VII 87: CSM II 60).

This picture of a divinely crafted system of mind–body correlations that generally works for our survival and welfare as human beings is threatened, however, by a further problem: that of the complex set of emotional states and dispositions that were known in Descartes's time as 'the passions'. Often—and this is an age-old issue in moral philosophy—feelings of anger, or arousal, or fear, or enthusiasm may lead us astray, making some good appear more important, or some evil more threatening, than it really is. The passions, as Descartes at one point puts its, often 'represent the goods to which they tend with greater splendour than they deserve, and they make us imagine pleasures to be much greater before we possess them than our subsequent experiences show them to be'. The result, all too familiar, is that giving rein to our passions can frequently lead to 'dissatisfaction, regret and remorse' (AT IV 285: CSMK 264).

Descartes's theocentric ethics, however, offers a way out. He maintained, as we have seen, that human beings are equipped, via the 'light of reason' with clear and distinct perceptions of the good, and that contemplating the good leaves us no choice but to wish to pursue it. Human concentration, however, is weak and limited, and we cannot always be focusing on the clear deliverances of the light of reason. Moreover, as embodied creatures we also have emotional responses, which, though generally conducive to our welfare (fear makes us flee from danger, anger helps us defend ourselves, attraction leads us to seek out friends and partners), can nevertheless sometimes lead us astray. But the solution to this, according to Descartes, lies in drawing on the results of Cartesian science: our scientific knowledge of the workings of the passions, and the way they are linked to physiological mechanisms, will enable us to manage and control them, so that they can be brought into line with what our reason perceives to be good, and thus become a source of joy (AT IV 285: CSMK 264).

The working out of this Cartesian moral theory, though quite subtle and complex in its ethical, psychological, and physiological detail,[17] leaves us in the end with a picture of the good life that is remarkably positive. There is a strong sense of a benevolent presence at the roots of our humanity. So far from being the product of 'fate or chance or a continuous chain of events' (AT VII 21: CSM II 14), our human nature bears the stamp of its Creator. Our intellect or 'light of reason' is directly God-given; and as for the sensory and emotional apparatus that derives in part from our embodied nature, once we learn to understand and control its workings, we shall see that there is 'absolutely nothing to be found there that does not bear witness to the power and goodness of God' (AT VII 87: CSM II 60).

5. Conclusion

In bringing this survey of the role of God in Cartesian philosophy to a close, it may be helpful to observe that what might be called the 'religious' flavour of much of Descartes's thinking should not be confused with the very different, faith-based, religious approach to philosophizing that is found, for example, in his contemporary Pascal, and, in a more extreme form in much later thinkers such as Søren Kierkegaard. Descartes does acknowledge, in addition to the natural light of reason, a 'supernatural light' of faith (AT VII 148: CSM II 106), but it turns out that the concept of faith does not play any significant role in his philosophical system. God is central, but it is a God who is established by reason, and who underpins the rationality of a system of science and morality that offers genuine power to human beings to ameliorate their lives (AT VI 62: CSM I 142). The darker struggles of the soul—the lonely existentialist thinker, abandoning the comforts of assured systems of philosophy and struggling to maintain a willed act of faith, 'out on the deep, over seventy thousand fathoms of water',[18] are light-years away from the Cartesian worldview.

Descartes, whom it remains quite appropriate to call the one of the inaugurators of modern science, has a measure of that optimism about our human nature, and our future, that is displayed by some of the breezier

---

[17] See Cottingham, *Philosophy and the Good Life*, ch. 3.

[18] Søren Kierkegaard, *Concluding Unscientific Postscript* [*Afsluttende Uvidenskabelig Efterskrift*, 1846], trans. D. F. Swenson (Princeton, NJ: Princeton University Press, 1941), 182.

modern advocates of science plus technology as the key to improving our lot. But for Descartes, unlike many present-day enthusiasts for science, this optimism is rooted in a cosmology that provides it with a secure anchor point. Given the assurance of a rationally ordered universe, and a supremely benevolent Creator, we can be sure we have the means at our disposal to achieve knowledge of the true and the good, and to regulate our lives in a way that allows us to be oriented towards that truth and goodness. The vision may not be as 'modern' as might be expected from a thinker who is often called the father of modernity; but it remains, for all that, an inspiring vision of what a philosophical system, grounded in religious belief, can aspire to articulate.

14

Descartes as Sage: Spiritual Askesis in Cartesian Philosophy

1. Introduction: The Cartesian Mask

In one of his earliest surviving writings Descartes says that just as actors put on masks (*personam induunt*), so he himself will enter the theatre of the world masked: *larvatus prodeo*.[1] 'Mask' was, of course, the original meaning of the Latin term *persona*—in Greek *prosōpon*: the false face of clay or bark that actors in the ancient world donned in order to come on to the stage. It is an odd figure of speech for a philosopher to adopt: both in Classical philosophical thought (from Plato's famous strictures against acting and role-playing),[2] and also in the Christian gospels (from Jesus' denunciation of those whose outward display did not match their inner thoughts),[3] the connotations of the term 'actor' (*hypocrites*) were far from favourable.

What *persona* did Descartes himself have in mind? We are apt, in the light of popular contemporary psychology, to think of a *persona* as some kind of false self-presentation;[4] but the ancient theatrical *persona* was a formal,

---

[1] *Praeambula* [1619], from Descartes's early notebooks (later dubbed the *Cogitationes Privatae*): AT X 213: CSM I 2.   [2] Plato, *Republic* [c.385 BC], 392c–398b.

[3] *Gospel according to Matthew* [c.AD 60], 6: 2–5.

[4] One thinks of Jean-Paul Sartre's famous account of how people wilfully imprison themselves in their official roles as a kind of escape from true self-realization: 'the waiter who tries to imitate in his walk the inflexible stiffness of some kind of automaton while carrying his tray with the recklessness of a tight-rope walker ... playing at *being* a waiter in a café ... There is the dance of the grocer, of the tailor, of the auctioneer, by which they endeavour to persuade their clientele that they are nothing but a grocer, an auctioneer, a tailor.' *Being and Nothingness* [*L'Être et le Néant*, 1943] (London: Methuen, 1957), ch. 2 p. 59. As Carl Jung observes (writing a few years before Sartre), 'the danger is that [people] become identical with their personas—the professor with his textbook, the tenor with his voice. Then the damage is done; henceforth he lives exclusively against the background of his own biography ... One could say, with a little exaggeration, that the *persona* is that which in reality one is not, but which oneself as well as others think one is.' 'Concerning Rebirth' ['Über Wiedergeburt', 1939, rev. 1950] in *Collected Works* (London: Routledge, 1959), ix. pt. I §221.

stylized device, whose purpose was not so much simulation as dissimulation. Going on stage is a daunting business, and the mask conceals awkwardness and embarrassment (a point that Descartes himself makes quite explicitly).[5] By hiding his nervousness, or simply the unprepossessing ordinary features that might be familiar to the audience, the actor could pronounce his lines with more confidence.

So it may be that the young Descartes is simply recording his shyness—his reluctance to make a stir. We know that his favourite motto was the Ovidian tag *bene vixit qui bene latuit*, a variation on the Epicurean maxim *lathe biosas*: 'get through life without drawing attention to yourself'.[6] And when he finally presented the public with an account of his 'method of seeking the truth in the sciences', together with some sample essays illustrating its results, he would not allow his name to appear on the title page.[7]

But there is more to it than this. Descartes may have been cautious and reticent, but he had a mission.[8] If the mask was there, it was one he wanted ultimately to shed, like the sciences themselves, of which he remarked that in his own epoch they were still 'masked' (*larvatae*)—veiled or constricted, as it were, in the formal stylized apparatus of scholasticism—but 'if the masks could only be shed', their true nature would 'appear in its full beauty'.[9] So to have a clear picture of the inaugurator of the early-modern age, we need to understand what Descartes saw himself as setting out to do, as he entered the world's stage: what he took his distinctive contribution to be, or what was his true self-conception as a philosopher.

In asking about the true self-conception of Descartes, or of any philosopher, we are moving to a richer and more positive sense of the term

---

[5] 'Comoedi, moniti ne in fronte appareat pudor, personam induunt.' ('Actors, taught not to let any embarrassment show on their faces, put on a mask.') AT X 212: CSM I 2.

[6] Letter to Mersenne of April 1634, AT I 285: CSMK 43.

[7] Published by Maire at Leiden, 8 June 1637, under the title *Discours de la méthode pour bien conduire sa raison, et chercher la vérité dans les sciences. Plus la Dioptrique, les Météores et la Géométrie qui sont des essais de cette méthode* ('Discourse on the Method of rightly conducting one's reason and seeking the truth in the sciences, and in addition the Optics, the Meteorology and the Geometry, which are essays in this Method.')

[8] The zeal and commitment is clearly apparent in, for example, the *Discourse on the Method* (especially throughout Pt. Six), and seems to have dated right back to Descartes's night of vivid dreams in November 1619, from which he awoke with the vision of inaugurating a comprehensive new scientific system, and made a vow of thanksgiving to visit the shrine of the Virgin at Loretto. Adrien Baillet, *La Vie de M. Des-Cartes* [1691], i. 85–6 (cf. AT X 180 ff. and AT X 216: CSM I 4).

[9] 'Larvatae nunc scientiae sunt: quae, larvis sublatis, pulcherrimae apparerent.' *Praeambula* (AT X 215: CSM I 2).

persona, one that takes us away from masks and acting towards something more 'personal', something connected not just with a 'career', but with the full moral and psychological dimensions of someone's chosen form of life. For alongside its ancient theatrical connotations, the Latin concept *persona* also has deeper and more serious resonances, deriving in part from early Christian theology. 'Tres personae in una substantia' (three persons in one substance) was Tertullian's formula in the third century for defining the unity and triplicity of God, *persona* being (in Hugh Pyper's apt phrase) 'a label for whatever accounts for the *distinctive identity* of Father, Son and Holy Spirit'.[10] Without going into the intricate theological controversies surrounding the mystery of the Trinity, one way in which the individual divine *personae* have long been understood is by analogy with the way in which a human being forms a true self-conception of him or herself.[11] For our present purposes, the *persona* of the philosopher may thus be said to involve the development and expression of a particular, distinctive identity, or sense of self—that which gives intellectual shape and moral significance to a given individual's life and work.

2. Philosophical Self-Conceptions and Their Evolution

The self-conception of the philosopher in something like the above sense was, until our own time, a serious and important matter—something we tend to forget in our philosophically somewhat degenerate age. A culture manifests its degeneration in part by bad faith, a telling instance of which is the undertaking of some philosophical pursuit not for itself, but merely instrumentally, for the sake of the practitioner's vanity or some other advantage. The sophists of ancient Greece, who claimed to teach virtue for money, were criticized by Socrates as a paradigm case.[12] Contrasted

---

[10] Tertullian, *Adversus Praxeas* [c.AD 213]. The gloss by Pyper (emphasis added) is from A. Hastings, A. Mason, and H. Pyper (eds.), *The Oxford Companion to Christian Thought* (Oxford: Oxford University Press, 2000), 531, s.v. 'person'.

[11] For this suggestion, deriving from St Thomas Aquinas, with earlier roots in Augustine, see B. Davies, *Aquinas* (London: Continuum, 2002), ch. 16 §2 ('Three Persons and one God'), pp. 167–8.

[12] The criticism is implicit in the heavy irony used by Socrates in his description of the sophists (in the course of his own defence against the accusation of corrupting the young): *Apology* [c.390 BC], 19d–e. For a more favourable interpretation of Plato's attitude to the sophists, see T. H. Irwin,

with this instrumental approach is the Platonic ideal of *philosophia*—love of wisdom for its own sake.[13] Familiarity with the label has perhaps dulled us to the passionate seriousness it originally conveyed—the seriousness that led Socrates, threatened with the death penalty, to insist that 'for a human being, the unexamined life (*bios*) is not worth living.'[14] It is often assumed nowadays that the critical enquiry that is the hallmark of the so-called Socratic method is of a purely logical character, having to do merely with the examination of concepts and definitions. But the oft-quoted slogan just cited should remind us that philosophical 'examination', for Socrates, involves the entire character of someone's life (*bios*). As Socrates goes on to explain in the *Apology,* his philosophical vocation was linked with unwavering allegiance to conscience, the 'god', as he put it, whose inner voice demanded his obedience.[15]

Contrast this moral seriousness with the climate inhabited by many of today's practitioners of philosophy—a climate whose character is aptly indicated by the kinds of question that seem to claim most attention. How do you know that you are really not sitting in this lecture room, but instead are just a brain floating in a vat of nutrients somewhere in the Andromeda galaxy? May it not be, for all you know, that the planet Earth and all its inhabitants are not real, but mere fantasies produced in your mind by a group of mad scientists in Andromeda, who have stimulated the nerve inputs of your floating brain in such a way as to give you all the appropriate sensations so as to create the convincing illusion that you are sitting by the fire reading this book, in a certain region of the Planet Earth, when in reality you are light years away, and don't have a body at all, and therefore no posterior to sit on in the first place.

Asking this sort of fantastic question might seem as silly a waste of time for grown people as one could imagine. Yet the present writer could testify (as no doubt could many other editors of mainstream anglophone philosophy journals) to receiving scores of submissions each year, highly

---

'Plato: the Intellectual Background', in R. Kraut (ed.), *The Cambridge Companion to Plato* (Cambridge: Cambridge University Press, 1992), 64 ff.

[13] 'Although we say many things are loved (*phila*) for the sake of something that is loved, we are evidently using an inappropriate word in saying that. It seems that the thing that is really loved is that in which all these things called loves come to an end... Then what is really loved is not loved for the sake of anything.' Plato, *Lysis* [*c.*390 BC], 220a7–b5. Cf. T. Irwin, *Plato's Ethics* (Oxford: Oxford University Press, 1995), 67 ff.   [14] *ho de anexetastos bios ou biōtos* (Plato, *Apology*, 38a5).

[15] Ibid. 40a2–c2.

intricate pieces of work, laboriously examining just one more variation on this 'brain-in-vat' scenario. Our philosophical culture, to be sure, perceives these enquiries as contributions to an important subject called 'epistemology'. But on reflection one may wonder whether this kind of work can be pursued only at the cost of a certain fragmentation, a split between one's job as a 'philosopher', and the more intimate concerns that structure the rest of one's life. The instrumental value of the work is clear, for on it depend promotions and grants and research ratings, and all manner of other appurtenances of modern academic life. And, in fairness, the intellectual puzzles involved may have a certain engaging intricacy that can be stimulating in itself, as well as provoking wider reflection on the nature and justification of knowledge claims. Yet for all that, are we not left with a certain sense of disquiet at seeing so much philosophical energy expended on examining the epistemic credentials of a science-fiction hypothesis that no human being, once they get outside the study or the seminar, could even begin to take seriously? One could of course *pretend* to care about it—pretend that one was passionately involved in making sure we know we are not on Alpha Centauri—but that would be hard to reconcile with the spirit of commitment and integrity that, since Socrates and Plato, has been thought of as fundamental to genuine philosophical enquiry.

In Harold Pinter's play, *The Homecoming*, a character called Teddy, who has escaped his East End, working-class background to become a philosophy professor in the USA, returns home to London on a visit. On his arrival, Lennie, his clever younger brother, who has stayed at home to become an accomplished pimp and thug, insolently asks him: 'What is a *table*, Teddy—*philosophically speaking*, I mean?'; and he proceeds to taunt his embarrassed elder brother with a barrage of questions about whether we should doubt the nature and existence of external objects.[16] The moral is clear: these are the kinds of vacuous question that get philosophy a bad name.

Many people might suppose that if this lamentable image of philosophy is to be laid at anyone's door, it must be that of René Descartes. For the last fifty years or so, at least in the anglophone philosophical world, the *persona* of the 'epistemologist' has been retrospectively fitted on to Descartes so tightly as to condition, for a large number of people, how his philosophy is

---

[16] Harold Pinter, *The Homecoming* [1965], Act 2; in Pinter, *Plays Three* (London: Faber, 1996).

examined and interpreted. The outlines of the story are very familiar. At the start of Descartes's most famous work, perhaps the most commonly used text in Introduction to Philosophy courses all over the world, the question of knowledge and its justification becomes *the* philosophical question par excellence; so the first steps in philosophy involve raising doubts about everything—even the existence of an 'external' reality. Asserting that he 'cannot possibly go too far in his distrustful attitude', the meditator supposes that 'the sky, the earth, and all external things' are merely 'delusions', which a 'malicious demon of the utmost power and cunning' has implanted in his mind in order to deceive him.[17] This last scenario is of course the precursor of today's brain-in-vat obsessions—the only difference being that Descartes developed it in an incorporealist mode, with the demon directly generating the deceptive sensations in a supposedly bodiless subject, while today's variant adopts the language of physicalism, with a story about the stimulation of brains and nerve fibres.

So entrenched has our vision become of Descartes as the purveyor of elaborate sceptical scenarios that the phrase 'Cartesian doubt' has passed into contemporary philosophical jargon as a shorthand for a whole mode of epistemological enquiry. There is someone called 'the sceptic', who has to be defeated; and although it has become unfashionable to accept Descartes's weapons for the victory (weapons that invoke divine power and goodness), he is at least credited with taking doubt to its limits, and showing us just what the anti-sceptic has to overcome. Nor is this epistemological image of Descartes merely the creation of those contemporary analyticians who have scant regard for historical context: Richard Popkin, very much a historian's historian of philosophy, takes a very similar line, observing that the introduction of Descartes's malicious demon pushes 'the *crise pyrrhonienne*' [the crisis of extreme scepticism] 'to its farthest limit',[18] and later defining the Cartesian revolution in terms of the centrality it accorded to the question 'Where does our knowledge come from, and what can we know and how certain is our knowledge?'[19]

---

[17] *Meditations on First Philosophy* [*Meditationes de prima philosophia*, 1641], First Meditation, AT VII 18, 19, 22: CSM II 12–15.

[18] Richard Popkin, *The History of Skepticism from Erasmus to Descartes* (New York: Harper & Row, 1968), 184.

[19] 'In questioning all of the theories in philosophy, science and theology of the time, the sceptics made it crucial for thinkers to find a satisfactory justification for their knowledge claims. Hence, the question Where does our knowledge come from, and what can we know and how certain is

But a careful look at how Descartes himself presents the sceptical issues in the *Meditations* is enough to cast serious doubt on this image of him as preoccupied with abstract epistemology. He himself described the sceptical doubts of the First Meditation as 'exaggerated' or 'hyperbolical', and 'deserving to be dismissed as laughable'—*explodendae* (literally, 'to be hissed or booed off the stage').[20] What is more, in the Synopsis published as an introduction to the first edition of the *Meditations* in 1641 Descartes explicitly disavows the role of a champion epistemologist holding the line against some supposed[21] 'sceptical crisis':

The great benefit of these arguments is *not*, in my view, that they prove what they establish—namely that there really is a world, and that human beings have bodies and so on—*since no sane person has ever seriously doubted these things*. The point is that in considering these arguments we come to realize that they are not as solid or as transparent as the arguments which lead us to knowledge of our own minds and of God.[22]

Descartes certainly wanted 'solid' and 'transparent' arguments; and certainly, like many of his immediate predecessors in the late sixteenth and early seventeenth century, he wanted to expose the vanity of what had passed for knowledge in the culture in which he had grown up.[23] But he was emphatically not playing the modern 'epistemological' game—inventing artificial positions (those of the 'the sceptic', the 'antisceptic', the 'realist', the 'antirealist', and so on) to see whether one is ingenious enough to refute the latest ploy in an introverted academic debate. His philosophical

our knowledge? became central. New theories of knowledge had to be offered to deal with the epistemological crisis brought on by the growth and spread of scepticism at the end of the Renaissance.' R. Popkin, 'Theories of Knowledge', in Charles B. Schmitt and Quentin Skinner (eds.), *The Cambridge History of Renaissance Philosophy* (Cambridge: Cambridge University Press, 1988), 684.

[20] 'hyperbolicae superiorum dierum dubitationes ut risu dignae sunt explodendae' (AT VII 89: CSM II 61).

[21] I have elsewhere expressed serious reservations about the account proposed by Popkin and others of a supposed *crise pyrrhonienne* in the late sixteenth and early seventeenth centuries; see J. Cottingham, 'Why Should Analytic Philosophers Do History of Philosophy?', in T. Sorell and G. A. J. Rogers (eds.), *Analytic Philosophy and History of Philosophy* (Oxford: Clarendon, 2005), 25–41.

[22] AT VII 15–16: CSM II 11 (emphasis supplied).

[23] Cf. e.g. Francisco Sanches in *Quod nihil scitur* [1581], which provides a remarkably frank description of the rambling mixture of anecdote and pseudo-explanation that passed for knowledge in the Renaissance world: 'Sufficiat nunc nosse nos nil plane nosse' (Suffice it for now to know that we know nothing at all); 'Misera est conditio nostra. In media luce coecutimus' (Wretched is our condition; in the midst of light we are blind). In F. Sanches, *That Nothing is Known*, ed. D. F. S. Thomson (Cambridge: Cambridge University Press, 1988), 57.

concerns had a far greater integrity, a far closer link to the goals of his life.

3. From Epistemology to Science?

In recent Cartesian scholarship, the long dominant image of Descartes the epistemologist has gradually given way to that of Descartes the scientist. In part, this is a reversion to an earlier view, held for example by the great Cartesian scholar and editor Charles Adam, that Cartesian metaphysics and epistemology are essentially subordinate to Cartesian science.[24] According to an interesting study by Desmond Clarke,[25] the key motivation behind Descartes's research programme is the desire to provide a new style of explanation that would replace the scholastic approach that prevailed in the world in which he grew up. Much of this is uncontroversial: Descartes frequently complains of the explanatory vacuity of the 'substantial forms and real qualities which many philosophers suppose to inhere in things',[26] objecting that they are 'harder to understand than the things they are supposed to explain'.[27] His own mechanistic accounts, by contrast, were supposed to have an immediate intelligibility, since they simply ascribed to the micro world exactly the same kinds of interactions with which we are familiar from ordinary middle-sized phenomena around us. If we understand the latter, then we already have a grasp of how the posited micro events operate ('imperceptible simply because of their small size'); and Descartes's key idea is that these give rise to the relevant explananda in a way that is (as he put it) 'just as natural' as explaining how a clock tells the time by reference to the little cogs and wheels inside it.[28]

There is no denying that a large proportion of Descartes's writings (vastly larger than is suggested by those passages typically selected for study in today's standard philosophy courses) is taken up with working out this mechanistic programme with respect to the animal and human nervous

---

[24] 'Descartes ne demande à la métaphysique qu'une chose, de fournir un appui solide à la vérité scientifique' (AT XII 143).

[25] Desmond Clarke, *Descartes's Theory of the Mind* (Oxford: Clarendon, 2003).

[26] *Principles of Philosophy* [*Principia philosophiae*, 1644], pt. IV art. 198.   [27] Ibid. art. 201.

[28] Ibid. art. 203.

system. In *Le Monde* and the *Traité de L'Homme* [1633] and the *Dioptrique* [1637], what we would nowadays call 'cognitive functions', such as visual perception, are investigated by Descartes in terms of brain events of a certain kind ('ideas as brain patterns', as Clarke puts it). And the same corporealist strategy is used by Descartes in his accounts of imagination and memory, and of the passions—an approach that receives its fullest treatment in his last published work, *Les Passions de l'âme* [1649]. But is it right, in the light of these extensive writings, spread over many years, to construe Descartes's primary role as that of the explanatory scientist?

One qualm about this interpretation is that it leads to a curiously awkward view of Descartes's notion of the *res cogitans*—the immaterial 'thinking substance' that he identifies in the central sections of his masterworks, the *Discours* and the *Meditationes*, as the indubitable subject of his metaphysical reflections. Construed as offering an explanatory theory of the mind, this notion of a 'thinking thing' tells us remarkably little; and indeed Clarke's interpretative framework, giving primacy to the *persona* of the scientist, leads him to mount a complaint against Descartes on precisely these grounds—that the notion of the *res cogitans* has no explanatory force. For given that the Cartesian quest, on Clarke's account, was for 'genuine' (i.e. mechanistic) explanations of seeing, hearing, remembering, imagining and so on, the programme 'ran into apparently insurmountable obstacles'[29] when it came to dealing with the perspective of the thinking subject; and the result, for Clarke, was a dead end. Descartes did not really have a 'theory' of an immaterial thinking substance; instead, his talk of a 'thinking thing' was 'true [but] uninformative', a 'provisional acknowledgement of failure, an index of the work that remains to be done before a viable theory of the human mind becomes available'.[30]

The talk of 'failure' is appropriate, Clarke suggests, because the Cartesian claims about thinking substances 'add nothing new to our knowledge' of them. Descartes is 'claiming no more than … that, if thinking is occurring, there must be a thinking thing of which the act of thinking is predicated'.[31] So the attribute of thinking can no more be of explanatory value than the Schoolmen's attribute of *gravitas* or 'heaviness' was any use in explaining why heavy things fall.

---

[29] Clarke, *Descartes's Theory of the Mind*, 241.   [30] Ibid. 257, 258.   [31] Ibid. 221.

The charge of explanatory vacuity seems right in one way, but in my view it is nevertheless misleading in so far as it tacitly assumes that Descartes must have approached the phenomenon of consciousness with a view to seeing if it could be *explained* after the manner of his mechanistic programme for physics. This is indeed what his contemporary Pierre Gassendi thought he should be doing: it is no more use telling us you are a 'thinking thing', he objected, than it would be to tell us that wine is 'a red thing'; what we are looking for is the microstructure that *explains* the manifest properties.[32] Descartes's reply is instructive: he was utterly scathing about the very idea that one might produce some 'quasi-chemical' micro-explanation of thinking.[33]

In the context of the argument of the *Meditations*, which is the focus of this sharp exchange, we should recall that Descartes's meditator has arrived at a self-conception of the mind that leads him directly forward to contemplate the 'immense light' of the Godhead, the infinite incorporeal being whose image is reflected, albeit dimly, in the finite created intellect of the meditator.[34] So whatever else the notion of *res cogitans* was or was not intended to do, it clearly played a central role in the meditator's journey towards awareness of God. Like Bonaventure before him, whose own *Itinerarium mentis in Deum* (*Journey of the Mind towards God*) was profoundly conditioned by the contemplative and immaterialist tradition of Plato and Augustine, Descartes has a conception of ultimate truth that required an *aversio*—a turning of the mind away from the world of the senses—in order to prepare it for glimpsing the reality that lies beyond the phenomenal world. Both Bonaventure and Descartes, following Augustine's famous slogan 'In interiore homine habitat veritas' (the truth dwells within the inner man), [35] undertake an interior journey. 'Go back into yourself,' says Augustine; 'let us return to ourselves, into our mind', says Bonaventure, 'that we may search for the "*lux veritatis in facie nostrae mentis*"—the light of truth shining in our minds, as through a glass, in which the image of the Blessed Trinity shines forth'.[36] 'I turn my mind's eye upon myself,'

---

[32] *Objectiones et Responsiones* [1641], Fifth Objections, AT VII 276: CSM II 193.

[33] Fifth Replies, AT VII 359: CSM II 248.   [34] Third Meditation, AT VII 51: CSM II 35.

[35] 'Noli foras ire, in teipsum redi; in interiore homine habitat veritas' (go not outside, but return within thyself; in the inward man dwelleth the truth). Augustine, *De vera religione* [391] 39. 72.

[36] 'Ad nos reintraremus, in mentem scilicet nostram, in qua divina relucet imago; hinc ... conari debemus per speculum videre Deum, ubi ad modum candelabri relucet lux veritatis in facie nostrae

says Descartes, and find the idea of God stamped there, like the 'mark the craftsman has set on his work'.[37]

Can this immaterialist metaphysics be merely a means to an end—a kind of propaedeutic to science in the way suggested by the thesis of Adam? Such a view is not, perhaps, beyond the bounds of possibility, though it would, I believe, be very difficult convincingly to explain the theistic reflections we find in the Third Meditation as simply part of an instrumental strategy; for it is striking that the style and flavour of the writing is often much closer to the language of devotion and worship than it is to the detached critical terminology of the analytician.[38] But there is another and more fundamental reason for being wary of the image of Descartes the scientist as the key to understanding the Cartesian system, namely that the very notion of 'the scientist' is fundamentally anachronistic when we transpose it back from our own time to the world of the seventeenth century. Descartes was deeply interested in physis and mechanics, of that there can be no doubt. But his interests were the interests not of a scientist in the modern sense, but those of the *natural philosopher*. And unpacking the *persona* of the natural philosopher discloses a role that is far more structured and systematic, and far more wide-reaching in its scope, than is readily graspable from the perspective of the fragmented and compartmentalized contemporary culture within which modern 'science' and 'scientists' find their place.

4. Philosophy, Knowledge, and Wisdom

The very term 'natural philosophy' immediately gives a strong clue to what the subject was in pre-modern times—not a separated discipline, in the manner of our contemporary academic and scientific specialisms, but rather a species of the genus *philosophy*. And philosophy, in the climate in which Descartes grew up, was by its very nature a synoptic or comprehensive

---

mentis, in qua scilicet resplendet imago beatissimae Trinitatis.' Bonaventure, *Itinerarium mentis in Deum* [1259], III. 1.   [37] Third Meditation, AT VII 51: CSM II 35.

[38] Cf. the following: 'Placet hic aliquamdiu in ipsius Dei contemplatione immorari ... et immensi hujus luminis pulchritudinem ... intueri, admirari, adorare' ('Let me here rest for a while in the contemplation of God himself and gaze upon, wonder at, and adore the beauty of this immense light'). Third Meditation, AT VII 52: CSM II 36. For more on this theme, see J. Cottingham, 'Plato's Sun and Descartes's Stove: Contemplation and Control in Cartesian Philosophy', in M. Ayers (ed.), *Rationalism, Platonism and God*. Proceedings of the British Academy, 149 (2007), 15–44; repr. as Ch. 15, below.

enterprise.[39] When he was a schoolboy of 13, there appeared a textbook that was rapidly to become a best seller, the *Summa philosophiae quadripartita*, a 'Compendium of Philosophy in Four Parts', which Descartes was later to describe as 'the best its type ever produced'.[40] Written by Eustachius, a Cistercian and professor of philosophy at the Sorbonne, it covered dialectic, morals, physics, and metaphysics. And in case we should think that the aim of this comprehensive summary was simply to impart to its readers an intellectual grasp of the essentials of each of the separate branches of philosophy, the object of the enterprise is stated very clearly: 'universae philosophiae finis est humana felicitas' (the goal of a complete philosophy is human happiness).[41]

The two principal features of philosophy that are prominent here, its all-encompassing character, and the link with how we can best live ('philosophy as a way of life', as Pierre Hadot has called it),[42] are in both cases explicitly recognized and adopted by Descartes for his own system. The celebrated metaphor of philosophy as a tree, which he uses in the French preface to his own comprehensive textbook, the *Principia philosophiae*, captures both the integrated or organic nature of the subject (metaphysics the roots, physics the trunk, the more specific disciplines—medicine, mechanics, and morals—the branches) and also its aspirations to yield fruit in our lives.[43] This last aspect is sometimes presented by Descartes in terms of the practical benefits or pay-offs of his philosophy, in contrast to the 'speculative' philosophy of the schoolmen';[44] in the *Discourse* and elsewhere, for example, he mentions the conquest of illness and the maladies of old age,

---

[39] For more on the 'synoptic' conception of philosophy, see J. Cottingham, *Philosophy and the Good Life* (Cambridge: Cambridge University Press, 1998), ch. 1.

[40] Letter to Mersenne of 11 November 1640, AT III 232: CSMK 156.

[41] Eustachius a Sancto Paulo, *Summa philosophiae quadripartita* [1609], Preface to pt. II. Translated extracts may be found in R. Ariew, J. Cottingham, and T. Sorell (eds.), *Descartes' Meditations: Background Source Materials* (Cambridge: Cambridge University Press, 1998), 68–96.

[42] Cf. Pierre Hadot, *Philosophy as a Way of Life* (Oxford: Blackwell, 1995). Originally published as *Exercices spirituels et philosophie antique* (Paris: Études Augustiniennes, 1987).

[43] *Principles of Philosophy*, Preface to French Edition [1647], AT IXB 14: CSM I 186.

[44] 'au lieu de cette philosophie spéculative, qu'on enseigne dans les écoles, on en peut trouver une pratique, par laquelle, connaissant la force et les actions du feu, de l'eau, des astres, des cieux et de tous les autres corps qui nos environnent, aussi distinctement que nous connaissons les divers métiers de nos artisans, nous les pourrions employer en même façon à tous les usages auxquels ils sont propres, et ainsi nous rendre comme maîtres et possesseurs de la nature.' ('Instead of the speculative philosophy taught in the Schools, we can find a practical one, whereby, knowing the force and actions of fire, water, the stars, the heavens and all the other bodies in our environment, as distinctly as we know the various crafts of our artisans, we could employ them in the same way for all the purposes for which

and even the artificial prolongation of life.[45] Here Descartes is adopting what is, to our ears, his most 'modernistic' *persona*—what we might almost now see as that of Descartes the 'proto-Californian'.[46] But if we bracket off these sometimes rather brash-sounding boasts about what the new mechanistic understanding of nature might achieve, Descartes's general philosophical orientation, one directed not only towards increased knowledge but also to the goal of a better way of life, was in fact part of a much older tradition that linked him, rather than separating him, from the scholastic predecessors he hoped in many respects to supersede.

Before exploring this further, we need first to be aware that even the contrast just made between knowledge on the one hand and one's way of living on the other can be radically misleading. The Thomist tradition, an important element in the philosophical culture that Descartes's teachers at La Flèche handed on to him, embodied a conception of knowledge that was much richer and less narrowly intellectualistic than our modern conception might suggest. Thomas Aquinas had divided the rational faculty into two categories, practical reason and speculative reason. The former involves the virtues of prudence and art (concerned respectively with doing and making what conduces to human good);[47] the latter involves the three virtues of *intellectus* or 'understanding' (the grasp of first principles), *scientia* or 'knowledge' (comprehension of things and their causes), and *sapientia* or 'wisdom' (awareness of how everything is related to the highest or ultimate causes).[48] But it is striking how far Aquinas departs from the original Aristotelian framework on which this classification is based; for although formally speaking these three virtues are excellences of speculative reason (which might suggest to us a certain neutrality and

---

they are appropriate, and thus make ourselves as it were masters and possessors of nature.') *Discourse on the Method*, Pt. Six (AT VI 61: CSM I 142).

[45] In the continuation of the passage cited in the previous note, Descartes observes that the new knowledge he envisages is 'desirable not only for the invention of innumerable devices which would facilitate our enjoyment of the fruits of the earth and all the goods we find there, but also and most importantly for the maintenance of health ... For whatever we now know in medicine is almost nothing in comparison with what remains to be known, and we might free ourselves from innumerable diseases, both of the body and of the mind, and perhaps even from the infirmity of old age, if we had sufficient knowledge of their causes and of all the remedies which nature has provided.' Ibid. (AT VI 62: CSM 142–3). See also Descartes, *Conversation with Burman* [1648], AT V 178: CSMK 353.

[46] Cf. J. Cottingham, 'Spirituality, Science and Morality', in D. Carr and J. Haldane (eds.), *Essays on Spirituality and Education* (London: Routledge, 2003), 40–54.

[47] Aquinas, *Summa theologiae* [1266–73] IaIIae (First Part of the Second Part), qu. 57 art. 2.

[48] Ibid. qu. 66 art. 5.

abstraction from the conduct of life), Aquinas's account places them within a richly structured religious and moral framework. Excellence of intellect, for example, is, as Eleonore Stump acutely observes, 'linked [by Aquinas] together with certain actions and dispositions in the will and also with certain states of emotion.'[49] And it follows that on Aquinas' view 'all true excellence of intellect—wisdom, understanding and *scientia*—is possible only in connection with moral excellence as well.'[50]

The idea of a complex interrelation between moral and intellectual excellence is reinforced once we begin to delve into the theological context of Aquinas's account of the virtues. There is explicit reference to the 'seven gifts (*septem dona*) of the Spirit', a doctrine based on the prophecy in Isaiah: 'And the spirit of God shall rest upon him, the spirit of wisdom and understanding, the spirit of counsel and strength, the spirit of knowledge and godliness, the spirit of the fear of God.'[51] Aquinas observes that four of the gifts pertain to reason, namely wisdom (*sapientia*), knowledge (*scientia*), understanding (*intellectus*), and counsel (*consilium*); and three to the appetitive faculty, namely strength or courage (*fortitudo*), godliness or piety (*pietas*), and fear (*timor*).[52] The result is that, despite Aquinas's stress on their different origins (natural and supernatural respectively), his discussion involves a considerable overlap, or 'twinning'[53] between the list of intellectual excellences and the list of gifts of the Holy Spirit. And indeed Aquinas's account constantly interweaves items from these lists, and also from other standard theological lists, including the famous enumeration in Paul's letter to the Galatians of the nine *fruits* of the Spirit, namely 'love, joy, peace, longsuffering, gentleness, goodness, faith, meekness, temperance'.[54] Aquinas also cross-refers us to the three great 'theological' virtues of faith, hope, and charity: two of the three intellectual virtues, *scientia* and *intellectus* are linked with faith, while *sapientia* is linked with charity.

---

[49] Eleonore Stump, *Aquinas* (London: Routledge, 2003), 353. In what follows about Aquinas I am heavily indebted to Stump's insightful and unusually wide-ranging treatment.   [50] Ibid. 360.

[51] Isaiah 11: 2, following the Greek text of the Septuagint version (LXX). The original Hebrew lists six gifts, and this is followed in the Vulgate: 'et requiescet super eum spiritus Domini, spiritus sapientiae et intellectus, spiritus consilii et fortitudinis, spiritus scientiae et pietatis.' But the LXX adds a gloss, 'the fear of God', which some commentaries construed as a seventh gift; hence the standard doctrine of the 'sevenfold gifts' of the Holy Spirit, reflected in Thomas's inclusion of *timor*.

[52] *Summa theologiae*, IaIIae qu. 68 art. 1.   [53] Cf. Stump, *Aquinas*, 350 ff.

[54] Galatians 5: 22–3: 'fructus autem Spiritus est caritas, gaudium, pax, longanimitas, bonitas, benignitas, fides, modestia, continentia' (Vulgate).

This interweaving is particularly striking in the case of *sapientia* or wisdom: although, if construed in purely secular or natural terms, it might be thought to be a 'morally neutral' virtue, and hence able to be present irrespective of the moral character of the agent, this ceases to be so if it is construed as a spiritual gift.[55] What had in Aristotle been understood in terms of the mastery of the first principles of metaphysics becomes in Aquinas associated with knowledge of the ultimate first principle, God, knowledge of whom is linked in many biblical texts to charity or love (which, of course, is far from being a purely intellectual matter).[56] Some of the ramifications of this are again brought out by Stump:

On Aquinas's account of wisdom…a person's moral wrongdoing will produce deficiencies in both her speculative and her practical intellect. In its effects on her speculative intellect, it will make her less capable of understanding God and goodness, theology and ethics. It will also undermine her practical intellect, leaving her prone not only to wrong moral judgement in general, but also to wrong moral judgement about herself and particular actions of hers, and so will lead to self-deception.[57]

The upshot of this is that although a certain image of Aquinas that is prevalent today sees him as a proto-analytic philosopher, concerned purely with abstract conceptual enquiries (together perhaps with certain quaint and abstruse theological puzzles, for example about the identity of angels), in reality his philosophy offers an integrated vision in which the pursuit of virtue and the cultivation of knowledge are closely interlinked, and in which even an abstract-sounding virtue such as wisdom or *sapientia* (the successor to Aristotle's *sophia*) emerges as central to a harmonious and integrated life. To quote from the *Summa theologiae*:

It belongs to wisdom, as a gift, not only to contemplate Divine things, but also to regulate human acts. Now the first thing to be effected in this direction of human acts is the removal of evils opposed to wisdom: wherefore fear is said to be 'the beginning of wisdom,' because it makes us shun evil, while the last thing is like an end, whereby all things are reduced to their right order; and it is this that constitutes peace. Hence James said with reason that 'the wisdom that is from above' (and this is the gift of the Holy Ghost) 'first indeed is chaste,' because it

---

[55] *Summa theologiae*, IIaIIae qu. 45 art. 4.   [56] See e.g. 1 John 4: 16.
[57] Stump, *Aquinas*, 353–4.

avoids the corruption of sin, and 'then peaceable,' wherein lies the ultimate effect of wisdom, for which reason peace is numbered among the beatitudes.[58]

5. Descartes as Sage?

Given that this traditional model exemplified by Aquinas and others—the model of philosophy as contributing centrally to how we should live—would have been absorbed at some fairly deep level by Descartes as part of his educational and cultural background, how far can we say that Descartes himself aspired to make his philosophy conform to it? And if, as has recently been suggested, the traditional *persona* of the philosopher (that of the 'philosopher as sage', as we might call it for convenience) had begun to come under serious attack in the early-modern period with the emergence of the new experimental science,[59] should Descartes be seen as joining that attack, or as holding fast to the older conception?

There is a certain amount in Descartes that may seem to point us towards the erosion (or indeed eradication) of the *persona* of the philosopher as sage, and its replacement by the harsher more modernistic *persona* of the technocrat—the controlling manipulator of nature, aiming to 'deliver the goods' as a result of the expertise provided by the new science. We have already mentioned the manifesto of the *Discours de la méthode*, which offers the hope that the new *philosophie pratique* will deliver mankind from the obstacles of disease and infirmity and make us 'masters and possessors of nature'.[60] And the way this programme is worked out in the writings of Descartes's later years seems at first to reduce morals to physiology and medicine: to use the new mechanistic knowledge to develop techniques to reprogramme the human affective system and thus, as it were, bypass the need for the traditional goals of spiritual discipline in the pursuit of the good.

At the heart of this technological vision is Descartes's idea of utilizing the results of physiological science in a blueprint for ethics. He told a

---

[58] *Summa theologiae*, IIaIIae qu. 45 art. 6 (English Dominican trans., 1947).

[59] See e.g. Stephen Gaukroger's account of Francis Bacon in 'The *Persona* of the Natural Philosopher in the Early to Mid Seventeenth Century', in C. Condren, S. Gaukroger, and I. Hunter (eds.), *The Philosopher in Early Modern Europe* (Cambridge: Cambridge University Press, 2006), 17–34.

[60] *Discourse*, Pt. Six (AT VI 61: CSM I 142), quoted above, n. 44.

correspondent in 1646 that his results in physics had been 'a great help in establishing sure foundations in moral philosophy';[61] and when he published his treatise on the *Passions* in 1649 he described it as breaking new ground by explaining the passions *en physicien*—from a physiological point of view, as we might say.[62] The ultimate goal here is to develop a scientific programme for the retraining of our psychophysical responses. Part of the background for this comes from ordinary observation: if the behaviour patterns of animals can be changed by training, might not human emotional responses, linked to similar types of physiological mechanism, be similarly altered? And if our early childhood experiences can set up automatic arousal or aversion mechanisms, might we not be able to delve back into these past causes, and learn how to overcome the conditioned patterns of response by restructuring them?[63]

Descartes's scientific ethics thus takes the general aim, voiced in his early manifesto, of becoming 'masters and possessors of nature', and proceeds to apply it not just to the external environment but to the internal world, to our own nature as human beings. Since the laws of operation of our bodies are no different from the mechanical principles operating everywhere else, and since the passions are intimately linked to bodily events in the nervous system, science can itself provide the solution to the ancient problems of how to achieve a virtuous life. The classical Aristotelian theory of virtue had had to rely on a large measure of luck: everything depended on being born into the right kind of ethical culture that would foster the right habits. But Descartes's new programme of training—of what at the end of *Les Passions de l'âme* he called 'guiding and controlling the passions'—envisages taking ingrained patterns of psychophysical response and redirecting them by the sheer application of technological know-how.[64]

---

[61] 'la notion telle quelle de la Physique, que j'ai tâché d'acquérir, m'a grandement servi pour établir des fondements certains en la Morale' (letter to Chanut of 15 June 1646, AT IV 441: CSMK 289).

[62] *Les Passions de l'âme*, Prefatory Letter of 14 August 1649, AT XI 326: CSM I 327.

[63] The details of Descartes's programme are examined at length in J. Cottingham, *Philosophy and the Good Life* (Cambridge: Cambridge University Press, 1998), ch. 3. For animal training, see *Passions of the Soul* [*Les Passions de l'âme*, 1649], art. 50; for patterns of emotional response acquired in early childhood see letter to Chanut of 6 June 1647 (AT V 57: CSMK 323); both these passages are discussed in Ch. 12, above.

[64] 'Ceux mêmes qui ont les plus faibles âmes pourraient acquérir un empire très absolu sur toutes les passions, si on employait assez d'industrie à les dresser et à les conduire.' (Even those with the most feeble souls could acquire an absolute mastery over all the passions if enough effort was employed in guiding and controlling them.) *Passions of the Soul*, art. 50.

All this might indeed seem to take us very far away from the search for wisdom and righteousness associated with the traditional *persona* of the philosopher as sage. But it is now time to notice that all these envisaged technical developments in the management of the passions have for Descartes an essentially subordinate role. For the passions are related to the good only, as it were, accidentally and contingently. Sometimes the objects they incline us to pursue are indeed worthy of pursuit,[65] but often they can mislead us into supposing that something's value is vastly greater than it is: 'Often passion makes us believe certain things to be much better and more desirable than they are; then, when we have taken much trouble to acquire them, and in the process lost the chance of possessing other more genuine goods, possession of them brings home to us their defects; and thence arise dissatisfaction, regret and remorse.'[66] This leads Descartes straight into an insistence on the 'true function of reason in the conduct of life', namely 'to examine and consider without passion the value of all the perfections, both of the body and of the soul, which can be acquired by our conduct'.[67]

Is what is here envisaged a kind of utilitarian calculus—the kind of rational instrumentalism that we have seen in more modern times, namely one that cuts free from any substantive vision of the good, and simply aims to maximize the 'preferences' of the agent, or of the community at large? Emphatically not. For Descartes never abandoned his allegiance to a strongly theistic metaphysics of value, one that construes goodness as an objective supra-personal reality, constraining the rational assent of human beings just as powerfully as do the clearly perceived truths of logic and mathematics.

At the centre of Descartes's metaphysics, resonantly expressed at the climax of his philosophical masterpiece, the *Meditations*, lies a vision of the eternal and infinite divine source of truth and goodness: 'Placet hic aliquamdiu in ipsius Dei contemplatione immorari ... et immensi hujus luminis pulchritudinem ... intueri, admirari, adorare' ('Let me here rest for a while

---

[65] This applies in particular to the legitimate pleasures that the soul has in common with the body: 'L'âme peut avoir ses plaisirs à part. Mais pour ceux qui lui sont communs avec le corps, ils dépendent entièrement des passions: en sorte que les hommes qu'elles peuvent le plus émouvoir sont capables de goûter le plus de douceur en cette vie' (The soul can have its pleasures of its own. But those which it shares with the body depend entirely on the passions, so that those human beings whom the passions can most move are capable of tasting the greatest sweetness in this life.) (*Passions*, art. 212.)

[66] Letter to Elizabeth of 1 September 1645. Descartes goes on to say that the passions often 'represent the good to which they tend with greater splendour than they deserve' and they make us 'imagine pleasure to be much greater before we possess them than our subsequent experiences show them to be', AT IV 284: CSMK 264–5.   [67] Letter to Elizabeth of 1 September 1645, AT IV 287: CSMK 265.

in the contemplation of God himself and gaze upon, wonder at, and adore the beauty of this immense light').[68] This vision, it needs to be emphasized, involves contemplation of the good as well as the true: following the lead of the Platonists, Descartes draws a strong parallel between how the mind responds to the *ratio veri* and to the *ratio boni*.[69] In the upward ascent of the mind from doubt and darkness to the light, whether of truth or of goodness, we first need to exercise our will to turn away from what is deceptive or unreliable. But once we free ourselves from illusion and focus on the objects revealed by the light of reason, then we arrive at our destination: the work of the will has been done, and it can now subside into automatic assent to what is revealed with the utmost clarity as good or as true: 'from a great light in the intellect there followed a great propensity in the will'.[70]

Once the importance of this powerful underlying metaphysics has been appreciated, we can see that Cartesian ethics, with its proposed techniques for the management of the mind–body complex, could not even get off the ground without the fundamental supporting role of reason. Philosophy can show us how to live because the divine light of reason, implanted in each of our minds, can, when used carefully and properly, make us aware of those genuine and lasting goods in the pursuit of which our true fulfilment lies. Because of the weakness of our nature (a recurring theme in Descartes)[71] we can easily be led astray, failing to focus on the light of truth and goodness, and allowing the false allure of lesser or specious 'goods' to attract our attention. But as long as we are determined to hold the image of the good before our eyes 'in so far as the eye of the darkened intellect can bear it',[72] then we can know the right way forward. And virtue follows in the wake of this, since its fundamental basis is a 'firm and constant resolution to use our freedom well, that is, never to lack the will to undertake and carry out what we judge to be best'.[73] This is the discipline, or *askesis,* that Descartes's philosophical

---

[68] Third Meditation, AT VII 52: CSM II 36.

[69] My spontaneous inclination to assent to the truth, or to pursue the good, is a function of my 'clearly understanding that reasons of truth and goodness point that way' ('quia rationem veri et boni in ea evidenter intelligo'); Descartes suggests that such inclinations may also be thought of as resulting from a 'divinely produced disposition of my inmost thoughts' (Fourth Meditation, AT VII 58: CSM II 40).

[70] 'ex magna luce in intellectu magna consequuta est propensio in voluntate' (Fourth Meditation, AT VII 59: CSM II 41).

[71] Cf. the last sentence of the *Meditations*: 'Naturae nostrae infirmitas est agnoscenda' ('We must acknowledge the weakness of our nature'), AT VII 90: CSM II 62.

[72] AT VII 52: CSM II 36 (end of Third Meditation).

[73] *Passions of the Soul*, art. 153 (speaking of the master virtue of 'generosity').

method requires, in morals as in metaphysics. And it is a discipline that, because of its theistically oriented character and its fundamental integration of the moral and epistemic domains in the quest for truth and goodness, it seems not inappropriate to call a genuinely spiritual one.[74]

Descartes's ambition for his own philosophy was for it to match the goals set by his scholastic predecessor Eustachius: 'the aim of a complete system of philosophy is human happiness'. And in so far as his theistic metaphysics is the key to securing this goal, he follows in the tradition of Aquinas, for whom *sapientia*, the highest of the intellectual virtues, operates properly when it is directed towards knowledge of the highest and most exalted cause, that is, God.[75] The key to discerning the *persona* of Descartes the philosopher has very often been understood in terms of his new vision of *scientia*. And that, of course, is a very important part of the story. But the full story discloses his even more important commitment to the ancient ideal of *sapientia*, with all the religious connotations that notion would have had for one brought up as he had been.

We began by calling attention to Descartes's earliest notebook, the *Prae-ambula*, where Descartes sees himself as entering the world stage masked, and goes on to describe the sciences themselves as masked. Peeling off the mask is no easy task when one is dealing with one of the most wary and private of the great philosophers. But if the argument of this chapter has been anywhere near the mark, Descartes's true philosophical *persona* is already strongly prefigured in the verse from the book of Psalms that he chose to inscribe as his motto at the very front of that first notebook: 'Initium sapientiae timor Domini'—'the fear of the Lord is the beginning of wisdom'.[76]

[74] There are many aspects of the *Meditations*, for example, that call to mind the model of a set of spiritual exercises. For more on these similarities (and some differences), see J. Cottingham *The Spiritual Dimension: Religion, Philosophy and Human Value* (Cambridge: Cambridge University Press, 2005), ch. 1.

[75] A recent most interesting study by Lilli Alanen has plausibly argued that from the time of the correspondence with Elizabeth onwards, Descartes became increasingly interested in the 'practical, moral and therapeutic' uses of reason: *Descartes's Concept of Mind* (Cambridge, Mass.: Harvard University Press, 2003), 166. Earlier in her book, Alanen acutely observes that Descartes's philosophical interests in *scientia* were closely connected to the traditional philosophical goal of *sapientia* (which, however, she glosses, somewhat narrowly it seems to me, as 'practical intelligence' (p. 7)).

[76] Psalm 110 (Vulgate); this corresponds to Ps. 111 in the numbering of the Hebrew Bible, which is followed by the Authorized Version (1611) and the Book of Common Prayer (1550, rev. 1662).

15

Plato's Sun and Descartes's Stove: Contemplation and Control in Cartesian Philosophy

1. Introduction

'Let no one unskilled in Geometry enter here.'[1] Descartes could have marched in boldly under the famous inscription over the portals of Plato's academy, since, as Thomas Hobbes reportedly remarked, he was set to be one of the best geometers of his age, had he not been diverted into philosophy.[2] The cosmological system that Descartes produced was, like that of Plato, heavily dependent on geometrical and other mathematical ideas, both in its fine detail and in its general principles.[3] Also like Plato, Descartes believed in the unity of the sciences, as against the separatist Aristotelian view of a plurality of disciplines each with its own methods and standards of precision.[4] Again, like Plato, he mistrusted and indeed

The paper that became this chapter was first delivered at the Dawes Hicks Symposium on 'Rationalism, Platonism and God', held at the British Academy, London, in May 2004. I am grateful to participants at the symposium for valuable comments and suggestions, and to Michael Ayers for helpful comments on the penultimate draft of the written version.

[1] *Mēdeis ageōmetrētos eisitō*. The tradition that this phrase was inscribed over the portals of Plato's Academy has not been traced back further than Joannes Philoponus, a Neoplatonic Christian philosopher who lived in Alexandria in the sixth century AD. See H. G. Liddell and R. Scott (eds.), *A Greek English Dictionary*, rev. H. S. Jones, 9th edn. (Oxford: Clarendon, 1996), s.v. *ageōmetrētos*.

[2] According to John Aubrey, Thomas Hobbes 'would say that had [Des Cartes] kept himselfe wholly to Geometrie he had been the best Geometer in the world but that his head did not lye for Philosophy' (*Brief Lives* [c.1680], ed. O. Lawson Dick (Harmondsworth: Penguin, 1962), 237).

[3] See René Descartes, *Rules for the Direction of our Native Intelligence* [*Regulae ad directionem ingenii*, c.1628], Rule Four (AT X 376–8: CSM I 18–19); *Principles of Philosophy* [*Principia philosophiae*, 1644], pt. II art. 64 (AT VIIIA 78–9: CSM I 247).

[4] See *Regulae*, loc. cit. (AT X 378: CSM I 19); *Principles of Philosophy*, Preface to French trans. of 1647 (AT IXB 14: CSM I 186).

repudiated the senses as a source of knowledge.[5] Finally, like Plato, Descartes argued for the immateriality of the soul and its resulting aptness to survive separation from the body;[6] and he wrestled with the implications of all this for the conduct of life.[7]

This is quite a list—and no doubt it could be augmented. And working with such a list, the historian of ideas could certainly construct a rich account of Platonic influences and sources for Cartesian philosophy, filling out the picture with reference not just to Plato's writings,[8] but to a host of texts from the succeeding centuries, from Plotinus to Augustine and on to the Neoplatonists of the Renaissance. Descartes hated to acknowledge predecessors, and reacted with stiff defensiveness when asked about his debts (he was reluctant, for example, even to admit that his Cogito had been inspired by St Augustine).[9] But no philosopher, even the most original, creates out of nothing, and it is always interesting to uncover some of the ingredients of the process.

My own aim in this chapter will, however, be somewhat different. I shall take in turn three principal areas of Cartesian philosophy, namely cosmology, metaphysics, and morals, and in each case I shall identify some important strands in Descartes's thinking that may broadly be characterized as 'Platonic'. But I want to examine these not simply from the perspective of the history of ideas—with a view to uncovering how Descartes drew on previous sources—but also with a partly proleptic eye, to see how (what we can now recognize as) Descartes's 'modernizing' tendencies pulled him forwards and away from his classical and medieval forebears. This will in turn throw into focus the curiously problematic link that obtains between today's philosophical outlook and that of the so-called 'father' of the modern subject. Descartes has unavoidably become for us the archetypal

---

[5] See e.g. *Principles of Philosophy*, pt. I arts. 68 and 69 (AT VIIIA 33: CSM I 217).

[6] See *Meditations* [*Meditationes de prima philosophia*, 1641], Second Set of Replies (AT VII 153: CSM II 209). See also J. Cottingham, 'Cartesian Dualism: Theology, Metaphysics and Science', in J. Cottingham (ed.), *The Cambridge Companion to Descartes* (Cambridge: Cambridge University Press, 1992), ch. 8.

[7] See letter to Elizabeth of 1 September 164 (AT IV 286: CSMK 264–5).

[8] When one contrasts Plato's own texts with subsequent 'Platonic' interpretations, it should not be supposed that it is a straightforward matter to derive from those texts an original core of doctrines that represent Plato's own philosophical views. One of the hallmarks of a truly great philosopher is the way in which his writings attract diverse interpretations, and, as Myles Burnyeat has elegantly demonstrated, Plato is an 'extreme case' of this. See M. F. Burnyeat, 'Plato', *Proceedings of the British Academy*, 111 (2001), 1–22.   [9] See Letter to Colvius of 14 November 1640 (AT III 247–8: CSMK 159).

Janus figure—the leading herald of our modern age whose thought was at the same time closely grafted onto the medieval and classical tradition that made it possible. By looking at our own relationship with him in this double light, by seeing both his proximity to us and his distance from us, we may perhaps gain a better sense of the distinctively philosophical (in contrast to the purely historical) point of studying his ideas. For in seeing which way Descartes himself turned (forwards or backwards, as it were) at certain crucial points in the development of his system, we may deepen our understanding of some of the tensions that still operate beneath the surface of our own contemporary philosophical worldview.

2. Cartesian Cosmology: from Order to Opacity

First, then, Descartes's cosmology. At least one commentator has recently drawn attention to possible links between the Cartesian theory of the physical universe and the Platonic cosmological tradition derived from the *Timaeus*, which had attracted considerable if sometimes erratic attention from assorted philosophical commentators in the centuries leading up to the early-modern revolution.[10]

When in his first published work Descartes described the basic character of his cosmological outlook, he wrote: 'I noticed certain laws which God has so established in nature, and of which he has implanted such notions in our minds, that after adequate reflection we cannot doubt that they are exactly observed in everything that exists or occurs in the world.'[11] The claim is the powerful one that the human mind is a divinely certified 'mirror of nature'.[12] In creating us, God structured our minds in such a way as to reflect the self-same rationally accessible parameters that operate in his other creation—the material universe. It is this match that ultimately

---

[10] Some of this background is fascinatingly described in Catherine Wilson, 'Soul, Body, and World: Plato's *Timaeus* and Descartes's *Meditations*', in S. Hutton and D. Hedley (eds.), *Platonism at the Origins of Modernity* (Dordrecht: Springer, 2007), 177–91.

[11] 'J'ai remarqué certaines lois, que Dieu a tellement établies en la nature, et dont il a imprimé de telles notions en nos âmes, qu'après y avoir fait assez de réflexion, nous ne saurions doubter qu'elles ne soient exactement observées, en tout ce qui est ou qui se fait dans le monde.' *Discourse on the Method* [*Discours de la méthode*, 1637], Pt. Five (AT VI 41: CSM I 131).

[12] For this phrase (albeit used in a wider sense), cf. Richard Rorty, *Philosophy and the Mirror of Nature* (Oxford: Blackwell, 1980).

makes science possible, since the 'external' rationality manifest in the created cosmos and the internal rationality of the human mind both stem from the same divine Creator. Now according to Stephen Menn, in his justly admired study of Descartes and Augustine, this is precisely the picture we find in Plato's *Timaeus*:

[For Plato] the world is governed by an intrinsically rational divine power, and this power is the source of rational order to the things it governs ... Heraclitus calls the source of rationality *logos*; Plato follows Anaxagoras in calling it *nous* ... Plato builds the physics of the *Timaeus* on this hypothesis, and the divine demiurge of that dialogue is identical with the world-governing *nous* that Plato invokes in the *Philebus* and also in passages of the *Laws* ... Nous is able to order the world, causing different portions of matter to participate in different intelligible forms at different times, according to a single all-encompassing rational pattern.[13]

It is not hard to see how there could be a fairly smooth transition between the Platonic cosmos so described and the Christian conception of a divine rationality at the heart of creation: 'In the beginning was the *logos*.' In the opening chapter of the Fourth Gospel, the *logos* is of course famously associated with light. And certainly in Descartes, the new science seems to be predicated on the idea of the divine light of reason, manifest in the workings of the material universe, and illuminating the minds of the human scientists who investigate its structure. This is not of course to say that there are not many important differences between Plato, St John, and Descartes. The standard Christian picture, adopted by Descartes, is of divine creative responsibility for all there is ('without Him was not anything made that was made'—John 1: 3): we have creation *ex nihilo*, rather than (as in Plato) the Demiurge imposing order on a pre-existing chaos. So while Plato can retain a dualistic picture, with a residual imperfection, a kind of raw unruliness of matter, set over against the divine impulse of rationality and order, Descartes as a Christian philosopher will follow the uncompromising Augustinian line: there is but one source of reality, and the explanation for any defects will have to be sought elsewhere.[14] But despite this and other

---

[13] Stephen Menn, *Descartes and Augustine* (Cambridge: Cambridge University Press, 1998), 87–8.

[14] In particular, for Augustine, in the bad use of our free will: 'everything called "evil" is either sin, or the penalty of sin' (*De Genesi ad litteram imperfectus liber* [AD 393], 1. 3); 'the cause of evil is the defection of the will of a being who is mutably good from the Good which is immutable' (*Enchiridion* [AD 423], 8. 23). Descartes adapts this theodicy in explaining the cause of epistemic error in the Fourth Meditation (AT VII 56 ff.: CSM II 39 ff.).

important differences, the parallel emphasized by Descartes in the *Discourse* between the divine ordering of the external universe and the ordering of the human mind seems to be appropriately characterized as a genuinely Platonic idea.[15]

This impression of continuity appears to be reinforced when we look at Descartes's earlier suppressed work, *Le Monde*, written only five years or so before the *Discourse*. For there an initial chaos makes it appearance—not, to be sure, as Plato's is, independent of or prior to God, but nonetheless not intrinsically possessing any order until, 'from the first instant of creation' God imparts certain motions into the parts of matter. Having done so,

he causes these parts to continue moving thereafter in accordance with the ordinary laws of nature. For God has established those laws in such a marvellous way that … they are sufficient to cause the parts of this chaos to disentangle themselves and arrange themselves in such good order that they will have the form of a quite perfect world.[16]

The picture looks at first to be broadly in harmony with both Plato and indeed the account in *Genesis*. An initial chaos—the world is *tohu bohu*—formless (Genesis 1: 2); and then the voice of God is heard and a perfect world is formed; 'and God saw that it was very good' (1: 31).[17] Or in Plato's *Timaeus*: 'As our world is the fairest of things that have come into being (*kallistos tōn gegonotōn*) so God is the best of causes (*aristos tōn aitiōn*); having come into being in this way, the world was fashioned according to what is graspable by rationality and intelligence.'[18]

Yet despite the parallels just noted (and now I come, as it were, to the antithesis), a closer scrutiny finds in Descartes passages that point in quite a different direction, prefiguring the bleaker, ethically blank universe so typical of our modern scientific world picture. Pascal famously said that he could not forgive Descartes for reducing God's role to that of giving the

---

[15] There are, inevitably, some caveats, the most significant of which was made by the great Plato scholar F. M. Cornford, who cautioned against an over-Christianized reading of the *Timaeus*: 'It is not fair either to Plato or to the New Testament to ascribe the most characteristic revelations of the Founder of Christianity to a pagan polytheist.' *Plato's Cosmology* (London: Routledge, 1937), 35. Cornford stresses that it is nowhere suggested that the Demiurge should be an object of worship: 'he is not a religious figure' (ibid.).   [16] *The World* [*Le Monde*, 1633], ch. 6 (AT XI 34: CSM I 91).

[17] The Greek Septuagint translation of Genesis uses the term *cosmos* to convey this order and goodness of the created universe: 'the heaven and the earth and the whole *cosmos* of them' (Genesis 2: 1).

[18] Plato, *Timaeus* [*c.*360 BC], 29A; my translation.

system an initial shove.[19] That particular criticism is in fact misconceived since Cartesian matter, being pure geometrical extension, has no power of its own to transmit, or continue in, motion; hence the motive power of God is continuously required to conserve as well as to create the motion in the cosmos.[20] But Pascal's general sense that the Cartesian deity is somehow remote in comparison to the living God of religious tradition nonetheless carries more than a germ of truth. The key to this lies in Descartes's remark (quoted above) that the different-sized particles of varying shapes that compose the initial matter of the universe are given certain initial motions and then caused to continue moving thereafter 'in accordance with the ordinary laws of nature' ('suivant les lois ordinaries de la Nature'). Although Descartes does not put it this way (and although, as just noted, the divine action is needed to conserve motion), nonetheless the thought has been planted that all one needs in order to provide an adequate explanation for the cosmos as we now find it is a set of initial conditions specifying certain quantities of matter in motion (its particles defined in terms of size and shape), plus certain universal laws governing the subsequent movement of those particles.[21]

Now although the *result* of the operation of these laws may be the magnificent universe we now observe—galaxies, stars, planets—the laws themselves do not appear to manifest any particular beauty (apart, perhaps, from their mathematical simplicity), nor indeed any intrinsic design or purposiveness. Isaac Newton, whose mathematical physics was in due course to supersede that of Descartes (and who adapted to his purposes some elements of the Cartesian system, for example the principle of rectilinear inertial motion), did indeed subscribe to the idea of design, observing that 'The most beautiful system of the sun, planets and comets could only proceed from the counsel and dominion of an intelligent and powerful Being [whom we know] by his most wise and excellent contrivances of things, and final causes...'[22] But Newton's reasoning for

---

[19] 'Je ne puis pardonner à Descartes: il voudrait bien dans toute la philosophie se pouvoir passer de Dieu; mais il n'a pu s'empêcher de lui donner une chiquenaude pour mettre le monde en mouvement; après cela, il n'a plus que faire de Dieu.' Blaise Pascal, *Pensées* [*c.*1660], ed. L. Lafuma (Paris: Seuil, 1962), no. 1001.   [20] See *Principles of Philosophy*, pt. II art. 36 (AT VIII 61: CSM I 240).

[21] Descartes reduces these laws to three—the principle of inertia, the principle of rectilinear motion, and the principle of the conservation of quantity of motion: *Principles*, pt. II arts. 37–40. For some contrasts between Descartes's system and the ancient atomism which it in some respects resembles, see *Principles*, pt. IV art. 202.

[22] *Philosophiae naturalis principia mathematica* [1687], trans. A. Motte (London, 1729), 344–6.

this invocation of divine ordering was that he believed that some kind of supernatural intervention would be needed to correct the celestial motions that would otherwise be perturbed as a result of the operation of gravity:

I do not think [the solar system] explicable by mere natural causes, but am forced to ascribe it to the counsel and contrivance of a voluntary agent... Gravity may put the planets into motion, but without the divine power it could never put them into such a Circulating motion as they have about the Sun, and therefore for this as well as other reasons I am compelled to ascribe the frame of this Systeme to an intelligent Agent.[23]

The counterfactual corollary is apparent: *were* it ever to turn out to be that case that one could, for example by modifying the theory of gravity or in some other way, discover a natural explanation for the actual perturbations of motions found in the solar system, then the intelligent interventions would be redundant.[24] But what at all events seems to be implicitly conceded by Newton in this passage is that the mere system of gravitational bodies moving subject to the law of inertial motion plus the inverse square law does not itself require a divine orderer, at any rate not in the sense of a purposive intelligence; the general pattern is, as it were derived simply from the natural disposition of things, explicable by 'mere natural causes'.

Talk of Newtonian forces such as gravitation of course takes us beyond Descartes's frame of reference; but the general point applicable to the Cartesian cosmological system remains. The universe that Descartes describes in *Le Monde* is not presented as possessing the kind of order that requires us to invoke a supernatural intelligence; rather, if we take it as axiomatic that particle interactions operate in accordance with the mathematical covering laws specified by Descartes in *Le Monde* and later in his *Principia philosophiae*, then we have, as it were, all that is needed to explain the natural world as we find it. The position is summed up in the opening paragraph of ch. 7 of *Le Monde* (though the language, which Descartes eventually decided should not see the light of day, is considerably more forthright than he later felt able to use when he published the *Principles*):

By 'nature' here I do not mean some goddess of any other sort of imaginary power. Rather, I am using this word to signify *matter itself,* in so far as I am considering it

---

[23] Letters to Bentley of 10 December 1692 and 17 January 1693.

[24] The more sophisticated system of Einstein (which encompasses perturbations unexplained in the Newtonian cosmos) arguably achieves just such completeness.

taken together with all the qualities I have attributed to it, and under the condition that God continues to preserve it in the same way that he created it. For it follows of necessity, from the mere fact that he continues thus to preserve it, that there must be many changes in its parts which cannot, it seems to me properly be attributed to the action of God (because His action never changes), and which therefore I attribute to nature. The rules by which the changes take place I call the 'laws of nature'.[25]

Not only is there explicit rejection of the need for any Platonic-style animating intermediaries (such as the 'world-soul' found in the *Timaeus* and in many Neoplatonic writings), but the divine presence in nature is reduced to a minimum; there seems to be more than a hint here of what will become the orthodox modern conception of physics, that the system of nature is pretty much autonomous, nothing more or less than 'matter itself', operating in accordance with suitably described covering principles. We are thus by now quite far away from the Christianized Platonism that was so vividly alive three centuries earlier, when Dante wrote:

> *Le cose tutte quante*
> *hanno l'ordine tra loro, e questo è forma*
> *che l'Universo a Dio fa simigliante.*
> *Qui veggion l'alte creature l'orma*
> *de l'eterno valore, il quale è fine*
> *al quale è fatta la toccata norma.*

> All things that do exist
> have order deep within, which is the form
> that makes the Universe like unto God.
> The higher creatures see in them the stamp
> of value everlasting, the true end
> for which this rule and order was decreed.[26]

---

[25] '[P]ar la Nature je n'entends point ici quelque Déesse, ou quelque autre sorte de puissance imaginaire, mais…je me sers de ce mot pour signifier la Matière même en tant que je la considère avec toutes les qualités que je lui ai attribuées comprises toutes ensemble, et sous cette condition que Dieu continue de la conserver en la même façon qu'il la créée. Car de cela seul qu'il continue ainsi de la conserver, il suit de nécessité qu'il doit y avoir plusieurs changements en ses parties, lesquels ne pouvant, ce me semble, être proprement attribués à l'action de Dieu, parce qu'elle ne change point, je les attribue à la Nature; et les règles suivant lesquelles se font ces changements, je les nomme les lois de la Nature.' *Le Monde*, ch. 7 (AT XI 37: CSM I 92–3).

[26] Dante Alighieri, *La Divina Commedia: Paradiso* [*c.*1300], Canto I; my translation.

Dante's universe is alive with the beauty and order of its Creator, rather like that later conceived by Leibniz, in which there is 'nothing waste, nothing sterile, nothing dead; no chaos, no confusions, save in appearance'.[27] In the Cartesian picture by contrast, the world is a neutral, inanimate, purely mechanical plenum, with even the biological domain reduced to a series of particle interactions that Descartes himself firmly proclaimed to be no different in kind from what occurs in any other part of the physical universe.[28]

There is, however, a final question to be raised by way of postscript, before we move on from Descartes's physics to other aspects of his system. I have argued that despite initial Platonic echoes, the general tenor of Cartesian cosmology is better seen as pointing forwards than backwards, to the autonomous physics of modernity rather than to the value-laden cosmos of the *Timaeus*. But a possible objection to this 'autonomizing' interpretation of Cartesian physics runs thus: does not the mere fact of a law-like, mathematically describable universe tend to support the idea of rationality rather than randomness, of intelligence rather than blind evolution, of *logos* rather than *tyche*? Descartes may have banished beauty, design, and finality from his physical cosmology,[29] but does not his firm commitment to the mathematicization of physics in itself constitute adherence to the idea of the ultimate rationality of the universe and its Creator?

This is, I think, a difficult question to answer, partly because modern philosophical debate has not really settled the question of whether the fine mathematical tuning of the cosmos is a deeply significant fact about its ultimate nature, perhaps even its divinely sourced nature, or merely (in Kantian spirit) a fact about the structure of the human mind, or again, more prosaically still, simply a banal truth about the contingent regularities that are a *sine qua non* for our being here to investigate them in the first

---

[27] G. W. Leibniz *Monadology* [*Monadologie* 1714], §69.

[28] 'I will try to give such a full account of the entire bodily machine that we will have no more reason to think that it is our soul which produces in it the movements which we know by experience are not controlled by our will than we have reason to think that there is a soul in a clock which makes it tell the time.' *Description of the Human Body* [*La Description du corps humain*, 1647/8], pt I (AT XI 226: CSM I 315). Cf. also *Treatise on Man* [*L'Homme*, c.1630], AT XI 202: CSM I 108.

[29] For Descartes's resolute rejection of finalism in science, see e.g. the Fourth Meditation: 'I consider the customary search for final causes to be totally useless in physics' (AT VII 55: CSM II 39).

place.[30] But if we keep the focus on Descartes himself, then there is a special complicating factor to be taken into account, namely his famous, or notorious, doctrine of the divine creation of the eternal truths—the doctrine, consistently maintained by Descartes, that God is the author of the truths of logic and mathematics, creating them by a sovereign act of will similar to that whereby he creates the material universe: he was wholly free to do otherwise.[31] This doctrine introduces a 'worm of contingency' into the Cartesian system.[32] For on Descartes's picture, although our minds are so structured that we cannot conceive of the eternal laws of mathematics as being otherwise, they remain, from God's perspective, wholly contingent on his creative will. It follows from this that the talk of a match between the human mind and the divine is in one sense misleading. We may have a clear and distinct grasp of the fundamental logical and mathematical principles by which the universe operates (as proclaimed in the resounding opening to Part Five of the *Discourse* with which we began this section), and in this sense we may think of the human mind as a mirror of nature. But because these truths are contingent on the divine will, the ultimate rationale for them, if any, must remain opaque to us. We cannot possibly conceive what it would be to create a logical or mathematical truth by an act of will, nor indeed how a truth so created could be a truth of reason in the sense in which we humans recognize such truths (namely as objects of thought that constrain the assent willy nilly).[33]

The upshot is that the Cartesian universe structured by such truths must be understood as diverging even more widely from the Platonic paradigm of a straightforwardly rational and value-laden cosmos. The Cartesian scientist

---

[30] The significance of the so-called 'anthropic principle' is still a subject of fierce debate. For a theistic/design interpretation, cf. the following: 'If we must make a forced choice between an unintelligent random process and an invisible Intelligence behind the scenes, as it appears we must, and if, furthermore, the chance against a random process accounting for the precise values of the basic constants of physics is well in excess of a billion to one, then a designer may be considered highly probable. In other words, the anthropic principle looks as if it might succeed ... in making highly probable the existence of a universal designer-creator.' (L. Stafford Betty with B. Cordell, 'The Anthropic Teleological Argument', *International Philosophical Quarterly* (1987); repr. in M. Peterson et al. (eds.), *Philosophy of Religion: Selected Readings* (Oxford: Oxford University Press, 1996), 198–210.)

[31] See letters to Mersenne of 6 May 1630 and 27 May 1630 (AT I 150, 152: CSMK 24, 25). It has to be said, however, that Descartes did not give the doctrine much prominence in his major published works.

[32] Cf. J. Cottingham, 'The Cartesian legacy', *Proceedings of the Aristotelian Society*, Supp. 66 (1992), 1–21; repr. as Ch. 2, above.

[33] For an elegant development of this point, see S. Gaukroger, *Cartesian Logic* (Oxford: Clarendon, 1989), ch. 2.

is in no position to apprehend the ground or basis for the universe's being the way it is: the rationale for the principles or laws of motion must be, as Descartes said of all God's purposes, ultimately 'shut up in the inscrutable abyss' that is the mind of God.[34] And the cash value of all this is that in the Cartesian system we have a worldview not all that different from the one envisaged by David Hume, when he said that the 'ultimate springs and principles of nature' must remain forever 'shut up from human curiosity'.[35] What Hume and Descartes in effect agree on is that the human intellect is capable of arriving at principles of maximum simplicity and generality which provide a framework for subsuming an indefinite range of observable phenomena.[36] But behind this remarkable systematizing success of human science lies what must remain for us a mere fiat: God simply willed, let it be thus and so. Beyond that, we cannot go. It is here that the Cartesian view of the status of human science goes a fair way to converging with our modern, post-Humean one: the gap between acknowledging an inscrutable divine fiat and simply accepting the unexplained explanatory postulates of modern secular physics seems to be wafer thin.

3. Metaphysics and the Return to God

The picture I have so far presented is, I think, accurate as far as it goes, but it now needs to be supplemented. I have just suggested that the divergence

---

[34] 'We cannot pretend that certain of God's purposes are more out in the open than others: all are equally hidden in the inscrutable abyss of his wisdom' (Fifth Replies: AT VII 375: CSM II 258). Cf. *Conversation with Burman* [1648], ed. J. Cottingham (Oxford: Clarendon, 1976), 19, 85 (AT V 158: CSMK 341).

[35] '[T]he utmost effort of human reason is to reduce the principles productive of natural phenomena to a greater simplicity and to resolve the many particular effects into a few general causes...But as to the causes of these general causes, we should in vain attempt their discovery...These ultimate springs and principles are totally shut up from human curiosity and enquiry.' *Enquiry concerning Human Understanding* [1748], sect. 4 pt. 1.

[36] This is not to deny important divergences between the Cartesian and Humean perspectives on science: Hume's scientific methodology, for example, involves generalizing from experienced particulars, while Descartes claims that at least some laws can be arrived at a priori. (It is worth noting, however, that Descartes does allow a considerable role for empirical hypothesis when it comes to finding the correct explanations for particular phenomena—a fact often ignored by those who caricature him as an 'armchair rationalist'. Cf. *Discourse on the Method*, Pt. Six: 'The power of nature is so vast, and [my] principles so simple and so general, that I notice hardly any effect of which I do not know at once that it can be deduced from the principles in many different ways—and my greatest difficulty is usually to know in which of these ways it depends on them, I know of no other means to discover this than by seeking further observations whose outcomes vary according to which of these ways provides the correct explanation' (AT VI 64–5: CSM I 144).

between the cosmological structure of Cartesian and of modern science is minimal. Epistemically speaking that may be more or less right; but ontologically speaking there is of course a crucial difference: whatever we may make of the precise significance of the deity within the Cartesian system, there is no doubt that Descartes, unlike his modern scientific successors, does explicitly assign an essential role to God as the source of all reality and truth. And if we go on to probe the metaphysical roots of Descartes's system, there is an even greater sense of divergence between the Cartesian and the modern picture. In Cartesian natural philosophy, there are distinct traces of Platonism, but I have suggested that they turn out under examination to be largely superficial; when we move to Cartesian first philosophy, by contrast,[37] the Platonism is powerfully integrated into the very structure of the thinking.

The journey recounted in Descartes's metaphysical masterpiece is too well known to need rehearsing at any length. At the start of the *Meditations*, the metaphysical enquirer follows the guidance of Plato in undergoing a process of *aversio*, or turning away from the senses, and in his struggle to find a way out of the cave, or what Descartes calls the 'inextricable darkness' of the sense-bound world,[38] he takes the particular version of the Platonic journey that was pioneered by Augustine, and looks for the truth deep within his own soul: 'in interiore homine habitat veritas'.[39] There follows, in the Third Meditation, an argument the terms of which (as one commentator has aptly remarked)[40] unmistakably 'manifest its Plotinan and Augustinian ancestry':

> I perceive this likeness, which includes the idea of God, by the same faculty which enables me to perceive myself. That is, when I turn my mind's eye upon myself, I understand that I am a thing which is incomplete and dependent on another and which aspires without limit to ever greater and better things; but I also understand at the same time that he on whom I depend has with him all those greater things, not just indefinitely and potentially, but actually and infinitely, and hence that he is God.[41]

---

[37] The term 'first philosophy' is of course the traditional Aristotelian term for metaphysics (see Aristotle, *Metaphysics* [*c*.330 BC], Book Gamma, 1004a9). The original title of Descartes's metaphysical meditations is *Meditationes de prima philosophia* ('Meditations on First Philosophy').

[38] 'inextricabiles tenebrae' (AT VII 23: CSM II 15).

[39] 'Noli foras ire, in teipsum redi; in interiore homine habitat veritas' (Go not outside, but return within thyself; in the inward man dwelleth the truth), *De vera religione* [AD 391] 39. 72.

[40] Menn, *Descartes and Augustine*, 288.   [41] AT VII 51: CSM II 35.

In the long discussion leading up to this conclusion, Descartes has invoked an explicitly Platonic idea (expressed in the terminology of Plotinus), observing that an investigation of the cause of his idea of God must sooner or later lead him to a primary idea, 'the cause of which will be like an *archetype* which contains formally and in fact all the reality or perfection present only objectively or representatively in the idea'.[42] The standard move we find in Plato is, for example, from particular beautiful objects, mere shadows or copies, to an archetype or pattern or form or idea of Beauty itself; the Cartesian move here is from a mental object (somewhat confusingly called an 'idea'[43])—a mental object with a certain representative content—to the original of which it is a copy. And echoing the broadly Platonic idea of a downward cascade of being from perfection to the lower realms, Descartes reminds us that 'the copy is like an image which can fall short of the perfection of the original but can never contain anything greater or more perfect'.[44] In inferring a divine source for the perfection found in his idea, Descartes (as Stephen Menn nicely puts it) 'confirms, for the case of Nous itself but not for the case of other particular *noeta* or Forms, the conclusion which [Plato in] the *Phaedo* had assumed...to hold in every case, that the ideal standard essentially possessing each intelligible perfection must exist in actuality.'[45]

Although the Platonic influences here are significant, it is not my purpose, as I remarked at the outset, to unravel the story of their transmission. And in the end, the occurrence of terminology which derives from a particular school of philosophy does not in itself tell us very much about its underlying philosophical (as opposed to historical) importance. Certainly in the Third Meditation the language suddenly becomes saturated with terminology that bears the imprint of the curriculum Descartes had studied at

---

[42] AT VII 42: CSM II 29 (emphasis supplied). The word 'archetype' (*archetypon*) does not actually occur in Plato, though it aptly conveys the role of a Platonic form as pattern or original (e.g. *Republic* [*c*.380 BC], 510 ff., 597 ff.), and is found frequently in Plotinus (*Enneads* [*c*.AD 250], 1. 2. 2 *et passim*), and in later writers in the Platonic tradition.

[43] Confusion might arise if the reader mistakenly equated it with a Platonic form, or with a purely psychological item of the kind often associated with Locke's use of the term. For the mistaken tendency of commentators to 'psychologize' Cartesian ideas, compare chs. 5 and 6, above.

[44] Third Meditation, AT VII 42: CSM II 29.

[45] Menn, *Descartes and Augustine*, 293. Some of the Neoplatonic developments of this idea (for example in Marcilio Ficino) are explored by Richard Popkin: 'Ficino tried to show that by contemplation we can reach illumination from Platonic ideas, thereby approaching ultimate knowledge, which is knowledge of God.' *The Cambridge History of Renaissance Philosophy*, ed. C. B. Schmitt and Q. Skinner (Cambridge: Cambridge University Press, 1988), 674.

La Flèche; but for every one Platonic resonance one could undoubtedly cite two or three pieces of characteristically scholastic terminology whose ultimate begetter is not Plato but Aristotle. Nevertheless, we cannot avoid recognizing how the Platonic language does indeed become prominent at key points in the development of Descartes's argument; and what seems to me crucial for understanding the relationship between the Cartesian outlook and our own contemporary worldview is the mindset that such language betrays—a mindset that can best be labelled *contemplative* as opposed to *controlling*.

Descartes's attraction to a contemplative mode of philosophizing becomes perhaps most unmistakable in the Fourth Meditation, where, in a strongly Platonic moment, we are presented with a match between how the mind responds to the *ratio veri* and to the *ratio boni*.[46] The metaphysical journey from darkness and confusion to divine illumination, whether in the pursuit of truth or of goodness, involves a cooperation between intellect and will: the will must be exercised first in rejecting what is doubtful and unreliable, and then in focusing attention on the innate indubitable deliverances of the natural light that remain. Once the eye of the soul, the *acies mentis*, is turned on the relevant objects, they reveal themselves with irresistible clarity to the perceiving intellect as good or as true, and the assent of the will (to affirm, or to pursue) follows automatically: 'ex magna luce in intellectu magna consequuta est propensio in voluntate'.[47]

The history of the underlying visual metaphor for intellectual illumination is well known; the pedigree, with its roots in Plato and also in the Fourth Gospel, stretches down, via Plotinus, to Augustine, and on to Bonaventure and beyond.[48] Descartes in fact directly follows Bonaventure in maintaining that the key to true illumination is the exercise of the will operating in conjunction with the light of the intellect. Our freedom of

[46] My spontaneous inclination to assent to the truth, or to pursue the good, is a function of my 'clearly understanding that reasons of truth and goodness point that way' ('quia rationem veri et boni in ea evidenter intelligo'); AT VII 58: CSM II 40.   [47] AT VII 59: CSM II 41.

[48] Plato, in the *Republic* [c.380 BC] had used the simile of the sun to describe the Form of the Good which makes manifest the objects of abstract intellectual cognition, just as the sun sheds light on ordinary visible objects (514–8). In St John's Gospel [c.AD 100], the *Logos*, the 'Word' or divine creative intelligence, is identified with 'the Light that lighteth every man coming into the world' (1: 9). And Augustine, in the *De Trinitate* [c.410], welding together Platonic and Christian ideas, asserts that 'the mind, when directed to intelligible things in the natural order, according to the disposition of the Creator, sees them in a certain incorporeal light which has a nature all of its own, just as the body's eye sees nearby objects in the ordinary light' (12. 15. 24).

the will, in respect of which (Bonaventure and Descartes agree) man is truly godlike, consists, in Bonaventure's phrase, in a 'concursus rationis et voluntatis';[49] and this cooperation between intellect and will brings the quest for enlightenment to fruition: 'nata est anima ad percipiendum bonum infinitum, quod Deus est; ideo in eo solo debet quiescere et eo frui'.[50] The rational soul finds salvation in the intellectual awareness of an object, the turning of the will towards that object, and the happiness of satisfied desire that comes to rest in it.[51]

The language of the soul's coming to rest in adoring contemplation of the light is one we associate more with the early Middle Ages than with the early-modern revolution, but such language still has an important place in Descartes. 'Placet hic aliquamdiu in ipsius Dei contemplatione immorari … et immensi hujus luminis pulchritudinem … intueri, admirari, adorare' ('Let me here rest for a while in the contemplation of God himself and gaze upon, wonder at, and adore the beauty of this immense light').[52] The meditator's voice here in the Third Meditation is the voice of the worshipper (or perhaps of the philosopher in the Platonic sense that implies a genuine love or yearning) rather than of the analytic philosopher; or perhaps we should more aptly say that Descartes is adopting a modality of thought vividly exemplified in the writings of many of the Christian fathers (Anselm particularly comes to mind)[53]—a mode in which analytic philosophizing and religious contemplation are inextricably intertwined. The tone and impetus of the meditating is less one of critical scrutiny than of humble submission. Just as for Augustine no salvation was possible without the gift of divine grace, so the scientific truth that Descartes seeks is dependent from the start on the 'immense light', mirrored in each individual soul,[54] or (to change the metaphor) the idea of God

---

[49] 'Ex concursu illarum potentiarum, rationis supra se ipsam redeuntis et voluntatis concomitantis, consurgit integritas libertatis.' *Breviloquium* [1257], 2. 9; in *Opera Omnia* (Quarachhi: Collegium S. Bonaventurae, 1891), v. 227b. Cf. E. Gilson, *La Philosophie de Saint Bonaventure* [1924], trans. I. Trethowan and F. J. Sheed (London: Sheed & Ward, 1938), 407.

[50] *Commentarii Sententiarum Petri Lombardi* [1248–55], 1. 3. 2 (*Opera*, i. 40); cited in Gilson, *La Philosophie de Saint Bonaventure*, 89.   [51] Gilson, *La Philosophie de Saint Bonaventure*, 47.

[52] AT VII 52: CSM II 36.

[53] Cf. G. Schufreider, *Confessions of a Rational Mystic* (West Lafayette, Ind.: Purdue University Press, 1994).

[54] For the light mirrored within each soul, see Bonaventure, *Itinerarium mentis in Deum* [1259], 3. 1 (*Opera*, v. 303): 'ad nos reintraremus, in mentem scilicet nostram, in qua divina relucet imago; hinc … conari debemus per speculum videre Deum, ubi ad modum candelabri relucet lux veritatis

being stamped there like the 'mark the craftsman has set on his work'.[55] And just as St Bonaventure's 'Journey of the Mind towards God', the *Itinerarium mentis in Deum*, depends on the vivid awareness of one's own creaturely imperfection, so Descartes's journey retraces a closely similar path, intertwining philosophical argument with the awareness of our own finitude that has always formed a key element in the religious impulse. *Dubito, cupio*— in the very act of doubting, of desiring knowledge, I recognize my defects; and this would be impossible 'si nulla idea entis perfectioris in me esset cujus comparatione defectus meos agnoscerem' ('if there were no idea of a more perfect being within me, by comparison with which I might recognize my defects').[56] Or as Bonaventure puts it, in phrasing so close to this that it is hard to believe Descartes was not directly influenced by it: 'Quomodo sciret intellectus hoc esse ens defectivum et incompletum, si nulla haberet cognitionem entis absque omni defectu? (How would the intellect know that this was a defective and incomplete being, if it had no awareness of a being free from every defect?)[57]

But despite all the parallels, there is between classical or medieval thinking on the one hand and the early-modern outlook on the other a great gulf fixed—a gulf shaped not so much by the enlarged scope of human knowledge, as by the possibility of developing a radically new *kind* of knowledge, more active, more dynamic than anything that had gone before. In the post-Renaissance world, it was becoming clear for the first time just how searchingly the book of nature could be interrogated, and the relationship of humankind to creation was thereby subtly altered. The triumphant activism of the *Discourse* contains Descartes's best-known declaration of the change: we are to become *maîtres et possesseurs de la nature*.[58] Just as striking is a crucial transition at the start of Part Three of

in facie nostrae mentis, in qua scilicet resplendet imago beatissimae Trinitatis' ('Let us return into ourselves, into our own mind, in which the divine image shines forth; here ... we should strive to see God as through a mirror, where, like the light of a beacon, the truth illuminates our minds, and the image of the most blessed Trinity is gloriously displayed.')

[55] AT VII 51: CSM II 35. The Christianized Platonic language occurring in this part of the Third Meditation carries echoes that go back as early as St Basil: 'Since through an illuminating power we reach forth to the beauty of the Image of the Invisible God, and through that come to the surpassing vision of the Archetype, this cannot take place apart from the presence of the Spirit of knowledge, who gives ... to those who love the vision of truth the power to behold the Image ...' Basil, *On the Holy Spirit* [*De spiritu sancto, c.*370], 28: 47, ed. C. F. Johnston (Oxford: Clarendon, 1892), 94–5.

[56] 'Qua ratione intelligerim me dubitare, me cupere ...?' (AT VII 46: CSM II 31).

[57] *Itinerarium* 3. 3 (*Opera*, v. 202).   [58] *Discourse on the Method*, Pt. Six (AT VI 62: CSM I 142–3).

the *Principles of Philosophy*, where we find encapsulated, in the space of two paragraphs, the move from the contemplative to the active critical mode. Acknowledging God's handiwork in creation, Descartes observes, may lead to 'Deum ob admiranda ejus opera suspiciendum'—adoring God for his marvellous works—but there immediately follows a description of the 'usus phenomenorum sive experimentorum ad philosophandum': it is to experiential phenomena that the philosopher must turn in order to explain and understand.[59]

This counterpoint between the contemplative and the controlling runs, in one way or another, through all or much of Descartes's work. If we are looking for symbols to sum up these two poles of Cartesian thinking, we might think respectively of the *sun* and the *stove*. On the one hand there is the Platonic image of the philosopher emerging to contemplate the sun, that is the Form of the Good, or in its Christian manifestation, the God who dwells in 'light inaccessible'.[60] This supreme perfection is an object of awe and worship, to be gazed on, as Descartes says, 'in so far as the eye of my darkened intellect can bear it'.[61] On the other side we have the image of Descartes's *poêle*—the stove that he used to keep warm during his troubled night of dreams in Bavaria where he had the vision of a new scientific system. No object of awe, but a mundane piece of machinery, put to use in the service of human convenience; this exactly corresponds to the physical universe as conceived of in Descartes's scientific manifesto—a lifeless series of mechanisms to be manipulated and controlled to our own advantage by the new *philosophie pratique*. Such a science, says Descartes, will enable us to understand and control all the objects in our environment as effectively as mechanics and artisans now manipulate their instruments, and so provide mankind with real power and control undreamt of by the contemplative and speculative philosophy of the past.[62]

---

[59] *Principles of Philosophy*, pt. III arts. 3 and 4 (AT VIIIA 81: CSM I 249).   [60] 1 Timothy 6: 16.

[61] Third Meditation, final para. (AT VII 52: CSM II 35).

[62] 'Au lieu de cette philosophie speculative qu'on enseigne dans les écoles, on en peut trouver une pratique, par laquelle, connaissant la force et les actions de … tous les … corps que nous environnent, aussi distinctement que nous connaissons les divers metiers de nos artisans, nous les pourrions employer en même façon, à tous les usages auxquels ils sont propres, et ainsi nous rendre comme maîtres et possesseurs de la nature.' 'Instead of this speculative philosophy taught in the schools, we may thus discover a practical philosophy whereby we could know the force and actions of … all the bodies in our environment as distinctly as we know the various crafts of our artisans, and use this knowledge in a similar way for all the purposes for which it is appropriate, so as to make ourselves as it were the masters and possessors of nature' (AT VI 62: CSM I 142).

One might think that history has vindicated the controlling voice of Descartes at the expense of the contemplative. We do not get from nature the kind of knowledge that can be of direct practical use if we contemplate her beauty and wonder, but only if we analyse and measure and interrogate. That is the message of Descartes's manifesto of 1637, and it still remains largely dominant today. Immanuel Kant famously identified the starry heavens above us as an enduring source of awe (*Achtung*),[63] but it is striking that Descartes never once, to my knowledge, adopts the awestruck or contemplative mode when referring to any part of the physical universe.[64] As a schoolboy in the chapel at La Flèche he must many times have heard the psalm *Caeli enarrant gloriam Dei*, but the only adoration found in his writings is that inspired by the results of the inward search for God within the recesses of his own mind.

4. The Moral Dimension: Manipulation or Meditation?

The sharp disparity between Descartes's metaphysical and his scientific modus operandi, the gulf between the contemplative and the controlling mindsets, seems to me to affect all parts of Cartesian philosophy; and it reappears prominently when we move to the moral branches of the system, which Descartes saw as bearing some of the principal fruits of his philosophy.[65] Here the tension emerges as a contrast between, on the one hand, a vision of the good life as a life of contemplative submission to the good (a kind of analogue of what theologians describe as openness to divine Grace), and, on the other hand, a more autonomous ideal of a life

---

[63] Immanuel Kant, *Critique of Practical Reason* [*Kritik der Practischen Vernunft*, 1788], conclusion. Trans. T. K. Abbott (London: Longmans, 1873; 6th edn. 1909). In *Kant's gesammelte Schriften*, Akademie ed. (Berlin: Reimer/de Gruyter, 1900–), 5. 161.

[64] Perhaps the nearest Descartes comes to this is in his account of the machinery of the body, where he comments on how far the ingenuity and intricacy of the divine craftsman exceeds that of the human artisan (*Discourse on the Method*, Pt. Five, AT VI 55–6: CSM I 139). But the point of this passage is not to express awe at the handiwork of God for its own sake, but rather to reinforce Descartes's argument that, since we know that ingenious automata can be constructed even by human hands, there is no bar in principle to explaining the automatic responses of human and animal bodies in just such purely mechanical terms.

[65] Morals is one of the branches of the Cartesian tree of knowledge from which the fruit may be gathered: *Principles of Philosophy, Preface to French edition* [1647], AT IXB 14: CSM I 186.

tailored for human needs and utilizing the resources of the new science to control and modify the mechanisms of the body.

The older contemplative view that held sway in the centuries before Descartes is perhaps best exemplified by the Augustine-inspired vision of Bonaventure. For the model of divine illumination that we have seen as pervading Bonaventure's metaphysics is fully carried over into his moral philosophy. There is (as Etienne Gilson acutely observes in his study of Bonaventure) a divine illumination of the virtues corresponding to the divine illumination of our ways of knowing. For Bonaventure, the virtues are divinely imprinted marks left on the will to render it good, just as theoretical ideas are marks left on the intellect to make it capable of attaining truth: 'they are imprinted in the soul by the exemplary light and produce their effect in the realm of feeling and action, just as in cognition'.[66]

In his influential exposition the virtues, St Ambrose, the bishop who had baptized Augustine in 387, isolated four as 'cardinal'—*prudentia, temperantia, constantia, justitia* (prudence or practical wisdom, temperance, firmness or fortitude, and justice);[67] the source for Ambrose was Cicero, whose typically derivative contribution in turn takes us directly back to Plato.[68] In the *Republic* Plato famously argues that on the individual level each human being, to lead a good and harmonious life, has to have a well-ordered soul; such an individual will be wise (with the wisdom of the rational element in control), courageous (with the 'spirited' element displaying bravery in the service of reason), temperate (with the desires properly subordinated to the rationally perceived good), and finally just (with each element working in harmony with the others).[69] Bonaventure, who will again serve as an apt spokesman for the tradition, summarizes the widely accepted rationale for the cardinality thesis with tolerable accuracy when he observes that temperance, practical wisdom, constancy and justice are called 'cardinal' for three possible reasons: 'because they are the gateway

---

[66] 'Haec imprimuntur in anima per illam lucem exemplarem et descendunt in cognitivam, in affectivam, in operativam.' Bonaventure, *In Hexaëmeron* [1273], 6. 10 (*Opera*, v. 362). Cf. E. Gilson, *La Philosophie de Saint Bonaventure*, 423.

[67] Aquinas, *Summa theologiae* [1266–73], IaIIae (First Part of the Second Part), qu. 61 arts. 1–5. Cf. ibid. Qus. 47–170.

[68] Cicero, *De finibus* [45 BC], 5. 23. 67; Plato, *Republic*, 427e; *Laws* [c.350 BC], 1. 631.

[69] *Republic*, 441–4.

to the acquisition of all the virtues; or because it is chiefly in them that each virtue is made whole; or because through them every aspect of human life has to be directed and regulated'.[70]

Steeped as he was in the Augustinian-Platonic tradition, one might have expected Descartes to plug into the doctrine of the four cardinal virtues when he came to develop his own moral theory. Given that the *Passions of the Soul* has as one of its key objectives the unfolding of how we may achieve a good life through the mastery of the passions, it might seem that the traditional quartet would be a highly appealing apparatus. An imaginary Descartes, inspired in this way, might perhaps have presented us with a quadripartite vision of *wisdom* (derived from the clear and distinct ideas of metaphysics) running the show; *firmness* or *constancy* displayed in resolutely focusing on the truths so illuminated; *temperance* manifested in the resulting control of bodily desires to bring them into line with the perceived good; and finally *justice* (perhaps anticipating the later line of Spinoza) shown in the collective cooperation of free men individually guided by reason. But it was not to be. Instead, in the *Passions de l'âme*, we find no breath of a mention of the cardinal virtues; in ignoring them, Descartes might almost be writing under the aegis of Aristotle, whom Bonaventure bitterly criticizes for his failure to grasp the importance of the cardinal quartet.[71] More alarming still to theological sensibilities, Descartes seems at times to have abandoned the very notion of the interiority of virtue, the Platonic intrapsychism that is so appealing to the Christian philosophers.

In many passages a far more dynamic or reactive conception of the good life emerges, premised partly on the idea of the value of training and habituation, found so prominently in Aristotle, but supplemented by a highly ambitious and radically new conception of what falls within the scope of such training. The key to this radical activism is Descartes's vision of how the results of physiological science could be harnessed to the service of ethics. He wrote to a correspondent in 1646 that his results in physics had been 'a great help in establishing sure foundations in moral

---

[70] 'Cardinales [sc. temperantia, prudentia, constantia, justitia] dicuntur tripliciter: vel quia per ipsas est ingressus ad acquirendum omnes virtutes; vel quia sunt principales in quibus integratur omnis virtus; vel quia omnis ratio vitae humanae habet dirigi et regulari per eas.' *In Hexaëmeron* 6. 11 (*Opera*, v. 362).

[71] *In Hexaëmeron* 6. 11 (*Opera*, v. 362): 'Aristoteles nihil de his sensit' (Aristotle knows nothing of them). For a different view, see D. S. Oderberg, 'On the Cardinality of the Cardinal Virtues', *International Journal of Philosophical Studies*, 7/3 (1999), 305–22.

philosophy';[72] and when he published his treatise on the *Passions* in 1649 he emphasized the novelty of his approach by underlining that he proposed to explain the passions *en physicien*—from the point of view of a physical scientist.[73] What Descartes has in mind here is a systematic programme for the retraining of our psychophysical responses. The details of this programme[74] are based partly on Descartes's observations of how the behaviour of animals can be modified by appropriate conditioning; partly on observations in his own case of how various patterns of emotional response can be triggered by an arbitrary physical stimulus previously associated with a certain outcome (a striking example is his description of how he freed himself from a tendency to be attracted to cross-eyed women, a conditioned erotic response caused by a forgotten childhood infatuation with a girl with a squint); and partly by his general investigations of the psycho-physiology of the affective system.[75]

Descartes's activist dream that human beings should become masters and possessors of nature thus now encompasses human nature as well. Scientific mastery will extend not only to the natural environment, but also to the mechanisms of our own bodies (indeed, the material structure, and the laws of operation are no different inside the body from what they are outside). And since the bodily events are inextricably linked to affective events (the passions of the soul), and since virtue is about a life of harmony between reason and the passions, science opens the door to a practical recipe for virtue. Habituation, as Aristotle foresaw, will be the key; but it will no longer rely on the luck of having a certain kind of childhood training, since it is now in our power to reprogramme ourselves, armed with scientific knowledge of how our psychophysical responses operate. 'Even those whose souls are most feeble would be able to gain an absolute mastery over all the passions, if enough effort were devoted to training and guiding them (*à les dresser et à les conduire*).'[76] The 'dressage' envisaged here,

---

[72] 'la notion telle quelle de la Physique, que j'ai tâché d'acquérir, m'a grandement servi pour établir des fondements certains en la Morale' (letter to Chanut of 15 June 1646, AT IV 441: CSMK 289).

[73] AT XI 326: CSM I 327.

[74] Examined at length in J. Cottingham, *Philosophy and the Good Life* (Cambridge: Cambridge University Press, 1998), ch. 3.

[75] Ibid. For animal training, cf. *Passions of the Soul* [*Passions de l'âme*, 1649], art. 50; for the girl with a squint, cf. letter to Chanut of 6 June 1647 (AT V 57: CSMK 323).

[76] 'Ceux mêmes qui ont les plus faibles âmes pourraient acquérir un empire très absolu sur toutes les passions, si on employait assez d'industrie à les dresser et à les conduire.' *Passions of the Soul*, art. 50.

at the end of part 1 of the *Passions of the Soul*, is aimed at nothing less than adjusting the pattern of brain movements (*les mouvements du cerveau*) and their associated feelings—a systematic reprogramming of our inherited and acquired psycho-cerebral responses.

This in turn opens up enormous scope for autonomous human action, in contrast to the essential quietism of the Platonic and Stoic inspired conceptions of moral philosophy that had formed much of the background to previous moral thinking. The quietist analysis of the human condition had rested on two pillars: the unalterability of the natural environment, and the danger posed by the passions to our tranquillity. And the cure was to accept with resignation the externals that we cannot change, and to cleanse our internal life of recalcitrant passion so that it can no longer lead us astray.[77] In Descartes's moral philosophy, by contrast, the externals no longer have to be taken as givens, since the power of science can control and modify them; and the passions no longer have to be feared or shunned, since they can be managed and redirected, so as to provide, without threat to our pursuit of the good, the pleasures they are naturally fitted to provide—the 'greatest sweetness this life has to offer' (*le plus de douceur en cette vie*).[78] This optimistic vision of the ethical future for mankind here in the concluding article of the *Passions of the Soul* is strikingly prefigured in a letter written a few months earlier, where Descartes vividly distances himself from the old strategy of suppression: 'La philosophie que je cultive n'est pas si barbare ni si farouche qu'elle rejette l'usage des passions; au contraire, c'est en lui seul que je mets toute la douceur et la félicité de cette vie.'[79]

---

[77] For the standard Stoic recipe for the control of the passions, see Cottingham, *Philosophy and the Good Life*, ch. 2 §4 (where some alternative interpretations of the Stoic view of the passions are referred to). The question of the Plato's attitude to the passions is an immensely vexed one, and I am well aware that to group the 'Platonic' and 'Stoic' approaches under the same broad heading is to ignore many complexities, particularly in Plato's writings on the passions and the good life. For some of the complexities, see e.g. Martha Nussbaum, *The Fragility of Goodness* (Cambridge: Cambridge University Press, 1986), chs. 5–7.

[78] 'L'âme peut avoir ses plaisirs à part. Mais pour ceux qui lui sont communs avec le corps, ils dépendent entièrement des passions: en sorte que les hommes qu'elles peuvent le plus émouvoir sont capables de goûter le plus de douceur en cette vie' ('The soul can have pleasures of its own. But the pleasures common to it and the body depend entirely on the passions, so that those human beings whom the passions can move most to the highest degree are capable of tasting the greatest sweetness of this life.') *Passions of the Soul*, art. 212.

[79] 'The philosophy I cultivate is not so grim or savage as to reject the use of the passions; on the contrary, it is here that I think all the sweetness and joy of this life is to be found.' Letter to Silhon of March or April 1648 (AT V 135).

In a persuasive analysis of the young Descartes's night of troubled dreams in his 'stove-heated room', the great Cartesian scholar Geneviève Rodis-Lewis sees the much-discussed symbol of the melon as representing the forbidden fruit of the tree of knowledge: 'ne s'agirait-il pas du péché suprême et originale: vouloir rivaliser avec Dieu?'[80] The new Cartesian ethic so far expounded does indeed seem to take us in that hubristic direction—towards the idea of a wholly autonomous human species, bringing under control all the recalcitrant externals that had hitherto threatened the search for fulfilment, and even modifying the conditions of its own affectivity by scientific manipulation.

But though this is a recurring theme in Cartesian ethics, it never completely swamps the older Platonic and Augustinian resonances that we have been hearing elsewhere in Descartes's system. The continued pull Descartes felt back towards the Augustinian fold is signalled with a flourish at the start of part III of the *Passions*: 'I observe but a single thing which could give us just cause to esteem ourselves, namely the use of our free will, and the dominion we have over our volitions' (art. 152). True virtue, Descartes proclaims in the following article, is a matter not of outward achievement but of the inner exercise of our will. 'Nothing truly belongs to us but the freedom to dispose our volitions, and we ought to be praised or blamed for no other reason than for using this freedom well or badly.'[81] And because it depends on such an inner resolve, rather than anything external, Descartes is able to add a universalist corollary that calls to mind his earlier allegiance in the *Discourse* to the Christian principle that salvation is open to all: those possessed of virtue so defined will rejoice in the 'virtuous will for which they alone esteem themselves, and which they suppose also to be present, or at least capable of being present, in every other person'.[82] The good life is not the autonomous power to recreate ourselves or the environment, but the use of our God-given free will to bring our lives into conformity with divinely generated truth and goodness.

---

[80] G. Rodis-Lewis, *Descartes* (Paris: Calmann-Levy, 1995), 67. Cf. the letter she cites, of 1 February 1647 (AT IV 608–9: CSMK 309).

[81] *Passions of the Soul*, art. 153 (AT XI 446: CSM I 384). The self-esteem of the Aristotelian *megalopsychos* was the satisfaction of one whose outward achievements match his sense of self-worth; the self-esteem enjoyed by the Cartesian *généreux* will depend on the 'firm and constant resolution to use our freedom well'.

[82] *Passions, of the Soul*, art. 154 (AT XI 446–7: CSM I 384; emphasis supplied). Cf. *Discourse*, Pt. One: 'the road to heaven is no less open to the most ignorant than to the most learned' (AT VI 8: CSM I 114).

5. Conclusion

There is no doubt a historical interest in mapping out classical and Christian strands in Descartes's philosophy, and comparing them with the revolutionary aspirations he has for his new scientific system. But if historians of philosophy are to be more than antiquarians, we must always ask what is the *philosophical* point of our enquiries. I do not mean by this that we should always try to force our historical materials through the fashionable mangle of 'up-to-date' analytic philosophy; for much modern work on ethics (in the anglophone tradition at least) runs a serious risk of becoming obsessive and short-sighted as it scrutinizes intricate conceptual puzzles in almost total abstraction from the cultural and philosophical tradition that delivered us where we are today. But equally, I would suggest that the history of philosophy can easily turn sterile if it lacks a sense of how the issues of the past are related to a continuing philosophical quest. Fruitful philosophical analysis, like individual self-discovery, operates at a point of interplay between the struggle towards a future not yet achieved, and the effort to recover and understand the past we have (partly) left behind.[83]

What is at stake, then, philosophically, in the efforts of Descartes as a 'modern' moral philosopher to come to terms with the different strands from his Christian and pagan antecedents? One of the main issues that I hope has emerged is the question of how far we can reconcile two distinct conceptions of how we should live—both in the practical sense of how we should conduct our daily lives, and also perhaps in the theoretical sense of how we should philosophize, how we should search for enlightenment. Should our posture be one of active, critical engagement with the conditions in which we find ourselves situated: should we be modifiers, changers, addressing ourselves to the world as would-be masters and possessors of our destiny? Or should we adopt the posture of submission and contemplation, rejecting the allure of control over externals as essentially irrelevant to the spiritual task of realizing our true selves?

Put in this perhaps somewhat portentous way, the question tends to answer itself. One cannot, in philosophy, any more than in life, go backwards. The scientific revolution that Descartes and his contemporaries

---

[83] I take this point from my General Introduction to *Descartes's Meditations: Background Source Materials*, ed. R. Ariew, J. Cottingham, and T. Sorell (Cambridge: Cambridge University Press, 1998).

inaugurated has irreversibly changed the relationship of humankind to its environment: the conditions of nature, the structures of our own bodies, are, whether we like it or not, now within our direct power to alter in very substantial and significant ways. To go back to the quietist, contemplative strategy is, in an important sense, no longer an option.

Yet even if we accept the Cartesian apologia for modernity and the new scope science affords for ameliorating our lot, a crucial question remains about what constitutes the central core of the good life for humankind; and this is a question that is by no means settled by the increased power over externals that modern man now enjoys. Descartes himself would have been well versed in at least three kinds of approach to this core question that were prominent in the ancient world. For the epitome of Aristotelian virtue, the *megalopsychos* or 'great-souled man', self-fulfilment realistically involved external achievement, a comfortable degree of success in the 'great and celebrated undertakings'[84] that are the appropriate display of excellence of character. For the Stoics, reverting to a more austere conception partly inspired by Plato, fame, fortune, and all such worldly perquisites of achievement, are simply *adiaphora*—perhaps worth pursuing under certain circumstances, and so 'to be chosen' (*lepta*), but not to be valued in themselves.[85] Finally, and in the starkest contrast of all to the achievement-oriented stance of Aristotle, we have the message of the Gospels in the first century AD: worldly wealth and success are not merely morally irrelevant to the virtuous life, but are positive *obstacles* to blessedness. Those picked out by the beatitudes in the fifth chapter of Matthew are precisely those who, in virtue of the circumstances of their lives, are at the furthest remove from the natural environment of the *megalopsychos*.

Compare now the final verdict reached by Descartes himself, when he reflects on the conditions for the good life and concludes that fulfilment lies not in the aggressive manipulation of the external conditions of our existence, but in the cultivation of moral integrity:

Provided the soul always has the means of happiness within itself, all the troubles coming from elsewhere are powerless to harm it. If anyone lives in such a way that his conscience cannot reproach him for ever failing to do something he judges to

---

[84] Aristotle *Nicomachean Ethics* [*c*.325 BC], 1124b.

[85] For the Stoic distinction between *adiaphoron* (indifferent) and *lepton* (to be taken), described in Diogenes Laertius and Stobaeus, see A. A. Long and D. N. Sedley (eds.), *The Hellenistic Philosophers* (Cambridge: Cambridge University Press, 1987), sect. 58.

be the best, he will receive from this a satisfaction that has such power to make him happy that the most violent assaults of the passions will never have sufficient power to disturb the tranquillity of his soul.[86]

The resounding conclusion reached here is reinforced by Descartes's final definition of virtue, a few paragraphs later, as a 'firm and constant resolution to use our freedom well, that is, never to lack the will to undertake and carry out what we judge to be best'.[87] In this sense, virtue is self-validating, because it gives us the way to be what we were meant to be, or what we can best become: human beings who fulfil our capacities for goodness, love, courage, generosity, and the like. And those capacities are realized in the moral character of the lives we can choose to lead, not principally by the degree of power we have over our bodies or their environment.

In the conclusions reached in his last published work, Descartes in the end moves the emphasis away from the ambition of command and control, and turns back to a distillation of what is best and deepest in Platonic, Stoic, and Christian thought—that the only thing that ultimately matters in our lives is the inner character of our response to goodness.[88] It is no accident that in this idea of subordinating our resolve so as to execute what we judge to be best, we are taken back to the theme of the divine light so prominent in Descartes's metaphysics. Deeply embedded in Descartes's philosophy is the idea that the good, once clearly perceived, compels our

---

[86] 'Pourvu que notre âme ait toujours de quoi se contenter en son intérieur, tous les troubles qui viennent d'ailleurs n'ont aucun pouvoir de lui nuire ... Car quiconque a vécu en telle sorte que sa conscience ne lui peut reprocher qu'il n'ait jamais manqué à faire toutes les choses qu'il a jugées être les meilleures ... il en reçoit une satisfaction qui est si puissante pour le rendre heureux, que les plus violents efforts des passions n'ont jamais assez de pouvoir pour troubler la tranquillité de son âme.' *Passions of the Soul*, art. 148. Despite the stress on *satisfaction* in this passage, it is in my view best construed *not* as asserting the shallow thesis that the value of virtue lies in the utility pay-off for the practitioner, but simply as making the important and encouraging observation that the virtuous life does indeed offer benefits for the agent. To make such an observation as part of the advocacy of the life of virtue is in fact quite compatible with allegiance to the more profound Stoic and Christian insight that virtue is valuable for its own sake—that, to use Kantian language, it shines like a jewel in its own right, irrespective of external accolades or even an internal psychic glow.

[87] *Passions of the Soul*, art. 153, speaking of the master virtue of 'generosity'.

[88] One might suppose that there is no irresolvable tension in the final position Descartes reaches here; for it could plausibly be argued that the mechanical manipulations of the scientist in modifying our psycho-physiology can be put to the service of the intellectual vision of the good: the ideal state for humans is when the passions are 'adjusted' so as to pull us in what our judgement independently perceives to be the right direction. Nevertheless the 'new-scientific' and the 'Platonic' strategies for ethics are logically distinct: the first envisages a bypassing of the need for temperance, through radical reprogramming of the passions; the second involves the more traditional model of gazing upon the good and exercising temperance so as to act in accordance with it.

allegiance, just as the truth compels our assent. The human ethical journey consists in training ourselves to have the resolve to continue on the right way, even though (because of the inherent weakness of the human mind) we cannot always be attending to the 'immense light' that shows us which direction to take. Here the Platonic motif he inherited from Augustine and Bonaventure exactly subserves for Descartes, as it did for his medieval predecessors, the faith he shared with them. The initial impetus and the final goal of the quest for virtue is the immense light of truth and goodness, the source of 'every good and every perfect gift'.[89]

---

[89] Bonaventure invokes at the very start of his own metaphysical journey 'the first principle from whom all lights descend, the Father of light [*Pater luminum*], who is the source of *every good and every perfect gift*' (*Itinerarium*, opening para.). The phrase recapitulates the Epistle General of James [*c.*AD 50], 1: 17: *pasa dosis agathē kai pan dōrēma teleion anōthen esti, katabainon apo tou patros tōn phōtōn* ('Every good and every perfect gift is from above, coming down from the father of lights.')

Bibliography

Standard Editions of Descartes

Œuvres de Descartes, ed. C. Adam & P. Tannery 12 vols., rev. edn. (Paris: Vrin/CNRS, 1964–76).

The Philosophical Writings of Descartes, trans. J. Cottingham, R. Stoothoff, and D. Murdoch (Cambridge: Cambridge University Press, 1985), i and ii.

The Philosophical Writings of Descartes, iii. *The Correspondence*, trans. J. Cottingham, R. Stoothoff, D. Murdoch, and A. Kenny (Cambridge: Cambridge University Press, 1991).

Other Editions of Descartes

ALQUIÉ, F. (ed.), *Descartes, Œuvres Philosophiques* (Paris: Garnier, 1963–73).

ANSCOMBE, E., and GEACH, P. T. (trans. and ed.), *Descartes, Philosophical Writings, A Selection* (London: Nelson, 1969).

COTTINGHAM, J. (trans. and ed.), *Descartes' Conversation with Burman*, trans. with introduction and commentary (Oxford: Clarendon, 1976).

CRESS, D. A. (ed.), *René Descartes, Meditations on First Philosophy* (Indianapolis: Hackett, 1979).

GILSON, ETIENNE (ed.), *René Descartes, Discours de la méthode*, ed. with commentary (Paris: Vrin, 1925).

HALDANE, E. S., and ROSS, G. T. R. (eds.), *The Philosophical Works of Descartes* (Cambridge: Cambridge University Press, 1911).

VEITCH, J. (ed.), *Descartes, Discourse on Method, Meditations and Principles* (London: Dent, 1912).

VOSS, S. (ed.), *Descartes, Passions of the Soul* (Indianapolis: Hackett, 1989).

Other Primary Sources (Works Written before 1900)

AQUINAS, THOMAS, *Summa theologiae* [1266–73], trans. Fathers of the English Dominican Province (London: Burns, Oates, & Washbourne, 1911).

ARISTOTLE, *Nicomachean Ethics* [c.325 BC], ed. T. Irwin (Indianapolis: Hackett, 1985). Also in *The Ethics of Aristotle*, trans. J. Thomson, rev. H. Tredennick (Harmondsworth: Penguin, 1976).

AUBREY, JOHN, *Brief Lives* [*c*.1680], ed. O. Lawson Dick (Harmondsworth: Penguin, 1962).

BACON, FRANCIS, *Novum Organum* [1620], in *The Philosophical Works of Francis Bacon*, ed. J. M. Robertson (London: Routledge,1905).

BAILLET, ADRIEN, *La Vie de M. Des-Cartes* [Paris: 1691] (repr. Hildesheim: Olms, 1972).

BASIL, *On the Holy Spirit* [*De spiritu sancto, c.*370], ed. C. F. Johnston (Oxford: Clarendon, 1892).

BERKELEY, GEORGE, *Philosophical Works*, ed. M. R. Ayers (London: Dent, 1975).

BONAVENTURE, *Itinerarium mentis in Deum* [1259] ('Journey of the Mind towards God'), in *Opera Omnia* (Quarachhi: Collegium S. Bonaventurae, 1891).

BRENTANO, FRANZ, *Psychology from an Empirical Standpoint* [*Psychologie vom empirischen Standpunkt*, 1874], trans. L. L. McAlister (London: Routledge, 1974).

DANTE ALIGHIERI, *La Divina Commedia: Paradiso* [*c*.1300], ed. G. Bickersteth (Oxford: Blackwell, 1981).

EUSTACHIUS A SANCTO PAULO, *Summa philosophiae quadripartita* [1609]. Extracts trans. in R. Ariew, J. Cottingham, and T. Sorell (eds.), *Descartes' Meditations: Background Source Materials* (Cambridge: Cambridge University Press, 1998), 68–96.

GALILEO GALILEI, *Le Opere*, ed. A. Favaro (Florence: Barbera, repr. 1968).

HEGEL, GEORG WILHELM FRIEDRICH, *Phänomenologie des Geistes* [1807], trans. by J. B. Baillie as *The Phenomenology of Mind* (London: Sonnenschein, 1910).

HUME, DAVID, *An Enquiry concerning Human Understanding* [1748], ed. T. Beauchamp (Oxford: Oxford University Press, 1999).

——— *A Treatise of Human Nature* [1739–40], ed. D. F. Norton and M. J. Norton (Oxford: Oxford University Press, 2000).

KANT, IMMANUEL, *Critique of Practical Reason* [*Kritik der Practischen Vernunft*, 1788], trans. T. K. Abbott (London: Longmans, 1873; 6th edn. 1909).

——— *Critique of Pure Reason* [*Kritik der Reinen Vernunft*, 1781, 1787], trans. N. Kemp Smith (New York: Macmillan, 1929).

——— *Kant's gesammelte Schriften*, Akademie edn. (Berlin: Reimer/de Gruyter, 1900–).

KIERKEGAARD, SØREN, *Concluding Unscientific Postscript* [*Afsluttende Uvidenskabelig Efterskrift*, 1846], trans. D. F. Swenson (Princeton, NJ: Princeton University Press, 1941).

LEIBNIZ, GOTTFRIED WILHELM, *New Essays on Human Understanding* [*Nouveaux essais sur l'entendement humain, c*.1704; first pub. 1765], trans. P. Remnant and J. Bennett (Cambridge: Cambridge University Press, 1981).

——— *Philosophical Texts*, trans. and ed. R. S. Woolhouse and R. Franks (Oxford: Oxford University Press, 1998).

_____ *Theodicy: Essays on the Goodness of God, the Liberty of Man and the Origin of Evil* [*Essais de théodicée sur la bonté de Dieu, la liberté de l'homme et l'origine du mal*, 1710], trans. E. M. Huggard (London: Routledge, 1951).

LOCKE, JOHN, *An Essay concerning Human Understanding* [1689], ed. P. Nidditch (Oxford: Clarendon, repr. 1984).

MALEBRANCHE, NICOLAS, *Recherche de la Vérité* [1674], *Entretiens sur la Métaphysique* [1687], and *Méditations chrétiennes et métaphysiques* [1683] in *Œuvres Complètes*, ed. A. Robinet (Paris: Vrin 1959–66), i–ii, xii, and x respectively.

MONTAIGNE, MICHEL DE, *Apology for Raymond Sebond* [1580], trans. M. A. Screech (Penguin: Harmondsworth, 1978).

_____ *Essais* [1580], in Montaigne, *Œuvres complètes*, ed. A. Thiabaudet and M. Rat (Paris: Pléiade, 1962).

NIETZSCHE, FRIEDRICH, *Beyond Good and Evil* [*Jenseits von Gut und Böse*, 1886], trans. W. Kaufmann (New York: Random House, 1966).

PASCAL, BLAISE, *Pensées* [1660], ed. L. Lafuma (Paris: Seuil, 1962).

POULAIN DE LA BARRE, FRANÇOIS, *The Equality of the Sexes* [*Discours Physique et Moral de l'Egalité des deux Sexes*, 1673], trans. D. Clarke (Manchester: Manchester University Press, 1990).

SANCHES, FRANCISCO, *Quod nihil scitur* [1581], Latin text established, annotated, and trans. by Douglas F. S. Thomson, with introduction and notes by Elaine Limbrick (Cambridge, Cambridge University Press, 1988).

SENECA, *De Vita Beata* [c.AD 58], *in Moral Essays*, ed. J. W. Basore (Cambridge, Mass.: Harvard University Press, 1932).

SPINOZA, BENEDICT, *The Collected Works of Spinoza*, ed. E. Curley (Princeton, NJ: Princeton University Press, 1985). (Referred to as 'C'.)

_____ *Ethics* [*Ethica more geometrico demonstrata*, c.1665], ed. and trans. G. H. R. Parkinson (Oxford: Oxford University Press, 2000).

_____ *Opera*, ed. C. Gebhardt (Heidelberg: Winters, 1925). (Referred to as 'G'.)

SUÁREZ, FRANCISCO, *Metaphysical Disputations* [*Disputationes metaphysicae*, 1597] (repr. Hildesheim: Olms, 1965).

All Other Works

ALANEN, L., *Descartes's Concept of Mind* (Cambridge, Mass.: Harvard University Press, 2003).

ALEXANDER, P., *Ideas, Qualities and Corpuscles* (Cambridge: Cambridge University Press, 1985).

ANSCOMBE, E., *Human Life, Action and Ethics*, ed. M. Geach and L. Gormally (Exeter: Imprint Academic, 2005).

ARIEW, R., COTTINGHAM, J., and SORELL, T. (eds.), *Descartes' Meditations: Background Source Materials* (Cambridge: Cambridge University Press, 1988).

AUDI, R., 'Doxastic Voluntarism and the Ethics of Belief', *Facta Philosophica*, 1 (1999), 87–109.

AUXIER, R. E. (ed.), *Essays in Honor of Marjorie Grene*, Library of Living Philosophers (Chicago: Open Court, 2003).

AYER, A. J., *Language, Truth and Logic* [1936] 2nd edn. (repr. London: Gollancz, 1962).

BENNETT, J., *A Study of Spinoza's Ethics* (Cambridge: Cambridge University Press, 1984).

BETTY, L. S., with Cordell, B. 'The Anthropic Teleological Argument', *International Philosophical Quarterly* (1987); repr. in M. Peterson et al. (eds.), *Philosophy of Religion: Selected Readings* (Oxford: Oxford University Press, 1996), 198–210.

BURNYEAT, M. F., 'Plato', *Proceedings of the British Academy*, 111 (2001), 1–22.

BUTLER, R. J. (ed.), *Cartesian Studies* (Oxford: Blackwell, 1972).

CARR, D., and HALDANE, J. (eds.), *Essays on Spirituality and Education* (London: Routledge, 2003).

CAVELL, M. *The Psychoanalytic Mind: From Freud to Philosophy* (Cambridge, Mass.: Harvard University Press, 1993).

CHAPPELL, V. (ed.), *Descartes's Meditations, Critical Essays* (Lanham, Md.: Rowman & Littlefield, 1977).

CHOMSKY, N., *Language and Mind* (New York: Harcourt, Brace & World, 1968).

CLARKE, D., *Descartes's Philosophy of Science* (Manchester: Manchester University Press, 1982).

—— *Descartes's Theory of the Mind* (Oxford: Clarendon, 2003).

COLODNY, R. G. (ed.), *Frontiers of Science and Philosophy* (London and Pittsburgh: Allen & Unwin and University of Pittsburgh Press, 1962).

CONDREN, C., GAUKROGER, S., and HUNTER, I. (eds.), *The Philosopher in Early Modern Europe* (Cambridge: Cambridge University Press, 2006).

COPLESTON, F., *A History of Philosophy*, 9 vols. (London: Burnes Oates, 1947–75).

CORNFORD, F. M., *Plato's Cosmology* (London: Routledge, 1937).

COTTINGHAM, J. (ed.), *The Cambridge Companion to Descartes* (Cambridge: Cambridge University Press, 1993).

—— *Descartes* (Oxford: Blackwell, 1986).

—— *A Descartes Dictionary* (Oxford: Blackwell, 1993).

—— 'The External World, "Nature" and Human Experience', in Vesey (ed.), *Philosophers Ancient and Modern*, 73–89. Repr. in Chappell (ed.), *Descartes's Meditations, Critical Essays*, 207–224.

—— 'Partiality and the Virtues', in Crisp (ed.), *How Should One Live?* 57–76.

_____ *Philosophy and the Good Life: Reason and the Passions in Greek, Cartesian and Psychoanalytic Ethics* (Cambridge: Cambridge University Press, 1998).

_____ *The Rationalists* (Oxford: Oxford University Press, 1988).

_____ (ed.), *Reason, Will and Sensation: Studies in Descartes's Metaphysics* (Oxford: Oxford University Press, 1994).

_____ 'The Role of the Malignant Demon', *Studia Leibnitiana*, 8 (1976), 257–64, repr. in Moyal (ed.), *Descartes: Critical Assessments*, ii. 129 ff.

_____ 'The Self and the Body: Alienation and Integration in Cartesian Ethics', *Seventeenth-Century French Studies* (1995), 1–13.

_____ 'Spirituality, Science and Morality', in Carr and Haldane (eds.), *Essays on Spirituality and Education*, 40–54.

_____ *The Spiritual Dimension: Religion, Philosophy and Human Value* (Cambridge: Cambridge University Press, 2005).

_____ 'Why Should Analytic Philosophers Do History of Philosophy?', in Sorell and Rogers (eds.), *Analytic Philosophy and History of Philosophy*, 25–41.

CRAIG, E., *The Mind of God and the Works of Man* (Oxford: Oxford University Press, 1987).

_____ (ed.), *The Routledge Encyclopedia of Philosophy* (London: Routledge, 1998).

CRANE, T., 'Intentionality', in Craig (ed.), *The Routledge Encyclopedia of Philosophy*.

CRISP, R. (ed.), *How Should One Live?* (Oxford: Oxford University Press, 1996).

CURLEY, E. M., 'Descartes, Spinoza and the Ethics of Belief', in Freeman and Mandelbaum (eds), *Spinoza: Essays in Interpretation*, 159–89.

_____ *Spinoza's Metaphysics: An Essay in Interpretation* (Cambridge, Mass.: Harvard University Press, 1969).

DANTO, A., and MORGANBESSER, S. (eds.), *Philosophy of Science* (New York: Meridian, 1960).

DAVIDSON, D., *Inquiries into Truth and Interpretation*, 2nd edn. (Oxford: Clarendon, 2001).

DAVIES, B., *Aquinas* (London: Continuum, 2002).

DELAHUNTY, R. J., *Spinoza* (London: Routledge, 1985).

DENNETT, D., *Consciousness Explained* (Boston: Little Brown, 1991).

_____ *Elbow Room* (Oxford: Oxford University Press, 1984).

DUMMETT, M., *Truth and Other Enigmas* (London: Duckworth, 1978).

ELIOT, T. S., *Collected Poems 1909–1935.* (London: Faber, 1963).

FRANKFURT, H., *Demons, Dreamers and Madmen: The Defence of Reason in Descartes's Meditations* (New York: Bobbs Merrill, 1970).

FREEMAN E., and MANDELBAUM, M. (eds.), *Spinoza: Essays in Interpretation* (La Salle: Open Court, 1975).

FREUD, SIGMUND, *Standard Edition of the Complete Psychological Works of Sigmund Freud*, ed. J. Strachey (London: Hogarth, 1953–74).

GARBER, D., *Descartes' Metaphysical Physics* (Chicago: Chicago University Press, 1992).

GARDNER, S., *Irrationality and the Philosophy of Psychoanalysis* (Cambridge: Cambridge University Press, 1993).

GARRETT, D., *Cognition and Commitment in Hume's Philosophy* (New York: Oxford University Press, 1997).

GAUKROGER, S., *Cartesian Logic* (Oxford: Oxford University Press, 1989).

—— *Descartes: An Intellectual Biography* (Oxford: Clarendon, 1995).

—— 'The *Persona* of the Natural Philosopher in the Early to Mid Seventeenth Century', in Condren et al. (eds.), *The Philosopher in Early Modern Europe*.

GIBSON, A. Boyce, *The Philosophy of Descartes* (London: Methuen, 1932).

GILSON, E., *Index scolastico-cartésien* (Paris: Alcan, 1916; 2nd edn., Paris: Vrin, 1979).

—— *La Philosophie de Saint Bonaventure* [1924], trans. I. Trethowan and F. J. Sheed (London: Sheed & Ward, 1938).

GOUHIER, H., *La Pensée religieuse de Descartes* (Paris: Vrin, 1934).

GRENE, M., *Descartes* (Brighton: Harvester, 1985).

GUEROULT, M., *Descartes selon l'ordre des raisons* (Aubier: Paris, 1968).

GUTTENPLAN, S. (ed.), *A Companion to the Philosophy of Mind* (Oxford: Blackwell, 1994).

HACKER, P. M. S., *Appearance and Reality* (Oxford: Oxford University Press, 1988).

HADOT, P., *Philosophy as a Way of Life* (Oxford: Blackwell, 1995). Originally pub. as *Exercices spirituels et philosophie antique* (Paris: Études Augustiniennes, 1987).

HARRÉ, R., *The Philosophies of Science* (Oxford: Oxford University Press, 1972).

HASTINGS, A., MASON, A., and Pyper, H. (eds.), *The Oxford Companion to Christian Thought* (Oxford: Oxford University Press, 2000).

HEMPEL, C. G., 'Explanation in Science and in History', in R. G. Colodny (ed.). *Frontiers of Science and Philosophy* (London and Pittsburgh: Allen & Unwin and University of Pittsburgh Press, 1962).

HOFSTADTER, D., and DENNETT, D. (eds.), *The Mind's I* (Harmondsworth: Penguin, 1982).

HUSSERL, EDMUND, *Cartesian Meditations* [*Kartesianische Meditationen*, 1931] trans. D. Cairns (Dordrecht: Kluwer, 1988).

HUTTON, S., and HEDLEY, D. (eds.), *Platonism at the Origins of Modernity* (Dordrecht: Springer, 2007).

HYMAN, J., *The Objective Eye: Color, Form and Reality in the Theory of Art* (Chicago: University of Chicago Press, 2006).

IRWIN, T., *Plato's Ethics* (Oxford: Oxford University Press, 1995).

JOHN PAUL II, *Memory and Identity* (London: Orion, 2005).

JOLLEY, N., *The Light of the Soul. Theories of Ideas in Leibniz, Malebranche and Descartes* (Oxford: Clarendon, 1990).

JUNG, CARL, *Collected Works* (London: Routledge, 1959).

KENNY, A., 'Aquinas: Intentionality', in T. Honderich (ed.), *Philosophy and its Past* (Harmondsworth: Penguin, 1984).

___ *Descartes* (New York: Random House, 1968).

___ 'Descartes on the Will', in Butler (ed.), *Cartesian Studies* (Oxford: Blackwell, 1972).

___ *The Five Ways* (London: Routledge, 1969).

KIM, J., and SOSA, E. (eds.), *A Companion to Metaphysics* (Oxford: Blackwell, 1995).

KING, P., 'Why Isn't the Mind–Body Problem Medieval?', in Lagerlund (ed.), *Forming the Mind*, 187–206.

KRAUT, R. (ed.), *The Cambridge Companion to Plato* (Cambridge: Cambridge University Press, 1992).

KRIPKE, S., *Naming and Necessity* [1972], rev. 2nd edn. (Oxford: Blackwell, 1980).

LAGERLUND, H. (ed.), *Forming the Mind: Essays on the Internal Senses and the Mind/Body Problem from Avicenna to the Enlightenment* (Dordrecht: Springer, 2005).

LEITER, B. (ed.), *The Future for Philosophy* (Oxford: Clarendon, 2004).

LIDDELL H. G., and Scott, R. (eds.), *A Greek English Dictionary*, rev. H. S. Jones, 9th edn. (Oxford: Clarendon, 1996).

LOEB, L. E., *Descartes to Hume* (Ithaca: Cornell University Press 1981).

LONG, A. A., and SEDLEY, D. N. (eds.), *The Hellenistic Philosophers* (Cambridge: Cambridge University Press, 1987).

LOWE, J., *A Survey of Metaphysics* (Oxford: Clarendon, 2002).

McGINN, C., *The Subjective View* (Oxford: Oxford University Press, 1983).

MACKENZIE, A. W., 'The Reconfiguration of Sensory Experience', in Cottingham (ed.), *Reason, Will and Sensation*, 251–72.

MARION, J.-L., 'Cartesian Metaphysics and the Role of the Simple Natures', in Cottingham (ed.), *The Cambridge Companion to Descartes*, 115–39.

___ *Sur la Théologie Blanche de Descartes* (Paris: Presses Universitaires de France, 1991).

MARITAIN, J., *Three Reformers* (London: Sheed & Ward, 1928, repr. 1947).

MENN, S., *Augustine and Descartes* (Cambridge: Cambridge University Press, 1998).

MOYAL, G. (ed.), *Descartes: Critical Assessments*, 4 vols. (London: Routledge, 1991).

NAGEL, T., *Mortal Questions* (Cambridge: Cambridge University Press, 1979).

___ *The View from Nowhere* (Oxford: Oxford University Press, 1986).

NORTON, D. F. (ed.), *The Cambridge Companion to Hume* (Cambridge: Cambridge University Press, 1993).

NUSSBAUM, M., *The Fragility of Goodness* (Cambridge: Cambridge University Press, 1986).

NUSSBAUM, M., *The Poetics of Therapy* (Edmonton: Academic Publishing, 1990).

ODERBERG, D. S., 'On the Cardinality of the Cardinal Virtues', *International Journal of Philosophical Studies*, 7/3 (1999), 305–22.

O'NEILL, O., *Constructions of Reason* (Cambridge: Cambridge University Press, 1989).

PARKINSON, G. H. R. (ed.), *A History of Western Philosophy* (London: Routledge, 1993).

PEARS, D., *Hume's System* (Oxford: Oxford University Press, 1990).

PENROSE, R., *The Emperor's New Mind* (Oxford: Oxford University Press, 1989).

PINTER, H., *The Homecoming* [1965], in *Plays Three* (London: Faber, 1996).

POPKIN, R., *The History of Skepticism from Erasmus to Descartes* (New York: Harper & Row, 1968).

PUTNAM, H., *Reason, Truth and History* (Cambridge: Cambridge University Press, 1981).

QUINE, W. V. O., *From A Logical Point of View* (Cambridge, Mass.: Harvard University Press, 1951).

REGAN, T., and SINGER, P. (eds.), *Animal Rights and Human Obligations* (Englewood Cliffs, NJ: Prentice Hall, 1976).

RICHARDSON, R. C., 'The Scandal of Cartesian Interactionism', *Mind* 91/361 (1982), 20–37.

RODIS-LEWIS, G., *L'Anthropologie cartésienne* (Paris: Presses Universitaires de France, 1990).

——— *Descartes* (Paris: Calmann-Levy, 1995).

RORTY, R., *Contingency, Irony and Solidarity* (Cambridge: Cambridge University Press, 1989).

——— *Philosophy and the Mirror of Nature* (Oxford: Blackwell, 1980).

RYLE, G. *The Concept of Mind* (London: Hutchinson, 1949).

SARTRE, JEAN-PAUL, *Being and Nothingness* [*L'Être et le Néant*, 1943], trans. H. Barnes (London: Methuen, 1957).

SCHMITT, C., and SKINNER, Q. (eds.), *The Cambridge History of Renaissance Philosophy* (Cambridge: Cambridge University Press, 1988).

SCHUFREIDER, G., *Confessions of a Rational Mystic* (West Lafayette, Ind.: Purdue University Press, 1994).

SEARLE, J., 'Intentionality', in S. Guttenplan (ed.), *A Companion to the Philosophy of Mind* (Oxford: Blackwell, 1994), 379–86.

SMITH, N. Kemp, *New Studies in the Philosophy of Descartes* (London: Macmillan, 1952).

SORELL, T. (ed.), *The Rise of Modern Philosophy* (Oxford: Oxford University Press, 1992).

_____ and ROGERS, G. A. J. (eds.), *Analytic Philosophy and History of Philosophy* (Oxford: Clarendon, 2005).

STUMP, E., *Aquinas* (London: Routledge, 2003).

VESEY, G. (ed.), *Philosophers Ancient and Modern.* Royal Institute of Philosophy Series, 20 (Cambridge: Cambridge University Press, 1986).

VOSS, S., 'Descartes: The End of Anthropology', in Cottingham (ed.), *Reason, Will and Sensation*, 273–306.

WATSON, R., *The Breakdown of Cartesian Metaphysics* (Atlantic Highlands: Humanities Press, 1987).

WILLIAMS, B., *Descartes: The Project of Pure Enquiry* (Harmondsworth: Penguin, 1978).

_____ *Problems of the Self* (Cambridge: Cambridge University Press, 1973).

WILSON, C., 'Soul, Body, and World: Plato's *Timaeus* and Descartes's *Meditations*', in Hutton and Hedley (eds.), *Platonism at the Origins of Modernity*, 177–91.

WILSON, M. D., *Descartes* (London: Routledge, 1978).

WITTGENSTEIN, LUDWIG, *Philosophical Investigations* [*Philosophische Untersuchungen*, 1953], trans. G. E. M. Anscombe (New York: Macmillan, 1958).

WOOLHOUSE, W., *The Empiricists* (Oxford: Oxford University Press, 1988).

ZARKA, L., *La Renaissance du stoïcisme au xvie siècle* (Paris: Champion, 1914).

Index